Clearing a Path for the Gospel

A Lutheran Approach to Apologetics

Arthur A. Eggert
Geoffrey A. Kieta

In Terra Pax Lutheran Publishing
Sun Prairie, Wisconsin

Cover photograph: Hell's Half Acre near Power River, Wyoming.
Photograph and added cross by Joan Eggert.

Copy editing: Kellie Eggert

All Scripture quotations, unless otherwise indicated, have been taken from the Christian Standard Bible®, Copyright © 2017 by Holman Bible Publishers. Used by permission. Christian Standard Bible® and CSB® are federally registered trademarks of Holman Bible Publishers.

Second Printing - 2022

ISBN: 978-0-578-22368-1
Library of Congress Control Number: 2019912099

Table of Contents

The Authors

Arthur Eggert has an extensive background in the physical and cognitive sciences. He received a PhD from the University of Wisconsin-Madison in analytical chemistry and taught chemistry at Duke University. For 41 years he was a tenure-track professor in the Department of Pathology and Laboratory Medicine at the UW-Madison and its Medical School. His research included the design of computer hardware and software, the flow of laboratory specimens and information in a medical environment, and the human-computer interface. Dr. Eggert concurrently served as the director of informatics for the clinical laboratories of the affiliated university hospital, eventually becoming the chief of the hospital's clinical pathology service and the administrative director of its clinical laboratories.

Arthur Eggert has been teaching Bible and doctrine classes in WELS churches in the Madison area for 30 years. He has served on the Self-Study Committee for WELS Ministerial Training Schools, the Western Wisconsin District Commission on Adult Discipleship, and the Wisconsin Lutheran Seminary Governing Board. He is the author of numerous articles that have appeared in *Forward in Christ*, *What About Jesus* and the *Wisconsin Lutheran Quarterly* and has presented three pastoral conference papers. Northwestern Publishing House is publishing his book *Simply Lutheran*, which was written to assist in congregational evangelism and retention efforts and as a resource to refresh the doctrinal fluency of long-time congregational members.

Geoffrey Kieta has served as a pastor in the WELS since he graduated summa cum laude from Wisconsin Lutheran Seminary in 1993. He spent five years as a world missionary in Bogota, Colombia, where he held the position of Director of Theological Education. Since returning to the United States, he has served parishes in Michigan, first in Muskegon and currently in Livonia.

Geoffrey Kieta is the author of *A Lutheran Looks at Methodists and Holiness Churches,* available from Northwestern Publishing House. He is also the author of Bible studies on Lutheran hymnody and the Smalcald Articles, two Lenten sermon series and articles in various publications. He has presented numerous papers to pastoral conferences and to conventions on a wide variety of topics.

Pastor Kieta currently serves on the Governing Board of Martin Luther College, on the WELS Translation Liaison Committee, as chairman of the Michigan District Pastor-Teacher Conference and as a circuit pastor. His past activities include chairing the board for Palabra de Vida de Detroit (which does Hispanic outreach), chairing the Michigan District Help Team, membership on the board of the Lutheran Association for Church Extension and service on many conference planning committees.

Reviewers and Commenters

Numerous people reviewed and commented on various parts of this book. The authors wish to thank all of them for their valuable insights but especially to thank

Rev. Shaun Arndt – Parish Pastor
Dr. Paul Boehlke – Professor Emeritus, Wisconsin Lutheran College
Rev. Dr. Kenneth Cherney – Professor, Wisconsin Lutheran Seminary
Rev Sam Degner – Professor, Wisconsin Lutheran Seminary
Rev. Luke Thompson – Parish Pastor
Sharon Grinyer – Technical proofreader
Emily Mandler – Technical proofreader

The authors also wish to express our deepest gratitude to our wives, Joan and Becky, mother and daughter, our helpmeets in life and in this project.

Introduction

In the early 1990's, a former pastor from the Evangelical Free Church attended a confessional Lutheran Seminary. He had studied Lutheran doctrine and had concluded that it gave the correct presentation of the biblical message. As a result, he went through the formal process of joining the synod as a pastor, which included spending some time at the seminary doing more in-depth study. Two students were very curious about his background, and they struck up a conversation.

> One of them asked, "How is our seminary different from the one you went to?"
> He thought for a moment and then said, "Well, you don't have an apologetics department."

Apologetics. That is what this book is about. At this moment in our history, there seems to be a rising tide of interest in this topic in confessional Lutheranism. That is notable all by itself, as for at least a couple of generations, the confessional Lutheran synods have not done much work in this area. In truth, Lutheranism in America has been noticeably absent from the world of Christian apologetics for a very long time. This wasn't always the case. In the 16th and 17th centuries, European Lutherans published a great deal about apologetics, but somehow in the New World, the topic dropped off our radar screens. Certainly, it would be an overstatement to say that no famous Christian apologist is a Lutheran. John Warwick Montgomery and his associates are probably the most acknowledged Lutheran apologists of our day.

Nevertheless, the apologetics discussion in America today has been dominated by Reformed voices, not least of all because much of the discussion has revolved around evolution and the response that many of these voices have given to that attack on God's Word. Unfortunately, their thinking has had a dramatic impact on the way theologically conservative Lutherans, both laypeople and called workers, have addressed these challenges to Christian teachings. We are not convinced that their approach has been consistent with Scripture or the Lutheran Confessions. The regrettable result of this reality: when our people are thirsty for apologetic resources, they often go to a different well—a well that doesn't always preserve Lutheran and scriptural truth. Consequently, in recent years more and more Lutherans have begun to make contributions to this area. This book is intended to add to this effort. It has not been written to change the world, but it has been written to contribute to, and hopefully advance, Lutheran apologetics.

We want to begin at the most basic level for several reasons. First, we believe that this is what most Christians need. They need and want help explaining their faith to people who dismiss it or attack it. Secondly, we believe that we Lutherans need to get back to the basics because our reliance on non-Lutheran work will cause problems in the long run. We are concerned that some of these problems are already rearing their ugly heads. Many of our members feel that their faith is under attack daily. Many Christian parents worry that their children will lose their faith while attending college or even in high school, and they want to prepare themselves to answer the tough questions and to guide their children in the way of God's truth. Many confessional Lutherans—including pastors and teachers—are desperate for materials that will help them defend what they believe. If they cannot find something that is solid and confessional, then they will use whatever they must. They don't want to go to a poisoned well. But they don't want to die of thirst in the desert either. We hope that this work will be a part of a broader effort to provide solidly scriptural, confessional Lutheran apologetic resources.

What is Apologetics?

Almost any introduction to apologetics will explain that the word comes from the Greek word *apologia*, which means "a defense". We Lutherans have a confession called the Apology to the Augsburg Confession. It is not a document that says, "We're sorry we wrote the Augsburg Confession." It is a document that defends what that earlier confession says. Apologetics, therefore, is about defending what we believe. For support, we turn to a commonly cited Scriptural passage on the topic, "But in your hearts regard Christ the Lord as holy, ready at any time to give a defense (Greek: *apologia*) to anyone who asks you for a reason for the hope that is in you."[1]

What then do we mean by a defense? What did Peter mean? Peter was using language that came from a Greek courtroom. He was talking about a situation in which people listen to an argument to find out what the truth is. But in the biblical context, Peter was not talking about winning an argument. He was talking about speaking in a way that persuades people of the truth. In the end, we Christians must always remember that the "reason" for our "hope" is the gospel. All true apologetics is really about finding a way to clear a path for the gospel.

Thus, maybe it is easier to say what apologetics isn't than what it is. It is not an attempt to prove that what the Bible says is true. In the end, we cannot do that. In fact, in the Lutheran Confessions we pledge ourselves to judge all teachers and teachings solely by the Scriptures.[2] Even more than 1 Peter 3:15, the key passage for all apologetic work is Hebrews 11:1: "Now faith is the reality of what is hoped for, the proof of what is not seen." Notice that faith focuses on what we cannot see. It focuses on what we hope for, and as St. Paul tells us, hope that is seen really is "not hope at all".[3] If we could prove the things that we trust in, that we hope for, we wouldn't need faith to believe in them.[4]

This is a key point for all our attempts to explain the reason for the hope that we have. We cannot convince anyone with a clever argument that Jesus paid for all the sins of the whole world. We cannot logically explain the doctrine of the Trinity and make it intellectually acceptable. We cannot prove creation by science or experiments. Faith is trusting in what we cannot prove. Faith is clinging to what God promises even when all the evidence we can see seems to contradict him and all the people we most love tell us that we are wasting our time. We know the truth because God has worked through the gospel and made us believers. No amount of posturing on our part can change the fact that only a believer will see these teachings as a perfectly rational position to hold.

---

1 1 Peter 3:15.

2 "Solid Declaration, Formula of Concord," *Concordia, The Lutheran Confessions, 2nd ed.* (Concordia Publishing House, St. Louis, 2006), 508, para. 3.

3 Romans 8:24.

4 The ministerial use of reason is discussed in Chapter 1.

Therefore, apologetics is not about winning arguments. It is not about convincing people that the Bible is true. It is about getting a hearing for the gospel. People don't want to listen to the truth. If they did, missionaries would have a much easier time. People don't want to believe that they are sinners who need a Savior so that they will not go to hell. They don't want to consider hard questions such as how a loving and all-powerful God can allow pain and suffering to happen. They don't want to wrestle with the love and the power of God. Instead, they bring up all kinds of objections that are really designed to avoid the law and the gospel. Apologetics is about dispensing with those objections so that we can get down to the real conversation, "What has Jesus done for you?"

Apologetics in a Postmodern World

It is certainly easier to say what needs to be done than it is to do it. There are reasons for this. One reason is a tremendous cultural shift that has taken place since the 1950's. Sociologists say that we have entered a *postmodern* age. One of the things they mean by this statement is that people's standards for judging what is true have changed. In the middle of the twentieth century, science and logic were considered the path to truth. The postmodern world has concluded that these approaches have failed. They did not give us unimpeachable truth, and they have not shown the path to a society that is just and free and prosperous. So many people today believe that truth is relative. "What's true for you might not be true for me." When it comes to faith, we sometimes encounter the most frustrating of all apologetic situations, the person who dismisses what we have to say as something that works for us but just isn't for them. They may even say that they respect our position and admire our sincerity, but they disagree with us and insist that this is their right.

So, where do they look for truth? Often to their feelings. Most Americans today would echo Obi-wan Kenobi and say one needs to stretch out with one's feelings. The only thing a person can count on as true is what is found in his or her heart. So, what do such people consider to be the purpose of a church? It is a community, a place of belonging. It speaks its own language and perpetuates its own traditions and maintains its own truth. If one chooses to belong to that community, one does so to fulfill some basic human need and in the process, one accepts the community's view of truth, at least to some extent. This view fails to recognize that the church's commission is to spread the message of salvation through Jesus Christ.

Thankfully, postmodernism does not mean that all people have completely turned off their brains. In fact, there may even be a rising reaction against the cynicism of the postmodern attitude. It is important to speak to people where they are. This book focuses on providing a solid, Scriptural response that can be employed in the world in which we live today to deal with apologetic questions.

The Importance of Not Knowing

When we're debating something that is really important, it is extremely frustrating when we don't know the answer to a question or to a challenge that the other person puts forth. Of course, that is why it is important for us to study God's Word in general and to be serious students of the culture in which we live. But part of the genius of the Lutheran Reformation was the realization that there is some information that God just didn't give us. This is hard, because we all like to have all the answers. Yet, humility often means trusting that God knows the answers and that when he chose not to tell us those answers, he was doing what is best for us. For example, we might think of a parent telling a young child that he or she is going to have a new baby brother or sister in a few months. That is certainly exciting news! Naturally, that young child has all kinds of questions. However, when it comes to the intimate relations between the father and mother that God used to bring that baby into existence, that little child doesn't need to know too many details. In fact, it could be confusing or possibly even unhealthy for that child to have too much information. In spiritual things, we are often like that little child.

There is more to faith than intellectual understanding. God doesn't always give us the information or the evidence we would like to have. Because we desire such information, we are tempted to look to archaeology, history, or science to supply the evidence needed to prove our faith. Certainly, there are times when these disciplines might help us to demonstrate that something the Bible says is true. But often, they only befuddle our apologetics. If we become obsessed with trying to find answers in these disciplines, we put our own faith at risk. How can this be? The most obvious way is that we begin to doubt God's Word because we cannot prove it. In addition, there is also a more subtle danger: we may begin to engage in intellectual dishonesty to uphold our position. We select facts from secular disciplines that seem to support what we believe and ignore those that don't. Eventually, we saddle ourselves with an ever-growing house of cards that needs constant reinforcement. One of the authors' driving concerns in writing this book is our desire to help Christians avoid the fallacy of relying on the brilliance of man to demonstrate the truth of God's Word.

Attempting to shore up the biblical witness with human planks also damages our credibility when people see through our efforts. It makes us look like the person who sticks his fingers into his ears and shouts, "I can't hear you!" any time some inconvenient piece of data comes their way. We further discuss the importance of truth in apologetics in Chapter 1.

Sometimes Christians have to say, "I don't know." God chooses what to tell us, and he lets us wrestle with things here. He calls us to trust that he knows what is best to share with us. Who is the one who decides what we can and cannot know? The Father who sent his Son to die for us. The Son who humbled himself even to death on a cross for us. The Holy Spirit who lives in our hearts and strengthens us through the gospel. That God of love is working for our good even when he hides things from us that we think we need to know. That God of love has built his power into the Scriptures. In the end, even when it comes to apologetics, he will work to accomplish his purpose through that Word.

What Are We Trying to Do?

The goal of apologetics is to speak and write in defense of the truth using logic[5] as well as Scripture. The mission of this book is to give apologists the tools they need to remove manmade obstacles which prevent people from hearing the message of Christ, thereby leaving the stumbling block of the cross itself as the only intellectual obstacle to faith. These tools will aid the apologist in disarming bad arguments against God and his Word, in undermining bad presuppositions and worldviews that are at odds with the biblical message and in stripping away all the peripheral attacks reason makes on the gospel, so that hearts may be confronted by the central claims of the gospel, both historical and theological, on its own terms.

---

[5] Logic, of course, must be used in its proper place, not as a judge or equal of Scripture, but as a tool that God gives us to understand His Word and the world which He has given us. This is explained in Chapter 1.

In creating this book, the authors have bound themselves to write nothing which conflicts with the Old and New Testaments of the Holy Scriptures or the Confessions of the Lutheran church. We have tried to use the highest standards of scholarship. We submitted our ideas to those with the expertise to judge the accuracy and quality of our work. We tried to always state our assumptions and those of our opponents clearly and accurately to prevent false agreement or false conflict. We avoided using *ad hominem* arguments, creating *strawmen* to avoid our opponents' real positions or engaging in lines of argumentation which they might reasonably recognize as containing fallacies.

Why did we do this? First of all, to be fair. Christ expects this of us. Second of all, because we believe that the truth can stand by itself. God doesn't need us to reshape his Word to make it more palatable to people in the 21st century (although we do need to speak to those people and to their concerns accurately and directly). Finally, it is not helpful to Christians who are trying to defend their faith if we present them with false targets. If we were able to edit what our opponents are saying—the way that a TV show often does when it is addressing an issue that is "timely" or "edgy"—it would be very easy for us to make unbelievers look foolish and all Christians look brilliant. That would be false security. When we came into actual contact with an unbeliever, we would not be prepared to address the questions and attitudes that were keeping him or her out of the kingdom of God.

As we have said, apologetics is a necessary discipline. It is all about getting a hearing for the truth. It is about engaging skeptics and doubters in a thoughtful way so that we can disarm their objections long enough for the Holy Spirit to perform a true miracle through the gospel. It requires calmness and a cool head. It requires an ever-growing knowledge of what God actually says in his Word. It requires serious study of the world around us and a real world understanding of the times we live in. It also requires an unflinching willingness to examine what we do say and to abandon favorite approaches that don't really help us in our efforts.

Above all else, it requires confidence in Jesus' promises. He promises that when we speak, he speaks.[6] He promises that he rules all things for the good

---

[6] [Jesus said,] "Whoever listens to you listens to me. Whoever rejects you rejects me. And whoever rejects me rejects the one who sent me." (Luke 10:16).

of his church.[7] He promises that when the unbelieving world attacks us, the Holy Spirit will give us wisdom that evildoers cannot contradict.[8]

A Note on the Bible Translation

We live in an age in which there are many English Bible translations available to us. To date, there is no consensus in confessional Lutheranism as to which translation best serves our work. (One of the authors of this book serves on the WELS Translation Liaison Committee [TLC] and tries to keep up with these issues.) We have chosen to use the Christian Standard Bible for this work because, to our knowledge, it has not been controversial among confessional Lutherans and because the publishers have invited confessional Lutherans to participate in its production, both through the TLC and by having Lutheran scholars on the committee charged with revising the translation. We believe, however, that our points could be made with any faithful translation.

[7] "And he subjected everything under his feet and appointed him as head over everything for the church, which is his body, the fullness of the one who fills all things in every way." (Ephesians 1:22-23).

[8] [Jesus said,] "I will give you such words and a wisdom that none of your adversaries will be able to resist or contradict." (Luke 21:15).

1

The Nature of Truth

Because the concepts of *truth* and *reason* will be used extensively in this book, we will begin by explaining our use of these terms. Christian apologists must speak the truth and speak only what is true, because we represent a God of truth.[1] St. Paul wrote, "Speaking the truth in love, let us grow in every way into him who is the head—Christ."[2] Jesus said, "You will know the truth, and the truth will set you free."[3] On the other hand, Jesus told us that the devil "is a liar and the father of lies."[4] Therefore, it is clear that if we are the children of God, we will seek to tell the truth. If we are willing to lie and deceive to accomplish our goals, we are children of the devil and not of God.

Telling the truth would seem to be easy because we simply tell things the way they are. Yet, how are things really? Our convictions of what is true could just be a matter of perception. We are faced daily with one person's idea of truth being different from another person's idea of truth. In fact, we will look at this psychological problem concerning the nature of truth in Chapter 9. In this chapter, however, we will concentrate on truth as a concept. In other words, how is truth defined and by what standards it is judged? In doing so, we will try to answer Pontius Pilate's question, "What is truth?"[5] Yet before

---

1 [Jesus said,] "I will ask the Father, and he will give you another Counselor to be with you forever. He is the Spirit of truth." (John 14:16–17a).

2 Ephesians 4:15.

3 John 8:32.

4 John 8:44.

5 John 18:38.

we can begin such a detailed examination of truth, we will need to review the proper role of reason in apologetics.

The Use of Human Reason

The fundamental source of our knowledge of Christian truth is the witness of the Holy Spirit in the Holy Scriptures, which will be discussed in chapter 3. Lutheran theologians say that this witness is *self-authenticating.* By this, they mean that there is no standard to which we can compare the Scriptures in order to prove that they are true. The Scriptures themselves are the standard. Or, to put it another way, we don't go through a series of logical arguments or proofs to demonstrate the truth of the Scriptures. The Holy Spirit works in our hearts, and he convinces—in the words of the Scriptures, "he makes us *know*" —that these words are true.[6] For the Christian, that is enough. We don't need to verify Scripture with science or history or archaeology. God has set the standard of truth for us.

The Christian faith, however, is not an incoherent set of beliefs, and we do not have to check our intellect at the door of the church. In fact, some of the deepest and most insightful writings in Western literature were inspired by the insights of faith. God does expect us to use our minds and our intellect, i.e., our *reason*, to use the theological term. Yet we need to understand the proper role of our God-given reason. St. Paul wrote, "We demolish arguments and every proud thing that is raised up against the knowledge of God, and we take every thought captive to obey Christ."[7] Notice that Paul did not say our thoughts are killed or hobbled or broken by the Word of God. No, they are taken captive by it.

As a result, Lutheran theologians talk about two approaches to the use of human reason. One is called the *ministerial use* of reason. This ministerial use of reason is its use as a servant, whether by a pastor or layperson. In other words, our reason recognizes that a master, namely Christ, is speaking in his Word and that all reason's efforts are under the authority of God's Word. This might not seem like much of a role. Yet the ministerial use of reason includes things such as studying Greek and Hebrew, mastering translation theory to learn how to best to express biblical teachings in English and learning the

---

6 "Then Jesus said to the Jews who had believed him, 'If you continue in my word, you really are my disciples. You will know the truth, and the truth will set you free.'" (John 8:31-32).

7 2 Corinthians 10:4b-5.

principles of biblical interpretation so that we can let Scripture interpret Scripture. It encompasses the study of the historic settings of the Scriptures, of the Reformation and of the Lutheran Church. It involves keenly studying the world today to identify the threats to the people of God and thinking creatively about how to touch people's hearts in sermons, in Catechism classes, in Bible classes and in Sunday school sessions. The ministerial use of reason enables a pastor, an elder, a counselor or a friend to diagnose what to say at the hospital bedside, at the graveside or in counseling someone with a troubled marriage. In reality, we could not study the Scriptures or teach the Scriptures without the ministerial use of reason.

The opposite use of reason is called the *magisterial use* because reason is used in a judgmental way. This use of reason places human intellect and thought above the Word of God. It subjects God's Word to our evaluation. While this might sound horrible to a believer, it is widely practiced in our culture. Students are taught to think critically, to evaluate every source they read and to ask, "Does this sound true to me? Can this be substantiated?" It's natural in our culture to think that the Bible should be subjected to the same standards of criticism and critical thinking that we would apply to any other document (see Chapter 8). Yet, doing so sets us and our minds over the Word of God. Jesus tells us that knowing God's truth will set us free. He commanded us to teach God's people to observe everything that he taught.[8] St. Paul tells us that the Word must take our thoughts captive. The magisterial use of reason, that is, any effort to make human reason the standard by which the Word of God needs to be validated, is clearly improper for the believer.

Apologetics is all about using God's gift of human reason in the service of the gospel. Good apologists engage their brains at every level to learn more about the Word of God and about a whole host of issues that we address in this book. Yet in the end, nothing stands above the Scriptures. The ministerial use of reason is the only use that we can legitimately employ in our efforts to defend the faith.

Setting the stage

As in all our labors in apologetics, we need to clearly establish the playing field by defining the terms and drafting the rules for discussion which we will

[8] Matthew 28:19-20.

use. This starts with formulating a satisfactory definition of truth, and that is not easy. That statement might seem surprising, but one needs to think about it for a moment. What does truth mean? Most people would say that truth means a statement that lines up with the facts. As a practical definition, this works most of the time. But what about when people disagree about what the facts are? What about when emotion clouds our judgment? What about the many situations that are simply too complex for a human being to know all the information that makes up "the truth"? What is truth then?

How much information do we need to have for a statement to be true? How much can we leave out before we have brought the truth of a statement into doubt? The difficulties that we have in defining *truth* are illustrated by the oath administered in many courts. People are asked to swear "to tell the truth, the whole truth and nothing but the truth" in an effort to bracket what might be the actual truth in the matter at hand. Yet even with that oath, testimony in court often presents only a contorted view of what actually is true because the attorneys' questions determine which information is brought forth in the witnesses' answers.

Many people think that they can recognize truth when they encounter it, even if they cannot put a precise definition of truth into words. Again, in everyday life, this probably works. However, when we actually have to defend the truth, we need more clarity so that we can hold the people whom we are engaging to a standard that prevents them from confusing the issue or distorting the evidence. Without a reliable definition of truth, we cannot avoid being deceived by false statements that only have the appearance of truth. Therefore, let us establish a number of key definitions which we will use in this book.[9]

***Truth** is something that conforms to a given standard.* This may seem like an unsatisfying definition, but its purpose is to make truth objective. Something isn't true because we believe it is true or we want it to be true. It is true because we can compare it to a standard. For example, any statement made about a triangle must be able to be validated against the definition of a triangle. Something can be true compared to one standard, of course, and not true compared to another. For example, a word spelled correctly according to

---

[9] Steven Gimbel, *An Introduction to Formal Logic* (The Great Courses, The Teaching Company, Chantilly, VA, 2016).

American English usage might be spelled incorrectly according to British English usage.

*A **standard** is a set of rules and/or procedures which are based on specific assumptions*. For example, the Internal Revenue Code is a standard by which all tax returns are judged to be correct (true) or incorrect (false).

*An **assumption** is something taken to be true based on its perceived reasonableness*. It cannot be proven because there is no standard by which to compare it. It is the point in a backward chain of reasoning where a person says, "I simply have to take this on faith." For example, we assume, i.e., take as a matter of faith, that the measuring devices which all the subcontractors use while building a house are correctly calibrated. ***Every system of truth eventually reaches the point where faith is required.*** A more restrictive assumption is often called a ***premise*** (or a ***proposition***). In argumentation, a premise is commonly asserted after assumptions have been made that define the scope of the discussion. A correct assumption or premise is said to be ***well-grounded***.[10]

*A **fact** in argumentation is something that everyone agrees is true, whether it is true or not*. The reason that the definition of a fact must be written in this way is that whether something is true may not be known at the time of a discussion. For example, 600 years ago everyone believed that the sun orbited the earth, so this was never mentioned in their discussions because it was regarded as a fact.

***Evidence** consists of specimens, artifacts, information and/or documents collected or created according to a pre-established set of rules requiring the collector or creator to note the time, place and circumstances of the collection or creation*. The type and nature of the evidence will vary greatly, depending on the nature of the argument for which it has been gathered.

---

[10] In his dialogue *The Sophist*, Plato refers to a perpetual battle between the gods and the Earth giants. The gods contend for knowledge, which is universal, necessary, and certain. In other words, the gods contend for the existence of absolute truth which is knowable to mankind. The Earth giants, on the other hand, claim that nothing can be known with certainty, but we can only know what we can touch and handle, for we cannot know which assumptions are necessary for us to gain knowledge of the truth. As Christians, we know that there is absolute truth because God is omniscient, but with Plato's Earth giants we must acknowledge that humans make assumptions because they seem reasonable in earthly terms but are not necessarily true in the absolute sense.

*A **conclusion** (or **consequent**) is the outcome of the process in which assumptions are made, evidence is presented and reasoning is done in an effort to determine the truth according to some standard.*

*A **line of argumentation** is the reasoning that connects the conclusion with the assumptions.* It is ***valid*** if it is free of inconsistencies and fallacies.

*An **argument** consists of a set of assumptions, which may be supplemented with evidence, a line of argumentation and a conclusion.* It is ***sound*** if the assumptions are well-grounded and if the line of argumentation is valid.

*A **fallacy** is a mistaken conclusion either unsupported by the evidence, based on false premises or derived from faulty reasoning.*[11,12]

Although most people assume that they are automatically right when they make an argument, what they offer as "truth" is seldom well-grounded or the result of valid reasoning. Now that we have established our key definitions, we can look at how reasoning is actually done and how conclusions are drawn. We will also consider some common fallacies and how to avoid them in our reasoning. To do this, we will examine what many people regard as the four most common systematic approaches to searching for truth: mathematical, philosophical, scientific, and theological. Understanding these approaches is critical for recognizing how people develop their arguments and draw their conclusions.

Truth in Mathematics (Deductive Truth)

We will start with what most people regard as the purest form of truth: *mathematical truth*. Mathematics comes from the Greek word *manthano* (I know) and is based on universally accepted definitions. Therefore, it can be said to be governed by this phrase: "Based on the assumed set of definitions, it follows that...." It is a discipline in which a mathematician establishes a domain or field of inquiry that includes various entities (numbers, sets, functions) and operators.[13] The mathematician carefully defines every entity and

---

11 Patrick Grimm, *The Philosopher's Toolkit: How to Be the Most Rational Person in Any Room* (The Great Courses, The Teaching Company, Chantilly, VA, 2013), Lect. 14.

12 Appendix 1 contains a table of many common fallacies.

13 Michael Starbird and Edward B. Burger, *The Joy of Thinking: The Beauty and Power of Classical Mathematical Ideas* (The Great Courses, The Teaching Company, Chantilly, VA, 2003).

every rule of operation. As a result, every theorem can be compared to the definitions that established the domain to prove whether it is true or false or indeterminate (i.e., no answer can be found). Its validity cannot be challenged by new discoveries of science or by new social theories, and so mathematical truth is reliable and unchanging. Integers (i.e., whole numbers) have the same properties today as in the time of Aristotle. Trigonometry works the same way in a democracy as it does in a monarchy. Those who do not play by these rules are not doing mathematics.

Because of this, we have all come to trust mathematics. We learned to count before we started elementary school and soon thereafter, we were taught arithmetic. Many of us found arithmetic to be satisfying because there was only one correct answer for each equation or problem. As we continued through other forms of mathematics, such as algebra, trigonometry and calculus, the same feeling of security in knowing that there was but one right answer remained. We may not have realized it, but our certainty that this was true was based on the fundamental assumption that all the terms and operators (e.g., addition, division) were precisely defined by mathematicians. This type of mathematics is called *numeric* and is an example of *deductive reasoning*. In such reasoning one *starts with known information, manipulates it by known rules and obtains a reliable and unique answer*.

Yet, despite the reliability of mathematics in theory, the answers in actual cases are not always correct. Even if we push all the right buttons on our calculators, for example, our answer will be wrong if the information with which we started is wrong. In other words, we will be wrong if one of our premises was incorrect. If we measure a door incorrectly (e.g., 7 feet 10 inches tall instead of 6 feet 10 inches) or reverse two digits when recording a number (e.g., 136 instead of 163), the mathematical calculation will be valid, but the answer will be wrong (not sound). Correct application of mathematics cannot compensate for bad input. Bad inputs can cause difficulties for us in apologetics as in any other area; we must look carefully when anyone desires to prove something using numerical information.

The greatest mathematical challenge in apologetics is when people introduce *probability* or *statistics* to support their arguments. Unless the person is an expert in the specific field being discussed and is also trained in probability and statistics, the information presented will almost always be wrong. Logical fallacies abound, even in simple cases. For example, Jim tells us that he has two children and that his oldest is named Frank. Sally tells us that she has two children and that one of them is named John. The probability that Jim has a daughter is 50%, but the probability that Sally has a daughter is 67%. While these cases sound alike, they actually create different sets of possibilities which yield different answers.[14]

The Jim-Sally problem is an example of the necessity of finding the right pool in which to go fishing for the correct answer. The total pool of people or items involved in a discussion is called the *population*, and the portion considered for analysis or presentation is called the *sample*. To be useful, the sample must be representative of the population. The size of the sample, where it is collected, and the possible influence of other factors must all be considered to determine the reliability of the results. If we pick a sample which is too small for this purpose, we are guilty of the fallacy of *hasty generalization*. If the sample is biased by an unrepresentative selection, then our error is the fallacy of *false attribution*, so named because the attributes (i.e., properties) of the sample do not match those of the population. As apologists, we often encounter people who engage in the fallacy of *cherry picking* by selecting only those few cases which support their argument and by ignoring the bulk of the data. Before we accept a statistical argument, we must insist on identifying the size of the population involved and on determining how the claims about it can be validated.

A second issue arises when someone uses large numbers (e.g., only 1 chance in 100 billion) to show that their opponent's case is ridiculous. There are two difficulties with such an approach. First, many of the numbers in science are very large, and this can be highly deceiving to people unused to it. For example, an ounce of water contains about 10^{24} (i.e., one million billion billion or 1,000,000,000,000,000,000,000,000) molecules. Even if only one molecule in 100 billion met a certain criterion, this ratio would mean that there would still be 10,000 billion molecules that did not in an ounce of water. This also is a large number, not the rarity that the original probability appeared to indicate. Second, in liquids and gases each molecule can collide with thousands of other molecules each second, so the number of reaction pos-

---

[14] Two children can be born in the order 1) boy-boy, 2) boy-girl, 3) girl-boy and 4) girl-girl. Since Jim's oldest child is a boy, only cases 1 and 2 can be true, so the chances are 50% that he has a girl. Sally has a boy born either first or second, so any of the first three cases can be true. Since the other child in two of these cases is a girl, the chances are 67% that Sally has a daughter.

sibilities is immense, a situation which somewhat offsets the probability that any single collision being successful appears to be extremely small. The apologist must put large numbers into the appropriate context and avoid being taken in by them. Instead, we must steer the conversation back to the underlying issue. The statement "interesting but irrelevant" is often the correct response to those trying to attack or defend biblical teachings with such data. The omnipotence of the Lord transcends even uncommonly large numbers.

The third issue which we face is that few people know how to compute probabilities or to understand their real meaning. To find the probability of something occurring, one must know all the pathways by which it could occur and then calculate the sum of the probabilities of its occurring by each of these pathways. Many times, in the real world, only a small fraction of all the possible pathways is known, their individual probabilities are not known with much or any certainty, or no simplifying equation exists to aid in the analysis. For this reason, unless a person is an expert in the technical field in which the probabilities are being calculated, we, as apologists, should refuse to accept as valid the information presented. It is pointless to argue against things that are meaningless.

Even a seemingly obvious situation in probability can have hidden consequences. Let's suppose that a medical test is positive 100% of the time when a disease is present in an individual, and negative 99% of the time when the disease is absent. This is an excellent test by medical standards. Yet, if a disease is present in only 10 out of 100,000 people, running the test on the whole population will, on the average, yield 1000 *false positives* (i.e., positive results for people who do not have the disease) as well as the 10 true positives for the people who do genuinely have the disease. Imagine the anxiety of the 1000 falsely positive people and the cost of treating them for a disease they don't have.[15] The existence of multiple factors affecting the results shows why building cases on probabilities must be left to the experts.

Finally, there are statistics. Numerous statistical models and tests of validity exist to handle the variety of possible situations. Yet, even if the correct model and test for reliability are employed, that does not actually mean that any specific individual will do what the overwhelming majority of the population does. In fact, some individuals can behave quite differently from

[15] This illustration is an example of an approach called *Bayesian analysis*.

the rest. If 99.9% of the population turns left, 0.1 % is still going to turn right. When we only look at a single example, we have no way of determining if it is the one in a thousand which doesn't "do the usual thing." When it comes to the God of the Bible, the apologist must realize that his actions can be an *outlier* (i.e., a case far from the average) in anything we can characterize by statistics. We should not try to hem in God with numbers of our own creation.

While mathematics in its essence is reliable at expressing the truth, the apologist should always remember the old adage, "figures don't lie, but liars do figure". In discussing the things of God, the introduction of numbers is often the fallacy of a *red herring*, something smelly to get us off track of the message that we really want to deliver. The Lord is a God of detail and precision, but his numbers are most commonly not things we can discern.

Formalized logic

In high school we encountered a special type of mathematics called geometry, in which much of the material was quite different from the numeric manipulation to which we were accustomed. We frequently had to prove certain statements to be true where no numbers were involved. Instead, we dealt with triangles and other figures for which we needed to show that some relationship was true by using a series of steps, each justified by some rule that was true for geometric figures. For example, we might have been asked to prove that the base angles of isosceles triangles are equal. Geometry, therefore, introduced us to a new[16] kind of mathematics, one in which some conclusion about the object of interest was sought rather than a numeric value. This mathematics is called *non-numeric.* Like numeric mathematics, its results are reliable, being the same no matter who does the problem-solving.

Long ago the Greek philosopher Aristotle concluded the type of reasoning used in geometry could be used to evaluate other intellectual problems as well. He developed *syllogistic logic*, another form of deductive reasoning.[17] This gave a means to reliably evaluate the validity of conclusions based on stated premises. Syllogistic reasoning was characterized by a major premise, a minor premise, and a conclusion. Throughout many centuries, students have

---

16 Geometry is in no sense "new." Euclid's *Elements*, a series of 13 books written about 300 BC in Alexandria, Egypt, derived all the common proofs used in high school geometry and much more about geometry and number theory.

17 Gimbel, ibid., Lect. 9.

learned the following argument:

> Major premise: *All men are mortal beings.*
> Minor premise: *Socrates was a man.*
> Conclusion: *Socrates was a mortal being.*

Because the premises in this syllogism are true, the conclusion must be true. All syllogisms have a *subject* (e.g., Socrates), a *predicate* (e.g., mortal) and a *middle term* (e.g., man). These three terms can be modified by the qualifiers "all", "some" and "no(t)."

Aristotle quickly realized, however, that syllogistic reasoning had its limitations. If the two premises were *Some Lutherans are tall* and *Trees are tall*, then the conclusion would be *Some Lutherans are trees*. Clearly, this conclusion is not true even though both premises are true. It is an example of a fallacy called the *undistributed middle*. To determine which of the many arrangements and types of subjects, predicates, middle terms, and qualifiers gave valid syllogisms, Aristotle developed five rules which guided this form of logic for 2000 years.

Syllogisms were the beginning of *formal logic*, which manipulates phrases with the same reliability that arithmetic manipulates numbers. Within the last century formal logic has been expanded far beyond syllogisms to methods such as *truth-functional logic* and *predicate calculus*. It has many uses in mathematics, philosophy, science, and theology because it always gives us valid answers, just as numerical mathematics always gives us valid answers if we follow the rules.

Formal logic is great for discussions among scholars, but not among the people with whom apologists most frequently deal. Such people want simple, easy-to-understand arguments, which is why they often accept reasoning that is totally nonsensical. Therefore, in presenting our case as apologists, we must be prepared to handle the difficulties of *false premise*s and invalid reasoning.

Even the best logic can give valid conclusions that are not sound. For example, "All Lutherans speak Mongolian." "Ben and Nancy are Lutherans." Therefore, "Ben and Nancy speak Mongolian." This conclusion is the result of valid reasoning, but it is not sound because the major premise is false (i.e., not well-grounded). Despite the validity of our reasoning, we will be led astray if we are duped into accepting a false premise. Similarly, we can fool ourselves if we assume a premise is being used although it was never actually stated. For example, if a product is labelled "reduced sodium" or "reduced fat," we tend to assume as a premise that the reduction is significant, not just 1%. That assumption might be wrong, however.

The second problem with formal logic is that the argumentation may not be valid. This happens when someone slips a *non-sequitur*[18] into the line of argumentation. These non-sequiturs break the logical chain between the premises and the conclusion, and they are a major problem in apologetics. Questioners and skeptics try to insert these to derail the apologist's line of argumentation for the purpose of defeating his case or building their own. Let us look at some common non-sequitur fallacies.

We have already seen an example of the undistributed middle fallacy above. In this fallacy, subject A (e.g., some Lutherans) and subject B (e.g., trees) are assumed to be part of the middle C (e.g., things that are tall), and then it is claimed that B contains A. In reality, items A and B are only known to share one common attribute (i.e., tallness), the one which gives them membership in C. They might not have any further relationships.

When Pastor Schmidt preaches a long sermon on Sunday morning, Frank takes a nap on Sunday afternoon. Frank is taking a nap this Sunday afternoon; therefore, Pastor Schmidt must have preached a long sermon this morning. This fallacy is called *affirming the consequent*. Simply because A causes B and B is true, it does not mean A is true. B may have other causes, such as Frank having played cards until midnight on Saturday night.

When three Lutheran women (Abby, Sandy, and Patty) go to church on Sunday morning, the mail carrier does not deliver mail on Sunday afternoon. Therefore, these women are preventing mail from being delivered by going to church. This is an example of the fallacy *post hoc ergo propter hoc*. It argues that just because B happens after A, B is caused by A. The related fallacy of *correlation implies causation* is often used to put the blame on A for causing B, when A and B are actually both caused by C. For example, when people wear swimsuits on the beach, ice cream sales go up in the city. People wearing swimsuits do not cause higher ice cream sales, but hot, sunny weather causes people to both wear swimsuits and to crave ice cream.

Space aliens wearing cloaking suits have been landing on Earth and are spying on Lutheran churches. If this isn't true, the government should prove it isn't. This is the fallacy called *onus probandi* (shifting the burden of proof).

---

[18] A non-sequitur is a statement that does not logically follow from the premises or evidence.

Ordinarily, when someone makes a claim contrary to what is currently accepted, that person bears the burden of showing that the commonly accepted belief is wrong. It is natural for people making such claims to want to gain credibility by demanding that they be disproven. This is a common tactic of conspiracy theorists and politicians. The apologist must not go for the bait.

When faced with any of these logical fallacies, as apologists, we must challenge and unmask the incorrect reasoning so that the claims being put forward are not taken as true by default, thereby becoming "facts" in future discussions (See the previous definition of fact).

It is also a common tactic for fanatics to prevent discussing any one argument that they have raised in detail, instead bringing up numerous other arguments, although these are often unrelated to each other or even in conflict. The goal here is to try to show that our position is so full of holes that any reasonable person would reject it. This is called *kettle logic* because a "whole kettle" of arguments is dumped into the discussion. The apologist must immediately challenge the kettle dumper to identify his or her best argument and insist the discussion be limited to that argument until it is resolved, and then proceed to his or her next best argument. After two or three of these self-chosen best arguments are dispensed with, the rest can be publicly dismissed because they are even worse than the ones already refuted, even according to the kettle dumper.

Finally, a common tactic of those who do not want to be forced to defend their position is to offer a *false compromise*, that is, a position which is seemingly in the middle to "avoid conflict," but which, in reality, requires the apologist to give up his or her key premise in the discussion. This is how Zwingli attempted to trap Luther at Marburg.[19] As apologists, we must know the scriptural positions on the issues under discussion and must not compromise them. We are witnesses to the truth, not free agents who can cut our own deals.

Let us next turn to the oldest way of seeking truth, namely philosophy, which comes from the Greek word *philosophia* (love of wisdom).

---

19 Martin Luther and Huldrych Zwingli met in Marburg in 1529 to try to resolve their religious differences. Zwingli declared himself ready to concede 14 of 15 points of disagreement if Luther would accept that Zwingli's teaching about the Lord's Supper was also correct. If Luther had made this compromise, he would have lost the Scriptural leverage against Zwingli's other 14 points, which his followers would then have quickly reintroduced.

Truth in Philosophy

The philosophical movement developed in ancient Greece about four to five centuries before Christ, beginning with such notables as Pythagoras, Plato, and Aristotle. These brilliant men hoped to use cognitive processes to find what was absolutely true about the universe so that mankind would be able to live in harmony with nature. They immediately ran into the problem that the terms needed to understand nature did not exist in some cosmic dictionary shared by everyone. Each philosopher could create his own definitions based on his experiences in an effort to seek the knowledge that he craved. Yet, everyone's experiences and—as was learned two millennia later—everyone's psychological makeups were not identical; therefore, their fundamental definitions were not necessarily the same either. Without a common definition base, finding knowledge of the absolute truth that was universal, necessary, and certain was impossible. Soon, various schools of philosophy developed in Greece as each great teacher sought to add his own understanding of the universe to what had gone before, only to often find that it was necessary to deconstruct some of the work of his predecessors. Schools like *Platonism*,[20] *Aristotelianism*,[21] *Stoicism*,[22] and *Epicureanism*[23] thrived in ancient Greece, but they had very different views of nature and mankind's proper relationship to it. An even greater divergence of philosophical thought exists today.

A good place to start our examination of how philosophy views truth is with Thomas Jefferson. In the Declaration of Independence, he wrote, "We hold these truths to be self-evident that all men are…." This sounds good to many Americans even though they are clueless as to what *self-evident truth* really is. Jefferson was not a Christian, and he believed that *philosophical truth* was formed directly in the human mind. Because the Bible did not meet his personal standard of truth, he edited it with a razor, producing what is called the *Jefferson Bible*. Copies of this Bible can still be purchased today.

The example of Jefferson shows us some of the basic elements of how classical philosophers search for truth. Jefferson used the fundamental under-

---

20 Charles H. Kahn, *Plato and the Socratic Dialogue: The Philosophical Use of a Literary Form* (Cambridge University Press, Cambridge, 1998).

21 Kelvin Knight, *Aristotelian Philosophy: Ethics and Politics from Aristotle to MacIntyre* (Polity Press, Cambridge, 2007).

22 John Sellars. *Stoicism* (Routledge, New York, 2006).

23 Timothy O'Keefe, *Epicureanism* (University of California Press, Berkeley CA, 2010).

lying assumption that classical philosophers use to seek what is true, namely, that the human mind is able to grasp the standard on which truth is based because that standard is self-evident. This means that, given a certain environment, the human mind on its own, or through the guidance of some nebulous divine being, will know how to judge whether something is true and right or false and wrong. The search for this type of truth is therefore governed by the phrase "It seems reasonable to me that...." Once the inherent reasonableness of an idea or a set of principles is established in the philosopher's mind, he or she can use various forms of valid logic to extend his or her system of truth to cover more cases. There are three difficulties in using this method of searching as our guide in determining the truth.

First, because what is reasonable to each person depends upon his or her background, as mentioned previously, classical philosophers were bound to differ both in their approaches to and in their conclusions about issues. Because in classical philosophy there are no commonly accepted definitions, as there are in mathematics, many radically different philosophical approaches (such as those of Immanuel Kant,[24] Friedrich Schleiermacher[25] and Karl Marx[26]) have developed and still have devoted followers today. More general approaches such as modernism, which appeals to science and reason, and postmodernism, which appeals to a sense of personal truth, have also arisen, each with numerous sub-schools of thought. Lacking a unifying standard by which all philosophical assertions can be judged, classical philosophy has been the source of bitter divisions, as we frequently see among people with differing political or moral philosophies.[27]

Second, classical philosophy is weaker than other methods of seeking truth. It lacks the divine authority of revelation. There is a fundamental difference between declaring "Thus says the Lord" and "Thus says Immanuel Kant," even if Kant didn't think so. Philosophy does not have the precise and universally accepted definitions and operative rules of mathematics. Debating over what the properties of a polyhedron might be is far different from proving

---

[24] Immanuel Kant, *Die Religion innerhalb der Grenzen der bloßen Vernunft* (Königsberg, 1793).

[25] Friedrich Schleiermacher, *Gesamtausgabe der Werke Schleiermachers in drei Abteilungen* (Berlin, 1834).

[26] Karl Marx and Friedrich Engels, *Manifest der Kommunistischen Partei* (London, 1848).

[27] Steven L. Goldman, *Science Wars: What Scientists Know and How They Know It* (The Great Courses, The Teaching Company, Chantilly, VA, 2006).

the properties of a polyhedron from its definition. Philosophical rationalizations can fall before the evidence of science, such as when Galileo's experimentation dethroned Aristotle's reasoning. No matter how reasonable it seems that a heavier object of a certain size and shape should fall faster than a lighter object of that same size and shape, actually dropping the objects settles the matter.

Finally, regardless of the merit of philosophical reasoning in academic debate and study—and certainly there is much to admire—those who try to use it in the public arena are prone to introduce fallacies simply because there are not universally enforceable definitions. Politicians, editorialists, humanists, religious gurus and others whom we see and hear in the media often make statements that are intentionally inaccurate abstractions or overstatements of what is known. These speakers are not so much interested in convincing us with evidence as they are in hoping to strike an emotional chord that will cause us to respond in the manner which they desire. An *appeal to emotion* is a logical fallacy because it biases our ability to impartially evaluate the evidence. By using such reasoning, the speaker tries to get us to accept his philosophy, and therefore, the truthfulness of his arguments, without providing well-grounded evidence or valid analysis.

While the ideas of numerous philosophers could be cited,[28] it is clear that ideas of truth in classical philosophy came from within the philosophers themselves. Seeing this problem, philosophers in the English-speaking world, since the beginning of the 20th century and under the leadership of such men as Bertrand Russell,[29] have migrated toward a new approach called *analytical philosophy*, which emphasizes a more systematic use of logic and more rigorous definitions.[30] While this has improved the process, the ideas of what is true in philosophy still differ greatly and are deeply rooted in Humanism. Therefore, philosophical reasoning is particularly dangerous when applied to matters of faith and morals because it sees them from the viewpoint of man rather than the viewpoint of God.[31] The Christian apologist must reject rather

---

28 Arthur Eggert, "What is Truth?" *Forward in Christ* (Northwestern Publishing House, Milwaukee, January, 2018), 10-11.

29 Bertrand Russell, *A History of Western Philosophy* (Simon & Schuster, New York, 1945).

30 Peter Hylton, *Russell, Idealism, and the Emergence of Analytic Philosophy* (Oxford University Press, Oxford, 1990).

31 "Be careful that no one takes you captive through philosophy and empty deceit based on human tradition, based on the elements of the world, rather than Christ." (Colossians 2:8).

than be taken in by the "cleverly contrived myths"[32] that such philosophers spin.[33] Sadly, classical philosophical reasoning is often used in searching for the truth by most people today, as it was by the Greek and medieval scholars, because it gives them a feeling of power to proclaim their own ideas of truth without having to support them with verifiable evidence.

We will see examples of philosophical efforts to prove the existence of God and the truthfulness of the Bible in the next two chapters. Other examples will occur in later chapters, often in conjunction with science and pseudo-science. We will show that, when the assumptions are not well-grounded or the arguments are not carefully structured within the requirements of the relevant standard, often other means of seeking truth degenerate to philosophical discussions.

Truth in Science (Inductive Truth)

When we considered truth in terms of mathematics and formal logic, we saw that these are examples of deductive reasoning. When using deduction, we learn no information that is not inherent in our premises. We are working within a well-defined box with well-understood tools. If we begin with premises which are true and follow the rules, then our conclusion will also be true. This is of great value for business and engineering, but it does not meet the needs of scientific investigation.

Science comes from the Latin *scio* ("I know"), and the driving motivation for scientists is to expand their knowledge of nature in their various fields of study. To do this, they often need to reach beyond the boundaries of what is stated in the premises of what they are studying. This involves what is called *inductive reasoning*, which goes from specific cases to a more general conclusion. For example, "Team X didn't make it to the World Series this year, last year or in any year that I remember. Therefore, Team X will not make it to the World Series next year." "Next year," however, is not within the initial set of information, so we are extrapolating when we make a statement about it. Such generalized conclusions run the risk of not being true, even though all the premises are true. Perhaps Team X will finally make it to the World Series next year. Even the Chicago Cubs did eventually. Unfor-

32 2 Peter 1:16.

33 David Brakke, *Gnosticism: From Nag Hammadi to the Gospel of Judas* (The Great Courses, The Teaching Company, Chantilly, VA, 2015).

tunately, *any system that relies on inductive reasoning will of necessity be limited by the fallacy of hasty generalization*. In other words, a conclusion may only appear to be correct because data-gathering was stopped too soon.

Nevertheless, much of science is based on inductive reasoning. This is because scientists are usually able to study only a small fraction of the cases that occur in nature (e.g., a small number of all the pebbles on America's Pacific coast). Only rarely, when they are able to actually investigate every possible case, can they say with certainty that something is true. All science is governed by the phrase, "Based on the available evidence, it can be said that…." Scientists require evidence that is obtained through making observations of the physical world. These observations are made and validated based on a set of rules (standards) which have been agreed upon *before* the observations are made, as previously discussed.

The goal of scientists is to create models which explain all their observations in terms of the natural properties of matter, energy, space and time. The *fundamental assumption of science* is that this can be done. This assumption excludes supernatural beings from being involved in anything that can be studied by science. This principle is first found in the 12th-century treatise *Natural Questions* by the English monk Adelard of Bath.[34] Because the conclusions of inductive reasoning can never be absolutely certain, scientists have developed a method of determining which models are more likely to be true than others. *Scientific truth* is therefore the result of the *scientific method.* This method requires that observations be made, a *theory* (i.e., *model*) be formulated to explain the observations, the model be submitted for review by the scientific community (*falsification challenge*) and the model be modified, as necessary, based on any relevant criticism. The process is then repeated until sufficient evidence exists for the model to be generally accepted (i.e., be scientifically true) or to be rejected.

As science does not have the absolute certainty of deductive reasoning behind it, the falsification challenge is critical to guarantee that the best analysts in the appropriate field see no reason why the theory is not true. Without this, one has only *pseudoscience*. Even so, scientific truth can be overturned if new evidence is found that does not fit the model. The results of scientific investigations are always *provisional*, although some are much less likely to be overturned than others.

---

[34] Goldman, ibid., Lect 2.

There are basically three kinds of science. In the *hard science* (e.g., chemistry, physics), it is possible to isolate the entity being studied (e.g., oxygen atoms) from the environment, thereby eliminating interferences. Experimenters then hold constant all independent variables except the one of interest (e.g., temperature) to study a dependent variable (e.g., pressure). The experiments can be exactly duplicated by others with similar equipment, thereby removing investigator bias and providing an easy way to falsify incorrect theories or results. Scientific models are built around mathematical models that seem to fit the evidence. While mathematical models are reliably valid, the scientific models underpinned by them might not be. This is because mathematical models are completely under the control of mathematicians, but natural phenomena are under the control of the Lord, not scientists.

Researchers can also do experiments in the *soft sciences* (e.g., sociology, pharmacology), but they cannot completely isolate the entity being studied (e.g., drug metabolism) from other factors (e.g., emotional stress). Experimental environments are extremely complex because they involve living beings who respond to multiple equilibria and stimuli with various reaction speeds.[35] Experimental results are often sensitive to the exact composition of the population (e.g., age, sex, culture, disease status) being studied. Repeating experiments can, therefore, yield significantly different results. This explains why medical guidelines often change as more or different factors are considered. Since it is susceptible to variations in experimental conditions, scientific truth from the soft sciences is not nearly as reliable as that from the hard sciences. Moreover, in some fields societal pressures can be used to set standards for what is normal and what is abnormal.

Finally, in *observational science* (e.g., cosmology, paleontology), the investigators are limited to what they happen to find. They can search where they hope to find new or confirmatory information, but they cannot produce new cases to study through experimentation. For example, economists cannot start financial depressions to experiment with methods of recovering from them, and astronomers cannot create new earthlike planets to test their

---

[35] When there are numerous entities present that can react with each other, each possible reaction will be governed by three factors—the energy it takes to start the reaction, the speed at which the reaction proceeds once it has started and the extent to which the reaction will proceed. Because the reactive capacity of every entity can have only one value at any time, the actual course of the reaction will be determined by the interplay of the rate and equilibrium equations that govern the three factors indicated.

models. Since its models often change due to new discoveries, the reliability of observational science research is generally overstated in the media. Since there is no rigorous way to test observational science models, they will always remain on a relatively weak footing.

When we are dealing with something that is claimed to be scientifically true, it is essential that as apologists we look at the type of science that is involved and ask, "Is it reproducible?" "Can it be tested by falsification?" While all scientific models are somewhat fragile and susceptible to being overturned by new discoveries, scientific truth in the hard sciences is much more reliable than in the soft sciences and much more testable than in the observational sciences.

There is still one more problem with scientific truth, however, and it is a big one. Theories are regarded to be provisionally true if they can explain what is observed. In other words, if theory A predicts result B, and result B is seen, this is taken as proof that theory A is correct. Unfortunately, result B might be the result of some process other than the one described in theory A. Accepting theories as correct based on their ability to explain observations is an example of the logical fallacy of affirming the consequent, which was previously discussed. Like the fallacy of hasty generalization, scientists are forced to live with this fallacy as well because they have no other alternative, and sometimes it does come back to bite them. For example, Newtonian physics were replaced by relativistic physics because the former's underlying assumptions were wrong even though they explained almost all observations for several hundred years. Regarding this situation, a Christian might say that all science is wrong because it cannot see the hand of the Lord behind the apparent laws of nature. Therefore, we should not be troubled by scientific truth because it is only a human explanation of the world, and it is limited by its fallacies. The Lord is in control. Everything that is inanimate does nothing without his command,[36] and everything that is animate does nothing without his permission.[37]

---

36 [Jesus said,] "For he [God] causes his sun to rise on the evil and the good, and sends rain on the righteous and the unrighteous." (Matthew 5:45b).

37 [The Lord said,] "The LORD of Armies himself has planned it; therefore, who can stand in its way? It is his hand that is outstretched, so who can turn it back?" (Isaiah 14:27).

Truth in Theology

While mathematical truth from deductive reasoning and scientific truth from inductive reasoning have value in this world, the most important truth for mankind is religious (i.e., theological) truth. Moreover, if people are not to grope around blindly in philosophical reasoning, hoping to find some sort of firm foundation, then there must be some source of theological truth and some standard by which to judge religious ideas. In other words, *theological truth* must be revealed to us because we cannot rise up to God.[38] Throughout history people have relied either upon some guru who claims insight of the divine (e.g., the pope or the oracle at Delphi) or upon some book of revelation (e.g., the Bible or the Qur'an) which claims to be God's Word. These are the standards of truth that are used in religion, and Lutheran apologists should be familiar with the other religious standards of truth that they might encounter. Of all these religious sources and standards of truth, only the Bible presents a God who freely delivers people from their sins and promises eternal salvation. All the rest make salvation dependent upon some course of action by which individuals must earn or contribute to their salvation through their own efforts.

With such a great offer, one would think that biblical Christianity would attract nearly everyone, but just the opposite is the case. People inherently want to take some of their own good deeds to the judgment throne of God when they are summoned to appear before him. They do not want free salvation because it means they must repudiate not only all their sins but also everything they view as their own meritorious works.[39] They are unwilling to accept the biblical declaration that they are *totally depraved* and have no works acceptable before the Lord.[40]Owing to their sinful nature, people attempt to change the message of the Bible by various means; this is the area in which the apologist will be most challenged.[41] While there are many nuances, they all are variations on a few themes.

The first theme is to muddy the situation by introducing some component

38 Romans 10:5-11.

39 *Luther's Works*, 79:196.

40 [Jesus said,] "I am the vine; you are the branches. The one who remains in me and I in him produces much fruit, because you can do nothing without me." (John 15:5).

41 While a proper understanding of how to interpret the Bible (called "hermeneutics") is extremely useful in apologetics, it is a broad topic and beyond the scope of this book.

of philosophy as a companion to the biblical standard of truth.[42] Some people seek a *rationalized truth* that is less clear-cut, one that leaves room for negotiation over issues of behavior and piety. Biblical truth becomes distorted when people try to mix philosophy derived from some form of self-evident truth into it.[43] The apologist must point this out, showing how this kind of mixture is of the devil. From the earliest days of the Reformation, Martin Luther recognized the inerrancy of the Bible and the importance of understanding it correctly because he knew that there can be no theological truth apart from the Lord's revelation. *Sola Scriptura* (from the Scriptures alone—see Chapter 10) became one of the pillars of the Reformation. Those who claim Luther did not regard the Bible as inerrant have not read enough of his writings.

A second theme is to edit Scripture much as Thomas Jefferson did, but perhaps without using a physical razor. Instead, some people and their teachers ignore those portions of the Bible that they feel uncomfortable using. With enough non-use, such parts of the Holy Scriptures become foreign to them and effectively cease to exist for them. Others overemphasize portions of the Scripture to make isolated passages into doctrinal sources and then twist the rest of Scripture to support their ideas.[44] Some put two teachings of Scripture in opposition to each other and synthesize a compromise that suits their fancy.[45] The apologist must identify such misuses of the Scriptures and argue for letting the Scriptures speak clearly without our manipulation. Today we use the phrase the *narrow Lutheran middle*[46] to indicate that we may teach no more and no less than is revealed in the Scriptures, as stated in both Deuteronomy 4:2[47] and Revelation 22:18-19.[48]

---

[42] Tyler Roberts, *Skeptics and Believers: Religious Debate in the Western Intellectual Tradition* (The Great Courses, The Teaching Company, Chantilly, VA, 2009).

[43] [Solomon said,] "Trust in the LORD with all your heart, and do not rely on your own understanding." (Proverbs 3:5).

[44] An example is how the Jehovah's Witnesses use the book of Daniel.

[45] An example is Matthias Loy's error in the Election Controversy, where he tried to reconcile God's desire for everyone to be saved with God's election of only some.

[46] Daniel D. Deutchlander, *The Narrow Lutheran Middle* (Northwestern Publishing House, Milwaukee, 2011).

[47] [Moses said,] "You must not add anything to what I command you or take anything away from it, so that you may keep the commands of the LORD your God I am giving you." (Deuteronomy 4:2).

[48] [St. John wrote,] "I testify to everyone who hears the words of the prophecy of this book: If anyone adds to them, God will add to him the plagues that are written in this book. And if anyone takes away from the words of the book of this prophecy, God will take away his

A third theme is to assert that theological truth changes as time passes.[49] In this view, God gradually leads mankind to greater truth as man becomes better able to handle complex ideas. In effect, the Lord showed himself to be a more punitive God to primitive peoples who were not ready to deal with him as the more gracious God whom he has revealed himself to be to more knowledgeable modern peoples. Due to the way God needed to reach out to mankind in the past, some of the things in the Bible should no longer be accepted as true. This idea has roots in both philosophy and science and ignores the biblical teaching that God is outside of time and as such, never changes.[50] As apologists, we must consistently stress that the God of the Bible is not a creature of time. Although this teaching already appears in Augustine's writings,[51] it is so foreign to people that they cannot easily grasp it. In a world in which everything changes, the thought that we can rely on a God who does not change should be a source of great comfort to the believer.

For the Christian, the ultimate theological truth is Christ. If one does not see the plenary saving work of Christ in the Scriptures, then the Bible is no different from any other book. It is only through the work of the Holy Spirit (which causes us to see Christ as our Savior as he is presented in the Bible) that the Bible becomes the sourcebook of our faith (as discussed in Chapter 3).

Giving Offense vs. Taking Offense

It is appropriate that we end this chapter on the nature of truth by discussing how the apologist will present that truth. When the apologist presents his or her defense of scriptural teachings, people will not always respond with an understanding heart or an indifferent shrug. Some will become visibly irritated. Therefore, we must consider the thorny issue of the difference between giving offense and taking offense. Cases of people be-

---

share of the tree of life and the holy city, which are written about in this book." (Revelation 22:18-19).

49 Brakke, ibid.

50 [A psalmist wrote,] "Long ago you established the earth, and the heavens are the work of your hands. They will perish, but you will endure; all of them will wear out like clothing. You will change them like a garment, and they will pass away. But you are the same, and your years will never end." (Psalms 102:25-27) / [The Lord said,] "Because I, the LORD, have not changed, you descendants of Jacob have not been destroyed." (Malachi 3:6).

51 Charles Mathewes, *The City of God* (The Great Courses, The Teaching Company, Chantilly, VA, 2016), Lect. 8.

coming offended have increased greatly in the 21st century, as America has become a society of people who tiptoe around numerous issues. *Political correctness* has been used to censor our speech. The ever-present possibility that something we say or do might find its way onto the internet makes many people positively paranoid. If someone claims to be offended by our words or actions, our society demands an apology.

As Christians, we cannot allow this mentality to muzzle us. We don't want to *give offense*; that is, we don't want to say or do anything that hurts someone else or that interferes with their ability to hear our witness. In theological terms, we don't want to do or say anything that leads someone into sin. On the other hand, we cannot worry about being humiliated in some forum by what people think of us. Jesus warned us, "Woe to you when all people speak well of you, for this is the way their ancestors used to treat the false prophets."[52] If we are faithful to God's Word, at times unbelievers are going to be offended. This isn't our fault. Lutherans call that type of response *taking offense*, by which we mean choosing to be offended over something that God says. The devil, the sinful world, and the sinful flesh of every human being on this planet hate the gospel and much of what God says. If we are faithful to his message, at times people are going to take offense. Sometimes, they may even retaliate against us for daring to speak it to them.

How we conduct our defense of our faith does matter. St. Peter said, "Conduct yourselves honorably among the Gentiles, so that when they slander you as evildoers, they will observe your good works and will glorify God on the day he visits."[53] Notice that God does want us to "live honorably among the Gentiles." He does want them to observe our good works, although they may not acknowledge them before Judgment Day. Hence, we want to avoid giving offense by being rude or thoughtless. An apologist who interrupts the person with whom he or she is speaking, who is clearly uninterested in what the other person has to say, or who insults or shouts at those with opposing views is not helping the gospel cause. In the same way, racism, insulting people with special needs and devaluing women have no place in the church. These are sins which the devil can use very effectively to discredit our testimony.

---

52 Luke 6:26.

53 1 Peter 2:12.

Summary

In this chapter we have considered the various meanings of truth and shown how people seek to find it. We have defined key terms used in that search and looked at some of the ways in which people fall into fallacies. This discussion has at times been heavy, but it is necessary background for the apologist. In the real world we are not facing strawmen of our own making, but flesh and blood opponents who have developed arguments—some well, some poorly—for their own positions. We will need to engage them in our quest to remove those obstacles that prevent them from hearing the message of God's great news of salvation. Let us start that quest with the thorny question of whether God even exists.

2

The Existence of God

"Is there really a god?" That's a good question, but it is the second question that needs to be asked. The first question must be, "What is a god?" As in all areas of scholarly study or even discussions among friends, in religious matters a clear definition of terms is critical. Therefore, let us begin by defining what gods are and how we will refer to them to maintain a distinction among the various types of gods.

Setting the stage

There are three different types of beings, objects or concepts that people treat as "gods." The first type consists of supernatural beings that do not form direct personal contact with people. "Mother Nature," "the Creator God," "the Final Scorer," "Lady Luck" and "the Man Upstairs" are examples of such gods. They are non-descript, and the extent of their power and influence is unknown even to those who make reference to them. While someone might occasionally venture to offer them a prayer, such prayers are more wishes than serious efforts to influence the god involved. We will refer to this type of god as a "generic god" and designate it by using a lowercase *g*.

A second type of god is one to which people devote a lot of time or on which they spend a large amount of wealth. Examples of such gods are the maintenance of a prized classic car, the pursuit of an outstanding physical appearance, a lucky pair of socks, a gorgeous vacation home or professional fame. Because this type of god is "created" by the individual who worships it, we will call these gods "private gods" and will also designate them by using a lowercase *g*. Lutheran theologians have called the service of these gods *secret idolatry*.

The third type of god is one with whom people form a personal relationship through worship and prayer and from whom they expect to obtain blessings here on earth and/or in the afterlife. Such a god has specific powers and moral expectations of its adherents. We will use an uppercase *G* to designate this type of being, even though the specific "God" might not actually exist, such as the divine beings of various organized religions (e.g., the "Gods" of Hinduism). Finally, there is the God of the Bible. When this God is being referred to, we will use the name "Lord" or "God of the Bible" to identify him, although we may use the more generic "God" once he has been identified.

The pronoun "it" will be used when referring to a "god," but the pronoun "he" when referring to a "God." Before looking at whether we can prove the existence of any god or God, let us briefly describe the God of the Bible to serve as a clear model for what the concept of a God means.

The God of the Bible

The Bible certainly does declare that a God exists[1] and that his name is Yahweh ("the LORD").[2] The Lord is a God who is much larger than any human can imagine or comprehend.[3] First, he is completely independent of the physical universe.[4] None of our human senses or our laboratory instruments can detect him.[5] Because we define the *physical universe* as everything which we can detect by our senses or our instruments, we call things related to the physical universe *natural*. Therefore, we say that the Lord, who is not part of the physical universe, is *supernatural*. We say the

---

[1] "Now to the King eternal, immortal, invisible, the only God, be honor and glory forever and ever. Amen." (1 Timothy 1:17).

[2] [God said,] "I am the LORD. That is my name." (Isaiah 42:8a).

[3] "'Am I a God who is only near'—this is the LORD's declaration—'and not a God who is far away? Can a person hide in secret places where I cannot see him?'—the LORD's declaration. 'Do I not fill the heavens and the earth?'—the LORD's declaration." (Jeremiah 23:23-24).

[4] [A psalmist wrote,] "Long ago you established the earth, and the heavens are the work of your hands. They will perish, but you will endure; all of them will wear out like clothing. You will change them like a garment, and they will pass away. But you are the same, and your years will never end." (Psalm 102:25–27).

[5] "Who alone is immortal and who lives in unapproachable light, whom no one has seen or can see, to him be honor and eternal power. Amen." (1 Timothy 6:16).

Lord is a *spirit,*[6] by which we mean that he does not have a physical body as we do. Moreover, the Lord is responsible for the existence of the physical universe, as is discussed in Chapter 5 on creation.[7]

It is best from a human viewpoint to describe the Lord with a series of attributes. He is omnipotent (i.e., all-powerful),[8] omniscient (i.e., all-knowing),[9] omnipresent (i.e., fully present everywhere),[10] immutable (i.e., incapable of changing),[11] purposed (i.e., has a will),[12] holy,[13] just,[14] wise,[15] truthful,[16] good,[17] loving,[18] merciful[19] and much more. He is absolutely perfect in

---

[6] [Jesus said,] "God is spirit, and those who worship him must worship in Spirit and in truth." (John 4:24)

[7] "In the beginning God created the heavens and the earth." (Genesis 1:1).

[8] "'I—I am the LORD. Besides me, there is no Savior. I alone declared, saved, and proclaimed—and not some foreign god among you. So you are my witnesses'—this is the LORD's declaration—'and I am God. Also, from today on I am he alone, and none can rescue from my power. I act, and who can reverse it?'" (Isaiah 43:11-13).

[9] "No creature is hidden from him, but all things are naked and exposed to the eyes of him to whom we must give an account." (Hebrews 4:13).

[10] [David wrote,] "Where can I go to escape your Spirit? Where can I flee from your presence? If I go up to heaven, you are there; if I make my bed in Sheol, you are there. If I live at the eastern horizon or settle at the western limits, even there your hand will lead me; your right hand will hold on to me." (Psalm 139:7-10).

[11] "Every good and perfect gift is from above, coming down from the Father of lights, who does not change like shifting shadows." (James 1:17) / "You [the Lord] will roll them up like a cloak, and they will be changed like clothing. But you are the same, and your years will never end." (Hebrews 1:12).

[12] "The world with its lust is passing away, but the one who does the will of God remains forever." (1 John 2:17) / [A psalmist wrote,] "The LORD does whatever he pleases in heaven and on earth, in the seas and all the depths." (Psalm 135:6).

[13] [The Lord said,] "Speak to the entire Israelite community and tell them: 'Be holy' because I, the LORD your God, am holy." (Leviticus 19:2).

[14] [Ethan the Ezrahite wrote,] "Righteousness and justice are the foundation of your throne; faithful love and truth go before you." (Psalm 89:14) / [David wrote,] "The LORD is righteous in all his ways and faithful in all his acts." (Psalm 145:17).

[15] "Oh, the depth of the riches both of the wisdom and of the knowledge of God! How unsearchable his judgments and untraceable his ways! For who has known the mind of the Lord? Or who has been his counselor?" (Romans 11:33-34).

[16] [Balaam, under the Lord's direction, said,] "God is not a man, that he might lie, or a son of man, that he might change his mind. Does he speak and not act, or promise and fulfill?" (Numbers 23:19).

[17] [David wrote,] "The LORD is good to everyone; his compassion rests on all he has made." (Psalm 145:9).

[18] "The one who does not love does not know God, because God is love. God's love was revealed among us in this way: God sent his one and only Son into the world so that we might live through him." (1 John 4:8-9).

[19] [Jesus said,] "Be merciful, just as your Father also is merciful." (Luke 6:36).

each of his attributes,[20] but he is still more. While a dog may have the attribute of brown fur, if that fur is shaved off the dog, it will still be a dog. The fur is a "non-essential" attribute. All God's attributes are an inherent part of God, so none of them can be removed from him. All of them are *essential attributes*. In effect, he is the union of all his attributes. We cannot play one of God's attributes off against another, such as his justice against his mercy, because he is, not just has, the perfect union of all of them. The Lord is thus beyond human comprehension.[21] More details about the Lord will be given in Chapter 4.

Moreover, the Lord interacts with the physical universe according to his will as discussed in Chapter 5 on creation and in Chapter 6 on miracles. He also interacts with the human race according to both his justice and his mercy as presented in Chapter 7. These interactions are driven by his will, so that everything will work together for his glory[22] and the good of those people whom he will bring from this physical world to his eternal kingdom of heaven.[23] He is, therefore, a God who is intimately involved with every aspect of every person living on Earth.[24] One cannot hide from him;[25] trying to ignore him is an eternal death sentence.[26] At the very mention of his name, every person should tremble because his or her fate in this temporal life and also in a future eternal life is totally in his hands.[27] Opposing his will is far worse than trying to step between a grizzly bear and her cub in the wilderness. The

---

20 [Jesus said,] "Be perfect, therefore, as your heavenly Father is perfect." Matthew 5:48).

21 "'For my thoughts are not your thoughts, and your ways are not my ways.' This is the LORD's declaration. 'For as heaven is higher than earth, so my ways are higher than your ways, and my thoughts than your thoughts.'" (Isaiah 55:8-9).

22 [David wrote,] "Blessed be his glorious name forever; the whole earth is filled with his glory. Amen and amen." (Psalm 72:19).

23 "We know that all things work together for the good of those who love God, who are called according to his purpose." (Romans 8:28).

24 [Jesus said,] "Aren't two sparrows sold for a penny? Yet not one of them falls to the ground without your Father's consent. But even the hairs of your head have all been counted. So don't be afraid; you are worth more than many sparrows." (Matthew 10:29-31).

25 [The Lord said,] "None of those who flee will get away; none of the fugitives will escape. If they dig down to Sheol, from there my hand will take them; if they climb up to heaven, from there I will bring them down. If they hide on the top of Carmel, from there I will track them down and seize them; if they conceal themselves from my sight on the sea floor, from there I will command the sea serpent to bite them." (Amos 9:1b-3).

26 "For God's wrath is revealed from heaven against all godlessness and unrighteousness of people who by their unrighteousness suppress the truth." (Romans 1:18).

27 [John the Baptizer said,] "The one who believes in the Son has eternal life, but the one who rejects the Son will not see life; instead, the wrath of God remains on him." (John 3:36).

Lord's jealousy for the honor of his godliness cannot be overstated.[28]

Scriptural Proofs for the Lord's Existence

Greek scholars had debated the existence and nature of god long before the time of Christ. By the Middle Ages, Christian theologians had progressively fused Greek philosophy with Roman Catholic theology. One result of this was the reintroduction of philosophical arguments to prove the existence of God. Martin Luther and Lutheran theologians recognized the danger of shifting our understanding of God to a source other than the Bible, whether that source be the pope or reason, and they dramatically scaled back their reliance on philosophical arguments.[29] That danger of over-reliance on philosophical arguments still exists today for the unwary.

The Bible is revelation, and its very existence is theological proof that the God who gave it exists, but it is not philosophical or scientific proof. These approaches to seeking knowledge have different standards of truth as was discussed in Chapter 1. While the Lord is not interested in proving to people that he exists according to their standards, nevertheless, in a handful of places, the Bible does make statements that have something in common with the philosophical arguments for God's existence. Outside the Scriptures themselves, which are the main witness and the only one that can truly point us to Christ, the Bible advances two witnesses for God's existence: the physical universe[30] and the conscience which propounds the law written in man's

---

28 [The Lord said,] "Do not have other gods besides me. Do not make an idol for yourself, whether in the shape of anything in the heavens above or on the earth below or in the waters under the earth. Do not bow in worship to them, and do not serve them; for I, the LORD your God, am a jealous God." (Exodus 20:3-5a).

29 Siegbert Becker, *The Foolishness of God* (Northwestern Publishing House, Milwaukee, 1982), 38.

30 [David wrote,] "The heavens declare the glory of God, and the expanse proclaims the work of his hands. Day after day they pour out speech; night after night they communicate knowledge." (Psalm 19:1-2) / Barnabas and Paul shouted, "People! Why are you doing these things? We are people also, just like you, and we are proclaiming good news to you, that you turn from these worthless things to the living God, **who made the heaven, the earth, the sea, and everything in them**. In past generations he allowed all the nations to go their own way, although he did not leave himself without a witness, since he did what is good by giving you rain from heaven and fruitful seasons and filling you with food and your hearts with joy." (Acts 14:15-17) / [Paul wrote,] "From one man he has made every nationality to live over the whole earth and has determined their appointed times and the boundaries of where they live. He did this so that they might seek God, and perhaps they might reach out and find him, though he is not far from each one of us. For in him we live

heart.[31]

These two witnesses have often been called "the natural knowledge of God" in Lutheran theology. St. Paul makes the point in Acts 14 that God's gracious ruling of the world in a way that provides for the physical needs of all mankind is a *witness* to God's existence. In Acts 17, it is noted that God controlled human history so that mankind would seek God and reach out for him. In Romans 1, God reveals his existence and his nature through creation. But immediately after, he goes on to condemn those who refuse to see that truth in the creation. In Romans 2, Paul makes the point that even Gentiles, who did not receive the moral law (see Chapter 7) on Mt. Sinai, often act in ways that are consistent with what God commanded in the moral law, with the result that their consciences both condemn and even defend them. So strictly speaking, they have a natural knowledge of the law and a conscience which judges their actions (see Chapter 7). Lutheran theologians have often made the point that God built this knowledge of the law and the conscience into the human heart, and that his actions tell us something about him, namely, that he is the judge and that all people will have to stand before him.

Strictly speaking, then, both the marvelous creation that God has given us and the interaction between our consciences and the natural law are witnesses

---

and move and have our being, as even some of your own poets have said, 'For we are also his offspring.'" (Acts 17:26-28) / "For God's wrath is revealed from heaven against all godlessness and unrighteousness of people who by their unrighteousness suppress the truth, since what can be known about God is evident among them, because God has shown it to them. For his invisible attributes, that is, his eternal power and divine nature, have been clearly seen since the creation of the world, being understood through what he has made. As a result, people are without excuse. For though they knew God, they did not glorify him as God or show gratitude. Instead, their thinking became worthless, and their senseless hearts were darkened. Claiming to be wise, they became fools and exchanged the glory of the immortal God for images resembling mortal man, birds, four-footed animals, and reptiles." (Romans 1:18-23).

31 "Although they know God's just sentence—that those who practice such things deserve to die—they not only do them, but even applaud others who practice them." (Romans 1:32) / "So, when Gentiles, who do not by nature have the law, do what the law demands, they are a law to themselves even though they do not have the law. They show that the work of the law is written on their hearts. Their consciences confirm this. Their competing thoughts either accuse or even excuse them." (Romans 2:14-15). The CSB translation of this last passage presents a minority view on its meaning. Most translations put the phrase "by nature" with the next clause, as in the NIV "Indeed, when Gentiles, who do not have the law, *do by nature things required by the law.*" Both translations are possible, but the authors agree with the majority view that the phrase is referring to the fact that Gentiles do by nature, that is, according to the way they are born, things that God commanded in the moral law.

of God's existence. God designed the human soul to see these witnesses and understand their meaning—hence St. Paul's point in Romans 1 that the Gentiles' "... thinking became worthless, and their senseless hearts were darkened."[32] The Lord inspired David to write, "The fool says in his heart, 'There's no God.' They are corrupt; they do vile deeds."[33] The Hebrew word *nabal*, often translated as "fool," doesn't indicate someone who lacks intelligence, but rather someone who lacks a moral compass. Natural man, because he is corrupt, does not believe in the God of the Bible, and he will tend to dismiss arguments based on revelation to lead him out of his folly. As the psalm continues, it pictures God looking down from heaven, searching for anyone who is "wise" and who "seeks God" and pointing out that "all have turned away" and "become corrupt."[34] God expects man to heed the witnesses he has given.

It is precisely at this point that the apologist runs into difficulty in using the witnesses God has given, as the Scriptures themselves indicate. Where the Scriptures do give tangible arguments for the existence of God, they tend to associate them with language which shows these arguments have not caused people to recognize God due to the total corruption of human nature. The classic example is Romans 1 and 2, where St. Paul notes that gross sinners do not see the majesty of the Lord in the physical world around them and that intellectuals do not recognize God's moral law within themselves even from the need for civil law and order. How can people miss something that God tells us they should see? The natural human capacity to miss obvious information was demonstrated by the famous "invisible gorilla" experiment.[35] The subjects of the experiment were asked to count the number of passes of a basketball by players wearing white shirts in a group where half the players wore black shirts. During the experiment a person in a gorilla suit walked conspicuously through the area of play, but half the experimental subjects did not notice the gorilla's presence. They had no excuse for not seeing him. At some level they did see him, but they did not see him at a conscious level. So it is with God's revelation through nature and conscience. Being created

---

32 Romans 1:21.

33 Psalm 14:1a.

34 Psalm 14:2-3. See also Romans 3:11-12.

35 DJ Simons & CF Chabris. "Gorillas in our Midst: Sustained Inattentional Blindness for Dynamic Events," *Perception* **28**:1029-1074 (SAGE Publications, Inc., Thousand Oaks, CA, 1999).

perfect, man had the natural knowledge of the existence of God infused in his essence, so that all of us are culpable if we do not retain it. We all are "without excuse." On the other hand, the degree of our conscious and subconscious knowledge of the existence of God from nature and conscience is affected by the age we attain and the environment in which we live.[36] A brief look at these two arguments will help establish their usefulness in philosophical discussions. Paul also noted that even those who have been given the written law cannot refrain from treating it in a ritualistic sense rather than as the revelation of the divine will.

The concept that the existence of the universe demands a creator is called the *cosmological argument*. Psalm 19:1-2 says: "The heavens declare the glory of God, and the expanse proclaims the work of his hands. Day after day they pour out speech; night after night they communicate knowledge." The verses that follow state that the voice of the heavens goes out into all the earth—every human being has the testimony that creation gives.[37] Once again, Scripture asserts that the very existence of the heavens makes a statement. The size and complexity of the universe does speak for itself. When people had only primitive tools and could build only simple structures, they knew they needed help in dealing with the universe, even if they did not recognize a specific creator. Hence, they practiced idolatry, hoping to gain the attention of some helper. Even to people as advanced in construction techniques as the Romans, St. Paul could point out the obviously greater majesty of the natural world around them.[38] Even today, if we camp out in the middle of the Great Plains, far from the light pollution of the cities, we will marvel at the glorious display of the heavens. Who can help but exclaim, "How could such complexity happen without some supernatural designer and builder being responsible for it?"

Yet many people today don't find this line of argumentation to be persuasive. In St. Paul's day, they suppressed this knowledge; they also find reasons to do so today. They may well argue that what humans have accom-

---

[36] Even if one is an infant, blind or living in a completely manmade environment where God's creation is never seen, we still are all without excuse because God originally created mankind with a knowledge of him.

[37] Psalm 19:3-4.

[38] "For his invisible attributes, that is, his eternal power and divine nature, have been clearly seen since the creation of the world, being understood through what he has made. As a result, people are without excuse." (Romans 1:20).

plished in the last century is strong evidence that a divine builder of the universe is unnecessary. Today, scientists develop new species of plants and animals, and engineers build things capable of flying in the air and traveling through space. They have produced incredible computing and communicating power that people can hold in one hand. None of this could have happened as recently as the 1890's. Today these things combine to make the existence of the "gorilla" invisible. Conversely, some will assert that the size and complexity of the universe are so great that no god could possibly be able to hold it "in the palm of his hand" and control it.[39] The apologist should certainly challenge this thinking by pointing out that it is easy to overstate the abilities of man,[40] which are frequently shown to be hopelessly inadequate to deal with natural forces. Likewise, it is easy for critics to downsize the ability of an almighty God to control what we see, or think we see, beyond the solar system.[41] The grandeur of what we see in the natural world still soars beyond what we can construct using the known laws of physics, and it always will. These are good points and consistent with the existence of a god or God, but the skeptic will point out that they are an example of the fallacy of affirming the consequent. "Being consistent with" is not the same as "proving".

The second biblical argument for the existence of God is the existence of conscience, which is called the *moral argument*. For example, when Adam and Eve sinned, the law which the Lord had written in their hearts caused them to hide in fear.[42] Jesus pointed out that people understand that they have an obligation to their children.[43] One of the thieves crucified with Jesus recog-

---

[39] This argument is called *flipping the warrant*, which means using the evidence presented by one's opponent to support one's own argument. In this case, the argument of size might be used against the existence of a god although presented by the proponents of such existence.

[40] "And they said, 'Come, let us build ourselves a city and a tower with its top in the sky. Let us make a name for ourselves; otherwise, we will be scattered throughout the earth.'" (Genesis 11:4).

[41] "Then the LORD answered Job from the whirlwind. He said, 'Who is this who obscures my counsel with ignorant words? Get ready to answer me like a man; when I question you, you will inform me. Where were you when I established the earth? Tell me, if you have understanding. Who fixed its dimensions? Certainly you know! Who stretched a measuring line across it? What supports its foundations? Or who laid its cornerstone while the morning stars sang together and all the sons of God shouted for joy?'" (Job 38:1-7).

[42] "Then the man and his wife heard the sound of the LORD God walking in the garden at the time of the evening breeze, and they hid from the LORD God among the trees of the garden." (Genesis 3:8).

[43] [Jesus said,] "Who among you, if his son asks him for bread, will give him a stone? Or if he asks for a fish, will give him a snake? If you then, who are evil, know how to give good gifts to your children...." (Matthew 7:9-11).

nized the respect owed to God even though he was a scoundrel.[44] Certainly, there is a sense of justice in man's nature which is not present in the animal kingdom.

Some people think that animals understand evil to a limited degree, as when a dog recognizes that its actions were wrong and senses estrangement from its master[45] or as when the gorilla Koko mourned the death of its pet kitten.[46] Yet, such reactions are emotional and not truly a conscience. Animals labor to survive the current day, the current cycle of life or the current season; they do not plan for a lifetime or an afterlife. Therefore, if they have a vague sense of guilt, it is transitory and does not have long-term repercussions. Humans, conversely, have a strong sense of right and wrong which, even when misguided, can drive their actions well into the distant future, and they have a fear of punishment that can last long after an event. This is a result of the law which God wrote into man's heart and to which St. Paul was referring in Romans.[47] Certainly the existence of conscience is consistent with the existence of God.

The underlying problem is that natural man is incapable of accepting the truth of revelation from the Lord in any form because of his depravity. So in an apologetic setting, what is the usefulness of these arguments? Lutheran scholars have long claimed that the cosmological and moral arguments present evidence that God must exist, a point the authors of this book accept. Yet, the fools of this world, blinded by their sinful natures, say in their hearts that there is no God. So, no matter how convincing we find that these arguments are to the regenerate man (and since they are God's Word, we accept them absolutely), they don't actually help us much when it comes to dealing with skeptics in this world, especially skeptics who are anchored in Humanism and steeped in scientific theories. They believe they have found the origin of the universe in cosmological models. They question outright whether

---

44 [One thief said,] "Don't you even fear God, since you are undergoing the same punishment? We are punished justly, because we're getting back what we deserve for the things we did, but this man has done nothing wrong." (Luke 23:40-41).

45 [The Lord said,] "The ox knows its owner, and the donkey its master's feeding trough, but Israel does not know; my people do not understand." (Isaiah 1:3).

46 C. McGraw, "Gorilla Pets: Koko Mourns Kitten's Death" (*Los Angeles Times*, December 12, 2012).

47 "When Gentiles, who do not by nature have the law, do what the law demands, they are a law to themselves even though they do not have the law. They show that the work of the law is written on their hearts. Their consciences confirm this. Their competing thoughts either accuse or even excuse them." (Roman 2:14-15).

all people really have a conscience and whether there is a universal moral code written into the hearts of men. Therefore, quoting a few Bible passages and claiming that we have proven God's existence will not likely have a positive effect. In fact, it may even end our chances of further witness.

This situation should not be unexpected or discouraging. Paul's point in Romans 1 and 2 was not to give proofs for the existence of God, but rather to declare that everyone will be judged. It does not matter whether one's rebellion is against the witness of nature, the witness of conscience or the Law of Moses, everyone is by nature in rebellion against God; therefore, God is righteous in punishing all forms of rebellion.

Narrowing the Focus

Having looked at the situation from the viewpoint of biblical revelation, we must now consider what we can say in the realms of philosophy and science. We already know that private gods are unique because they are created by the people who worship them, and they exist only to the extent that those people are willing to give them their service. We will therefore look at this type of god when we discuss atheism and agnosticism later in this chapter. As for the other types of gods, let us define them as being *supernatural beings*, that is, as *beings who are not defined or constrained by the laws of the physical universe*. This separates the concept of a divine being from that of a galactic superhero who *is* bound by the laws of nature. As previously demonstrated, the Lord is a supernatural being.

When we are asked whether we can prove that a supernatural god exists using science, we are forced to answer "no". Why? When using deductive reasoning, one can never prove the existence of something outside the domain in which one is working. For example, if one lived in a two-dimensional world, one could not prove the existence of a third dimension. Anything that happened in the third dimension that impacted one's two-dimensional plane would be interpreted as an event that happened in that plane by those living there. It might be highly confusing to them, but the residents would strive to give the best explanation of what had occurred that they could devise. While they might speculate about higher dimensions, none of their instruments could detect them or measure anything in them. Similarly, if one is working in the domain of rational numbers (those that can be represented as the quotient of two integers), one cannot create an irrational number (i.e., a non-repeating decimal number, such as π) using only the operations allowed for rational numbers (i.e., addition, subtraction, multiplication, and division). One would need a transcendental operator (e.g., square root or infinite summation) to create an irrational or imaginary number.

In the same way, when one is working in the natural domain of the physical universe, one has no logical operators or scientific methods that can reach out from that domain into the supernatural domain in which God exists. No matter how clever one's reasoning or how complex one's proof, one always ends up with something in the physical world, unless one unethically inserts a hidden assumption about the existence of the supernatural into the proofs. This creates the fallacy of circular reasoning, which is often triggered by the fallacy of the *argument from ignorance* (i.e., claiming that something cannot exist in the physical world became it is not currently known). Unless one uses the assumption of the natural knowledge of God having been written in our hearts, an assumption that an unbeliever will not accept, one has no operator or pathway that will allow one to connect the physical and supernatural realms.[48] This is the reason why all arguments that endeavor to prove the existence of God are a waste of effort, even though we are firmly convinced that God exists.

Couldn't a supernatural being reach into the physical world to make its existence known? Unfortunately, not in a way that would be recognized by science. Even if a god were to interact with the physical world, those actions could not be traced to that god, as the pathway leading to it would leave the physical world and thus would be undetectable by means available within the physical universe. As in the two-dimensional world above, the god's actions, no matter how spectacular, would be assumed to be the result of some force of nature with which scientists were not yet familiar.[49] This concept of separation between what is natural and observable and what is supernatural and

48 "If the Natural Law had not been inscribed and placed by God into the heart, one would have to preach a long time before the consciences are touched; to a donkey, horse, ox, cow, one would have to preach 100,000 years before they would accept the Law in spite of the fact that they have ears, eyes, and heart, as man has; they can also hear it, but it does not touch their heart." (*St. Louis Edition. of Luther's Works III*:1053).

49 Sometimes the Lord did demonstrate his power to people through miracles, and the Scriptures do indicate these eye-witness accounts are important. Yet, without some word of the Lord to the people observing these miracles, their meaning would have been lost in the superstition of the time and, without their being recorded in the Bible, we could not deduce that they were acts of God from the physical evidence that we see today.

unobservable will be referenced several times in this book because it is essential to the understanding of why proving or disproving the existence of a divine being through scientific means is impossible.

Philosophical Efforts to Prove the Existence of God

Various philosophical arguments have been advanced to prove the existence of a god, yet these arguments have weaknesses, such as false premises, hidden assumptions, invalid reasoning, or lack of physical evidence, which has made the conclusion unsound. As apologists, we must recognize this situation and should not advance such arguments, lest we appear to have a religion which is based on human reason instead of divine revelation. If we were to base our belief for the existence of God on a philosophical or scientific argument and that argument were later shown to be false, would we give up our belief in God? If we wouldn't, then why should we use an argument that is irrelevant to our faith? It is as if we put down our college diploma and a few dollars on the counter at Starbuck's and asked for a cup of coffee. They will readily give us the coffee if we place down the money alone. Why would we want to risk slopping coffee on our diploma if it has no bearing on the transaction? In the same way we should not risk harming our faith by human arguments.

In arguing for the existence of God, the burden of proof lies on those who are proposing such existence. The opponents merely need to demonstrate logical inconsistencies or give counterexamples. Let us examine some commonly proposed arguments for the existence of God and the difficulties that are involved in them.

Ontological Argument (St. Anselm): It is possible to imagine a perfect being who has all the highest levels of the best characteristics of every good thing and none of the evil characteristics that exist in the world. Moreover, such a being could not be perfect unless its essence included actually existing. As a result, a perfect being must exist, and that being is God. **Rebuttal:** Anselm's argument illegitimately moves from the existence of an idea to the existence of a thing that corresponds to the idea. Anselm tries to define something into existence, but that is a fallacy called *mind projection*.[50] We cannot create a thing simply by defining it, no matter how reasonable the thing is or how much we want it to exist. If we could, we would all be rich.

Cosmological Argument (Aristotle/Aquinas): Everything that moves must have something to move it (i.e., a mover). One can therefore follow the chain of movers backwards until the first (i.e., prime) mover is found. Because the prime mover is not set into motion by any other mover, it must be a god. **Rebuttal:** This argument is an example of the fallacy called *begging the question*,[51] but the fallacy is hidden by the poor statement of the premises (i.e., the assumption that there is a supernatural realm is hidden). All observable items that are moved are entities in the *physical world*, and the movers are also *physical* entities. The first mover must therefore also be an entity in the physical world, and thus it cannot be supernatural; consequently, it cannot be a god. To claim that this first physical mover can only be moved by a supernatural mover requires we further assume 1) that such a supernatural mover exists and 2) that it can influence something in the physical world. But this puts us back at the start and means we have not proven a supernatural mover must exist. Moreover, Isaac Newton's discovery of the laws of physical motion showed that the first premise is false, meaning the argument contains the fallacy called *false premise*.[52] Newton's third law of motion states if object **A** applies a force to object **B**, then object **B** applies an equal force to object **A**. As a result, the objects move each other, and a first mover is not necessary to begin the process. Discoveries in quantum and relativistic mechanics reinforce the principle that objects in nature are continually engaging in mutual influence on each other and that therefore there is no need for a "first mover" to start the process.[53]

Cosmological Argument (Leibniz): The non-existence of the universe would require no explanation, but the existence of the universe requires an

---

[50] Mind projection is a fallacy asserting that the way one sees, or wishes to see, the world reflects the way the world really is, going as far as assuming the real existence of imagined objects.

[51] Begging the question is a fallacy where the conclusion and one of the assumptions are really the same, so the argument proves nothing.

[52] False premise is a fallacy in which one or more of the assumptions is not true, so the validity of the conclusion cannot be determined.

[53] Richard Wolfson, *Einstein's Relativity and the Quantum Revolution* (The Great Courses, The Teaching Company, Chantilly, VA, 2000).

explanation, and that explanation is a god. **Rebuttal:** While this argument might have theological merit (see previous discussion), it does not have philosophical merit. We have seen "existence" but never seen "non-existence." Why is an explanation for existence required? The perpetual existence of the universe is as reasonable as the universe not having existed at some time in the past. Such perpetual existence has been believed by many since the ancient Greek philosophers. In fact, it is no less unreasonable than that a god exists perpetually. As often occurs in philosophy, what is reasonable to one person is not reasonable to another, so nothing can be proven. This argument is an example of the fallacy of *wishful thinking.*[54]

Cosmological Argument (Kalam/Craig): This argument is a syllogism: 1) Whatever begins to exist has a cause; 2) the universe began to exist; 3) therefore, the universe has a cause, which must be a god. **Rebuttal:** As with Aristotle's argument, there is a clever fallacy in the problem statement. To resolve a syllogism, the middle term must have the same meaning in both premises, i.e., "began to exist" must have the identical meaning to "begins to exist." In the second premise this meaning is that something comes into existence from nothing (*ex nihilo*). If its meaning in the first premise is not the same, the conclusion is automatically unsound because there is no linkage between the premises (called the *four-term fallacy*). If "begins to exist" does mean the same, then whether or not the first premise is true is unprovable because we do not have any observations of something coming into existence from nothing nor is it likely that such observations will occur. The premise is therefore not well-grounded, and the argument is unsound. Whether or not the second premise is well-grounded will depend on the development of a definitive and universally accepted grand unification theory of all physics,[55] which is unlikely to occur in the foreseeable future. Moreover, even if the argument were sound, it would be worthless to Christian apologists because it would only show that a god must have existed and acted billions of years ago. Deists who would believe in such a god would merely enter hell by a different door than atheists who don't. The existence of the god that people are trying to

---

[54] Wishful thinking is a fallacy in which one wants something to be true, and therefore concludes it is true, without evidence to support the conclusion. It tries to "wish" something into existence. It is often used synonymously with mind projection.

[55] Don Lincoln, *The Theory of Everything: The Quest to Explain All Reality* (The Great Courses, The Teaching Company, Chantilly, VA, 2017).

prove in this argument is not the God of the Bible. As Solomon said, this argument is a "chasing after wind."[56]

Teleological Argument (William Paley): The cosmos is well ordered, well-balanced and extremely complex. In fact, if certain natural constants differed significantly from their observed values, the universe as we know it could not exist. Life would be impossible. Just as one can recognize the existence of a skilled watchmaker from the existence of a precise timepiece, one can recognize the existence of a god from the precisely organized universe (see Chapter 5). **Rebuttal:** While the odds may be a billion-to-one against any specific ticket winning a national lottery, eventually someone will get a winning ticket. Even if it now appears that the odds are astronomically low for any particular universe existing out of all possible universes, yet at least one of these many universes clearly does exist now. If we were not in that universe, then we would not exist to be considering the issue! Someone might even argue that every universe failed until the one we live in came along (i.e., nature finally won the universe lottery). Conversely, it may be that the critical universal constants so necessary for life are, in fact, forced to have their specific values by the very nature of matter, energy, space and time. If that were the case, the existence of the universe as we know it would not be improbable at all, perhaps it would even be the default case. Scientists are actively seeking to learn whether the natural constants are, in reality, intrinsic properties of existence rather than of a particular universe's unique specifications.[57] Simply because we do not know something now does not mean it is unknowable. The fallacy at the root of this argument is called the *argument from ignorance*.[58]

Thermodynamic Argument: The second law of thermodynamics states that the randomness in nature, measured as *entropy*, must always increase. As a result, complex molecules like DNA could not have come into existence from simpler ones by natural processes. Therefore, without a god, life could not have evolved, so there must be a god. **Rebuttal:** The nature of evolution and creation will be discussed in detail in Chapter 5. However, this particular

---

[56] Ecclesiastes 1:14.

[57] Lincoln, ibid.

[58] Argument from ignorance is a fallacy which claims that because an answer is unknown, perhaps even by the experts, therefore, it is unknowable and an alternative explanation is as reasonable and must be accepted.

argument is based on a fundamental misunderstanding of the second law of thermodynamics. Entropy is a measure of the number of microstates in a particular system,[59] not the degree of organization of any specific microstate in that system. Therefore, some components of a system can become more organized while others become less organized during a reaction process, as long as the entropy of the overall system remains constant or increases. For example, when it snows, snowflakes of complex shapes and symmetries form naturally out of the extensive disorganization that exists in a storm cloud. Entropy is only one factor that determines whether and how a particular process will occur. Each system must be evaluated on its own merit, and such evaluation involves a complicated set of equations when systems are complex. This argument is an example of a false premise fallacy.

Experiential Argument: A substantial number of people claim to have had personal religious experiences with a god or other-worldly being, particularly in near-death situations. Therefore, a god must exist. **Rebuttal:** Not everything which a human mind is convinced it has experienced is based on reality. Dreams and hallucinations can seem very real, particularly when a person believes himself to be dying. Moreover, research in cognitive psychology (see Chapter 9) has shown that the subconscious mind will develop programs (called *scripts*) to deal with critical situations, and these may explain many of the perceived religious encounters.[60] When a pre-stored script is activated, it feeds the conscious mind information which can be at variance with its inputs from the physical senses. The conscious mind tries to reconcile the differences, often with unexpected results. This explains why people witnessing crimes often get the details wrong and why near-death experiences vary by culture. Claims of religious experiences cannot be investigated because they are not repeatable and cannot be tested or verified, even though they may seem to be very real to the people at the time.[61] The experiential argument is an argument from ignorance.

---

59 The entropy (S) is equal to the Boltzmann constant (k_B) times the natural logarithm of the number of microstates (Greek letter Ω).

60 Dean Mobbs & Caroline Watt, "Near-Death Experiences Explained be Science," Trends in Cognitive Psychology **15**:447-449, 2011.

61 Michael Shermer, *Skepticism 101: How to Think like a Scientist* (The Great Courses, The Teaching Company, Chantilly, VA, 2013), Lect. 7.

Pragmatic (Moralistic) Argument: Human society requires an ethical basis to survive. Ethics are more effectively enforced if people fear a God and eternal punishment and have a hope for eternal life. Therefore, God must exist because humans need to have such an ethical framework. **Rebuttal:** The expediency of a belief does not prove its truthfulness. Moreover, even the promise of heaven and the threat of hell do not prevent crime or build just societies. The fear of immediate consequences and the promise of immediate reward are much stronger motivators, and these can exist even in a totalitarian society. Because of the existence of contrary evidence, this is an example of the false premise fallacy. Objective morality, in terms of God's moral law, will be covered in Chapter 7.

Subjective Awareness Argument: Subjective awareness is quite unlike anything we have encountered in the physical universe. The weirdness of consciousness and our inability to understand it have given rise to the notion of substance dualism between the mental and the material. Subjective awareness had to be given to man by a supernatural being. **Rebuttal:** The existence of something currently unexplained in the physical universe does not mean that it does not have a natural explanation. Most things known today were at one time mysteries to the people who encountered them. While this argument is consistent with the existence of a God, it does not prove such existence, because subjective awareness could simply be an attribute caused by some gene in human DNA. Since this is an area of active study in which supporting and contrary evidence may yet be found,[62] this argument is an argument from ignorance.

None of the arguments above would prove the existence of the God of the Bible even if they had the possibility of being logically sound. From the viewpoint of Christianity, the real limitations in these arguments are that they leave us no closer to proclaiming the message of Christ and that they may even ensnare us in other issues in the process of making such arguments. As such, they are of no value to us.

---

[62] Andrew Newberg, *The Spiritual Brain* (The Great Courses, The Teaching Company, Chantilly, VA, 2012).

Efforts to Disprove the Existence of God

We will next consider the arguments advanced against the existence of a God. These are arguments that we must be ready to refute philosophically. In this case, however, the burden of proof is on those who deny the existence of a God, and we can use Scripture in fashioning our counterexamples. This is because the proponents must disprove the existence of all gods, including the God of the Bible. Nonetheless, we must beware lest we mix theology with philosophy in our response and corrupt our standard of truth. We must keep these arguments separate even if they both apply. Philosophical arguments are given in this chapter, and theological arguments are presented in later chapters.

The Omnipotence Paradox: If God were omnipotent, he could do anything. he could, therefore, make a rock so heavy that he could not lift it. If he could not make such a rock, then he would not be omnipotent. If he could not lift such a rock, he also would not be omnipotent. Since God cannot be omnipotent in either of the only two possible cases, therefore an omnipotent god cannot exist. **Rebuttal**: This is a clever example of the false premise fallacy, using an inaccurate definition. The correct definition of omnipotence is that God can do anything *consistent with his will.* Since it is inconsistent with God's will to perform "parlor stunts" devised by sinful human beings, this argument can be rejected based on its fallacy.

Existence of Evil Argument: Because evil exists, God cannot be simultaneously omnipotent, omniscient, loving and good. Therefore, there is no god. **Rebuttal**: We must begin by recognizing that there are two types of evil. Moral evil (i.e., sin) is whatever is against the will of God. It exists because the Lord gave the angels and humans the freedom to choose between good and evil, and they chose to sin. The "why and how" of God allowing this to happen is a theological issue on which we have limited revelation. Moral evil, which affects man's relationship with God, is not however the issue at hand. The "evil" in this argument is philosophical, something that is defined relative to some human standard, for example, something regarded as being to the disadvantage of some or all people. But this definition creates a problem. What if the omnipotent, omniscient, loving, and good god's favorite creature was the leopard seal, the oak tree or slime mold, and that god regarded mankind as an invasive pest? Then being good to its favorite creature would mean that that god would give mankind grief to keep it under control. It is human arrogance to claim that a god must define "good" in terms of what is good for humanity. We, after all, do not define "good" in terms of what is good for bindweed or mosquitoes. There is no reason why what is evil by human standards cannot serve the will of a loving and good God.[63] The existence-of-evil argument is based on the fallacy of wishful thinking. We cannot wish something out of existence because it does not meet our standards any more than we can wish something into existence because we find it desirable. Although this argument fails on logical grounds, the existence of evil is an important topic for the Christian apologist and will be discussed in more detail in Chapter 4.

Injustice Argument: People are treated unfairly because skills, living environments and rewards are not allocated on the basis of merit or equality. The good and bad things of life are distributed either arbitrarily or with an advantage to those who already have good things. People suffer evil and pain independent of whether they deserve it or not. Therefore, God cannot be omnipotent, omniscient, and just, and he does not really exist. **Rebuttal**: The psalmist Asaph wrote, "For I envied the arrogant; I saw the prosperity of the wicked. They have an easy time until they die, and their bodies are well fed."[64] For centuries even believers have wondered why the Lord could treat his followers so poorly and the wicked so well. One can only grasp this in terms of how abhorrent sin is to God.[65] In the eyes of a perfect God, all people, including their children, would be repugnant rebels. None of them would deserve anything but his wrath. In fact, they would all deserve severe punishment for acting against his will. That he would give anyone anything better than that is pure mercy, and no one has a right to mercy.[66] Who gave frail human beings the right to impose their standards on the behavior of an omnipotent God? They are the ones who befouled his perfect world. Bad

---

63 [Solomon wrote,] "Do not despise the LORD's instruction, my son, and do not loathe his discipline; for the LORD disciplines the one he loves, just as a father disciplines the son in whom he delights." (Proverbs 3:11-12).

64 Psalm 73:3-4.

65 "When the LORD saw that human wickedness was widespread on the earth and that every inclination of the human mind was nothing but evil all the time, the LORD regretted that he had made man on the earth, and he was deeply grieved." (Genesis 6:5-6).

66 [The Lord said,] "I will cause all my goodness to pass in front of you, and I will proclaim the name 'the LORD' before you. I will be gracious to whom I will be gracious, and I will have compassion on whom I will have compassion." (Exodus 33:19).

things do not happen to good people; bad things happen to bad people because there are no good people by the standards of a perfect God. That is a bitter statement for humans to accept, but it is reasonable behavior for a just God. This argument is therefore a false premise fallacy.

Inconsistent Revelation Argument: Since the various religions have Gods that differ widely in their attributes based on different sources of revelation, only one of these religions, at most, can be right about God. **Rebuttal**: Of course, but what is the problem with that? There are often conflicting claims to what is true or to whom a piece of property belongs. Those claims are resolved in a court of justice, and it is completely reasonable that the real God will resolve claims about who is right in his court of justice. If he has told people the truth, then it is people's fault if they do not recognize this truth and instead believe in false and worthless deities. This argument is a red herring in the question of the existence of a God because it is immaterial to that issue.

Simplicity Argument: Because god is undetectable by human observation or by laboratory instruments, and because the universe is no different if he exists or doesn't exist, therefore, by Occam's Razor, the simplest explanation must be correct, and that explanation is that no god exists. **Rebuttal**: Occam's Razor states that the simplest explanation is usually the best. It is not a law or rule, but a practical guideline that doesn't always work, as every doctor, scientist, etc. knows. It is only a human formulation, put forward, oddly enough, by a monk. God's existence cannot be legislated away, even if all people agree that it should be. Moreover, there is no way we can test whether the universe would be different with or without the existence of God, so one of the premises is unverifiable. It is a case of the false premise fallacy, namely applying a human standard to a supernatural being.

Finally, philosophical arguments against the existence of a god invariably run into the fallacy of *conflicting premises*.[67] One of their underlying assumptions is that only evidence that exists or has credence within the physical world can be considered. But another fundamental assumption is that there is no supernatural influence on the physical world. How can a supernatural god make itself known in the physical world if every action that it performs is

---

[67] Conflicting premises is a fallacy in which all the premises cannot be true at the same time because the truthfulness of one of the premises precludes the truthfulness of another.

regarded as an act of nature? Consequently, these arguments must be rejected on the grounds both of conflicting premises and of the relevant fallacy underlying each specific argument. One cannot disprove the existence of a supernatural being philosophically any more than one can prove its existence.

False Beliefs about God

Agnosticism is the belief that the existence and the identity of God cannot be determined. Agnostics have abandoned the search for the truth about God because they have become convinced that they can never find that truth with certainty. Anything which they might be led to believe could well be false and, as such, a waste of time and emotional energy. While they believe that they cannot rationally deny the existence of a god and/or of the supernatural, they feel the risk of neutrality on religious faith is better for them than adherence to something about which they could never be completely certain.

More and more, agnosticism is becoming the default position of Americans today. Such phrases as "all roads lead to heaven" and "all gods are really the same" characterize the attitude of those who prize their freedom to remain uncommitted. Those who are content with this situation are poor mission prospects. We can maintain contact with them, let them see our life of faith and inject the law into our conversations at appropriate moments, but they are likely to be unresponsive as long as they think their approach to life is working.

Agnostics become better mission prospects if life challenges the certainty of their beliefs. Death, disease, economic trouble, or relationship issues can make the "one can never know" position about God less comfortable. Lack of certainty or continuity has a way of making a person wonder about his or her life and whether there will be an accounting for those things which were mishandled. If we have kept a good relationship with an agnostic and if that person has been able to see the confident Christian life which we are living, the agnostic may start giving us subtle signals that he or she would like to have our resilient lifestyle as well. It is then time to switch from the apologetics mode to the outreach mode and to see whether an "I'm a sinner; you're a sinner" approach will work to get them to open up about their hurts and fears. If this begins to bear fruit, we can make a full-scale evangelism effort. If not, then we must fall back to watching and waiting for a future opportunity.

Atheism is the belief that there is no god. Specifically, atheists reject the existence of a God with whom one can communicate. Some atheists are very hostile to God and even actively attempt to spread their unbelief. Attempting to reason with such people or to reach them with the gospel will certainly be like casting pearls before swine. Here we must be prepared to answer their arguments against the existence of God and against the evil of religion. The former are in the preceding material of this chapter, while the latter are in Chapter 10 on the Christian church. Our goal must be to prevent them from leading others astray through phony reasoning or bullying. We must not let them give the impression that they are the people with the enlightened arguments, while we are superstitious morons. We should expect name-calling, and we should be quick to point out that those who have legitimate arguments do not have to resort to such gutter tactics (i.e., *ad hominem* arguments[68]). We must keep cool and rebuke them if they fume. We should be willing to settle for a draw in which we concede nothing. These people have made themselves very religious in being anti-god.

Many atheists are not nearly so hostile, or they are against God and religion for very specific reasons. Faced with this situation, the first job of the apologist is to determine the real issue for unbelief in God. Some have never thought much about God. Atheism is the default position they learned, and they have never doubted it. With such people, we must explore the consistency of their atheism. What is the basis of their moral sense of right and wrong? Do they feel an obligation to anyone besides themselves and, if so, why? If they are self-centered, there is little hope for making progress with the message of Jesus. If they feel any significant obligation to family, friends, or community, then we can explore these to show them that these are inconsistent without a belief in a God that places an obligation on us to care for our fellowmen. If we can reach a point with them where they acknowledge a sense of knowing that they ought to be held accountable on these matters, the door may be open to evangelism.

Some atheists have suffered misfortune and feel that if a merciful God exists, the misfortune would not have happened. Here we need to show sympathy. The world can be a difficult place. There are many things that are harmful and some people who are overtly evil. We need to assure them that

---

[68] An *ad hominem* fallacy is an attack on the personal character of the speaker, either directly or through those associated with him, rather than on the arguments which he presents.

the Lord does care about what happens in the world, but that because he has given people the ability to make their own worldly decisions, he has to let things play themselves out. Would they want God to intervene in their lives continually, checking every one of their actions to determine whether he should let them do such things? It is unlikely that they would want that. Yet, if he doesn't so intervene, people will do dumb things, and misfortunes will occur. Sin makes the world a troubling place in which to live. The God of the Bible can help us in this world to deal with the misfortunes that occur to us, and he can eventually take us somewhere where bad things never happen. These ideas might be used as an opening to begin to talk about a Savior God over the course of future conversations.

Some people have had bad experiences with organized religion or with a cult of some sort. We must be quick to assure such people that we are not a cult with secret rituals that tries to separate them from their family and friends. Rather, we are people with a message of good news for everyone, and spreading that message is our whole purpose. We should be ready to share with them any part of that message that they appear ready and willing to hear. We should also acknowledge that no member of any church is perfect in his or her behavior. The church is an organization made up of people who are still sinners and who have not yet reached perfection. Thus, our congregations are composed of repentant sinners, who understand that the Lord expects our light of Christian love to shine to the world. If these troubled individuals are willing to listen at all, they may have questions that this book can help answer. We will need to win their confidence, but we must never be willing to compromise on biblical teachings just to get them sitting in our pews. Their bad experience with organized religion may have arisen from their insistence that they had a right to commit certain sins and that they did not need to repent of such sinful behavior.

Private gods are a troubling problem which every apologist encounters. Even many people who claim to be Christians can practice secret idolatry, just as many people in the Old Testament did.[69] The only difference might be that in the Old Testament people had idols representing their household gods, and today people have things that serve the same function but are given more

---

69 Michael A. Lockwood, *The Unholy Trinity*: *Martin Luther against the Idol of Me, Myself, and I* (Concordia Publishing House, St. Louis, 2016).

socially acceptable names. When dealing with people who raise questions about Christianity, we must always probe for these false gods, which can be the real source of spiritual uncertainty. People can mistakenly believe that being culturally part of a church and having a head knowledge of what the church professes are sufficient, even while their time and attention are directed elsewhere. Private gods take people away from God and his Word.

We expect that unbelievers will fill their time with such gods because they naturally seek their fulfilment outside of Christ's church. Yet, it is important that we point out to unbelievers that they really do have gods which gobble up their time and resources. Moreover, these private gods will be of no help to them when life gets difficult and when death arrives. The initially apparently comfortable road of life will eventually become rocky and then plunge over a cliff.

For some, such a message may be a wakeup call. Every Christian also must realize the danger in devoting time and treasure to things that take them away from their Lord. If the hobby, the possession, the TV program, the internet, the children's sports activities, or the job is preventing the Christian from devoting the time and the resources to the Lord which he has the right to expect from us, then these things are private gods of our own making, and we are worshiping them. Unlike supernatural gods, their existence cannot be questioned, and their influence is undeniable. The apologist must make the case as Jesus did that one cannot love God and the things of this world.[70] Moreover, like the Israelites in the Old Testament, people are likely to be very defensive about their right to do as they please and still expect the Lord to bless them.[71]

Summary

We have examined the question of the existence of God and have seen that that existence is unprovable through philosophical arguments. It is a matter of faith, and that is good. If our faith in a supernatural being depended on making the right assumptions, then it would always rest on a human action.

---

70 [Jesus said,] "No one can serve two masters, since either he will hate one and love the other, or he will be devoted to one and despise the other. You cannot serve both God and money." (Matthew 6:24).

71 [The Lord said,] "Do you steal, murder, commit adultery, swear falsely, burn incense to Baal, and follow other gods that you have not known? Then do you come and stand before me in this house that bears my name and say, 'We are rescued, so we can continue doing all these detestable acts'?" (Jeremiah 7:9-10).

We could never be certain that what we believe today would not be shown to be false tomorrow. In our apologetics, therefore, we must always frame our arguments so that they point toward our certain source of knowledge, the Holy Scriptures. Depending on the person with whom we are dealing, we may have to shape our arguments to deal with their issues. It is of utmost importance, however, that we never direct people away from the Scriptures to some human argument lest we put them on the path of trusting their own reason for their salvation.

3

The Bible

As stated in Chapter 1, theological truth comes through revelation. As a result, revelation is the standard by which all ideas about the nature of God and his will must be judged. Why is this so? God is supernatural, that is, beyond the laws governing the natural world. While a supernatural being is not by definition excluded from reaching into the natural world to contact its inhabitants, the human mind is excluded from reaching out of the natural world into the supernatural world to initiate that contact. If it could do so, it would itself be supernatural. Therefore, revelation must originate with God who works through a human or other agency to provide the divine message. If such a message is not accepted in its entirety as the standard of divine truth, then human ideas, e.g., philosophy, must be used to revise it. The reason why people who claim to belong to the same religion differ in what they believe is that they mix some of their own ideas, e.g., their philosophical standards, with the standard of revelation that they claim came from their God. When they do this, their standard of truth is no longer divine revelation, but their own philosophy, which they have superimposed upon the revelation of their God. In this process, they have reshaped their God in their own image, not as he appears in their source of revelation.

In this chapter, we will discuss the Bible as the standard of truth concerning the Lord God[1] and the apologist's role in defending this standard. As part of

[1] [A psalmist wrote,] "Your word is a lamp for my feet and a light on my path." (Psalm 119:105).

that defense, it is wise, when the situation permits, to encourage people to read specific sections of the Scriptures to allow the Holy Spirit to work directly on their hearts. At the end of the chapter, we will touch briefly on other sources of supposed revelation and why they cannot be set beside the Bible as other sources of God's Word.

Setting the Stage

To defend the teachings of the Bible, one must know the teachings of the Bible.[2] Most people who claim that they believe what the Bible teaches do not know what the Bible teaches, often even in critical matters of faith. This leads people to try to defend what the Bible never says. Sadly, it is not only laypeople who have this problem. The Bible is a book of faith, but it is also a book of knowledge.[3] If faith gets separated from knowledge, then what is being defended is not the Word of God but the ideas of men.[4]

First, let us consider how easy it is to overstate or understate what the Bible really says by examining the question, "How many wives did Adam have?" Many pious Christians will quickly answer "one," but this answer adds to what the Bible teaches. The Bible gives us very little information about the life of Adam. It is possible, for example, that Adam married one of his great granddaughters to have more children, perhaps after Eve's death. The Bible does not give us enough information to judge the truth of such an assertion. People might try the answer "I don't know," but this answer admits less than the Bible teaches because we know that Adam was married to Eve. The correct answer is "at least one," which states no more and no less than what the Bible tells us. This example should convince the apologist that he or she must study what the Scripture actually says about a subject before rushing into the fray.

---

[2] [Moses said,] "These words that I am giving you today are to be in your heart. Repeat them to your children. Talk about them when you sit in your house and when you walk along the road, when you lie down and when you get up. Bind them as a sign on your hand and let them be a symbol on your forehead. Write them on the doorposts of your house and on your city gates." (Deuteronomy 6:6-9).

[3] "All Scripture is inspired by God and is profitable for teaching, for rebuking, for correcting, for training in righteousness, so that the man of God may be complete, equipped for every good work." (2 Timothy 3:16-17).

[4] "But the LORD said to me, 'These prophets are prophesying a lie in my name. I did not send them, nor did I command them or speak to them. They are prophesying to you a false vision, worthless divination, the deceit of their own minds.'" (Jeremiah 14:14).

Second, in apologetics we must be diligent in deciding what we are defending and to whom. There is a difference in how we should defend the Bible as our source of revelation to an unbeliever and how we should defend the integrity of biblical teachings to someone who claims to be a Christian but wants to keep a spiritual foot outside of the Holy Scriptures. We need to ask, "Are we facing wonderers or wanderers?" The apologist must determine whether the goal should be to impart information, argue the reasonableness of the Christian belief about the Bible or confront the straying with the indefensibility of their position. We will address these considerations in terms of the various challenges to the Holy Scriptures that we encounter on our heavenward journey.[5]

The Bible as Revelation

A common challenge the apologist will meet is that Christianity is based on the fallacy of *circular reasoning.* Christians claim to believe that the Bible is true because it is the Word of God, but they also believe in God because the Bible teaches about him. The apologist must respond to this challenge by asserting that we believe that the Bible is the Word of God because it convinces us that it is the Word of God. We, therefore, take it on faith that it is the Word of God, just as physical scientists take on faith that they can explain all observations of nature in terms of mass, energy, time and space. It is our fundamental assumption, and it is certainly as reasonable as the fundamental assumption of science. We say that the Bible is self-authenticating, because when we study it, the Holy Spirit works through what we read to convince us that it is actually the revelation of God. Consequently, an important part of the revelation which is contained in the Bible is that the Lord gave us the Bible.[6]

---

[5] A related concern is defending the faith of our fellow Christians who are troubled by the attacks of skeptics or false teachers. To some extent, this is the point of all Christian education. However, we would not be writing a book like this if we did not recognize that the faithful need to face attacks from unbelievers. Sometimes, those attacks "get under their skin," and they need solid apologetics to keep them from being harmed spiritually. We won't spend a lot of time on this in our discussion, but it is in the background of all that we are writing.

[6] "Jesus said to them, 'How foolish and slow you are to believe all that the prophets have spoken! Wasn't it necessary for the Messiah to suffer these things and enter into his glory?' Then beginning with Moses and all the Prophets, he interpreted for them the things concerning himself in all the Scriptures." (Luke 24:25-27).

We must readily acknowledge that we cannot prove the Bible is the Word of God based on external sources. If we could, then these external sources would be our real standard of belief and not the Bible itself. This is an extremely important point. If we appeal to reason, history, science, archeology, etc., then we can be attacked from those quarters because we have tried to build upon their real estate. In the process, we have increased the number of flanks that we must defend. If something in one of those areas appears to contradict the Bible, then even if it is later found to be false, the damage will have been done: our defenses will be breached, and we will be in retreat. Consequently, the Bible must stand on its own. It will appear to fall if whatever material that we have used to buttress it fails. And we can count on anything that is devised by humans to eventually fail.[7]

To be successful, the apologist must use what the military calls a "cordon defense" and not a "defense in depth." A cordon defense requires that everything be defended. The defensive perimeter is set so that everything of value is within the perimeter, and nothing outside the perimeter will be defended. This is the type of defense which one uses when one has an impregnable position, such as the rock which is the Holy Scriptures. The enemy must spend its strength on attacking that position and gaining nothing. On the other hand, a defense-in-depth approach allows one to attempt to strengthen one's position by increasing the territory being defended. If the defenses in some areas are breached, then one can fall back to more essential positions, abandoning what can no longer be maintained. While the latter approach has advantages when awaiting reinforcements or a peace settlement, it is disastrous when applied to biblical apologetics. There are no reinforcements coming to our aid, and there will be no peace settlement with the forces of Satan. If we argue for things beyond what Scripture teaches, thereby deluding ourselves that they will help us, then when those things later are shown to be incorrect, we will have lost the strategic position that all our doctrine is true, and we will be forced to concede more and more biblical teachings to maintain our viability.[8]

---

[7] [A psalmist wrote,] "A king is not saved by a large army; a warrior will not be rescued by great strength. The horse is a false hope for safety; it provides no escape by its great power." (Psalm 33:16-17).

[8] [Moses said,] "Be careful to do everything I command you; do not add anything to it or take anything away from it." (Deuteronomy 12:32).

Biblicism (the "Paper Pope")

While some accept that we should not expand our position beyond the Scriptures to incorporate other information, they argue that we should soften doctrinal positions in the light of social changes. They insist that the Lord never intended that his Word should be bound but that it should have free course to reach people in every age. Such people wish to be called Christians, but they do not want to be hemmed in by the teachings of the Bible. They feel that a wise and loving God would not bind current generations to the limitations which he might have had to impose during more primitive times. Such people deride the Bible as a "paper pope."[9] They claim that just as the pope has put the Roman Catholic Church into a doctrinal bind by insisting that he is infallible in matters of faith and life, so Christianity is put into a doctrinal straightjacket by our insistence that the Bible must be the only source and norm of doctrine.

As apologists, we must reject this idea because it replaces the Bible as our standard of truth with the notion that consensus can be used as a standard of revelation (historically called the *Vincentian Canon*).[10] What is being proposed by those who want to reinterpret the Bible in the light of modern science and social theories is not a standard of truth at all. It is a pseudo-standard based on what the "enlightened community" wants to be true, and it will constantly be in flux. This approach is a logical fallacy called *appeal to the masses* because the disposition of the masses, rather than sound reasoning, is used to establish the conclusion. Apologists must not yield to ridicule and give this proposal any credence, because it rapidly undermines every teaching of the Bible.

The apologist must recognize that what is wrong with the pope is not his inflexibility, but that he has abandoned the Scriptures for his own ideas. Our defense of the Bible in this matter must be based on two unchangeables—the will of God and the nature of man. As we will discuss in Chapter 4 on the nature of God, God never changes, so his will never changes.[11] Man's nature

---

9 Karl Barth, *Church Dogmatics, Vol I.* (T & T Clark, London, 1969), *525*.

10 St Vincent of Lérins established a threefold test of catholicity, namely "what has been believed everywhere, always, and by all." In other words, ecumenicity, antiquity and consent legitimize doctrine.

11 [Samuel said,] "Furthermore, the Eternal One of Israel does not lie or change his mind, for he is not man who changes his mind." (1 Samuel 15:29).

also does not change, but remains totally corrupt.[12] While the outward manifestations of man's corruption might change from generation to generation, man's perverse nature continues to remain persistent under various guises of civic righteousness.[13] Cain did not like the Lord's message and neither did the people at the time of the Exodus, of the judges, of the kings, of the returning exiles or of Jesus' ministry. In fact, when people are happy with the message they are hearing from God's preachers, it is a sign that the preachers are preaching falsely.[14] The apologist's message is that we can count on the Scriptures being God's Word because they will be understood in the same way in different eras by readers using sound principles of interpretation. Thanks to the Scriptures being a rock and not sand,[15] we know we can trust the God who gave them.

The Canon

It is fair to ask how people knew which books belonged in the Bible. While the *Qur'an* and the *Book of Mormon* were each the product of one man, the Bible was written over a long period of time by multiple writers. It is not unreasonable, if one views the Bible from outside of the church, to assume that it is thus a collection of spiritual ideas recorded over many years which some editor thought to be profitable for the common people and consequently put into one volume. In fact, because the parts of the Bible were gathered in at least two eras, it would seem that there must have been multiple collectors involved. Moreover, because some extant religious documents in the eras both before and after Christ were excluded, it would appear that the collectors clearly had a bias toward certain religious ideas to the exclusion of others. From this point of view, the *canon*[16] of the Bible is arbitrary. The apologist should recognize that this is a reasonable position for the unbelieving scholar to take because the Bible cannot be proven to be the Word of God from outside sources, as noted previously.

---

12 [The Lord said,] "I will never again curse the ground because of human beings, even though the inclination of the human heart is evil from youth onward." (Genesis 8:21b).

13 Civic righteousness (*coram mundo*) is righteousness in the eyes of the world, that is, good behavior which pleases one's neighbors but is not motivated by a love of the Lord.

14 [Jesus said,] "Woe to you when all people speak well of you, for this is the way their ancestors used to treat the false prophets." (Luke 6:26).

15 Matthew 7:24-27.

16 The canon, as a technical term, means those books which make up the Bible and none others.

To someone convinced that the Bible is the Word of God, that which is included in the Bible is not at all arbitrary. The Bible centers on Jesus of Nazareth who is the Christ (Greek) or the promised Messiah (Hebrew). The Old Testament was intended to prepare one chosen group of people, so that they would understand the need for a Savior from sin and would be ready to accept him and proclaim him when he arrived. It gives the history (primarily from a spiritual viewpoint) of the descendants of the patriarchs, Abraham and Israel, who were the people the Lord chose for this task. It contains the wisdom literature that was to help them live godly lives and the writings of the prophets that showed them how they were failing to live such lives.[17] It contains prophecies which told of the coming Savior so that they would recognize him.[18]

The New Testament is the record of the teachings and works of Jesus and of his personally chosen messengers, i.e., the apostles. Three men–John, Paul, and Luke–wrote 20 of the 27 books of the New Testament, so the idea that the books of the New Testament are an unstructured collection rather than a cohesive body of teachings is false. Concerning the rest of the books, three were written by apostles, two by Jesus' brothers and the other two by members of the early missionary teams. These books comprise a mutually supportive lattice of teachings about Jesus (See EndNote).

The key point for the apologist is that, while the Bible was written by numerous penmen, it had but one author, the Lord himself. This is clear from the cohesive set of doctrines taught throughout the Bible. The central theme of the almighty, unchanging, just and merciful God and of his dealings with a depraved, rebellious mankind runs through the whole Bible from the first chapters of Genesis to the last chapters of Revelation. There are no human superheroes in the Bible, and even God's chosen agents often had feet of clay. This is not how authors write if they want to gain a mass following or create a national hero. The Lord does not want those who believe in him to identify with rugged individualists who can accomplish great things because of their superior characters, but rather to identify with disgusting sinners who can only

---

17 [Jesus said,] "Therefore, whatever you want others to do for you, do also the same for them, for this is the Law and the Prophets." (Matthew 7:12).

18 "The Spirit of the Lord GOD is on me, because the LORD has anointed me to bring good news to the poor. He has sent me to heal the brokenhearted, to proclaim liberty to the captives and freedom to the prisoners; to proclaim the year of the LORD's favor, and the day of our God's vengeance; to comfort all who mourn." (Isaiah 61:1-2).

accomplish things through the Lord's help and can only be saved by his power.

The Lord claims to have chosen his penmen[19] and to have moved them to write what he wanted written, using words that reflected the chosen writer, but words still given by God to communicate his ideas. The Bible itself says so.[20] And if the Lord went to that much trouble rather than dropping a book directly from heaven, it follows naturally that he would lead these agents to include only those things in the Bible that he wanted included. That this is the case can be seen if one studies other religious writings of the late Old Testament[21] and early New Testament[22] periods. These apocryphal books all contain inconsistencies with the theology of the Bible and/or with the history they present. Some of them are very fanciful. The attentive reader now, as in times past, would reject them as not speaking in the same spirit as the books which are included in the biblical canon. The Lord has, through the various words that he had written and through the Holy Spirit, guided those assembling the Bible to choose only those books, and all those books, that the Lord wanted us to have. The Lord's plan of salvation would be worthless to mankind if mankind did not have a clear and trustworthy revelation of it.[23]

Unfortunately, since ancient times, many different writings have made claim to being inspired and therefore worthy of inclusion into the canon. The Roman Catholic Church recognizes a group of books that other Christian churches do not recognize. These are called the *apocrypha*, and in Catholic Bibles they are scattered throughout the Old Testament. In addition, there are

---

19 For example, calligraphers make works of art out of words. They have special pens with special tips. Each pen/tip makes different, unique effects when a skilled artist writes with them. True calligraphers do not randomly grab different pens and different tips. They decide on the desired effect for their artwork and then carefully choose the pen and tip that will best create it. If they don't have a tip that will do the job, really skilled calligraphers will make their own new and unique pen/tip that does that job. Not only did God decide exactly what He wanted the Scriptures to say and exactly which words to give to the writers, He also created the penmen themselves. He made Paul an educated, logical, professor-like writer and Peter a fisherman whose Greek was sometimes rough. He made Isaiah a soaring poet and Moses a man who could transcribe complicated law codes. So, both the message and the means He used to transmit the message are the work of God.

20 "No prophecy ever came by the will of man; instead, men spoke from God as they were carried along by the Holy Spirit." (2 Peter 1:21).

21 *The Apocrypha* (Revised Standard Version), (Thomas Nelson & Sons, New York, 1957).

22 *The Lost Books of the Bible* (Bell Publishing Company, New York, 1979).

23 [Jesus said,] "But the Counselor, the Holy Spirit, whom the Father will send in my name, will teach you all things and remind you of everything I have told you." (John 14:26).

quite a number of writings that have laid claim to being part of the Bible but which the church has never recognized. These are sometimes called *pseudepigrapha.* Some of these writings purport to belong to the Old Testament and others to the New Testament.

The apologist should be aware of at least two challenges that arise in this area. One is simply to assert that the church determined which books were in and which ones were out. This view denies the supernatural intervention by the Holy Spirit which produced the inspired Word of God. A more subtle approach argues that Christians and Jews had a more "open" view of the canon in the past (see Chapter 8). This position has many different variations and applications. It points to very limited pieces of information in the historical and archaeological record and makes assumptions that say more about the bias of the interpreter than they do about the evidence that is actually present.

For the Old Testament books, the testimony of the New Testament is the standard to which we point. Paul speaks of the church being "built on the foundation of the apostles and prophets."[24] Jesus repeatedly quotes the Old Testament as the Word of God and even goes so far as to say, "The Scripture cannot be broken."[25] How do we know that he was working with the same Old Testament that we are? Jewish rabbis traditionally divide the Old Testament into three sections: the Law of Moses (Genesis, Exodus, Leviticus, Numbers and Deuteronomy), the Prophets (which includes different books than we might include: Joshua, Judges, 1 and 2 Samuel, 1 and 2 Kings, Isaiah, Jeremiah, Ezekiel and the twelve Minor Prophets) and the Writings (Hebrew *kethubhim)*, which is dominated by the Psalms and includes all the rest of the Old Testament books (wisdom literature like Ecclesiastes and Song of Songs, history like Ruth and 1 and 2 Chronicles, and prophetic writings like Daniel). Jesus references this three-fold division in Luke 24:44.

The New Testament presents a somewhat more difficult challenge, but from the apostolic age on, the church recognized those books which are inspired. Jesus' words to the apostles at the Last Supper point to the role that the apostles would play in certifying those books which had the authority of Scripture.[26] The Holy Spirit would remind them of Jesus' words (so the Gos-

---

24 Ephesians 2:20.

25 John 10:35.

26 [Jesus said,] "I have spoken these things to you while I remain with you. But the Counselor, the Holy Spirit, whom the Father will send in my name, will teach you all things and remind you of everything I have told you." (John 14:25-26) See also John 16:7, 13-15.

pels are not just the product of imperfect human memory written down years later), and he would teach them all things so the epistles (which explain the meaning of Christ's life and often present the most direct statements of doctrine) give us the teachings God wanted us to have. Since ancient times, one of the key tests of inclusion was the association of a book with one or another of the apostles.[27] Already in New Testament times, while the apostles were still alive to object to any false writings, there is evidence that books were being collected[28] and shared[29] among churches. Likewise, the apostles themselves warned of false writings, again demonstrating their role in identifying the true Scriptures.[30]

After the time of the apostles, questions arose about which books should be included, and we do have some record of the investigations and the efforts of the early church to correctly identify those books having apostolic authority. Some New Testament books, like James or Revelation, have come under more scrutiny than others. But ultimately, they withstood the criticism and are recognized as Scripture today.[31]

The Authenticity of the Bible

The authenticity of the Bible is attacked in two ways. First, some claim that even if God did inspire men to write his Word accurately, the original manuscripts have been lost. Therefore, we cannot be sure that we have texts that contain the real words of God today.[32] Second, some claim that the Bible was not written as it indicates that it was written, but that some of the books were composed in different eras or by different people than those the Bible indicates. Let us first consider the issue of having a reliable text.[33]

---

[27] See statements like those of Paul regarding his apostolic authority in Romans 1:1, Romans 11:13, 1 Thessalonians 2:13 and Peter's claim in 1 Peter 1:1 and 2 Peter 1:1.

[28] See, for example 2 Peter 3:15,16 which refers to Paul's letters as Scripture.

[29] See, for example 1 Thessalonians 5:17 and Colossians 4:16.

[30] See, for example, 2 Thessalonians 2:2.

[31] Wilbert Gawrisch, "How the Canonicity of the Bible was Established," *Our Great Heritage, Vol. 1* (Northwestern Publishing House, Milwaukee, 1991), 99-125.

[32] For an example written on a popular (as opposed to a scholarly) level, see Bart D. Ehrman, *Misquoting Jesus: The Story Behind Who Changed the Bible and Why* (HarperCollins, New York, 2005), 75-100.

[33] Brian Keller, *Bible, God's Inspired, Inerrant Word* (Northwestern Publishing House, Milwaukee, 2002), 125-158.

While the Western church was without good manuscripts of the Scriptures in their original languages from the time of St. Jerome in the 4th century to the time of the Reformation in the 16th century, that situation rapidly changed after Desiderius Erasmus prepared a new manuscript of the Greek New Testament (first published in 1516). Since that time, dedicated scholars have searched for older and hidden manuscripts of the Greek and the Hebrew portions of the Bible. There are now many hundreds of copies and partial copies of the New Testament dating from the early centuries of the church.

The argument that we can't know what the original texts said is based on the fact that before printing was invented, the Bible was hand copied, and we do not have a single original copy (e.g., an actual letter written by Paul or an actual psalm written by David). All we have are copies of copies. There are literally tens of thousands of differences—called variants—between these copies. However, the situation is not quite as bleak as that. First, no one has ever produced an authoritative count of variants or list of variants because no one can decide what constitutes a variant or how to count them. If manuscript A misspells a name, is that one variant, or do the other fifty manuscripts that have the name spelled correctly count as fifty more variants? Some would say yes, some no.

While it is true that there were various copying errors in the corpus of manuscripts and even occasional notes added by scholars, this is not nearly the problem that some people represent it as being. First, the overwhelming majority of the differences are things such as spelling errors, leaving out a word or similarly obvious and understandable errors. When you have hundreds of copies to compare, those types of things are easily dealt with. Second, the existing manuscripts tend to fall into families based on the path through which they were produced. By studying these manuscript families, it is often possible to determine what the original text was, based on the oldest and most widespread readings. Most disagreements can be resolved, but it is true that there are some places where it is not possible to be absolutely certain what the original reading was. However, none of those verses have any impact on even a single biblical doctrine. The New Testament text today can be regarded as accurately representing what was first written, even if some variants are unresolvable.

The Old Testament text is more challenging because we do not have as many copies of it, nor do we have copies that are so near in time to when its originals were written as we do with the New Testament. Yet, we can have strong confidence in the current Old Testament text for three reasons. First, the Levitical scribes who copied the Hebrew text were obsessed with treating God's Word with the highest respect. They developed character-counting methods to guarantee that each line did not have missing or added words. These efforts led to remarkable consistency. Second, the Hebrew Bible was translated into Greek in Alexandria, Egypt during the 2nd and 3rd centuries BC. This required the text of the Hebrew Bible to have been verified for correctness by the scholars involved. This gives us a means of judging the "sense" of the Hebrew text by comparing it to its Greek translations, the best known of which is the *Septuagint*. Finally, soon after World War II the discovery of the Dead Sea Scrolls and other early Hebrew manuscripts from isolated sites allowed scholars to compare these texts with both the Hebrew texts that come through more formal Jewish channels and the Septuagint. As a result, scholars' confidence in the quality of the current composite Hebrew manuscript has grown during the 20th and 21st centuries[34] [35] (see Chapter 8). Apologists using these efforts to establish more reliable biblical texts is an example of the proper use of scholarship in regard to the Holy Scriptures. But above this, we believe that we can count on the Lord to preserve what he created so as to bring his elect to himself in heaven.[36]

These efforts contrast with those of scholars who are intent on destroying the Bible as a credible standard of divine truth. Early in the 19th century, scholars at German universities began to question the assumption that the Bible was the inspired Word of God, and in the process, they denied outright that it was inerrant, particularly when it came to questions of scientific and historical information. This questioning was based on several assumptions. They questioned whether God ever communicated directly with humans at all and, as time passed, this questioning led to an assumption that such direct revelations never happened. Certainly, they deemed as absurd the idea that

---

34 Keller, ibid., 147-156.

35 Siegbert Becker, "Verbal Inspiration and Variant Readings," *Our Great Heritage, Vol. 1* (Northwestern Publishing House, Milwaukee, 1991), 164-183.

36 [David wrote,] "The words of the LORD are pure words, like silver refined in an earthen furnace, purified seven times. You, LORD, will guard us; you will protect us from this generation forever." (Psalm 12:6-7).

God gave every word of the Scriptures to the men who recorded them, not the least because he does not do anything like that now, nor has he done so in the last two thousand years. Having drawn this conclusion, the assumption quickly followed that true prophecies of the future are impossible. Therefore, portions of the Old Testament prophets like Isaiah that clearly speak of events after the time the writer lived must have been edited into the text later.

Along with these ideas came the assumption that the Scriptures should be treated like any other ancient document. This has come to be called *higher criticism* (as opposed to *lower criticism* which deals with the issue of variants discussed above). At first, treating the Bible like any other ancient document might not sound too alarming, but there is a problem, namely, that ancient documents are very rare. We know the names of many hundreds of ancient works that have been lost and are only quoted in other works. Numerous ancient works are fragmentary—that is, only parts of them have survived. They have all been recopied, so we don't know with certainty what the original author wrote. When such works are quoted, scholars spend a lot of time puzzling over how complete or accurate the quote is. Finally, all ancient documents have a bias. Historians argue at length about the reliability of every ancient source document we have (see Chapter 8). Starting in the 19th century, these German scholars began to subject the Bible to the same kinds of criticism as all other ancient documents. This approach made all references to miracles suspect. It also caused scholars to compare dates and records and people and events in the Scriptures to extra-biblical references and to accuse the Scriptures of error. Finally, it led to viewing most of the Old Testament and significant parts of the New Testament (especially the Gospels) as being the products of a long process of editing and merging and reediting documents. Very few secular scholars today would view Moses as the author of the Pentateuch, Isaiah as the author of his work or the Gospels as having been written by Matthew, Mark, Luke, and John.

As apologists, we need to avoid getting sucked into a meaningless debate about these issues. In contrast to the physical sciences, it is very hard to gather conclusive evidence for the development of scriptural texts. We only have what is preserved. Despite the scholarly consensus that the Bible is the product of a process of evolution, no one has ever produced even a page of one of the so-called source documents. Sometimes, the Dead Sea Scrolls are held up as evidence. Yet, an honest evaluation of them only confirms the reliability of the texts we have, as we will discuss in Chapter 8.

The burden of proof is on those who claim that there is some defect in the Bible. We must not let them shift the burden of proof to us. The Bible exists, and all the evidence points to the text that we have as being sound and reliable. When dealing with ordinary Christians tempted to believe such mudslinging about the reliability of the Scriptures, the apologist should point out higher criticism's poor track record in proving any of these assumptions. The scholarly world has been unable to come to a final opinion about how the Scriptures were produced (since they have no real evidence) and about the underlying assumptions about God that drive this entire approach to studying his Word.

In the end, most of higher criticism relies on internal evidence—that is, on what the scholars see, or think they see, within the text itself. The believer, however, can make the point that the unity of the biblical message is clear and demonstrable and that it is strong evidence that there is one author of God's Word. As is the case with science, however, the point is not to win an argument. The point is to clear the field to talk about the gospel.

Internal Conflicts

Critics of the Bible like to claim that the Bible contradicts itself. There are three reasons why there appear to be contractions in the Bible. We will look at each of them and outline a strategy for the apologist in dealing with them. Due to the many things that can be brought up, writing a suitable answer for each of the challenges is beyond the scope of this book. Instead, we will concentrate on the principles to be used to develop responses and consider sample cases.

The first reason for apparent contradictions is the practice of assuming a contradiction must exist and then interpreting two sections of the Bible in such a way as to make them seem to conflict with each other. For example, if one assumes that there are different versions of the creation account in Genesis 1 and Genesis 2, then one will read them in a manner to find things that can be shown to be different and, therefore, in conflict with each other. One can argue over the order of how things were created, pointing out that while man is created last in chapter 1, he is created earlier in chapter 2. This, however, is a result of ignoring the different purposes of chapters 1 and 2. The intent of chapter 1 is to give an historical account of God's actions. The context is time. The intent of chapter 2 is to highlight God's treatment of man, the centerpiece of his creation. The context is purpose. If one person stands at the end of a valley and another person stands on a hill overlooking the valley, they will describe the valley differently based on what they see. Nevertheless, they are seeing the same valley. In the same way, different camera angles at a football game show the same play but not the same details. These analogies are important for the apologist to remember when facing what appear to be inconsistencies in the scriptural record.

Alleged contradictions are common any time two portions of the Bible discuss the same historical events. Some examples are how the statements and actions of Jesus are presented in the four Gospels, the depth of the historical details among the books of Samuel, Kings and Chronicles, and how theological issues are presented by the prophets as compared to how they are presented by Moses. The apologist's job when such alleged contradictions are raised is to identify the critical factors in the two accounts involved. This includes the actors and the recorders, the audiences, and the purposes of the accounts. Someone telling a friend about an auto accident that she saw would give a much different account of the incident from that of a police officer testifying in court, even though both accounts might be true. Their vantage points may have been the same, but the purposes of their accounts differ. The apologist, therefore, always asks, "What might have occurred that led to these apparently differing accounts?" rather than "How can I show that these accounts are in conflict?" The goal is not to find a definitive answer that goes beyond what the Bible says, but rather to show that there are situations where the two accounts would not be in conflict. The burden of proof is on the people making that claim that there is no explanation that would reconcile the two accounts, not on the apologist, and this point must be pressed. The more the apologist knows about the culture and intentions of those involved in the biblical account, the better he or she will be in pointing out possible ways that apparently differing accounts can be harmonized.

Often apparent discrepancies in the Bible are the result of a lack of our knowledge of the culture of the people who recorded the events. For example, Matthew wrote that Jesus was on the cross at the sixth hour of the day,[37] while

---

37 Matthew 27:45.

John wrote that he was still before Pilate at the sixth hour.[38] How could this be? One possibility is that Matthew, writing for the Jewish Christians, used Jewish time, which was in use in Palestine, while John, writing much later and in Asia Minor, used Roman time, which was in common use there. For the apologist, there is no substitute for knowing the laws given by Moses and the culture of the 1st century Jews, Greeks and Romans. The Holy Scriptures were not written in the 21st century, and there is only so much that the translators can do. The biblical writers penned their words assuming their readers possessed a particular set of knowledge. Today's readers often lack that knowledge, so apologists must rely upon theologically sound commentaries when addressing apparent discrepancies in the Bible, both for their own edification, as well as for that of the people to whom they are speaking. Moreover, there are rare cases for which we do not know enough to explain why the apparent differences exist, and we must be willing to acknowledge our lack of knowledge in such cases. However, we must not let our challengers use the fallacious appeal to ignorance to claim that because we do not know the correct explanation, therefore, there is no such explanation.

The third reason that apparent discrepancies exist is that Christians want to read things into the Bible that are not there. The question about the number of Adam's wives is an example of this. Christians want the answer to be "one," so in their minds they make it "one." Similarly, when Jesus said to Peter, "I will give you the keys of the kingdom of heaven,"[39] Roman Catholics want the word "only" to exist before "you," and they mentally put it there. Yet, Jesus' statement does not mean that he did not say similar things to his other disciples at other times.[40] These examples should convince the apologist that he or she must be a *minimalist*. While apologists must have due concern over subtracting from the Scriptures, they must have an even greater concern over adding to the Scriptures. This is because whatever is added to the Scriptures must be defended, and such defenses can set up apparent conflicts with things which really are mentioned in the Scriptures or which can be undeniably observed in the world. Apologists cannot afford to become like the

---

38 John 19:14.

39 Matthew 16:19.

40 [Jesus said to all his disciples,] "Truly I tell you, whatever you bind on earth will have been bound in heaven, and whatever you loose on earth will have been loosed in heaven". (Matthew 18:18).

Pharisees, who built a hedge around the Law of Moses to make sure they never offended against it.

Other Revelations

There is a movement among the world's intellectuals to push for the unity of all religions (e.g., COEXIST bumper stickers), starting with an effort to gain acknowledgement that all their holy books present the will of "God," differing only according to the cultures. These Humanists hope that such unity will bring about an earthly utopia where people of all backgrounds will live and prosper together. It is a modern version of the effort to build the tower at Babel.[41] Alas, the nature of man and the limited resources of the earth will prevent this from ever happening. Every Christian should regard any effort to equate the Word of the Lord to the babblings of pagans as an act of blasphemy.[42] Let us consider a few cases.

Because its sacred scripture is the Hebrew Bible, i.e., the Old Testament, it would seem that Judaism does indeed have the true Word of the Lord. Yet appearances can be deceiving. While religious Jews like to parade with the Torah, i.e., the five books of Moses, they do not accept what it says. According to the Torah, they are all unclean and cut off from the people of the Lord. Because Jews came to see the Law of Moses as no longer applicable to their lives after the destruction of the temple, in the 3rd through the 6th century AD, they developed a new book, the Babylonian Talmud,[43] which has become the real guiding authority of Jewish teachings and life. This 22-volume set contains the opinions of the rabbis concerning what they think the Hebrew Bible really means, and that meaning often bears little resemblance to the literal meaning of the text in its historical setting. Their "scripture" has become a set of rules which are diametrically opposed to the grace of God as presented in the New Testament. Already in the Old Testament, Isaiah condemned such

---

41 "And they said, 'Come, let us build ourselves a city and a tower with its top in the sky. Let us make a name for ourselves; otherwise, we will be scattered throughout the earth.'" (Genesis 11:4).

42 [The Lord said,] "I am the LORD. That is my name, and I will not give my glory to another or my praise to idols." (Isaiah 42:8).

43 *The Babylonian Talmud: A Translation and Commentary*, Jacob Neusner, ed. (Hendrickson Publishers, Inc., Peabody MA, 2005).

reliance on human teachings as false worship.[44] Religious Jews tend to follow individual rabbis (i.e., teachers), although there are numerous official branches of Judaism which have more formal standards. In dealing with religious Jews, the apologist will find the Law and the curses, as given in Deuteronomy, and the Gospel, as presented in Isaiah, to be his or her greatest assets.

The Arab prophet Mohammed spoke the suras (i.e., sayings, chapters) which were eventually written down and became the holy book, the *Qur'an* of Islam.[45] Mohammed claims that Abraham's son Ishmael was the real son of promise and that the Arabs are descended from him. Mohammed accepted many of the Old Testament and some New Testament biblical accounts, in somewhat altered form, and that Jesus was a great prophet who lived a sinless life. In fact, Jesus is the second greatest prophet in Islam. Originally, Mohammed hoped that the Jews and the Christians would accept his work as simply an Arab version of what their religions taught. The problem is that Mohammed did not understand the concept of free and reliable grace. As a result, Muslims must work hard and faithfully for their salvation, but there is no guarantee even then that they will receive it, unless they are killed fighting for Islam in a holy war. This is why desperate Muslims are in such danger of becoming radicals. They have come to believe that their eternal prospects are better through dying in a fight than through exemplary living. While there are many sects in Islam, Muslims tend to follow individual clerics (variously called "mullahs" or "imams") because most sects of Islam have no formal clerical organization. In addition to the *Qur'an*, Muslims also revere the *Hadith* (accounts of Mohammed written by others) and other sources, depending on their sect. The apologist needs to start with the high respect that Muslims have for Abraham and the holiness of Christ and move, as possible, to the importance of having a faith in which entering heaven is a certainty.

Joseph Smith was a New England farm boy who claimed to have been visited by an angel who loaned him sacred writings to translate while he wore special glasses. Smith's alleged translation of these writings is now called the

---

[44] [The Lord said,] "These people approach me with their speeches to honor me with lip-service—yet their hearts are far from me, and human rules direct their worship of me." (Isaiah 29:13).

[45] *The Generous Qur'an*, Usama K. Dahdok, tr. (Usama Dahdok Publishing, LLC, Venice FL, 2009).

Book of Mormon.[46] The plot of the *Book of Mormon* is that a band of Jews escaped Judah before the Babylonian Captivity and made their way to America. There they built a new temple and tried to establish a new Israel. The book is filled with tales of warfare among these immigrants over religion and apostasy. Jesus came to visit them after his resurrection to teach them his ways, but they eventually destroyed their whole population and disappeared. The *Book of Mormon* establishes the principle of continuing revelation through future prophecy, and the Latter-Day Saints have established the office of prophet to continue that tradition. Smith used this office to write many of the current teachings of Mormonism into a book called *Doctrine and Covenants*, and additional rules have been introduced by later prophets. Some small groups have broken off from the main body. Mormonism is a works-righteousness religion, although Mormons often use Christian terminology. When approached by Mormons, the apologist must keep pointing these "missionaries" back to the Bible, which they claim to accept "in so far as it is correctly translated". They are peddling a religion of good works and family values, but they need to be reminded that these are not nearly good enough to avoid the wrath of the Lord.

We could give a brief overview of the sacred writings of other major religions, but these can easily be found on the internet. All these books share the goal of showing people how to improve their behavior so as to build a better world and/or to gain eternal happiness. From the view of the apologist, therefore, they differ little. They may be similar to each other in this regard but not to the Bible, which has a radically different approach to salvation. To announce that people are saved by grace through the work of God is a unique message which is counter to what humans generally think. The message of the Bible is wonderfully different.

Summary

We cannot reason someone into accepting the Bible as the Word of God because the message of the Holy Scriptures, apart from the work of the Holy Spirit, is nonsense.[47] All the other holy books offer some way for people to

---

[46] *The Book of Mormon*, Joseph Smith, tr. (The Church of the Latter-day Saints, Salt Lake City UT, 1980).

[47] "For the Jews ask for signs and the Greeks seek wisdom, but we preach Christ crucified, a stumbling block to the Jews and foolishness to the Gentiles." (1 Corinthians 1:22-23).

atone for their sins and thereby hope to obtain their God's favor. The Bible places the whole burden of salvation upon the Lord himself. Therefore, the Bible will always be under attack by those who value their own good works and who do not want a book telling them that God will not deal with them on that basis. They also do not want to hear that those who accept the Bible as the inerrant Word of God will not strike a false compromise with them for the sake of making people feel good and of establishing an earthly utopia. The apologist is not a negotiator, but a witness to the teachings of the Lord that we have received in the Bible.

EndNote: Both the Old Testament and New Testament have a central set of writings. In the Old Testament it is the Torah (the five books of Moses), and in the New Testament it is the Gospels. The rest of the writings revolve around these basic writings and apply and explain them. Each Testament has a historical section, but these sections don't present history the way in which a modern professional historian would. They don't attempt to relate all that the writers knew about each subject. Rather, they relate how God interacted with his people and how he moved his plan of salvation forward. In the Old Testament, the history section is quite lengthy, since it covers eleven hundred years from the death of Moses until the return from exile (roughly 1500 BC to 400 BC). It comprises Joshua, Judges, Ruth, 1 and 2 Samuel, 1 and 2 Kings, 1 and 2 Chronicles, Ezra, Nehemiah, and Esther. In the New Testament, the history section is limited to the book of Acts, since it covers only the first generation after the ascension of Christ. Each testament has books that explain and apply the teachings of the central books in a way that make it possible for us to understand the point that God was making in those initial narratives. These writings allow us to make firm doctrinal statements about what God wants us to know. In the Old Testament, they are usually called "the prophets" (Isaiah, Jeremiah, Ezekiel, Daniel, Hosea, Joel, Amos, Obadiah, Jonah, Micah, Nahum, Habakkuk, Zephaniah, Haggai, Zechariah and Malachi). In the New Testament, they take the form of letters, generally from the apostles, which we call "epistles" (Romans, 1 and 2 Corinthians, Galatians, Ephesians, Philippians, Colossians, 1 and 2 Thessalonians, 1 and 2 Timothy, Titus, Philemon, Hebrews, James, 1 and 2 Peter, 1, 2 and 3 John and Jude). The New Testament ends with Revelation, which is not usually called an epistle, but which serves this same function. Finally, in the Old Testament, where God was very direct in the way in which he set up Israel's worship system, there are books that are very artistic in nature. These reflect the worship (the psalms), the emotional impact of the triumphs and tragedies of God's people (Lamentations, Song of Songs), and also their attempts to apply God's wisdom to their lives (Proverbs and Ecclesiastes). Taken together, all these writings revolve around the central theme, which tells the account of how God saves his people.

4

The Nature of the Lord God

In Chapter 2 we introduced the Lord, the God of the Bible, as an example of a personal God with whom someone can form a relationship. A number of the attributes of the Lord were presented to give an overall impression of his immenseness and the complexity of his being. In this chapter we will discuss the Lord as the Supreme Being and how we must present him to others. As apologists, we must grasp the incredible magnitude of his being so that we do not end up understating him in an effort to make him saleable to those to whom we give a defense of our faith. The material in this chapter will be most useful in discussions with those who have a belief in some sort of god and/or are struggling to grasp the nature of the God portrayed in the Bible. Because of its reliance on the Holy Scriptures, it will be of less use when dealing with those who reject the concept of revelation.

Framing the Discussion

As the Lord reveals himself in the Hebrew Bible, he is scarily big. If we read the Old Testament in the context of the people to whom God first showed himself, rather than in the context of cynical twenty-first century Americans, our whole bodies tremble. We hide with Adam in the bushes as we wait in fear for the Lord to come and execute his promised death sentence upon us.[1] We struggle with an overmatched Noah in the middle of an unbelievably

[1] Genesis 3:8.

strong storm as his small crew tries to manage thousands of animals on a boat built using only primitive tools and materials.[2] Our hearts pound as if they will burst as we enter Abraham's skin and await the question we know is coming from our son Isaac, "But Father where is the lamb?"[3] We stand as bewildered flatlanders as we hear the deafening noise, feel the shaking ground and see the raging smoke and fire on the top of Mount Sinai.[4] There we hear some of our sins labeled with a word so bad that we know they disgust the Lord to the fiber of his being. God could not be more emphatic about how great he is and how worthless we are. The language of the Bible is direct, and it is clear. The gulf between the Lord and us is unfathomably great, and we are babbling fools if we think we have any standing whatsoever on our own before God.

As we read on in the Old Testament, we also find that the Lord is incredibly merciful.[5] He is willing to give the human race and its members grace that they do not deserve, and he is willing to give it to them in abundance. But even in his mercy, the Lord makes clear that it is *his* mercy and not our due from him. It is *he* who decides when and how and to whom his mercy will be extended.[6] There is no appeal from his decisions, and he is not open to our advice or solicitous of our opinions. He is life in and of himself, and we have life only through his divine pleasure.

To discuss the God of the Bible as his apologists, we must understand him ourselves, as least as far as our human abilities permit. We must portray him as he is, not as we or our audience might like him to be. We must ride the clouds with him and watch as he works his wonders. He made us in his image; we must not try to remake him in our image, lest we find we are only holding a handful of dirt as our god. Let us begin by first considering the gods that we encounter in our daily lives, those would-be competitors of the Lord for people's minds and hearts.

The Gods of Society

No matter what their politics or sense of morality, everyone is looking for, or at least willing to take, available advantages. People like to have friends in

---

[2] Genesis 7:17-24.

[3] Genesis 22:7.

[4] Exodus 20:18-19.

[5] Exodus 34:6-7.

[6] [The Lord said,] "I will have mercy on whom I will have mercy, and I will have compassion on whom I will have compassion." (Exodus 33:19).

appropriate places who can help them obtain their goals more easily. Friends in high places are particularly useful, and there is no higher place than the realm of a god. This is why non-descript religions and various forms of spirituality are so popular among those who are far too erudite to want to mingle with the traditional Christian crowd. This trend is nothing new but dates to seventeenth century England.

Deism began attracting intellectuals because it "allowed God to be God" without bothering men. In effect, God was allowed to be the great Creator of the universe and the Giver of moral directives, but then he was relegated to permitting the universe to run under the laws of nature, except for occasional tweaks to keep things from spinning out of control. This idea dates back at least as far as Isaac Newton. The Masons adopted it, and Voltaire carried it to France and to the intellectual circles on the European continent. It became firmly embedded in American culture because men like Thomas Jefferson, George Washington, Benjamin Franklin, and numerous other Founding Fathers were Masons. The spirit of deism is evident in the Declaration of Independence and in other documents of the period. While most of these early patriots attended Christian churches, their hearts were not with the God of the Bible.

Deism continued to guide the thinking in both Great Britain and the United States during the nineteenth century. In Britain it showed itself in the drive for obtaining "an empire on which the sun never sets". This was done because it was the "white man's burden" to civilize the world by persuasion when possible and by force when necessary. In America the same philosophy was carried out under the slogan of "manifest destiny." It was under this banner that the Native Americans were driven from their lands, nearly half of Mexico was annexed, the Philippines and Puerto Rico were seized from Spain and even to some extent the Civil War was fought. It continued to guide the thinking of English and American leaders through two world wars as they worshipped the god of "our far-flung battle line".[7]

For many centuries there has been an even more nebulous god than that of deism, namely the enigmatic force behind astrology. Astrology is based on the idea that the celestial bodies control the lives and events of all the people on Earth. The stars and the other heavenly bodies supposedly place babies upon a directed path at the time of their birth and control how events occur at

[7] From "Recessional," a poem by Rudyard Kipling.

various times during their lives. Throughout history, many political and even some Christian leaders have sought the "direction of the stars" and favorable omens in making their plans. Today, newspapers still print the predictions of the zodiac signs for those who believe in them, bookstores are loaded with New Age books, and the practitioners of astrology are not going to go broke even in this highly educated era.

In more recent times, another kind of impersonal god has become popular. The technical term for this concept is *pantheism*, which means seeing "god" in all things or seeing the universe itself as god. This is a very common form of belief in the entertainment industry, and the all-pervasive influence of TV and movies has made this a very popular and respectable kind of thinking. One version is evident in the beliefs of the Jedi in the Star Wars franchise. "*The force*" is a power that moves through the whole universe and holds it all together. It isn't a god that can be prayed to, and yet, "the force" can be "with you." It partially controls a person and yet is subject to personal control. Another very popular approach is to view "the universe" as god. Quite often, TV characters will talk about "the universe" wanting something or making something happen. For example, the main characters met and fell in love because "the universe" wanted them to.

The main attraction of pantheism—in whatever form it takes—is that it relieves one from having any responsibility to have a relationship with "the force" or "the universe." Even though it has some kind of purpose and will, it is not thought of as a being that can be prayed to or to which one is answerable. So long as a person maintains a generically "moral" lifestyle, "the universe" will be favorably disposed to work for his or her general advantage.

Another variation of this kind of thinking shows itself among people who practice no kind of faith at all, but say, "I'm praying for you." They assume that whatever god or god-like entity is out there will listen if we bother to pray to him, her or it. An even blander form often shows itself on television news programs or talk shows, when someone says, "We're sending good thoughts out" to the victims of some tragedy. Or they combine the two ideas and say, "Our thoughts and prayers are with you." Notice how unconsciously, even the prayers are directed at the people who are in difficulty, rather than to the God of the Holy Scriptures who alone can help them. Even if the people who are saying this are personally religious, they revert to this formula in public speech so as to avoid offending any religious group or individual. Hence, they make a god that is as generic as possible. And in the process, they make it as impersonal as possible.

It is not uncommon that people who believe in these generic gods think they indeed believe in the same God who appears on the pages of the Bible, but that they merely recognize him in a different form. In fact, when they are asked about whether "*In God we trust*" applies to their god as well as the gods of others, they may seem startled that there could be any doubt of this. The apologist must separate the God of the Bible from the generic gods by declaring his attributes and his insistence to be recognized with these attributes, not with any set of attributes that people care to assign to the entity they desire to be their god. We will thus look at the attributes of the Lord which are so misunderstood by so many, in order that, as apologists, we may give the Lord the honor due to him as we talk about him.

The Lord's Power

When Elijah faced a people who were confused about the identity of the real God they should be worshiping, he could challenge his opponents to a show of power between the Lord and Baal.[8] Everyone understood whom Elijah worshipped and whom these priests of Baal worshipped. Today, we cannot draw such a clear-cut distinction between the God of the Bible and the challengers to his deity. Thanks to deism, astrology, pantheism and many poorly trained nominal Christians, most modern people don't even know the nature of the god they claim to worship. The generic title "god", often capitalized, is spread over any being that has vague hints of divinity.

The power of the God of the Bible, therefore, is not well-understood by most people. People generally regard their god as capable of doing what they ask it to do, provided that they are not too greedy. They might ask for material goods, for a favorable outcome to an endeavor or for health for someone who is ailing. Most try to keep their requests reasonable (at least in their own minds) but occasionally someone will ask for something that would require an overt miracle to accomplish. These "stretch" prayers, like hail-Mary passes, are often offered with little hope that their god will, or even can, grant them, although the media keeps the idea of fanciful "Christmas miracles" alive. People's desire to limit the power of their god is understandable because

[8] 1 Kings 18:20-40.

they do not want to appear too helpless or too desperate in their god's presence.

The issue of how much power the biblical God really has is a troubling topic for many people. They look at a world that does not function in a way that they would regard as ideal, and they ask the question, "Why doesn't God do something about it?" The implication in this question is clear—either God doesn't have the power to act (i.e., he is not *omnipotent*) or he doesn't have the will to act (i.e., he is disinterested or malevolent). Since they want to think well of the god they worship and perhaps hope to obtain some assistance from it, they tend to reject the latter idea. They would rather imagine their god is limited in power, although still more powerful than they are. The apologist should expect to find this underlying attitude frequently, even if it is not well articulated by people.

In stark contrast, the Bible proclaims the Lord, a God who truly can do anything he pleases.[9] He is not in the slightest degree nebulous, but he has clearly announced who he is. He is the God of gods and Lord of lords.[10] The Bible contains numerous examples of the extent of the Lord's control of nature. For example, he confused the languages at the tower at Babel,[11] sent plagues on the Egyptians in order to rescue his people[12] and parted the Red Sea.[13] He affected the earth's rotation or the flow of time,[14] made an iron axe head float,[15] struck an entire army with blindness[16] and slaughtered 185,000 soldiers as they besieged Jerusalem.[17] In the New Testament there was the virgin birth,[18] the curing of many diseases and handicaps, the calming of the

9 [A psalmist wrote,] "For I know that the LORD is great; our Lord is greater than all gods. The LORD does whatever he pleases in heaven and on earth, in the seas and all the depths." (Psalm 135:5-6).

10 [Moses said,] "For the LORD your God is the God of gods and Lord of lords, the great, mighty, and awe-inspiring God, showing no partiality and taking no bribe." (Deuteronomy 10:17).

11 Genesis 11:1-9.

12 Exodus 7:19-12:32.

13 Exodus 14:21-28.

14 Joshua 10:12-15.

15 2 King 6:5-7.

16 2 Kings 6:18.

17 2 Kings 19:35.

18 Luke 1:26-38.

lake,[19] the feeding of large crowds[20] and the raising of the dead.[21] The number of miracles that Jesus performed was so large that it was clear even to his opponents that he was not a normal man, limited by the laws of nature.[22] Together, these miracles show a God whose power is absolutely limitless.[23]

The Lord is indeed omnipotent, and he will not share the glory of his power with anyone. He demands that people call on him by *his Name*, not by some pseudonym, because he will not recognize and respond to any other name.[24] Most people have real trouble grasping this. Even those who are willing to grant that God has power over the whole Heaven and Earth often fall short in their understanding of omnipotence. They still think of God as only a terribly powerful dude, more powerful than anyone else, and this may cause them to approach him with deep respect. Nevertheless, they do not comprehend that God really has *all* the power. Nothing else has *any* power at all. None. Zero. Zilch. Everything from subatomic particles to large galaxies can do nothing without the Lord's active support;[25] in fact, they cannot even continue to exist without his constant command to do so.[26] Without the delegated power from the Lord, not a star shines, not a stream flows, and not a muscle moves. Not until people understand the real magnitude of the Lord's power can they comprehend the God of the Bible.

The apologist must be prepared to spend time helping people grasp this point. It is here that real mission work must begin. People with a god smaller than the Lord will not feel totally helpless in their god's presence. They will think there is a good chance that they can placate their god and cut a deal on favorable terms with it. After all, if they believe that they have any power of their own, it is natural for them to think that they can put up a fight. Because

---

19 Matthew 8:23-27.

20 Matthew 14:19-21, Matthew 15:35-38.

21 Luke 7:11-15, Mark 5:35-43, John 11:1-44.

22 John 11:47-48.

23 [The Lord said,] "I am he alone, and none can rescue from my power. I act, and who can reverse it?" (Isaiah 43:13).

24 [The Lord said,] "I—I am the LORD. Besides me, there is no Savior. I alone declared, saved, and proclaimed—and not some foreign god among you." (Isaiah 43:11–12).

25 [Solomon wrote,] "Unless the LORD builds a house, its builders labor over it in vain; unless the LORD watches over a city, the watchman stays alert in vain." (Psalm 127:1).

26 [A psalmist wrote,] "The heavens were made by the word of the LORD, and all the stars, by the breath of his mouth. He gathers the water of the sea into a heap; he puts the depths into storehouses. Let the whole earth fear the LORD; let all the inhabitants of the world stand in awe of him. For he spoke, and it came into being; he commanded, and it came into existence." (Psalm 33:6-9).

they almost invariably ascribe "being loving" to their god, they expect that it would rather avoid a fight, even one that it is certain to win. This causes people to be resistant to their god's commandments. The smaller they have made their god, the less they are willing to bow to its perceived desires. Therefore, the apologist must methodically sell the true nature of omnipotence. People will never totally abandon themselves to the Lord so long as they think there is a way to maintain some pride in themselves. Counterfeit Christianity begins with only partial repentance based on people's belief that they have something to offer which the god that they worship would be willing to accept. Their self-made god might, but the Lord won't.

"But why doesn't God, if he is almighty, do something about the condition of the world?" they will ask. "There is terrible evil in the world! Everyone knows that! How can God be good?" This is one of the strongest challenges to the Christian's belief in God. The Lord does not give us the complete answer, but he does emphatically indicate his attitude toward sin. Due to sin, death and destruction exist throughout the natural world. Consider the animal kingdom. Big fish eat little fish, a real injustice if one is a little fish. A zebra injures his foot and is killed by a predator. A calf gets tangled in the afterbirth and suffocates. A rockslide closes the entrance to a mountain lion's den, and it starves. The early bird gets the defenseless worm and feeds it to its fledglings. A range fire outruns and kills cattle. Pain is suffered by all of God's creatures because sin exists in the world. We may not like that explanation, but the Lord has a message about his abhorrence for sin that he needs to deliver, and people are blockheads when it comes to listening. Sometimes being an apologist is just stating things the way they are.

"But aren't we greater in God's sight than the animals?" Yes,[27] but do we give God any more honor than the animals do?[28] While animals do what is necessary for the survival of their species, humans often take advantage of fellow members of humankind for their own benefit. How much of the evil that befalls people is their own fault because they do foolish or sinful things? People break laws. They engage in dangerous sports. They build houses on floodplains and hillsides. They spend more money than they make. They drink too much and take illegal drugs. They engage in things harmful to their

---

[27] [Jesus said,] "So don't be afraid; you are worth more than many sparrows." (Matthew 10:31).

[28] [The Lord said,] "The ox knows its owner, and the donkey its master's feeding trough, but Israel does not know; my people do not understand." (Isaiah 1:3).

health. Much of the evil in the world is a direct result of people individually or collectively doing bad things to themselves and to each other. Should God stop people from doing as they please? Wouldn't that be the worst form of paternalism? Those who complain about biblical teachings on this matter cannot have it both ways.

"What about disease and injuries which happen haphazardly to people?" Certainly, God could control that, but would people thank him for it? People are happy to take personal credit for everything that they receive from the Lord.[29] Should the ruler of the universe be enslaved by human desires and then accept criticism for not meeting their every wish? What gives such a very disobedient creature the right to blame the Creator[30] because the creature continually craves more than he or she needs for this body and life? Because Adam and Eve sinned, we all will deteriorate physically and die. Our first parents knew the penalty, and they disobeyed anyway. Are we any less willing to attempt to circumvent God's laws today? If some must suffer more than others, is it not perhaps God's way of telling us that by nature none of us has the righteousness to stand before him and demand justice? Job thought he did, and God personally showed him his inadequacies.[31] God is not human, and his justice cannot downplay sin as humans do. Human suffering in this life serves as a warning of the far greater suffering that all will endure in hell if they do not repent of their sins and repudiate their shameful selves.[32] The switches on our backs are hard to bear now, but they are nothing compared to what will befall those who think that their humanity gives them rights before God.

The Lord's Knowledge

As more and more places use security cameras and as more and more data from online websites are archived, the privacy of the world's citizens is continually diminishing. Even the signal from a person's cellphone can be used to track his or her movements. While few people are actively being spied on

---

[29] Deuteronomy 6:10-12.

[30] [The Lord said,] "You have turned things around, as if the potter were the same as the clay. How can what is made say about its maker, 'He didn't make me'? How can what is formed say about the one who formed it, 'He doesn't understand what he's doing.'" (Isaiah 29:16).

[31] Job 38-41.

[32] "Then Jesus said to his disciples, 'If anyone wants to follow after me, let him deny himself, take up his cross, and follow me.'" (Matthew 16:24).

by American security agents, foreign governments or freelance meddlers, the fact that any group which gets its hands on someone's personal information can disturb his or her life leaves many people deeply concerned over how they can maintain any privacy. While "Big Brother"[33] may not have enough agents to be continually watching everyone, he can quickly find out who has been naughty or nice should he chose to do so.

Yet, with all their sophistication, those today trying to monitor dangerous and criminal activities in society are nowhere close to having the knowledge of the behavior of every individual that the Lord possesses. The Lord literally knows everything about the universe—past, present, and future. The writer to the Hebrews noted that nothing is hidden from him.[34] David testified that the Lord knew everything about him.[35] The Lord spoke to Job and claimed a thorough knowledge of the forces of nature.[36] Jesus pointed out to his disciples that not a sparrow dies without the Lord's knowing it and that the very hairs on people's heads are numbered by the Lord.[37] Therefore, the Bible teaches that the Lord is *omniscient* (i.e., all-knowing).

The implications of the Lord's total knowledge of the universe are overwhelming. For example, because the Lord knows everything, it is impossible for Him to be caught by surprise. He knows where every component of the universe is now, regardless of its size. Moreover, he knows what its exact location and velocity has been since the time of its creation, despite the law of nature that makes knowing both of these at the same time impossible.[38] He also knows the future course of every component of the universe. Because he already knows all things, there is never anything new for him to learn. More importantly for us, he knows the attitudes of every human heart from the moment of a person's conception until the moment of his or her death. What is more, he knows exactly how people would react to a situation, even if they never experience that situation. David summed it up: "LORD, you have

---

33 A character in George Orwell's *Nineteen Eighty-Four* (Harvill Secker, London, 1949).

34 "No creature is hidden from him, but all things are naked and exposed to the eyes of him to whom we must give an account." (Hebrews 4:13).

35 Psalm 139.

36 Job 38-41.

37 [Jesus said,] "Aren't two sparrows sold for a penny? Yet not one of them falls to the ground without your Father's consent. But even the hairs of your head have all been counted." (Matthew 10:29-30).

38 Werner *Heisenberg, "Über den anschaulichen Inhalt der quantentheoretischen Kinematik und Mechanik," Zeitschrift für Physik **43**:172–198, 1927.*

searched me and known me. You know when I sit down and when I stand up; you understand my thoughts from far away. You observe my travels and my rest; you are aware of all my ways. Before a word is on my tongue, you know all about it, LORD."[39]

The omniscience of the Lord frightens many people. Some would like to hide from him. Others would like to have a god that they can "educate" to their way of thinking. They would like to try to fool it by offering it deals which they never intend to keep. The Lord's perfect knowledge of the future makes people helpless to finesse Him. Many, therefore, reject what the Bible says and try to reengineer the Lord into a god who has much less ability to thwart their plans. The apologist needs to point out that such blasphemy of the Lord is grave folly. It is like claiming Niagara Falls is only five feet high and then expecting to find it to be that way. It is the fallacy of wishful thinking. They may not believe our witness, but they need to hear the truth whether they believe or not.[40]

Some people are indignant with the idea that the Lord is omniscient. "If he knows about all the terrible things that are going to happen before they happen," they ask, "why doesn't he stop them? Certainly, he could intervene in some unseen way to avert natural disasters like tsunamis and manmade disasters like Nazism!" Indeed, he could! Who knows how many more disasters would have happened if he had not intervened—perhaps more than one a day. Perhaps he has blocked greater than 99% of the evil things that would have happened if he had not intervened.[41] Who knows? The apologist needs to point out the numerous good things that happen to people every day, which are then completely ignored so as to focus on the bad things. In fact, people are happy to take credit for the good[42] and blame God for the bad.[43] How often do we curse God for letting us slide into the ditch when that was the only way to prevent us from being killed by going off the embankment where the bridge

---

39 Psalm 139:1-4.

40 "This is what the Lord GOD says, 'Whether they listen or refuse to listen—for they are a rebellious house—they will know that a prophet has been among them.'" (Ezekiel 2:4–5).

41 [A psalmist wrote,] "For he will give his angels orders concerning you, to protect you in all your ways." (Psalm 91:11).

42 [Moses said,] "When the LORD your God drives them out before you, do not say to yourself, 'The LORD brought me in to take possession of this land because of my righteousness.'" (Deuteronomy 9:4).

43 [The Lord condemned the Israelites for blaming him by saying,] "The fathers have eaten sour grapes, and the children's teeth are set on edge." (Jeremiah 31:29).

had collapsed! The children of Adam are a thankless lot. They trust their gut but not their God. That the Lord is omniscient means that he can manage things for our ultimate good even when our path goes "through the darkest valley."[44] The point is this: the Lord knows everything, and we know next to nothing. Let us rejoice in his knowledge and not berate him for it.

The Presence of the Lord

From the references to the Lord's presence in the Bible, we realize that he is present in numerous ways, such as his presence in the Sacrament of the Altar, his presence within our hearts, his presence in the work of the church and his presence in the burning bush that confronted Moses. Yet, it is his sustaining presence, which underlies his omnipotence and omniscience, that most interests people. We call this his *omnipresence* and, like all the attributes of the Lord, it is not easy to understand.[45]

The place to start is by asking, "Where does God dwell?" A psalmist tells us that "Our God is in heaven and does whatever He pleases."[46] In fact, there are many references to God's being in heaven.[47] But what does this mean? Eternity is where the Lord dwells in his full godliness. He is the only eternal being, so there is none other who can be in his presence in the eternal sense. Moses quotes the Lord, "See now that I alone am he; there is no God but me."[48] St. Paul affirms the incredibleness of the Lord's presence when he writes, "He is the blessed and only Sovereign, the King of kings, and the Lord of lords, who alone is immortal and who lives in unapproachable light."[49] Therefore, when the Lord created the universe, he also created a heavenly realm[50] where he would dwell with his holy ones and where the angels could continually behold his face.[51]

But if God dwells in heaven, how can he be with us on earth? The Bible does not explain this in any detail, so we need to try to grasp how he might do this by considering how we understand our existence on earth. Historically,

---

44 Psalm 23:4.

45 Arthur Eggert, "The Presence of the Lord" (Central Conference of the Western Wisconsin District, Watertown, WI, January 8, 2018).

46 Psalm 115:3.

47 For example, Deuteronomy 4:39, 2 Chronicles 20:6, Psalm 2:4 and Lamentations 3:41.

48 Deuteronomy 32:39.

49 1 Timothy 6:15-16.

50 "In the beginning God created the heavens and the earth." (Genesis 1:1).

51 Matthew 18:10.

we have thought of the physical universe as existing in three dimensions, often called "length," "width" and "height." We can travel in any direction and return to our previous place in this three-dimensional space. We also experience time, which is like a road which can only be traveled in one direction. We can never return to a previous point in time. We mark events along the road of time, which we call a *timeline*. We might say that we are all trapped in time and forced to travel down this timeline. As we move along it, we change and decay. In the twentieth century physicists discovered that time and space are not independent of each other but form a complex system they call *spacetime*. How things move through spacetime is not always obvious because space is curved and time does not flow at the same speed at all points.

Regardless of the complexity of the universe in which we dwell, the Lord is separate from it; he is not contained within its physical space and time[52] because he is not of the same substance as the matter and energy he created.[53] However, he can act within time and space, as is often described in the Bible. Let us first consider God's relationship to time. Psalm 102 says that the earth will wear out, but that the Lord is always the same (*immutable*) and will never cease to exist (*eternal*). Malachi agrees that God does not change.[54] Peter quotes Moses saying "with the LORD one day is like a thousand years, and a thousand years like one day" (*timeless*).[55] In fact, God has been able to foresee all of human history at once, even before he had created the world.[56] He chose people to carry out his plans, and he set them apart before they existed.[57] From these verses, it is certain that unlike us, who see the past hazily and the future only in hope, the Lord sees clearly whatever has or will happen. It is as if the Lord sees our timeline of the universe end-on, as a single point, with all history effectively simultaneous before the Lord. This is important to us because it implies that the Lord will never fail to do what he has promised. When he is making a promise at one point in human history, he already foresees

---

52 [Solomon said,] "But will God indeed live on earth? Even heaven, the highest heaven, cannot contain you, much less this temple I have built." (1 Kings 8:27).

53 *Luther's Works* **1**:11.

54 Malachi 3:6.

55 2 Peter 3:8.

56 "For those he foreknew he also predestined to be conformed to the image of his Son, so that he would be the firstborn among many brothers and sisters." (Romans 8:29).

57 "The word of the LORD came to me: 'I chose you before I formed you in the womb; I set you apart before you were born. I appointed you a prophet to the nations.'" (Jeremiah 1:4-5).

himself fulfilling it at some later point.[58] He is not "slow" to fulfill his promises as people reckon slowness,[59] but he has placed their fulfilments at the times in human history so as to make his plan work as he intends.[60]

In a similar way, God's relationship to space is not the same as ours. We, and everything we can see or detect, occupy a defined amount of space at a fixed position. Two physical things cannot occupy the same space at the same time, and one object cannot be at multiple places at the same time. God, however, is completely present everywhere. Luther wrote, "Nothing is so small but God is still smaller, nothing so large but God is still larger, nothing is so short but God is still shorter, nothing so long but God is still longer, nothing is so broad but God is still broader, nothing so narrow but God is still narrower, and so on. He is an inexpressible being, above and beyond all that can be described or imagined."[61] The Lord not only fills all space, he saturates it with his presence. When David asks, "Where can I go from your Spirit? Where can I flee from your presence?" in Psalm 139:7, the answer is "nowhere". A mathematician might say that God maps or projects his whole being to every point in space and time.

For the apologist, the Lord's omnipresence is much more difficult to explain than his omnipotence and omniscience. It poses hard questions. How can anything be completely present everywhere at the same time? How can anything span intervals of time? Clearly, God cannot be defined in terms of "here" or "there," "was" or "will be." He is beyond our understanding. Yet in some ways, this attribute of the Lord makes his previously discussed attributes easier to comprehend. If he is at every point in the worldly realm, then knowing everything follows because he is at every point where anything happens. The apologist can use the omnipresence of God to help people understand how he can exercise effective control over the universe. Nothing can get out of hand because God is immediately present to prevent any problem from developing, and nothing can fail to act as God wills it to, because God is there

---

58 [Balaam, under the Lord's control, said,] "God is not a man, that he might lie, or a son of man, that he might change his mind. Does he speak and not act, or promise and not fulfill?" (Numbers 23:19).

59 "The Lord does not delay his promise, as some understand delay, but is patient with you, not wanting any to perish but all to come to repentance." (2 Peter 3:9).

60 "When the time came to completion, God sent his Son, born of a woman, born under the law, to redeem those under the law, so that we might receive adoption as sons." (Galatians 4:4-5).

61 *Luther's Works*, **37**:228.

to direct every action. We must realize that we play out our whole lives on a stage where God is sitting front row center, watching our every action. There is no secret to which he is not a party.

How do people react to the omnipresence of the Lord? Most ignore it, even if they nominally claim to believe it. They assume that God is going to let them go about their daily lives without his active intervention, and they hope to avoid his parental gaze when they want to do something of which he does not approve. Who wants to go on a date with one's parent as a chaperon? In the same way, who wants to live their lives with the Lord as a chaperon? By ignoring the presence of God, they hope that he will also ignore their behavior. They only want God to be watching when they encounter a situation requiring his help.

The God of the Bible, however, is neither a genie nor room service. He is not someone who is absent except when summoned by a prayer. He is not off engaging in some more godly matters until we need him. No, the Lord is always present with us, no matter where we are,[62] even though he is invisible. Moreover, he is not just invisible like air, but he is a spirit.[63] That is, he is supernatural and, therefore, cannot be detected by our senses or by any scientific measuring device.

Finally, people might ask, "Doesn't the Bible talk about God having human qualities?" Yes. Although the Lord has no physical body, he is all-powerful, so he is capable of assuming a physical form if he has a reason to do so. Indeed, the Bible gives several examples in the Old Testament when he did take on a physical form.[64] Such a physical form, however, is not an essential attribute of the Lord, as are his justice and his mercy, and he can dispose of it when it has served his purpose. (Note: In Chapter 7, we will discuss why the physical body of Jesus is permanent.) When the Bible describes the

---

62 [David wrote,] "Where can I go to escape your Spirit? Where can I flee from your presence? If I go up to heaven, you are there; if I make my bed in Sheol, you are there. If I live at the eastern horizon or settle at the western limits, even there your hand will lead me; your right hand will hold on to me." (Psalm 139:7-10).

63 [Jesus said,] "God is spirit, and those who worship him must worship in Spirit and in truth." (John 4:24).

64 Examples of God in human form are Genesis 18, Joshua 5:13-15 and Judges 6.

Lord in human terms by talking about his eyes,[65] his ears[66] and his arms,[67] it is using picture language to help us relate God's activities to concepts that we can grasp because how he actually acts is far beyond human understanding.

The Jealous God

When we hear the word "jealousy," our immediate response is predictably negative. We think of the "green-eyed monster" who wants everything for itself. It is the envy of neighbor Bert's expensive new car which we cannot afford. It is the covetousness over the beautiful new dress our friend Melissa just bought and which we had planned to buy for ourselves or our spouses, but now wouldn't dare. It is the resentment over the promotion for which we had hoped but which went to Darrin. It is the suspicion that Jill is getting things that we want because she somehow is cheating. It is the distrust of good advice simply because it was not our idea. Jealousy is a bad word which we associate with those whose motives we dislike. Jealousy is something we project to others but rarely see in ourselves.

Let's consider the other side of the issue. Suppose a man is the owner of a medium-sized business in his city, and the committee trying to build a new youth center comes to him to fund the project. He knows it's important, so he digs deep into his pocket to find the money to cover the building's cost. Then, when the building is dedicated for use, it is named after his toughest competitor instead of him. Would he be jealous? Absolutely. His good deed had been credited to another. This story shows the situation that God faces who, in truth, does own everything, when what he provides to people freely is credited to others or not recognized at all. When the Bible quotes the Lord saying that he is "jealous,"[68] it is referring to this.

The Lord is jealous in three ways. The first way is in terms of his godliness. He **is** the only God,[69] and the Creator of all things. He has given us not only

---

[65] "King Joash didn't remember the kindness that Zechariah's father Jehoiada had extended to him, but killed his son. While he was dying, he said, 'May the LORD see and demand an account.'" (2 Chronicles 24:22).

[66] [David said,] "I called to the LORD in my distress; I called to my God. From his temple he heard my voice, and my cry for help reached his ears." (2 Samuel 22:7).

[67] [Moses said,] "Then the LORD brought us out of Egypt with a strong hand and an outstretched arm, with terrifying power, and with signs and wonders." (Deuteronomy 26:8).

[68] [The Lord said,] "For I, the LORD your God, am a jealous God." (Exodus 20:5).

[69] [The Lord said,] "I am the LORD, and there is no other; there is no God but me." (Isaiah 45:5).

everything that we have, but also our very lives themselves. For this, he deserves all our thanks and praise, as Martin Luther notes in his explanation of the first article. In fact, the Lord demands our thanks and praise,[70] not because he needs them,[71] but because we need to set our hearts on him as the source of ultimate goodness rather than on the things of this world which are only pale imitations of that goodness. The first commandment, to which the statement of God's jealousy was attached at his giving of the Law, clearly states the Lord's expectation.[72] He alone is to be worshipped because he alone provides. Nothing else we might worship has any ability to help us.[73] The Lord is not interested in sharing the credit for our blessings when it is only he who gives those blessings.

As apologists, we will be faced with people who resent the Lord's insistence that he be in first place in their lives. Even among Protestants, only 23% answering a survey were willing to give God first place.[74] It is natural for every person to want to hold the first position in his or her own life. Everyone wants to "watch out for number one". The Lord makes it clear that if such is our attitude, then we are his enemies.[75] There is only one throne in our hearts, and if we or some other god is sitting on it, then the Lord isn't. It is here that Jesus' statement about not being able to serve two masters needs to be employed.[76] The argument that "I can still be a good person and not have to submit to the Lord in everything" is just plain wrong. The Lord is not interested in human arguments about why he does not deserve the honor clearly due him as the Owner and Ruler of the universe. He is the one, the only and the great God. "It's all about me" has no place in the life of a Christian.

Secondly, the Lord is jealous about his law. To preserve his perfect creation, he enacted a perfect law which would have preserved perfect harmony

---

70 [The Lord said,] "I am the LORD. That is my name, and I will not give my glory to another or my praise to idols." (Isaiah 42:8).

71 Psalm 50:7-15.

72 [The Lord said,] "Do not have other gods besides me." (Exodus 20:3).

73 [A psalmist wrote,] "Their idols are silver and gold, made by human hands. They have mouths but cannot speak, eyes, but cannot see. They have ears but cannot hear, noses, but cannot smell. They have hands but cannot feel, feet, but cannot walk. They cannot make a sound with their throats." (Psalm 115:4-7).

74 Lockwood, ibid., 81.

75 Parable of the rich man. Luke 12:16-21.

76 [Jesus said,] "No one can serve two masters, since either he will hate one and love the other, or he will be devoted to one and despise the other. You cannot serve both God and money." (Matthew 6:24).

among his creatures had it been followed. Man could never have devised such a law. God, therefore, wanted his law perfectly obeyed, and he gave his creation, including man, the ability to keep this law.[77] The law is the image of the perfection of God himself. When man sinned, the perfect law of God was fatally soiled. It could no longer accomplish its intended purpose to guide people to live righteously before God. Instead, it became a curb on man's evil[78] and a mirror to show him his sin.[79] The Lord continued to emphasize his law for these two purposes throughout the Old Testament. The Lord is jealous of the fact that he gave man the way to happiness and life but that man chose another way which leads to misery and death. The Lord's jealousy here is that he does not want his Name sullied by the accusation that he is somehow responsible for man's folly. The apologist needs to point out that the Lord did everything necessary to keep evil out of the world, but it was man who insisted on bringing it in (see Chapter 7).

Finally, the Lord is jealous about his gospel. When man sinned, God immediately acted by promising a plan of complete and free salvation.[80] The plan was ingeniously crafted and cost God dearly to carry out.[81] It was exactly what man needed done but was helpless to accomplish by himself.[82] Like the creation and like God's law, God's plan of salvation was perfect. To allow everyone to learn about and accept this plan of salvation, the Lord commissioned believers to spread the news of it to everyone in the world.[83] Once again, however, the plan that was promulgated had to be the perfect plan of

---

77 [David wrote,] "The instruction of the LORD is perfect, renewing one's life; the testimony of the LORD is trustworthy, making the inexperienced wise. The precepts of the LORD are right, making the heart glad; the command of the LORD is radiant, making the eyes light up. The fear of the LORD is pure, enduring forever; the ordinances of the LORD are reliable and altogether righteous." (Psalm 19:7-9).

78 "When they had heard all the words, they turned to each other in fear." (Jeremiah 36:16).

79 "For no one will be justified in his sight by the works of the law, because the knowledge of sin comes through the law." (Romans 3:20).

80 [The Lord said,] "I will put hostility between you and the woman, and between your offspring and her offspring. He will strike your head, and you will strike his heel." (Genesis 3:15).

81 [Jesus said,] "The Son of Man will be handed over to the chief priests and scribes, and they will condemn him to death. They will hand him over to the Gentiles to be mocked, flogged, and crucified, and on the third day he will be raised." (Matthew 20:18-19).

82 "For while we were still helpless, at the right time, Christ died for the ungodly." (Romans 5:6).

83 [Jesus said,] "Go, therefore, and make disciples of all nations, baptizing them in the name of the Father and of the Son and of the Holy Spirit, teaching them to observe everything I have commanded you." (Matthew 28:19-20).

the Lord, not some smudgy copy soiled by man's additions and subtractions. The Lord is jealous that what he did for people's salvation should not be credited to them because they think they can contribute something to it, and it should not be regarded as a common right of mankind.[84] He justly demands all the glory for providing a way for our salvation and for our accepting that salvation on his terms. The apologist needs to stress the magnitude of the Lord's actions for fallen mankind and point out the arrogance of anyone who feels he or she has anything to contribute to this great undertaking (see Chapter 7).

Summary

The apologist will frequently be confronted by the argument that the Lord cannot be the way the Bible describes him. According to this reasoning, a god either cannot or would not be of this nature. People want a god that is more amenable to their way of thinking. Stripped of all their rationalizations, they really want a voice in how God is constructed. The Lord will have none of this. On the other hand, some people are merely functionally ignorant of what a god is. They need to be enlightened to the incredible magnitude of the Lord and how he really does have the power and knowledge to control everything in the universe.

This chapter has been aimed at helping the apologist deal with the ignorance and arrogance of the human mindset when trying to come to grips with the nature of the Lord. It has emphasized the greatness of the Lord because the people of the twenty-first century have lost their awe of him. It has laid the foundation for discussing God's control over nature in the next two chapters on creation and miracles and his plan of salvation in Chapter 7.

---

84 "For you are saved by grace through faith, and this is not from yourselves; it is God's gift—not from works, so that no one can boast." (Ephesians 2:8-9).

5

Creation and Science

In Chapter 4 we saw the incredible power and majesty of the Lord as he is described in the Bible. Now we need to look at the methods and strategies of physical and biological scientists in their quest to accomplish their goal of explaining all observable phenomena in terms of the inherent properties of matter, energy, space, and time. In the process, we will determine which arguments that are used in evolutionary theories can be challenged by evidence and reasoning and which things cannot. The theater of activity is large, so we will stick to the key points. The last section of the chapter will deal more generally with dreamers, pseudo-scientists, and deniers.

We must reasonably start with the question "What is science?" Many people in modern society have difficulty answering this question, and that difficulty leads to a misuse of science and a misplaced fear and even resentment of science by some Christians—perhaps even resulting in some misdirected attempts to discredit science. Science is nothing more than an approach or a methodology for exploring the physical universe. As such, it is only a tool, which can be used poorly or well, for good purposes or for bad. One widely held misunderstanding of science is that it produces absolute truth (see Chapter 1). In reality, science follows a zig-zag course as the gathering of new data continually causes the modification or rejection of previously held models, as well as the creation of new theories. In the long run, scientific models get better, but in the short run, things are frequently messy and contentious.

In the modern world, the work of science is often used to give a false impression by those with their own agenda, such as Humanists. Humanism is a belief system—even a religion.[1] It asserts that science can produce absolute truth. It claims that science has disproved the existence of God. One of its underlying assumptions is that, given enough time, man will discover everything necessary to know about our universe to be his own savior. Man will solve all the problems of life and will achieve a manmade paradise on Earth.

The apologist must be able to distinguish in his or her own mind the difference between the discipline of science and the way in which Humanists use science. The apologist must also recognize that most people with whom he or she talks, both inside and outside of the church, are not aware of this distinction and will not be careful to observe it. Nevertheless, the apologist should not concede such a blurring of this distinction, because insisting on the proper role of science and of its theories and formulations will limit the illegitimate attacks which are brought against the gospel.

Framing the Discussion

The sciences began as part of philosophy in ancient Greece. Philosophers like Plato and Aristotle crossed from one area of study to the other without much concern.[2] Such men believed if it was reasonable, then it was true.[3] No one bothered to experimentally test many of their statements about the physical world for validity for almost 2,000 years. One might say they did theoretical science rather than experimental science.

Experimental science using a more refined scientific method was introduced in about 1600 by Galileo Galilei, Johannes Kepler and other inquisitive people.[4] Galileo ran into severe opposition from the Roman Catholic Church, which had effectively elevated the Greek philosophers to doctors of the church.[5] For most of the next century, a mixture of theological and philosophical ideas continued to dominate scientific thinking, until Isaac Newton

---

1 What is called "Humanism" has changed a lot over its history, from the time of Plato and Aristotle to the time of the Reformation to modern times. Humanism will be discussed in more detail in Chapter 10.

2 Goldman, ibid., Lect. 1.

3 Greeks emphasized geometry and logic. While some Greeks did count and observe, they lacked algebra and, therefore, did not seek to develop rigorous models through experimentation.

4 Herbert Butterfield, *The Origins of Modern Science* (Macmillan Free Press, New York, 1957).

5 In some ways the Reformation opened the door to scientific investigation because it challenged artificial authority and directed people back to original sources.

developed calculus and formulated laws of nature that were easy for people to test, use and teach.[6] This began a revolution in the physical sciences which has continued into the twenty-first century. The study of the biological sciences accelerated with Charles Darwin's *Origin of the Species* in 1859 [7] and Gregor Johann Mendel's work in genetics in the 1860s.[8] Work in astronomy and geology also began to intensify at the same time. During the nineteenth century the opinion that the earth was older than a few thousand years progresssively gained strength among the scientific community, but scientific methodology was still inadequate to collect sufficient evidence to experimentally verify this idea.

Three events caused many fields of science to take gigantic strides forward during the twentieth century. First, Albert Einstein published four key papers in 1905 which directed physics away from its Newtonian roots to what has come to be called "modern physics."[9] Second, World War II caused the Americans, British and Germans to intensify scientific study as part of their war efforts. Finally, the launching of the first artificial satellite by the Soviet Union in 1957 ignited a panicked response by the American government, which then trained hundreds of thousands of scientists in the following two decades. As a result, in the last quarter of the twentieth century, key scientific disciplines made astonishing advances in technology and in the gathering and processing of information. The scientific knowledge of people who studied science as undergraduates in the 1960s and 1970s is as obsolete in the twenty-first century as is the rotary-dial telephone.

Before we can look at what can and cannot be used by apologists vis-à-vis the evidence and theories of science, we need to discuss how various key fields of science have developed and their impact on how we draft our positions in response. For anyone to gain enough knowledge and understanding to speak to the theories and ideas that dominate scientific thought today, he or she needs to take numerous college level courses in diverse scientific fields. Because scientific models are in a constant state of development, such people need to engage in a broad-based program of continuing education, or they will

---

[6] William Dunham, *Great Thinkers, Great Theorems* (The Great Courses, The Teaching Company, Chantilly, VA, 2010), Lect. 13-15.

[7] Stephen Nowiscki, *Biology: The Science of Life* (The Great Courses, The Teaching Company, Chantilly, VA, 2010), Lect. 17.

[8] Nowiscki, ibid., Lect. 14.

[9] Wolfson, ibid.

find themselves arguing about scientific history rather than current scientific thinking.

The Status of Science

Physics is the study of matter, energy, space and time at its most fundamental level. Classical physics, the type we learned in high school and early college courses, makes sense to the logical mind. It is the basis for most of the technology that we employ in our daily lives. Modern physics has more of the feeling of being Alice in Wonderland, yet its strange models are verifiable by reproducible experimentation. In quantum physics one is forced to deal with wave functions that collapse into matter only when they are observed.[10] The members of the "particle zoo" in particle physics have properties and interactions that bear no relationship to the nature of balls and marbles which we understand.[11] In special relativity, time does not flow at a constant rate, and the order of events can depend on the frame of reference of the observer.[12] In general relativity, matter tells space how to bend and space tells matter how to move.[13] Why is this stuff important to us? The global positioning system would not work without taking into consideration the effects of velocity and gravity on time flow, and computer design is affected by the speed of light. While physics is not a direct player in evolutionary theories, its models of nature underpin cosmology, which is. While apologists do not need to be physicists, they must be aware that the validity of what is actually observed in the physical world cannot always be judged by common sense reasoning.

Informatics includes artificial intelligence (AI), computer learning, simulation, modeling, information flow management, data concurrency, multiprocessing, numerical analysis, and systems design.[14] AI is responsible for human-computer verbal interfaces and the growing smartness of numerous appliances. Computer simulation is used extensively in facility design, pro-

---

[10] Dan Hooper, *What Einstein Got Wrong* (The Great Courses, The Teaching Company, Chantilly, VA, 2017), Lect. 8.

[11] Wolfson, ibid., Lect. 22.

[12] Sean Carroll, *Mysteries of Modern Physics: Time* (The Great Courses, The Teaching Company, Chantilly, VA, 2017), Lect. 1-8.

[13] Benjamin Schumacher, *Black Holes, Tides, and Curved Spacetime: Understanding Gravity (*The Great Courses, The Teaching Company, Chantilly, VA, 2013).

[14] *Artificial Intelligence: A Modern Approach, 3rd ed.* (Stuart Russell and Peter Norvig, eds., online).

cess flow and training. Supercomputers with modeling software have allowed scientists to gather billions upon billions of pieces of evidence and to use them to optimize theories automatically. This has made challenging many scientific models impossible for anyone without access to the overwhelmingly large pools of data in areas such as geology, climatology, and astronomy and to the computing power to analyze them.

Analytical Chemistry develops and refines the measurement methodology and instrumentation to weigh, count, measure and identify substances for many of the physical and biological sciences, as well as their sampling strategies and their information validating criteria. Developments in microelectronics, information theory and light manipulation technology now allow measurements to be made with precision undreamed of in the 1970s.[15] Like physics, analytical chemistry is not a direct player in evolutionary models, but it has given numerous fields the ability to collect and precisely analyze evidence used in building such models.

Geology is the study of the earth, its functioning, and its physical history. The development of the plate tectonics model and the overwhelming evidence gathered which supports it have allowed geologists to unite many diverse strands into a solid model of how the earth functions.[16] Numerous high-tech sensors over the earth's surface feed data directly into computers holding the tectonic models, allowing for continuous refinement. The movement of the tectonic plates and the changes in the earth's surface features are known with high precision. Shockwaves from the numerous earthquakes that happen daily are now used to map the internal structure of the earth. Geology has become an evidence-based science to the extent that its theories of Earth's history are no longer challengeable by amateurs.

Astronomy is the study of what exists in the universe beyond the earth.[17] With the exception of the solar system into which astronomers have been able to send physical space probes, the only thing that astronomers have to work

---

[15] *Analytical Instrumentation Handbook, 2nd ed.*, GW Ewing, ed. (Marcel Dekker, Inc, New York, online).

[16] John J Renton, *The Nature of Earth: An Introduction to Geology* (The Great Courses, The Teaching Company, Chantilly, VA, 2006).

[17] Alex Filippenko, *Understanding the Universe: An Introduction to Astronomy, 2nd ed.* (The Great Courses, The Teaching Company, Chantilly, VA, 2007).

with is the radiation they can detect coming from the sky. This is very limiting, but they can observe the whole electromagnetic spectrum, and things appear quite different across the various wavelengths of radiation. In addition, advancements in physics, instrumentation and supercomputers have greatly increased the astronomers' ability to study these celestial objects. Space telescopes, interplanetary probes, and computer compensation for atmospheric interferences for earth-based telescopes have allowed astronomers to collect an unfathomable amount of data. The study of exoplanets has become an area of particular interest, and the techniques developed to verify their existence are ingenious.[18] Evolutionary theories of the lifecycles of stars and planetary formation are staples of astronomy, but they can only be evaluated by observation and not by experimentation.

Cosmology attempts to explain the nature of the universe and its history.[19] It is the most speculative of the physical sciences because it faces severe challenges in data-gathering. Not only does it have all the limitations of astronomy in terms of tremendous distances that it cannot traverse to study objects up close, but it also cannot traverse time to see if currently unknown factors might have influenced the development of the universe. Despite these limitations, cosmology is wildly popular with the media, being best known for the Big Bang theory. In addition, it has discovered the cosmic microwave background, dark matter (which is causing deviations from the theory of universal gravitation) and dark energy (which is challenging the law of the conservation of energy). It has dabbled in string theory and a multiverse, both of which are currently untestable. Being a young field, its key theories are likely to be in flux for some time.

Genetics is the study of how traits are passed between generations.[20] For a long time, genetic research was limited to breeding members of the various species of plants and animals. Since the discovery that the genetic material is held in DNA molecules on genes that are part of chromosomes, rapid progress has been made in understanding the nature and relationships of genetic ma-

---

[18] Joshua N. Winn, *The Search for Exoplanets: What Astronomers Know* (The Great Courses, The Teaching Company, Chantilly, VA, 2015).

[19] Sean Carroll, *Dark Natter, Dark Energy: The Dark Side of the Universe* (The Great Courses, The Teaching Company, Chantilly, VA, 2007).

[20] David Sadava, *Understanding Genetics: DNA, Genes, and Their Real-World Applications* (The Great Courses, The Teaching Company, Chantilly, VA, 2008), Lect. 1-9.

terials across species. The entire human genome (3 billion base pairs) has been sequenced, so the blueprint of human life is in the hands of scientists. This genetic map, along with similar maps for plants and animals, has created many research opportunities. For example, people's ancestries can now be identified, and DNA testing can be used to connect criminals with their crimes and to free innocent people.

Molecular Biology allows the molecules of life, particularly DNA, to be manipulated like other molecules.[21] DNA material can now be cut and pasted to move genes from one species to another, thereby creating new forms of life. For example, cells have been manufactured specifically to produce human insulin and other key biological products. In addition, major advances in understanding how to identify and fix genetic problems have occurred. The research in this area presents moral concerns because of the growing ability to make new forms of living things, including intermingling human genetic components with plant and animal components to create races of mutants.

Evolutionary Biology has existed since Charles Darwin proposed that species evolve through chance mutations and natural selection. The decoding of the human genome and the genomes of animals and plants will allow evolutionary biologists to create more complete models of how life apparently developed through genetic mutations. It is a daunting project, as origin-of-life researchers are well aware, but computing resources might facilitate rapid advances in this field. Such advances will offer significant challenges to the biblical apologist.

Understanding how Scientists Seek Truth

As explained in Chapter 1, any "truth" can only be asserted relative to a standard of truth. A *standard* is a set of assumptions.[22] The fundamental assumption of science is that all observations made in the natural world can be explained in terms of the inherent properties of matter, energy, time, and space. It follows from this assumption that no supernatural being (i.e., no god) can do anything in the natural world, and as a result, effectively does not exist. For all scientists, even for those who are Christian, this is an essential working

---

[21] Sadava, ibid., Lect. 10-24.

[22] Goldman, ibid.

assumption.[23] Why is this the case? Suppose a woman is trying to bake ten dozen chocolate chip cookies. Further suppose several hungry teenagers periodically wander into her kitchen and grab some of the cookies. As a result of these random agents, she cannot know how many cookies she will have when she finishes baking. If any of the observations which scientists make are the result of a god acting by supernatural means, their models will be unreliable for explaining events. *The interference of a god renders even the best scientific model only as reliable as the god wants it to be*. (Note: This last sentence is a key argument for apologists.) Without this primary assumption, science would be reduced to the philosophical methods of Aristotle. All aspects of engineering and medicine would become speculative.

If we talk to good scientists, they will tell us that what drives them to study nature is that they feel previous models of nature are inadequate to explain all observations. They, therefore, want to develop new and more complete models. Because science is highly competitive, every scientist would like to be the first to find such inadequacies and to propose a new model to explain them. Fame, promotions, grant money and Nobel Prizes hang in the balance. Yet the scientific road is not completely smooth. Scientists, like all of us, are sinful and therefore prone to *confirmation bias*, that is, reading their own data in too positive a light. In addition, the conclusions of inductive reasoning can never be absolutely certain.[24] As a result, to receive the recognition they seek for their work, scientists are required to submit their theories and data to the rest of the relevant scientific community to give that community the opportunity to disprove their work (i.e., a *falsification challenge*). Only those theories which survive this challenge are regarded as scientifically true. Even so, scientific truth is always provisional and can be overturned if new evidence is found that does not fit the model. As the famous University of Wisconsin–Madison statistics professor Dr. George Box observed, "Basically, all models are wrong, but some are useful."[25]

In the long run, scientists do hope that the results of their experiments do not completely verify current models, but that they show areas in which model

---

23 In all human activities, and science is a human activity, all players must obey the rules. In American football, for example, players knock other players to the ground, although this is otherwise not good Christian behavior.

24 See section on science in Chapter 1.

25 George Box, "Science and Statistics," *Journal of the American Statistical Association*, **71**: 791–799, 1976.

refinement is necessary. It is here where scientists build their reputations. Each scientist is driven to be suspicious of every other scientist's work and is continually probing it, looking for shortcomings. Therefore, for anyone to try to hide evidence that does not support their theories is professionally dangerous.

What troubles a lot of Christians is that many scientists seem dedicated to the concept that the universe evolved and was not created by God. As was just shown, science ceases to be science if God is introduced into its theories. Supernatural actions cannot be correlated with what is observed in nature. All theories then become, "Well, God did something here." It is hard to build bridges and cure diseases with that approach. All scientists react to what they observe, and they observe that things change, which is a synonym for evolve. They believe that such changing (evolving) has always occurred, and they try to build models of how the changes occurred to produce the cumulative effects which we observe. That, in a nutshell, is macroscopic evolution, which assumes only natural causes.

Further, scientists are faced with undeniable evidence that the earth has an apparent age of several billion years (see the next section). Some use this evidence as the backbone of their explanations of macroscopic evolution. Moreover, there is extensive evidence from numerous areas of research that is generally consistent with this model, even though the picture is far from complete. As is well known in science, however, simply because evidence is consistent with a model does not prove that model. Arguing otherwise is to commit the fallacy of affirming the consequent. This is an important point for apologists to remember. While Humanists may proclaim the gospel of macroscopic evolution with religious zeal, to most scientists it is merely an environment in which they do their research, much of which has nothing to do with anything evolving over long periods of time. Whether one believes in macroscopic evolution or in six-day creation is really irrelevant to most scientific work. Everyone needs to collect evidence according to the same rules and to submit theories to the same review. We will consider the implications of this for apologetics when we look at the individual issues that science raises.

There are six broad areas in which science operates: outer space, the physical planet Earth, life, the mind, the sub-atomic world, and the nature of social interactions. We will discuss key issues of the first three areas in this chapter and discuss the mind in Chapter 9. The other two areas are not within the scope of this book.

What is the Age of the Earth?

To understand the challenge that we face as apologists, we must first fashion a definition of age. To gain the perspective to do so, let us consider the following scenario. Suppose we have a friend who works for a major movie studio in California. While we were visiting this friend, he was able to get us passes to see the set of a big-budget movie about Louis XIV that his studio was making. When we arrived on the set, after-hours and with a guard, we marveled at the amazing furniture in several of the stage rooms being used for the filming. We asked our friend, "From where were they able to borrow this beautiful 350-year-old furniture?" Our friend replied, "It's more like 35-day-old furniture. There's a shop a couple blocks from here that makes the furniture for all our sets." Appearances can be deceiving. The director wanted the set to look old and authentic for his movie, but that did not mean that what was on the stage really came from that ancient period. This story shows us the difference between *actual age* and *apparent age*. The first is reality; the second is what we can observe. If we realize that the Bible tells us the former, but science can only measure the latter, then we do not have to get bogged down in the creation-versus-science conflict over the age of the earth.[26]

Next, let's suppose we could have a noted internist examine Adam on the day after his creation. He would likely report that Adam was an extremely healthy adult male, apparently in his twenties. His actual age, however, was but one day old! If a veterinarian examined the birds and mammals on the same day, he would also report that they were healthy adults of their species with an apparent age of one to multiple years old. Their actual ages were one or two days old. If, on the seventh day, a soils scientist were to examine the soil that was hosting the lush vegetation of the Garden of Eden, he would report that the soil was of excellent quality and that, depending upon which type of rock it had developed from and what agents were available to aid its development, it would have taken many thousands, if not millions, of years

[26] Consider how easy it is for people to be deceived about age. Joshua 9:16-27 gives us an account of how the Gibeonites deceived the Israelites about the age of their clothing and supplies when the latter did not consult the Lord.

to reach its observed state.[27] An atmospheric scientist who analyzed the nature of the air on the seventh day would report that it was of a composition that would have required many million years to evolve planet-wide, depending on the degree of plant cover and other factors affecting its oxygen content.[28] In reality, both the land and air were less than 7 days old, but they would have an apparent age that was much greater to the eyes and instruments of the scientists. Finally, an astronomer would examine the sky the night of the seventh day and report that he could detect stars that were millions of lightyears away,[29] even though the light had had only 3 days to travel toward Earth after the stars were created and, as such, could not have reached it by natural means.

What is clear from the first chapter of Genesis is that the Lord created a planet and a universe in six days, but with an apparent age, that is, in a form, that would appear to people and their instruments to be much older than their actual age. This is good because on a completely new planet, nothing would grow, one could not breathe the air and the radiation levels would kill every

---

27 The development of soil from rock masses is a highly studied process. Material goes through many steps from rock mass to boulder to cobble to gravel to sand to silt to clay. But this is only the geological side of the conversion. The inorganic clay must attract bacteria that can absorb the metal ions from it and then die to leave carbon behind. Over time, as the amount of organic carbon grows, larger forms of life are attracted to the clay and add nutrients to it. It is a bootstrapping process in which as time passes more and more of the ingredients are deposited that make the clay into fertile soil. Photosynthesis, nitrogen-fixing and aeration are all needed to be provided by living creatures, either plant or animal, to improve the soil quality so it may grow a beautiful garden. There are literally thousands of small steps in the process, but fortunately geologists and soil scientists can study them in parallel. They can visit tens of thousands of sites where the process of soil production is in different stages and study how long each step takes. Then, by adding together the time periods for each of the steps to occur, they can get an estimate of the minimum time the natural process of soil development takes. This is the apparent age of the soil. Of course, it could take longer if steps were inhibited by unfavorable conditions.

28 Oxygen is a very reactive element. It reacts with elements in the earth, such as iron, to form oxides, and it dissolves in water. If oxygen were not being continually added to the atmosphere by the photosynthesis in plants, it would gradually decline and disappear. Earth's atmosphere is 21% oxygen, and many, but not all, animals depend on such a high level of oxygen. If Earth's atmosphere started with 0% oxygen, which would be its normal state, then it would require a tremendous amount of work by plants to build it up to its current level. This is because as they produced oxygen, a significant amount of it would be lost to oxidation or to being absorbed into the oceans. A great number of large plants would be needed, which in turn would require a lot of soil development. It, therefore, would take a long time to reach the current level of oxygen in equilibrium. The best estimate of how long this would take is the apparent age of the atmosphere.

29 To be seen, the light emitted by a star must travel to Earth. This is not instantaneous. Light travels at a fixed speed in a vacuum. A lightyear is the distance that light travels in one year, which is 5.879 trillion miles.

living thing. As apologists, we need to accept this reality. Similar to the director in the Louis XIV story, the Lord created a stage set on which the drama of mankind is to be played out, and he found it desirable to make it a stage set with a significant apparent age. While we can use the genealogical records in the Bible to make an estimate as to how long ago the Lord created the universe, he did not explicitly tell us. We cannot defend an exact date. Moreover, the Lord did not specifically mention in Genesis 1 and 2 that the created earth had an apparent age or what it equals. But he also didn't tell us that he put the earth and the planets in orbit around the sun. He just told us that he made the rest of the heavenly bodies on the fourth day. The Lord does not owe us an explanation of what he does or why he does it in a particular way. As apologists, we talk about what he has revealed, not what he might have done but did not reveal.[30]

When scientists try to measure the ages of things on the earth, they can only detect their apparent values. There are three general approaches that can be used. The first is to measure the isotopic content of the earth as it exists now. Some atomic isotopes are stable, while others have decay half-lives ranging from less than 10^{-20} second to more than 10^{20} years. A *half-life* is the time necessary for one-half of the current amount of a particular material to disappear through radioactive decay. After a second half-life, only one-fourth remains, and after three half-lives only one-eighth remains. After fifteen half-lives, an isotope is reduced to the level of effective undetectability. For example, an isotope with a half-life of 1000 years would effectively have disappeared after 15,000 years. When isotopes are gathered from all over the earth, all the stable isotopes (250 of them) are found to exist. All radioactive isotopes (30 of them) consistent with the earth being between 1.2 and 11 billion years old are also found to exist, but none of the radioactive isotopes (46 of them) consistent with the earth being less than 1.2 billion years old are found to exist.[31] This analysis uses common laboratory equipment and has been repeated many times. The chances that someone will perform this experiment and get a different result are vanishingly small. Therefore, an apparent age of the Earth of between 1.2 and 11 billion years old is consistent with the evidence, while a younger age is totally inconsistent with the evidence (see

---

30 "For we walk by faith, not by sight." (2 Corinthians 5:7).

31 Radioactive isotopes that do not exist naturally can be made artificially using nuclear reactors, and these are widely used in medical procedures.

Appendix II for a more detailed discussion).

The second approach to measuring the Earth's age is to gather up specific rocks, extract selective elements that form a radioactive decay series (see Appendix II) and then do measurements of the relative isotopic abundance to determine how long the radioactive decay in the rock has been occurring. This analysis works because before rocks solidify, the decay products of radioactivity can escape, but once the minerals of the rocks solidify, the decay products are trapped in the rock's crystal structure until the rock erodes away or is analyzed.[32] Using current measurement technology, such as mass spectrometry and atom-probe tomography, it is possible to get very precise ratios between different isotopes and to even count single atoms or small clusters of them. This permits dating rocks very accurately and even detecting whether a specimen has somehow become contaminated. The oldest rocks have been dated at over 4.3 billion years old and, as a result, 4.6 billion years is generally regarded as the age of the Earth. While rock dating once was sometimes compromised by inadequate collection documentation and inappropriate specimen handling, these issues have disappeared with better training and strong competition among researchers.[33] The apologist should note well that rock dating differs from carbon dating, which will be discussed later.

The third approach to dating objects is based on their rate of mass wasting (e.g., rock splitting by the freeze-thaw cycle), erosion, sedimentary buildup, or similar geological processes.[34] These methods are less reliable because the rates at which these processes work can change. Nevertheless, they can be

---

32 The dating of mineral zircon ($ZrSiO_4$) is a good example of the radioisotope dating process. Uranium atoms fit readily into its crystal structure in place of zirconium atoms, but lead atoms do not. When zircon crystals formed, therefore, they were contaminated by small amounts of uranium but by no lead. Yet, we often find zircon in nature with lead mixed in. Why? Uranium of atomic mass 238 (U^{238}) [half-life 4.5 billion years] decays eventually into lead of atomic mass 206 (Pb^{206}), while U^{235} [half-life 700 million years] decays eventually into Pb^{207}. By measuring how much of each of these four isotopes is present and comparing the lead/uranium ratio to the length of the half-lives for these two different decay series, it is possible to determine when the samples of zircon were apparently formed. In fact, because the two decay series are independent of each other, scientists can check the results for consistency. Other radioisotopes are used for other minerals, depending on the chemical composition of the minerals.

33 To maintain credibility with their customers, most analytical laboratories are part of accreditation programs from which they periodically receive unknown samples which they must analyze. They then submit their results for comparison with a master reference laboratory and with each other. Customers can access this information.

34 Renton, ibid., Lect. 14-22.

used to make estimates of relative age if markers of known age can be found in or with them. One of the common markers is the fossils of plants and animals found in rock and soil layers. If the age of a particular type of fossil has been established because it is also found in rock formations that have been accurately dated by radiological methods, the fossil can be used as a secondary standard for dating other materials, with the understanding that such dating will be less reliable. On the other hand, if one is only trying to establish general trends, this may be good enough.

The apologist must not get hung up on the apparent age of the earth. After all, it is the Lord who gave the earth its apparent age, and we need to accept that estimates of its value are the result of repeatable measurements made by a large number of highly trained people. Evolutionists will use the apparent age for their own purposes, but that should not cause us to deny what can be demonstrated before our eyes in the laboratory. The Lord determined that the apparent age which he gave the earth was the correct age for his purposes. We need to point out that it is not inconsistent with the Bible because already in Genesis 1, an older apparent age of the earth is indicated. God's revelation trumps the meaning of human measurements, but God also gave us the ability to make the measurements because he has a purpose in allowing us to do so. It seems evident that God didn't feel that we needed to know that purpose.

A note of caution is in order, however. It is always possible that someone will make an unwarranted assumption, use bad sampling technique, or poorly prepare a sample for analysis. While such cases sometimes gain an extraordinary amount of publicity, they are becoming progressively rarer. All scientific claims are viewed with suspicion by the rest of the scientific community, and false claims soon become obvious. We should allow the experts to sort out these issues rather than issuing opinions based on limited knowledge.

Science and Revelation

At this point we need to again review the meaning of truth. The scientific standard of truth is established in terms of what can be weighed, counted, measured, and identified by reproducible measurements. Science is a human enterprise, and therefore, it is limited by human frailties. Scientists cannot detect the hand of the Lord working in nature when that hand is supernatural and hidden. In contrast, the Christian standard of truth is the Bible, which is the Word of God. Therefore, it can, if God so chooses, give us information about the supernatural actions of God which scientists cannot see. Truth measured by these two standards will not be the same. Things true according to one of them might be false according to the other. Science can only measure things as they appear, not as they really are. Therefore, there cannot be anything called "true science" which will find precisely what the Bible says. Efforts of sinful human beings simply cannot duplicate the revelation of the Lord.

Further, intensive scientific investigation is not something commanded by the Lord.[35] It thus has no promise attached to it. Nowhere has the Lord promised that he will allow man to determine how he actually made the world and manages it. In fact, in Job 38-41 God effectively declares that how nature works is known to him only and far beyond us. By poking around in nature, we cannot force him to allow us to discover what he is doing with his hidden hand, which is not restricted to operate according to the laws of nature. If we could so force him, then we would have control over him. None of the props we find in this world need to have the meaning we assign to them.

For example, scientists have come to describe stars as orbs similar in many ways to the sun. The Bible never gives a definition of a star, describing them only as giving light,[36] having splendor,[37] being numerous[38] and someday falling to Earth.[39] The only things scientists know about the spatial realm beyond our solar system are what they deduce from its radiation that reaches the Earth and, extremely rarely, from a gravitational wave front.[40] What has been detected is certainly consistent with there being "100 billion stars in each of 100 billion galaxies" as many cosmologists currently believe,[41] but it is also consistent with "the heavens" being merely an elaborate backdrop for the Lord's stage set on planet Earth. How is that possible? It is because we cannot actually "see" stars; rather all we can do is detect the ends of the beams of light

35 While the Lord commanded mankind to "subdue" the earth in Genesis 1:28, our first parents, as well as the original readers of Moses' writings, would certainly have understood this to mean that God was directing them to employ practical methods to manage the earth's resources. Organized scientific study is a much more recent invention of man.

36 Philippians 2:15.

37 1 Corinthians 15:41.

38 Genesis 15:5.

39 Mark 13:25.

40 Filippenko, ibid., Lect. 1.

41 Filippenko, ibid., Lect. 69.

that reach us. Scientists quite reasonably assume that that light came from actual physical orbs, but the Lord could have in some or all cases created the light beams independent of the existence of physical stars. (Special effects are not necessarily limited to Hollywood film studios.) Moreover, unless we learn some radically new laws of physics which would allow us to send probes over the great distances of space, we will never verify what is truly out there. It is blasphemy to charge the Lord with deceiving us if he didn't set up the universe or even the earth in the way that our investigational logic tells us it should be.[42] Consider that the Tree of the Knowledge of Good and Evil does not make either scientific or philosophical sense, but it was nevertheless a purposeful creation of the Lord. Sometimes, as apologists, we must point out that if we have food, clothing, shelter, and enough knowledge of the physical things of this world so we can live our lives in service to the Lord, then we have enough. We should not be overly desirous of trying to pin God down by our measurements of what he has done.

Carbon-14 Dating[43]

Unlike the isotopes used to date rocks, carbon-14 is a replenishable radioactive isotope (*radioisotope*) produced by the collision of cosmic rays with nitrogen-14 in the earth's atmosphere. Although its half-life is only 5,730 years, it maintains a steady concentration on the earth's surface based on its rates of production and decay.[44] Carbon-14 isotopes are chemically the same as stable carbon isotopes and are incorporated with them into the substance of living plants and animals based on what they draw from the soil or the air or otherwise consume.[45] When a plant or animal dies, no more carbon-14 is added to the remains of, nor any product made from, that plant or animal. The

---

42 In this regard, creation science is like decision theology. It causes us to look to our abilities rather than accepting that the Lord moves to perform his wonders in ways hidden to our intellect and senses. Dr. Siegbert Becker beautifully described why Luther rejected this Reformed approach in the second chapter of *The Foolishness of God* (Northwestern Publishing House, Milwaukee, 1982), 13-25.

43 "Radiocarbon dating" (Wikipedia, online).

44 Despite its relatively short half-life, carbon-14 continues to exist in nature because of what is called the *bathtub effect*. If one fills a bathtub partially full of water, opens the drain and turns on the faucets to match the drainage flow, a level of water will continue to remain in the tub even if the original water would have long ago drained out if it were not being replenished. Production of carbon-14 from cosmic rays equals the loss from radioactive decay.

45 Carbon is present in all organic materials, such as plants and flesh.

carbon-14 isotopes decay back to nitrogen-14 which, because of its ubiquity, cannot be uniquely identified. Therefore, the age of the original plant or animal cannot be calculated as the ratio of the parent isotope and its daughter decay product isotope as with rock dating. Instead, it is calculated based on the ratio of the assumed initial amount of carbon-14 that existed when the plant or animal was alive and the measured amount in its remains or product made from it. For example, this method might be used to date a piece of linen to determine whether it was made in the first century BC or the thirteenth century AD.

There are obvious limitations to the use of carbon-14 dating. First, because of its relatively short half-life, it cannot be used to date anything that appears to be more than 40 to 50 thousand years old. Second, the assumption that the original fraction of carbon atoms that were carbon-14 has been constant throughout history may not be true, particularly for older samples. When materials of known ages are available, scientists can use them to calibrate their measurements to eliminate this problem. This is only doable for the last few thousand years for which we have materials of known ages. Finally, trying to date non-carbon materials on the basis of carbon-containing materials found in their vicinity is questionable unless everything is found together in a sealed environment. This is because contamination can come from environmental carbon, particularly carbon ash from any fire. Carbon-14 dating is reliable, provided its limitations are respected and the analysis is performed by experts in such analysis.

The Big Bang Theory[46]

When the ten non-linear equations of Albert Einstein's theory of general relativity are solved for the universe as a whole,[47] the solution indicates that the universe must be either continually expanding or contracting. Evidence currently available is consistent with its being in a state of expansion and with that expansion occurring at an increasing velocity. This being the case, sci-

---

46 Carroll, *Mysteries*, Lect. 22.

47 All theories in physics are written in the form of sets of equations, each of which contains constants, variables, and frequently variables in differential form. To solve the equations for special cases simultaneously, boundary conditions must be set. Often solutions can only be determined by making successive approximations of the variables by numerical methods until a stable set of values is found. Apologists need not worry about the details which are often challenging even to mathematical geniuses.

entists have extrapolated the universe's history backward to the point where all the matter and energy in it would have been concentrated in a tiny ball. Based on current estimates, this would have been about 13.8 billion years ago. The basis of the Big Bang is not that materials are moving away from each other through space, but that space itself is expanding, carrying its contents with it. The Big Bang model has been worked out in great detail to tiny fractions of a second from when the process is hypothesized to have started. In the abstract, it is a theory that seems to fit its assumptions and data well in terms of apparent time.

The apologist should not be overly concerned about the theory because it is young and highly likely to change. The theory requires that the laws of physics worked in the way that we now understand them under conditions which we have never seen. In past cases of extreme conditions, our models of the physical laws have sometimes proven inadequate to explain what was happening, and they have had to be revised. The necessity to postulate the existence of dark (i.e., unknown) matter and dark energy whose quantities far exceed the matter and energy which we can detect may be a clue that the Big Bang model will need major revisions before it gives a completely satisfactory explanation. In any event, this model is irrelevant to how the Lord actually brought the universe into existence and governs it. The universe is only a backdrop to the earth, which is the real stage of the human drama. The apologist needs to point out that making cosmological models is like doing a 12-star-rated Sudoku puzzle. It is extremely challenging intellectually but of no practical usefulness. Someday, the Lord will roll up the whole universe and toss it away.[48]

Exoplanets[49]

"*These are the voyages of the starship Enterprise…*" are words that have greeted science fiction fans since the 1960s. The concept of planets elsewhere in the universe, which may contain life, goes back much further, however. Today, scientists believe that most stars may have one or more planets, but measurements are extremely difficult to make. Variations in Earth's atmosphere reduce the clarity of the light from the stars in terrestrial observations,

---

48 "All the stars in the sky will dissolve. The sky will roll up like a scroll, and its stars will all wither as leaves wither on the vine, and foliage on the fig tree." (Isaiah 34:4).

49 Winn, ibid.

and space-based telescopes, which do not have such limitations, are extremely expensive. Due to the brightness of any star in comparison with any planet that might be orbiting it, planets can only be detected by indirect means, such as dimming of the star's radiation during *planet traversal*,[50] *wobble* in the star's position[51] or the *Doppler Effect*,[52] all of which are very small. Learning much about the attributes of planets which are discovered is extremely challenging, and verifying such information is impossible because of the great distances to even the nearest stars. An unmanned probe traveling at 100 million feet/second would take more than 40 years to reach the nearest star and 4.3 years to radio back to us what it found.

The idea of finding a planet with intelligent life on it is still science fiction, and scientists currently do not have any even remotely plausible technical path to make such a discovery. There are also numerous unique features about Earth that make finding a suitable twin planet to it in our region of the universe exceedingly unlikely. A few of these special features are the earth's magnetic field, its size and composition, the inclination of its axis, its speed of rotation, its surface temperature, its abundance of water, the amount of nitrogen in its atmosphere, its distance from its star, the stability of its star and the radiation intensity and spectrum produced by its star. None of the planets and moons in our solar system has more than one or two of the earth-like factors which are critical to advanced life forms, and relatively few stars are both similar to the sun and also not in a binary star system. For example, Earth's "twin" in size in the solar system is Venus, but it is hardly habitable. Its atmosphere is deep and toxic, and its surface temperature is over 800° F.

The apologist should not be tempted by "what if" questions about life on other planets. Until evidence shows up, the fact that life could happen else-

---

50 Planet traversal is when a planet passes between the star and the Earth, thereby blocking a tiny percentage of the star's light.

51 Wobble is caused by the planet's gravitational effect on the position of its star as the planet moves from one extreme of its orbital position to the other.

52 The Doppler Effect is the wavelength shift that occurs when a light source is moving toward or away from the observer rather than remaining at a constant distance.

where is pure speculation.[53] The scriptural position is that man is the special creation of the Lord and that the rest of the universe exists for his benefit.[54]

Fossils and Geology

When we visit natural history museums, we see a great variety of *fossils* from animals and plants, large and small. Of course, only an extremely low percentage of living things become fossilized, and only those which have a structure that can somehow be preserved are candidates for fossilization. Conditions need to be within a narrow range in regard to many factors to permit fossilization rather than decay to occur. As apologists, we might be tempted to throw up our hands in despair or feel obligated to find a way to attack every claim we find on those neatly printed cards attached to the exhibits. Neither extreme will advance our cause.

We need to begin by considering how fossils originated. To the evolutionist, this is not much of a challenge to explain in general, but sometimes more difficult in particular cases.[55] Evolutionists believe that fossils are a record of the development of the plant and animal kingdoms since the beginning of life on Earth. In reality, the fossil record does not reach back to the time life supposedly began because those early creatures were too flimsy to be fossilized, but it does appear to reach back a long way. Evolutionists have used fossil data to develop a detailed history of the evolution of life, with new species being added as their fossils are found. They have dated the fossils based on the time when the rocks holding them appear to have been formed. As previously mentioned, the dating of rocks can be done fairly precisely, so in recent years these family trees of plant and animal life have become well established.

To the Christian, the source of these fossils is also clear; namely, the God of the Bible put them where we are finding them. Many will respond, "That's just plain crazy! Why would God do such a thing?" Well, for one thing, he is

---

53 "Instruct certain people not to teach false doctrine or to pay attention to myths and endless genealogies. These promote empty speculations rather than God's plan, which operates by faith." (1 Timothy 1:3-4).

54 In Genesis 1, which tells how he made the world, the Lord declared that man was made in his image. In Genesis 2, he tells how his act of creation was shaped for the purpose of accommodating man.

55 Robert M. Hazen, *Origins of Life* (The Great Courses, The Teaching Company, Chantilly, VA, 2005), Lect. 5 and 6.

God. He can do whatever he pleases and owes us no explanation, as the old poem goes, "God in his wisdom made the fly and then forgot to tell us why." If that answer sounds flippant, it isn't. The Lord does what he knows to be best for us, and he tells us that he will give us whatever we truly need in this life.[56] Yet, like our original mother Eve, we have an insatiable curiosity, and it does not always work out well. We have no divine command to search for fossils and explain what they mean; we are just curious. Yet, fossils can be useful in showing us the relationship among the components of plants and animals and how the various parts in one species are manifested differently than in another. Perhaps this was God's reason for creating them; perhaps he wanted to show us what other creatures he could have given us to deal with in our lifetimes; perhaps he did it to test us to see if we trust his Word; perhaps he had some reason that we would never guess on this side of eternity.

We might be further curious to learn when God buried the fossils around the earth. The Bible does not tell us; therefore, it is not important for our salvation. Certainly, he could have done it at creation;[57] he could have done it after the fall, he could have done it in conjunction with the Flood. Or he could have done it over a period of many years. Not only do we not know when or how he did it, but we have no ability to learn this information. What we can be sure of is that it did not happen primarily by the natural processes of which we are now aware. Geologists have gathered evidence from many thousands of sites and have been able to create a model of how the world works which is consistent with the fossils being buried naturally over the course of almost a billion years.[58] Obviously, God did not use this process, so he must have used a supernatural process or changed the rules of nature. Although anyone is, of course, free to suggest a natural process to explain the burial of the myriads of fossils, that process would have to account for the whole mountain of evidence that has been discovered about the geology of Earth. It cannot explain just a few choice items, and it must appear feasible to experts in geology.

---

56 "If we have food and clothing, we will be content with these." (1 Timothy 6:8).

57 Some might object that because God created a perfect world, it could not have had death in it in any manner, for death is associated with sin. Yet, when Adam picked fruit to eat on the first day, the fruit died, and fertile soil, at least as we know it, requires decaying plant or animal remains in it. If the fossils are merely props which had never been part of living creatures, then no death would have been involved in their generation. God cannot be limited by how we establish our definition of "perfect." If he did choose to do it this way, then his creation was still perfect in his eyes.

58 Renton, ibid.

The only thing that such an effort to forge a different explanation will do is to draw us away from the Great Commission that Christ gave to the Church.

But, did the animals and plants whose fossils we now find live at one time? How could the answer not be "yes"? Of course, it could be "yes" based on what was stated in the previous paragraph. Yet, if we recall that the Lord is the set director for the human saga, then there is no need that the props which he provided for us must be real, only that they must look real. As previously discussed, we cannot constrain the Lord to act in the way we would like him to act, nor can we explain how he acts when he does not tell us.[59] [60] Once again, apologists are tempted to throw up their hands and exclaim, "How am I to defend a God whose behavior I cannot know or explain?" The answer is, "Stop trying!" We are merely to say what God has told us and point out that as the Lord God Almighty, he is not under obligation to us except when he places himself under such obligation.[61] We do not have to, nor can we, explain how God acts when he acts supernaturally. No one can challenge his ability to act supernaturally, but they can challenge any argument that we make if we try to explain his actions through natural means. By faith, we must let God be God.[62]

Life from Life

Perhaps one of the strongest ideas that has been driven into our minds is

---

59 "For this reason God sends them a strong delusion so that they will believe the lie, so that all will be condemned—those who did not believe the truth but delighted in unrighteousness." (2 Thessalonians 2:11–12).

60 Some have suggested that for the Lord to have created fossils of animals and plants that never existed would be to intentionally deceive us. But how is this so? The Lord never commanded us to dig up fossils and study them. That has been man's choice. Is this any different from the Lord's creating geological age without running all the surface materials of the Earth through the rock cycle of geological evolution? Is it any different from the Lord bringing starlight to our sky which could not have possibly traveled to it since creation because of the distance to the stars? Who gives us the right as sinful humans to establish the bar that the Lord needs to meet to get our stamp of approval on his creation? This is the fallacy of *false premise* because we cannot establish such requirements for the Lord.

61 "'Though the mountains move and the hills shake, my love will not be removed from you and my covenant of peace will not be shaken,' says your compassionate LORD." (Isaiah 54:10).

62 "Stop your fighting, and know that I am God, exalted among the nations, exalted on the earth." (Psalm 46:10).

that life can only come from life.[63] Moreover, Genesis 1 tells us that a specific kind of life can only come from that specific kind of life.[64] St Paul also points out that there is a fundamental difference between the various kinds of life.[65] These ideas are being challenged by what has been demonstrated, and is, therefore, undeniable, in the areas of biochemistry, genetics, molecular biology and cell biology.

Already in the 1990s, chemists were able to synthesize enzymes from raw inorganic materials, have them fold appropriately and then function as naturally occurring enzymes when put into cells.[66] Since that time, scientists have developed the technology to cut apart DNA and paste it back together again.[67] This allows genes to be reengineered and placed into chromosomes, changing the genetic characteristics of plants and animals. Useful genes can be moved between species, and cells can be assembled that not only reproduce themselves, but also act as chemical factories for numerous substances that can be synthesized biochemically. Designer plants and animals are currently being introduced into the real world. The use of this technology to make human babies with specific characteristics is very possible. Cell-cloning technology has advanced to the point of being able to take certain adult cells, convert them into stem cells and use them to grow new tissue and even new organs for transplanting into the cell donor. This could solve the organ availability and tissue rejection problems, but it could also lead to people attempting to gain eternal existence by having their whole bodies cloned. Many related advances could be given, but the central matter is that humans now possess the ability to make new forms of life and to produce radical changes in old forms. What Christians have always considered the domain of God is now in the hands of humans.

---

63 "Then the LORD God formed the man out of the dust from the ground and breathed the breath of life into his nostrils, and the man became a living being." (Genesis 2:7).

64 "So God made the wildlife of the earth according to their kinds, the livestock according to their kinds, and all the creatures that crawl on the ground according to their kinds." (Genesis 1:25).

65 "But God gives it a body as he wants, and to each of the seeds its own body. Not all flesh is the same flesh; there is one flesh for humans, another for animals, another for birds, and another for fish." (1 Corinthians 15:38–39).

66 Kaufman, D.L., Houser, C.R., Tobin, A.J. "Two forms of the γ-aminobutyric acid synthetic enzyme glutamate decarboxylase have distinct intraneuronal distribution and cofactor interactions," *Jour. of Neurochemistry*, Wiley Online Library, 1991.

67 Sadava, ibid., Lect. 14.

This forces the apologist to face the general issue of when is the Bible stating an eternal truth and when is it only giving an explanation of some principle in terms that were understandable to the people who first read or heard it. For example, God said to Job "Do you understand how the clouds float?"[68] "Have you traveled to the sources of the sea or walked in the depths of the oceans?"[69] "Do you know when mountain goats give birth? Have you watched the deer in labor?"[70] These are part of a series of questions, challenging the power of Job, and the answers to all the questions were to be "no." But the answer to some of God's questions is now "yes." Jesus said, "The wind blows where it pleases, and you hear its sound, but you don't know where it comes from or where it is going."[71] This was true for Nicodemus to whom Jesus was speaking, but it is not true for meteorologists today. It would appear that God was speaking in these instances, where he is being directly quoted, in the way that a pastor does in sermon illustrations. The pastor must work within the level of understanding of his audience so that its members comprehend the point he is making. He is not necessarily providing them with an unchanging truth. Nevertheless, God's point still holds because each answer that scientists find only generates more questions. Let us consider the matter of life in this context.

When God breathed life into Adam,[72] he gave him "the breath of life." What does this mean? In Genesis 7:22, God uses an almost identical term to speak of both animals and people.[73] In general, Lutherans have held that God imparts a kind of "life force" to all living creatures. But it is not identical in all creatures. In Genesis 2, God does something unique with Adam: he personally blows the breath of life into his nostrils. Forever after that, the Scriptures speak of man's having a soul or a spirit. Ecclesiastes 12:7 makes it clear what death really is: the separation of the soul and the body.[74]

At creation, life was indeed a gift of God, extended to all plants and ani-

---

68 Job 37:16.

69 Job 38:16.

70 Job 39:1.

71 John 3:8.

72 "Then the LORD God formed the man out of the dust from the ground and breathed the breath of life into his nostrils, and the man became a living being." (Genesis 2:7).

73 "Everything with the breath of the spirit of life in its nostrils—everything on dry land died." (Genesis 7:22).

74 "And the dust returns to the earth as it once was, and the spirit returns to God who gave it." (Ecclesiastes 12:7).

mals. However, it does not follow from this that every living creature has some kind of "divine spark." Those who claim this are leaving behind what God's Word truly says and entering the realm of philosophy. Man is unique in that he has a soul/spirit, but all living creatures have a life force that animates their bodies and that they pass on to their offspring. The question is whether man can create a living thing without a direct intervention from God. As described above, man is now manipulating life which God created in ways that were unimaginable to the men whom God used to write the Scriptures. Yet, God never specifically said that only he can make a living thing in the immediate (i.e., without an agent) sense.[75] So is it possible that scientists will at some point make a totally new living creature out of inorganic materials? Nothing in the Bible rules out that possibility. Even if they do succeed at this, however, they would still be using materials that God created which function according to the rules he set in his creation.

In Genesis 1:24, God stated that the animals he created would reproduce according to their own *kind*. But what is a kind? A donkey can mate with a horse to give a mule. Are three kinds involved here or one? The Bible does not define "kind." Perhaps Jesus' words will help when he says, "You'll recognize them by their fruit. Are grapes gathered from thorn bushes or figs from thistles?"[76] We must recognize that the biblical statements about "kind" and "flesh" are not statements about genetics, but about our ability to trust God to behave in predictable ways. When we plant a particular kind of seed, we will not be surprised by the type of plant that grows. When we breed two dogs, we will not get a pelican. This is no different from the Lord's message after the Flood, "As long as the earth endures, seedtime and harvest, cold and heat, summer and winter, and day and night will not cease."[77]

While the Lord has told us how he will act in regard to certain aspects of his creation, he does not tell us how we must act, but he has given mankind the right to rule over all the other creatures. In terms of what scientists are capable of doing, this rule clearly does extend to the kinds of genetic engineering referred to above. It may even be possible for people to artificially

---

75 Jesus is called "the source of life" (Acts 3:15) [Greek: "originator of life"] and he does say that he has "life in himself" (John 5:26). In context, this means Jesus has the power to conquer even death and restore life, so he is the true giver of all life.

76 Matthew 7:16.

77 Genesis 8:22.

extend human life someday to lengths that seem almost impossible today.[78] However, what would be God-pleasing is another matter. While that is a little outside the scope of our discussion here, nothing in this "rule" prevents people from reshaping the "kinds" as long as they do not try to change the nature of man.[79] Man is God's special creation and is in his hands alone.[80] The rest of the things on Earth are here for mankind's wise use and can be manipulated for its benefit. We are not restricted in our bioengineering by the Bible beyond this.

Irreducible Complexity

Before we proceed further, it is best that we look at two objections to biological evolution. Some biological entities are extremely complex. The human body is such an entity, with highly integrated anatomical components, biological mechanisms, and chemical processes. A similar degree of complexity exists in systems which contain a symbiotic relationship, that is, in which two (or more) organisms are linked in a mutually supportive affiliation, and, therefore, neither of them can live independently of the other. In some of these systems there is currently no known way in which the components could develop independently. As a result, some argue that the evolution of such systems would have been impossible due to their *irreducible complexity*.[81] This is sometimes called the teleological argument (see Chapter 2).

The argument is based on the logical fallacy of appeal to ignorance. Simply because we do not know today how something happens does not mean that the relevant information for how it happens will not be known in the future. The claim that something cannot be true because we have no explanation for it is an example of what is known in mathematics as the *halting problem*. In such problems, one tries to search for an entity in an unbounded domain, but one does not know whether the entity (e.g., an explanation) actually exists or not. Is there a way to determine when one has searched long enough to prove

---

78 Of course, the Bible itself records incredibly long lives in the Old Testament.

79 By saying this, the authors are in no way condemning genetic engineering to repair malfunctions that cause disease in humans.

80 [The Lord said,] "I will require a penalty for your lifeblood; I will require it from any animal and from any human; if someone murders a fellow human, I will require that person's life. Whoever sheds human blood, by humans his blood will be shed, for God made humans in his image." (Genesis 9:5-6).

81 Michael J. Behe, "Irreducible Complexity Obstacle to Darwinian Evolution" (Lehigh, 2004).

that the entity does not exist? In 1936 Alan Turing proved mathematically (i.e., with certainty) that the answer to this question is "no."[82] Unless one can find that the existence of the entity would violate a fundamental law of nature, one cannot assert that it does not exist, because by looking long enough it might be found. This is the reason the appeal to ignorance is a fallacy.

A counterexample is in order. At the end of the nineteenth century, certain observations of the physical world were inconsistent with Newtonian physics. Physicists' efforts to explain them had reached such a high level of complexity that a systematic resolution of these issues seemed impossible. Yet, during the twentieth century new models of nature supported by ingeniously designed experiments have led to an understanding of previously inexplicable phenomena. The processes of nature as explained by quantum mechanics and the theory of relatively often do not make logical sense, as all of us who have studied them can attest, yet they are demonstrable by reproducible physical experiments. When faced with experimental evidence, the argument "it does not make sense" simply cannot be employed. God's mechanisms by which the universe operates are far more complex than people had imagined in the past. Yet, what is too complex for us to understand today may be regarded as "obvious" at some point in the future.

Genetic Entropy

If we look at the living things around us, we see that they all grow old and die. Since man's fall into sin, all macroscopic life forms grow, deteriorate, and die naturally (if they are not eaten by something else first). Change and deterioration happen at the genetic level as well as the observable physical level. As a life form's genetic material is reproduced, errors sometimes occur, and the organism may then show signs of illness and aging. Moreover, in the reproduction of some chromosomes, ends of their DNA tails are shortened, so a small part of the buffer regions in their tails is progressively lost with each reproduction. While the genes are protected, the robustness of the chromosomes may be reduced. In addition, the negative changes to genes on chromosomes from errors or damage far outnumber the positive changes that

---

82 Alan Turning, "On Computable Numbers, with an application to the Entscheidungsproblem," Proceeding of the London Mathematical Society (2), 43: 230-265 (1936-37).

occur.[83] Some people thus claim that there is a *genetic entropy* which causes species to deteriorate rather than to evolve to be genetically better,[84] and these people use the evidence that on the internet one can find many more cases of bad genetic effects than good effects.

There are four relevant issues here. First, genetic errors do occur, but living creatures have developed numerous processes to find and correct many of such errors. The remedial processes work at various stages of the reproductive cycle, either by repairing the damage or by destroying the damaged copy of the DNA to prevent further harm.

Second, the reproduction of species occurs through special organs that generate the female eggs and male sperm cells. Only cellular errors produced in these organs can affect the genetic makeup of the offspring. Once again, corrective mechanisms exist to repair the errors or to eliminate the cells with damaged genetic material. While females typically produce one or a relatively small number of eggs which are of significant size at any specific time, males produce many millions of small sperm cells. There is strong competition among the sperm cells to fertilize the available eggs, a competition which favors those with the best characteristics. This process helps to weed out genetic errors, which are further reduced by the death of the embryos or their failure to implant in the uterus if they are genetically defective. All of these safeguards help to protect the viability of a species.

Third, even if the negative genetic mutations are more numerous than the positive ones at the point of birth or hatching, natural selection begins to play its significant role. Genetically stronger members of animal species are at an advantage in this brutal world where many offspring never reach adulthood, and thus the stronger are left to breed the next generation. Conversely, widespread healthcare among humans may actually be causing negative evolution by helping more people with negative genetic mutations survive long enough to breed.

Finally, the fact that many more cases of negative human mutations are highlighted in the media does not mean that they are more significant. People with health issues caused by negative genetic mutations rush to their doctors for help and lobby Congress to appropriate money to address such problems.

---

83 Caleb E. Finch & Rudolph E. Tanzi, "Genetics of Aging," Science, 278:407-411 (American Association for the Advancement of Science).

84 John Sanford, *Genetic Entropy & the Mystery of the Genome, 3rd ed.* (FMS Publication, Waterloo, NY, 2008).

How many people with positive genetic mutations rush to their doctors to be treated for better-than-average health? Positive mutations are therefore significantly underreported. The argument for genetic entropy needs to be demonstrated in controlled population studies and in laboratory experiments, not presented to the technically untrained public (a logical fallacy called *appeal to the masses*).

The apologist should point out that just because an argument makes sense philosophically does not mean that it is true scientifically, where the standard of truth is reproducible experimental results. Trying to prove that life could not have arisen through evolution goes beyond what the Bible teaches. *The Bible does not say the universe and life could not have evolved through natural processes; it merely says they didn't.* It is blasphemous to say that the Almighty God could not have established the laws of nature so that macroscopic evolution was possible. Perhaps he didn't, but perhaps he did, yet chose not to use that mechanism for reasons known only to him. This being the case, the effort to attack the viability of macroscopic evolution is a useless distraction from the mission of the church.

Research in Biological Evolution

We know that life and the species we see did not evolve through natural means because the Bible says that they were created during the third through the sixth day of Earth's existence. The issue in considering the evidence gathered by scientists is whether these things could have evolved by natural means had God allowed them to do so. It is best to split the evolution of life into three stages and look at the difficulties.

The first stage is the path from simple chemicals—water, carbon dioxide, methane, ammonia, phosphates, and such—to some sort of a primitive nucleic acid structure that could reproduce itself.[85] This is a problem of chemical synthesis, and various options are available. Each individual step in the process is quite feasible at the molecular level, but the huge number of steps needed is mind-boggling. To have any chance of success, the process would have to occur in a confined space with structural catalysts and sufficient energy to facilitate the reactions. It would have to occur in an environment where there was an abundance of the raw materials, such as a shallow pool where organic

---

[85] Hazen, ibid., Lect. 9-22.

chemicals were concentrated by evaporation or at a tectonic plate juncture on a mid-ocean ridge. The likelihood of this happening is incredibly small at any particular location, but on the microscopic scale there are also an incredible number of sites and many billions times trillions of reactions possible over a billion years at each site. While enough research has been done to sketch the major steps, it is still unclear if there are insurmountable barriers to this occurring. Those who argue that this stage of evolution is statistically impossible are engaging in the logical fallacy of appeal to ignorance. Scientists do not know all the pathways through which this phase of evolution might be accomplished, so there is insufficient information to do a statistical analysis. In 1910, everyone would have said that something with the size and characteristics of a smart phone was technically, statistically, and even scientifically impossible. Can we say the same today?

The second stage is for the primitive nucleic or ribonucleic acid to gain the ability to organize the chemical environment around it, to produce a cell membrane, to begin the process of absorbing nutrients and to start dividing into new cells.[86] Somewhere in the process the primitive genetic material would have to become a double-stranded DNA (deoxyribonucleic acid). Since the nature of the primitive ribonucleic acid is speculative, whether these things are very likely, or even possible, to happen is unknown. Certainly, if it were in a location where it could propagate a large number of copies of itself, these copies might drift to places where opportunities for development were better. While the likelihood of any one of the copies evolving to the point of becoming a viable cell might seem to be greater than the original formation of the primitive ribonucleic acid, this is completely speculative because research in this origins-of-life area is meager.

The last stage is the diversification of the original cells into the plethora of plant and animal species that exists today.[87] Because this stage starts with a much greater degree of organization than the previous two, it would seem that it is more likely to occur. Charles Darwin postulated that small differences among members of the same species would lead to those members with better characteristics surviving to breed at a higher rate and to come to dominate the species over time. This is called *natural selection*. It is the basis of what most people think of as the only process of evolution. But, things are more com-

---

86 Hazen, ibid., Lect. 16-18, 23-24.
87 Nowicki, ibid., Lect. 20-25.

plex. The observable characteristics in a species are called its *phenotype*. The major evolutionary changes of a species must occur through its *genotype*, that is, through changes in its genetic code. The genotype is not always completely expressed in the phenotype, which greatly complicates studying the evolutionary process. For example, a child with the genetic capability to be tall might be of only average height if he suffered from malnutrition at a key point in his growth cycle. Then too, consider the caterpillar that metamorphoses into a butterfly. The genotype of the animal remains the same, but the phenotype becomes radically different as different parts of its genetic code are turned on and off.

Scientists have learned that the actual method of evolutionary change involves more than just natural selection. Factors such as *genetic drift* (pure chance), mutations (e.g., mistakes or viral additions) in the germinal cells (body cells do not count), population mating structure (barriers between populations, population size, sexual selection) and culture (where medical advances and sanitary practices guard genotypes with lower fitness) can all contribute to changing the phenotype and/or underlying genotype of a species. This is the reason why arguing that a specific change could not occur purely through natural selection might be true, but it might also be irrelevant if other factors are involved in the pathway for such a change. As biological research continues, the quality of the models for this stage of biological evolution will improve.[88]

---

88 Let us consider one way in which an exotic trait might be added to a species. We will represent the genetic code that produces the trait with T. DNA molecules contain large numbers of base pairs, many of which are not directly involved in gene expression. For those that are, amino acid production is coded for by successive three-base groups (which we will represent by letters: ABC DEF GHI …). The amino acids formed are then joined together in order to form a protein (often an enzyme), which does the chemical work within a cell. If an extra base X is placed into the DNA molecule by accident (ABC DXE FGH I…), the sequence of amino acids produced will be radically altered because new groupings of three bases will form down the DNA molecule. Almost always this produces a nonsensical series of amino acids which creates a protein of no value. It is possible, however, that one or more bases accidentally inserted into the DNA molecule at point X would actually produce a protein to be made that would cause the trait T to be expressed in the phenotype if that expression happened in cells throughout the organism. Here is a sequence which would allow this to happen: An egg cell has an appropriate X inserted in its DNA by some mechanism. The cell is fertilized and grows into an adult female. If trait T is recessive, it will not be expressed because it is only on one gene of the gene pair. The female mates and some of her offspring carry the recessive trait T. If these offspring mate with each other, some of their offspring will have trait T on both of their genes, and it will be expressed. If species members with trait T preferentially mate with other members with trait T, soon a

As apologists, we are tempted to look at biological evolution, to draw a line in the sand and to say, "It didn't happen because scientists will never be able to do X or explain how Y could have happened." This temptation must be resisted. If a major breakthrough occurred and scientists were suddenly able to do X or explain Y, what would happen to our credibility on other subjects once an it-can't-be-done claim we had made was shown to be false? Many previously drawn lines claiming something to be impossible by misguided apologists have been crossed, leaving us all tarred as Luddites. The apologist's attitude toward biological evolution needs to be the same as his attitude toward geological evolution, namely, "Just because humans can give an explanation of how something could have happened naturally, does not mean that is how it happened." That is, science cannot avoid the fallacy of affirming the consequent in its models, as discussed in Chapter 1. Trying to slug it out in the quagmire of current scientific theories will never leave us victorious, but it will always leave us incredibly soiled. Apologetics based on the sciences of men rather than on the revelation of God is always sitting on the slippery slope of new discoveries just above the quicksand pit of folly.

Dreamers, Pseudoscientists and Deniers

All scientists attempt to reach beyond what is known. They are standing on the shoulders of the giants of previous generations and straining their eyes to see beyond the horizon. That is what inductive reasoning is all about. Nothing is ever 100% certain. Some models of nature are very well supported by evidence, while other models' support is meager, but perhaps they are the best models that can be made with the data available. Dreamers are scientists, humanists and writers who start with legitimate science and then create visions that may have little to do with what is possible. For example, in the 1950s dreamers claimed that within 20 years much of the world's energy requirements would be met by the use of "clean hydrogen fusion". It didn't happen because the technology for controlling superheated hydrogen plasmas proved unworkable. When the first men landed on the moon in 1969,

---

subpopulation with trait T will emerge. If trait T is particularly useful, such as flight feathers or a prehensile tail, species members with trait T will come to dominate the population or will split off to form a separate population. While such major changes are extremely rare, they only need to happen once to add useful characteristics to a species. Research studies at this level of detail are in their infancy.

dreamers claimed that there would be a moon-base in 20 years and that efforts to colonize Mars would be in full swing by the beginning of the twenty-first century. The lack of suitable raw materials on these celestial bodies to build structures and sustain life has made permanent bases on them too costly, causing these projects to be deferred indefinitely.

Today's dreamers talk about finding intelligent life on planets in other parts of the universe and about developing a utopian society on Earth. These ideas are more fantasy than they are science, however. Unless some new principle of physics is discovered to allow people to traverse the great distances of space in short time intervals, visiting planets around other stars to look for life is impossible. Likewise, human self-centeredness and the limited resources of planet Earth will radically limit the quality of any planet-wide community. The apologist needs to remind people there is a big difference between predictions of improvements in those technologies which exist and can be enhanced and in those technologies which do not exist and need to be invented. While the former can be anticipated, the latter are no different from the predictions of the fortunetellers,[89] no matter what the past accomplishments have been of those doing the predicting. Until solid scientific evidence appears to support them, such ideas are fairy tales.

Pseudoscientists are people who use scientific terms and make claims about scientific matters, but who are not willing to have their claims tested in the laboratory by experts in the relevant fields. People continue to believe in UFO's, yetis, and alien abductions, but these believers in their existence have not produced testable evidence to verify their claims. Creation science has also been a fertile area for these claims. For example, suppose someone claimed that radioactive dating is not reliable because the natural constants, such as the speed of light, are changeable. If someone could show this particular claim by reproducible experiments, he or she would be a shoo-in to win a Nobel Prize in physics. In fact, many of the claims of pseudoscientists would win their advocates considerable fame in the scientific community if they could be demonstrated experimentally. Their failure to do so is strong evidence that their claims are bogus. Pseudoscientists use the general lack of scientific knowledge on the part of their audiences to gain adherents.

---

[89] Steven Novella, *Your Deceptive Mind: A Scientific Guide to Critical Thinking Skills* (The Great Courses, The Teaching Company, Chantilly, VA, 2012), Lect. 23-24.

As apologists, we cannot teach people to be scientists so that they are capable of evaluating such claims, but we can urge them to consult those educated in the appropriate fields of science with their questions. In fact, it is a good idea for people to develop a friendship with a college or knowledgeable high school science teacher who could give them background information on various claims. The key question people need to ask is "What would someone have to do to prove this claim?" Testing claims both for and against one's current beliefs is essential so that one does not become a victim of confirmation bias.[90]

Finally, deniers are people who attack scientific methods by claiming that the scientists using them have made mistakes, so therefore the methods themselves are unreliable.[91] In reality, any measuring technique can be misused. One can get the wrong result using a yardstick to measure length if one does not think things through carefully, but that does not make a yardstick an unreliable tool. Geological dating methods are the most commonly attacked measuring methods because they are the most threatening to young-Earth creationism. However, scientists are also aware of the possible sources of error in their measurements, and they vigorously examine every result that is new or unexpected compared with previous data. Unfortunately, the media often publicizes results early in the validation process for things that are novel. If the results later are found to be unverifiable, deniers claim that this shows the methods used were unreliable rather than pointing to the real reason, namely that the experimenters were careless or overzealous in their claims. More about denialism will be discussed in chapter 9.

Deniers gain credibility by telling the Christian community what it wants to hear, namely that the science behind evolution is highly flawed and its measuring methods are unreliable. Deniers use the fallacy of kettle logic (see Chapter 1) by putting forth numerous claims of measurement failure, often non-relevant, without showing that the measuring methods themselves are flawed even with proper use. The apologist must avoid using these techniques because they are dishonest. They compromise our position that the Bible is the Word of Truth. When dealing with the speculation of dreamers or the claims of pseudoscientists, the apologist needs to attack their real assertions

---

[90] Indre Viskontas, *Brain Myths Exploded Lessons from Neuroscience* (The Great Courses, The Teaching Company, Chantilly, VA, 2017), Lect. 9.

[91] Novella, ibid., Lect. 20.

and underlying assumptions, not attack caricatures of their arguments as deniers do.

Summary

In dealing with scientific models that contradict the Bible, apologists have a strong hand and need not resort to pseudoscience. There are three unalterable reasons for this which no new research or theory can ever undermine. First, scientists can never be completely sure of the validity of their models because they cannot examine all the possible cases which these models cover. Their models, therefore, can always only be accepted as provisionally true, and scientists cannot be sure that they have not committed the fallacy of hasty generalization in creating these models. Second, even if a particular model appears to perfectly explain all observations, scientists cannot claim it is the true explanation without committing the fallacy of affirming the consequent. Something other than the proposed explanation might be the real explanation for the observations. Third, the fundamental assumption of science implies there is no god, but as any fundamental assumption, it is unprovable and may be false. Apologists can point out that if an Almighty God exists, then the fundamental assumption of science is indeed false, and the meaning of all the carefully gathered evidence is uncertain. In short, apologists must emphasize that all science, even that of much practical value, is limited by its two inherent fallacies and by the validity of its fundamental assumption. No amount of research, no matter how good, can remove these limitations.

Looking at it another way, in dealing with the challenges raised by the physical and biological sciences, we must remember we are defending only what the Bible says in regard to what scientists have actually discovered, not what we wish the Bible had said or how we wish the Lord had created the universe. We must separate the legitimate evidence, which we are foolish to challenge because of the overwhelming ability of the scientific establishment to gather and validate such evidence, from the uses of that evidence in evolutionary models. We need not argue over whether scientists can accurately measure the apparent age of Earth or whether they have actually developed new "kinds" of plants and animals by genetic manipulation. We do need to state the position that the Lord created the universe in six days, conceding that he gave it an apparent age, and we do need to maintain that he created plants and animals that faithfully reproduce themselves according to the genetic patterns which they have. Our purpose is not to explain scientific evidence better than the scientists, but to proclaim that no scientific discovery will shove the Lord off his throne as the Creator and the Preserver of the universe. We must make clear that everyone is still accountable to him, and that is why his law and his gospel matter as much as ever.

One final matter should be considered: science is a long-term enterprise. There are many thousands of open questions for which scientists are seeking answers. Every year many articles are published, and some of these articles make major challenges to the current understanding of the scientific community. A number of these articles will be verified by others, causing core models of science to change. A larger number will be shown to be false by other investigators and fall from favor. Occasionally, portions of the scientific community will be misled by these articles and head off in the wrong direction. Nevertheless, after some period of time, the mistakes in these articles will be found, and the affected fields of science will resume their previous direction. Because claims can take years to work their way through the scientific method, the apologist should not be deceived by articles that seem to undermine evolutionary models. If they are right, the evolutionary models will merely be reshaped to take the new evidence into consideration. If they are wrong, it would be foolish to build one's case on a research mistake. One must build one's case on what does not change, namely, the Lord's revelation.

6

Miracles

Questions about miracles are common because we do not see miracles happening around us. This does not mean that they do not happen, but it only means that if they happen, they are not seen. Moreover, when people claim that a miracle has occurred, there usually turns out to be a logical explanation based on natural causes, or it is merely something unlikely to happen but something which is statistically quite possible. When we are amazed by things out of the ordinary, they are almost always unfamiliar things which were created by man, not special acts of God. Issues raised about the miracles that are recorded in the Bible include challenges to their possibility, claims that they were a result of the ignorance of the observers, assertions that they were fables, and allegations that they were invented to bolster the reputation of Moses, Jesus or some other biblical figure. Sometimes there are questions about how particular miracles could have happened. Rather than starting with the individual issues people might raise, we need to look at the root from which all the questions and objections arise.

Setting the Stage

Jason and Melissa Kiefer[1] have been happily married a dozen years and have two children in elementary school. Melissa works mornings at a nearby

---

1 A fictitious couple.

business but is home in the afternoons. Jason works at a company about four miles down the expressway. He finishes at 4 pm every day, punches out, always gets onto the expressway and drives home. Jason is a creature of habit; Melissa can practically set her watch by the time at which he arrives home.

One day Jason arrived 15 minutes later than usual and said that he had decided to come home via Chase Street to see how the building of the new Menards hardware store was coming along. Should Melissa believe him? Let's examine the evidence. Jason's leaving time is fixed. He is certainly capable of driving on side streets as well as the expressway. Driving past the Menards site on the side streets would take several minutes longer, particularly at rush hour. Menards would be a place at which Jason might want to shop once it was completed. Yes, Melissa should believe Jason. What he did was unusual for him, but it was certainly something that he was capable of doing and that was logical for him to do for the stated reason. We are all familiar with "creatures of habit" who occasionally step out of their normal pattern of behavior when they have an appropriate incentive to do so.

Now let's recall what we said about the God of the Bible in Chapter 4. Because he has all the power that exists anywhere, no one can do anything unless he gives the actor the strength to do it.[2] It means that gravity does not work, that the winds do not blow and that the sun does not shine unless he provides the power for these things to happen.[3] From the lowliest sub-atomic particles and energy fields to the largest galaxies, nothing does anything unless he empowers the actions.[4] Natural things act only at his command and only with that power that he gives them. In fact, nothing even exists unless he

---

[2] [Isaiah wrote,] "The LORD of Armies himself has planned it; therefore, who can stand in its way? It is his hand that is outstretched, so who can turn it back?" (Isaiah 14:27) / [Solomon wrote,] "Unless the LORD builds a house, its builders labor over it in vain; unless the LORD watches over a city, the watchman stays alert in vain. In vain you get up early and stay up late, working hard to have enough food—yes, he gives sleep to the one he loves." (Psalm 127:1-2).

[3] [A psalmist wrote,] "The LORD does whatever he pleases in heaven and on earth, in the seas and all the depths. He causes the clouds to rise from the ends of the earth. He makes lightning for the rain and brings the wind from his storehouses." (Psalm 135:6). / "By faith we understand that the universe was created by the word of God, so that what is seen was made from things that are not visible." (Hebrews 11:3).

[4] [The Lord said,] "Can you fasten the chains of the Pleiades or loosen the belt of Orion? Can you bring out the constellations in their season and lead the Bear and her cubs? Do you know the laws of heaven? Can you impose its authority on earth? Can you command the clouds so that a flood of water covers you? Can you send out lightning bolts, and they go? Do they report to you: 'Here we are'?" (Job 38:31-35).

gives it the power to exist.[5] It is hard to comprehend the power of such a God. He would seem to be extremely dangerous, in that he could turn the universe into utter chaos by directing its components to behave in a haphazard fashion. What if he suddenly dropped the temperature by 80° F, changed the piece of land on which we were standing into an ocean or caused the sun to dissolve into nothingness? Although he could do these things, he doesn't.[6] Instead, like Jason in the story above, the God of the Bible makes himself known to us as a being of habit. We call his habitual ways of behavior within our world "the laws of nature."

But what if, like Jason, God had a good reason to do things differently? Certainly, being almighty, God would be able to do things in a different way if he chose.[7] It would be no more difficult for him to do so than for him to do things in the "regular" way, because he supplies the power for everything that happens anyway.[8] When God does things differently, we call it a *miracle*. A miracle is "abnormal" behavior on the part of God, but no big deal for him, only different. In fact, because all mankind can only observe a very, very few things that are happening in the universe at any particular instant, God might be doing an extremely large number of miracles every minute, and we would never notice them. Moreover, through his absolute control of nature, the God of the Bible is able to direct events in our lives without our even realizing what is happening.[9] Based on this situation, we ought to believe that miracles can occur for the same reason that Melissa should believe that Jason engaged in abnormal behavior by driving home by a different route. That is, it is well

---

5 [A Psalmist wrote,] "All of them wait for you to give them their food at the right time. When you give it to them, they gather it; when you open your hand, they are satisfied with good things. When you hide your face, they are terrified; when you take away their breath, they die and return to the dust. When you send your breath, they are created, and you renew the surface of the ground. May the glory of the LORD endure forever; may the LORD rejoice in his works. He looks at the earth, and it trembles; he touches the mountains, and they pour out smoke." (Psalm 104:27-32).

6 [The Lord said,] "I will never again strike down every living thing as I have done. As long as the earth endures, seedtime and harvest, cold and heat, summer and winter, and day and night will not cease." (Genesis 8:21-22).

7 [A psalmist wrote,] "Our God is in heaven and does whatever he pleases. (Psalm 115:3).

8 Francis Pieper wrote, "Whatever God wills He accomplishes in one of two ways: either by His appointed means (*causae secundae, potentia ordinata*) or without them (*poentia absoluta, immediata*). *Christian Dogmatics, vol. I* (Concordia Publishing House, St. Louis, 1950), 459.

9 [The Lord said,] "I am about to put a spirit in him, and he will hear a rumor and return to his own land, where I will cause him to fall by the sword." (2 Kings 19:7).

within God's ability to do so and he has a good reason for doing so.

If one believes in the Lord, the God of the Bible, believing in miracles follows naturally. How can one believe that God is able to do miracles and that he claims to have done miracles and yet deny that he did do them? It is this question that guides the apologist when responding to people who deny that God or Jesus did the miracles in the Bible.

Dealing with the Questions and Objections

In dealing with questions and objections about miracles, the apologist will recognize a few common threads. First, most people don't really know that much about the Bible. What they're likely to say about these miracles probably reflects what they've heard or read, not conclusions they have reached on their own. In fact, they often don't know what the Bible says really happened. While we must use tact, we must not be afraid to explain to them what the Bible does or doesn't say about a specific miracle. They may find some of their objections are harder to sustain once they discover what God really says.

Another common thread is that skeptics today often challenge biblical miracles as being scientifically impossible or lacking "real world" credibility. In the paragraphs that follow, we will address these kinds of challenges. Yet, there are basic spiritual truths that must be remembered. The Lord made the universe, and he still runs it. He can work through the laws of nature, or he can suspend those laws. As a result, whether what God did is scientifically impossible should not bother us. As apologists, we must keep going back to the one who is doing the work. Concerning the reliability of Scripture, the biblical writers themselves were aware of how impossible these miracles were.[10] Despite this, they still recorded them, because they were part of God's message to his people. The apologist needs to point out to the skeptic that the biblical writers weren't stupid. They expected to be criticized over their accounts,[11] but they gave their testimony anyway.

The first question to ask in any discussion about miracles is "What do you think a miracle is?" We know from the previous discussion that a miracle is

---

10 "For we did not follow cleverly contrived myths when we made known to you the power and coming of our Lord Jesus Christ; instead, we were eyewitnesses of his majesty." (2 Peter 1:16).

11 [Jesus said,] "You are blessed when they insult you and persecute you and falsely say every kind of evil against you because of me." (Matthew 5:11).

just the almighty God doing things in a different way, but what do the people who raise the questions about, or objections to, miracles believe about them? They may regard them as fairy tales or magic. Perhaps, they have never thought of a miracle as just being a different way for God to accomplish something that he wanted done or as a manner of doing it so as to convince the observers that he was genuinely in charge of the laws of nature. It is possible that once people realize what a miracle really is, their attitude about miracles will change or at least they might be willing to discuss them with a less hostile attitude.

The second question to ask is "What is your attitude toward God?" Options may have to be spelled out for them. Do they believe that a god or gods exist? If they are atheists or agnostics, we need to abandon the discussion of miracles and change the topic to their beliefs about the nature of the universe without a god, which is discussed in Chapter 2. They certainly are not going to believe in miracles if they do not believe in a being that can do them.

If they do believe in a god, the next thing to determine is whether their "god" is one with whom they can interact (i.e., a personal God) or whether it is a disinterested being who ignores the human plight. If the latter is the case, then we need to leave the discussion of miracles and proceed to discussing the material in Chapter 4 on deism. If we can establish that the skeptics believe in a God with whom they can interact, then we must determine whether they have questions or doubts about just specific miracles or about all miracles in general. If their concern just involves specific miracles, then we can proceed to the section on various miracles later in this chapter.

If people believe in a God with whom they can communicate, but they do not believe in miracles, it is necessary to inquire about the nature of the God in whom they believe. What can their God do or not do? It is possible that they have never thought through the nature of the God in whom they believe. In this case we need to ask specific questions about what their God's characteristics are. What are their God's abilities and limitations? How much does he know? How available and reliable is their God? How did they learn about their God? Does he reward and punish? Is their God always good, always evil or a mixture of both? Is their God similar to them, only more powerful? Is their God just based on their own feelings or do they have a source for the beliefs that they hold about their God? The goal of these and similar questions that we might ask is to understand into which category their God fits so that we can see where to go next in our discussion with them.

Suppose they claim that they really are good Christians, but they don't think that they need to believe everything that the Bible says. If this is the case, we should move to a discussion of the nature of the Bible using the materials in Chapter 3.

Suppose they claim that they believe in Jesus, but they just don't understand how God can do miracles or why he doesn't do them anymore. Presenting to them the material from the beginning of this chapter will allow us to help them see that miracles are just a different way that God sometimes choses to do things in the universe as part of his plan for managing it for the good of Christians. We need to explain the nature of his almighty power. Certainly, if these challengers are willing to trust God for their salvation, they should be willing to trust him when he tells them some of the things which he did as part of his plan for their salvation. Our emphasis should be that God has the power to do the miracles and he has claimed to have done the miracles, so how can we doubt that he did do the miracles? We may need to have more discussion sessions with them to help such people. They may have additional reasons, which are hidden, as to why they doubt miracles, or they may simply be struggling to change their opinion about miracles.

Suppose we learn that the people have a different standard of religious truth such as the pope, the *Book of Mormon* or the *Qur'an*. Then we need to use the material in the appropriate sections of Chapter 3, because miracles are not the real issue of contention.

Those yet unclassified are people who have created idols out of their own thoughts.[12] Their god is as phony as any idol made from wood or stone. They do not believe in miracles because they do not want to believe in miracles. They have made a god which is an image of themselves, and that god does not deal in miracles, although it often does deal in fantasy. We can politely point this out to them and help them try to realize what they are really doing, but this will seldom work. It is perhaps best to terminate the discussion but to leave the door open because the Lord may later give us another chance to witness to them.

---

[12] [The Lord said,] "Even though the inclination of the human heart is evil from youth onward." (Genesis 8:21).

Specific Miracle Questions in the Old Testament

The Flood[13]: There are three issues that are commonly raised about the flood. The first is that the extensive geological evidence which has been found does not support the occurrence of an earth-wide flood happening five to six thousand years ago. There is no legitimate reason to doubt the quality of the bulk of the scientific evidence, but there is good reason to doubt its relevance. If one reads the descriptions of the earth from before[14] and after[15] the flood in the Bible, it appears that the Lord may have done some reconstruction of the environment on the earth as part of the flood or shortly thereafter. He did not tell us what he did, so we do not know the extent of the changes which he made. We do know that he gave us the world as it now is, having wiped the fingerprints of his actions from the final product. If he could create the universe out of nothing, he could certainly rearrange the furniture without leaving tracks on the floor.

The second issue is how Noah with primitive tools could have built a seaworthy boat which was 450 feet long, 75 feet wide and 45 feet high and which had three decks.[16] Certainly with modern tools for construction, computer modelling and ripple tanks to test prototypes, a boat of such dimensions could be built. Noah's ark, however, was not built to rest on land as a tourist attraction, but to float on an ocean under adverse conditions.[17] Although certain things about building smaller ships were perhaps known at his time, Noah had to get a much larger boat right the first time. Failure to do so would have meant death.

Numerous ways exist for wooden ships to fail, and the ark was bound to be stressed by the heavy rains and rolling seas. It seems very likely that the Lord supplied Noah with more building details than are listed in Genesis 6. But Noah had something even more important than detailed plans; he had the promise of the Lord's protection in this voyage by sea that he had been commissioned by the Lord to undertake.[18] The whole Flood account is a series of miracles, and it was the Lord's miraculous power that guaranteed the ark

---

13 Genesis 6:9-8:19.

14 Genesis 1-3.

15 Genesis 9:1-17.

16 Genesis 6:14-16.

17 Genesis 7:11-20.

18 [The Lord said,] "But I will establish my covenant with you, and you will enter the ark with your sons, your wife, and your sons' wives." (Genesis 6:18).

would survive the stormy weather of the flood even if the boat, as Noah had been able to build it, might not have survived a crossing of Lake Winnebago on a calm day. When David faced Goliath, he said, "This whole assembly will know that it is not by sword or by spear that the LORD saves, for the battle is the LORD's. He will hand you over to us."[19] Not by the clever construction of the ark, but by the Word of the Lord Noah's family and the animals were spared.

The third issue is how all the animals could be fitted into an ark the size of the one described in Genesis.[20] There are more than 5 million land animal species[21], ranging in size from microscopic to the African elephant. Even if young members of species were initially placed on the ark, many of them would grow substantially over the course of the year during which they were imprisoned on the ark. It is clear that rapid evolution and speciation would have needed to occur after disembarking from the ark so as to allow only a representative group of animals to have been fitted into the ark. Such rapid changes would not have been natural. It required a series of miracles by the Lord to give us the present diversity of species which we see. The management of even a significantly reduced number of animals would have been incredibly challenging for a crew of eight under the circumstances existing in the ark. The animals required food, drink, bedding, removal of solid and liquid waste, temperature control, ventilation, exercise, and protection from other animals, all under conditions where there was little or no light while on a rolling sea. Once again, the Lord's miraculous hand needed to be present to prevent disaster. Yet, when one has a covenant with the God of the Bible, as noted above, he does take care of all necessary things.

Trying to rationalize the flood and the ark in human terms is tempting, but it is dangerous spiritually to do so. The Lord stated that it was an event over which he had total control.[22] It did not occur naturally, and it is presumptuous

---

19 1 Samuel 17:47.

20 Some conservative Christians have argued that the ark was large enough to easily accommodate all the species of animals on the earth, but this is not at all realistic. Making statements like this undermines our credibility with people who realize that such statements are foolish.

21 Camilo Mora, Derek P. Tittensor, Sina Adl, Alastair GB Simpson and Boris Worm, "How Many Species Are There on Earth and in the Ocean?" *PLoS Biology* **9**:8 (2011).

22 [God said to Noah,] "I have decided to put an end to every creature, for the earth is filled with wickedness because of them; therefore I am going to destroy them along with the earth." (Genesis 6:13).

to assume that there was anything natural about it. It was the Lord's show from beginning to end. By faith Noah built the ark and got on it,[23] and we need to accept the biblical account by faith, not in terms of how we think that it could have been pulled off.

The Plagues on Egypt[24]: Except for the death of the firstborn, the plagues that are recorded in Exodus could have been natural occurrences. Some people have attempted to develop scenarios which would account for them, such as a comet's tail sweeping through the earth's atmosphere or a volcanic eruption somewhere in the Mediterranean basin. Yet the severity of the plagues, the swiftness of their beginnings and endings and the fact that the apparent plague-masters Moses and Aaron were not simply seized and killed by the angry Egyptians all undermine these efforts to ascribe the plagues to natural causes. The last plague[25] is a real killer, both literally and figuratively, to such rationalizations. Moreover, the fact that Moses and Aaron were both flawed characters in the events of the exodus adds to the credibility that these plagues were not a later concoction to promote the greatness of the Israelites. No one except the Lord looked very good in this account. The miracles are credible because the Lord had the power to do them and he had a good reason for doing them.

The Crossing of the Red Sea[26]: When the Israelites were trapped by the Egyptians against the Red Sea,[27] the Lord opened a passage through the sea to permit them to escape, and then he allowed the sea to flow back to drown their pursuers. The Lord's specified agent to accomplish the parting of the sea was "a strong east wind". Some will point out that a wind strong enough to part the waters in such a manner is probably physically impossible and, if possible, would have blown away the Israelites and their possessions too. Here again, as in the case of Noah's ark, a physical element that could not have done the job by itself was used as a cover by the Lord as he worked a miracle.

---

23 "By faith Noah, after he was warned about what was not yet seen and motivated by godly fear, built an ark to deliver his family. By faith he condemned the world and became an heir of the righteousness that comes by faith." (Hebrews 11:7).

24 Exodus 7:14-12:39.

25 "Now at midnight the LORD struck every firstborn male in the land of Egypt, from the firstborn of Pharaoh who sat on his throne to the firstborn of the prisoner who was in the dungeon, and every firstborn of the livestock." (Exodus 12:29).

26 Exodus 14:15-31.

27 Also referred to as the "Sea of Reeds."

As Lutherans learn concerning Holy Baptism and Holy Communion, when the Word of the Lord combines with a physical element, great things can be accomplished. Certainly, the Lord could have rescued his people in another way, but the Lord used this way as a teaching event to show the Israelites that not even the laws of nature could prevent their God from saving them. Like Jason's drive past Menards, the Lord engaged in abnormal behavior one day at the Red Sea. In a similar manner, God also dried up the Jordan River at flood stage to let Israel pass, this time into the land of Canaan.[28] These miracles not only got the Israelites where they needed to go, but they spread the terror of the Lord among their enemies. It was therefore quite reasonable for the Lord to perform such miracles.

The Sun Standing Still[29]: If there is any miracle in the Old Testament that should be challenged by the skeptics, it is the sun and moon ceasing to move across the sky for nearly a full day. No cleverly devised tale can explain this away as some sort of natural event. If the Lord had merely stopped the earth from rotating, it would have caused catastrophic results around the world unless it was accompanied by an incredibly large set of miracles. All the particles composing the Earth and its environment down to the size of the atom would have had to be reprogrammed or time would have had to be stopped at some places while continuing to flow at others. It is easy to say, "Well, the day just seemed to drag on forever." But the results of the battle that day could not have been completed in a normal day, so the Lord created an abnormal day. Can we produce physical proof that it occurred? No. Yet, such a miracle is characteristic of the events in the whole campaign to clear out Israel's enemies from Canaan, during which the Lord intervened in creative ways to

---

[28] "Now the Jordan overflows its banks throughout the harvest season. But as soon as the priests carrying the ark reached the Jordan, their feet touched the water at its edge and the water flowing downstream stood still, rising up in a mass that extended as far as Adam, a city next to Zarethan. The water flowing downstream into the Sea of the Arabah—the Dead Sea—was completely cut off, and the people crossed opposite Jericho." (Joshua 3:15-16).

[29] "On the day the LORD gave the Amorites over to the Israelites, Joshua spoke to the LORD in the presence of Israel: 'Sun, stand still over Gibeon, and moon, over the Valley of Aijalon.' And the sun stood still and the moon stopped until the nation took vengeance on its enemies. Isn't this written in the Book of Jashar? So the sun stopped in the middle of the sky and delayed its setting almost a full day. There has been no day like it before or since, when the LORD listened to a man, because the LORD fought for Israel." (Joshua 10:12-14).

give victory to his people.[30] That the Israelites were more fully committed to the Lord at the end of this period than at any other time during their entire history indicates that they had seen the Lord's hand in action.[31] A similar demonstration of the Lord's control of nature occurred when the Lord actually backed up time to show his commitment to the health of Hezekiah.[32] No magician could perform such a trick, and it would be a silly thing to record this incident in two places in the Bible if it were not a significant event.[33]

Jonah[34]: People often condemn the account of Jonah because they argue that not only is the throat of a whale not big enough to swallow a man, but also that a person could not survive inside a whale's stomach for three days. However, we must read the text of Jonah carefully before jumping to such conclusions. Jonah 1:17 reads, "The LORD appointed a great fish to swallow Jonah, and Jonah was in the belly of the fish three days and three nights." The implications of the Hebrew word translated "appointed" indicates that this sea creature was especially chosen for this purpose, perhaps a special creation capable of this task. Because it was the intention of the Lord to keep Jonah imprisoned for three days so that he would have time to think and to repent of his sins, it would have been natural for the Lord to internally equip the sea creature so that it could contain Jonah without doing him serious harm. The point of the account is not to assert that people can survive for three days in the bellies of fish, but that the God of the Bible can use unusual means to lead people to repentance. If the Lord is indeed almighty, then he could certainly provide a sea creature that would perform as in this account, so the issue becomes whether he did so or did not do so. Since he said that he did so and he had a good reason for doing so, why would we doubt that he did do so if we believe in the Lord?

---

30 Examples: Passing through the Jordan River on dry land—Joshua 3:15-17 / The walls of Jericho collapsed—Joshua 6:20 / The complete destruction of the huge army of northern Israel in one battle—Joshua 11:1-9.

31 "So the people said to Joshua, 'We will worship the LORD our God and obey him.'" (Joshua 24:24) / "Israel worshiped the LORD throughout Joshua's lifetime and during the lifetimes of the elders who outlived Joshua and who had experienced all the works the LORD had done for Israel." (Joshua 24:31).

32 "Then Hezekiah answered, 'It's easy for the shadow to lengthen ten steps. No, let the shadow go back ten steps.' So the prophet Isaiah called out to the LORD, and he brought the shadow back the ten steps it had descended on the stairway of Ahaz." (2 Kings 20:10–11).

33 Isaiah 38:8.

34 Jonah 1-4.

What people often fail to notice is that there are three other major miracles in the account of Jonah. In the first chapter of this account, the Lord showed his complete control of nature by creating a severe storm in order to force the crew of a ship to jettison Jonah into the sea. Then, the Lord abruptly ended the storm when the seamen did so, and they were terrified by the power of the Lord.[35] If the Lord could do this, then bringing forth a large sea creature would have been no problem for him.

The repentance of the contemptable people of Nineveh was also a far greater miracle than the sea creature account. These were blood-thirsty humans who killed and enslaved all their neighbors. The Word of the Lord is truly powerful.[36] The miracle of Jonah and the plant shows just how hard-hearted people can be even if they know the Lord and how he will intervene in love to try to bring them to back to himself.[37] Once again, God used natural agents under his direction to deliver his message. The account of Jonah dramatizes the lengths to which the Lord will go to accomplish his plans.

Elijah and Elisha: The miracles performed by the Lord through these prophets are astounding. At the word of Elijah, a three-and-a-half year drought destroyed virtually all the vegetation in Israel.[38] To bring an end to the drought, Elijah called on the Lord to send fire to consume an offering, which permitted Elijah to destroy the prophets of the idol Baal.[39] Later, when a king tried to have Elijah arrested, he twice called down fire to destroy those seeking to take him into custody.[40] Finally, God snatched Elijah from the earth in a whirlwind.[41] When an iron hammerhead was lost, Elisha used a stick to make it float.[42] At the request of Elisha, God restored a young boy to life.[43] The Lord

---

35 "Then they picked up Jonah and threw him into the sea, and the sea stopped its raging. The men were seized by great fear of the LORD, and they offered a sacrifice to the LORD and made vows." (Jonah 1:15-16).

36 "Then the people of Nineveh believed God. They proclaimed a fast and dressed in sackcloth—from the greatest of them to the least." (Jonah 3:5).

37 Jonah 4.

38 1 Kings 17:1-18:2.

39 1 Kings 18:20-46.

40 2 Kings 1:9-12.

41 "As they continued walking and talking, a chariot of fire with horses of fire suddenly appeared and separated the two of them. Then Elijah went up into heaven in the whirlwind." (2 Kings 2:11)

42 "When he showed him the place, the man of God cut a piece of wood, threw it there, and made the iron float." (2 Kings 6:6).

43 2 Kings 4:32–37.

struck a whole army with blindness at the prayer of Elisha.[44] These accounts and numerous other miracles which the Lord performed through these two men were intended to make the people realize that the God who had brought them out of Egypt was still alive and interested in them. He was continually trying to get all the people of Israel to abandon idol worship. As at the time of Moses, he was using miracles to demonstrate his power, but the people continued to ignore even his greatest signs and wonders. As a result, the miracles themselves became signs that God's destruction of the people of Israel was just, due to their impenitence. Here again, we see the reasonableness of the Lord's approach to the use of his power.

Daniel in the Lion's Den[45]: While this account is well known, some view it as not much of a miracle. Perhaps the lions just weren't hungry. This, however, is proven to be false: when Daniel was pulled out of the den and his opponents were thrown in, these opponents were immediately attacked and eaten. Clearly, the Lord had told his creatures that they did not have his permission to eat Daniel, and they could not act against the Word of God.

The Three Men in the Fiery Furnace[46]: This account is also well known, and the power of the Lord is emphatically demonstrated. Someone might have survived a lion's den, but no one was going to survive the flames in a superheated furnace. They killed the guards who only came close enough to shove the prisoners into it. Saying that this could not happen is silly. What good is an almighty God if he cannot do things which are totally impossible for human beings? When faced with such an account we might ask, "Does this make sense in the Lord's terms?" If God wanted to demonstrate to a king who thought that he had all authority on Earth that he didn't really have such authority, wouldn't such a rescue have delivered that message? It certainly seems to have done so, because King Nebuchadnezzar quickly changed his attitude toward the servants of the Lord. Once again, a miracle of God is shown to be quite a reasonable way for him to carry out his purpose.

While we could look at other miracles in the Old Testament, the above miracles are those which are most likely to be questioned or challenged. Our

---

44 "When the Arameans came against him, Elisha prayed to the LORD, 'Please strike this nation with blindness.' So he struck them with blindness, according to Elisha's word." (2 Kings 6:18).

45 Daniel 6:1-24.

46 Daniel 3:8-30.

answers to such objections always must be built around this same formula: an almighty God would have the power to do what the Bible says he did; there was at least one valid reason for him to do the deed; his plan of salvation benefited from his action. If people do not find this convincing, then: 1) they do not accept that an almighty God exists; 2) they reject that he would use his power to advance his agenda through any means other than the laws of nature; 3) they reject that he would give us an accurate account of the events of history. Each of these issues is covered in other chapters of this book.

Specific Miracle Questions in the New Testament

Before the Lord brought the Israelites out of Egypt, he produced a flurry of overt miracles,[47] and he continued to produce them at various times during Israel's travels to Canaan, the land that he had promised Abraham.[48] Soon after the Israelites entered Canaan and conquered the land, however, the number of visible miracles declined substantially, except when God decided to use them to rescue his people from their enemies.[49] This pattern persisted throughout the Old Testament. The Lord used miracles to demonstrate to his people that he was a reliable source of help and to designate that particular people were his chosen leaders and messengers.

The advent of the Messiah in the New Testament again caused the Lord to produce a flurry of overt miracles. He wanted to demonstrate that Jesus Christ was the one promised to Eve,[50] Abraham,[51] Moses,[52] and David.[53] For this

---

47 Exodus 7:14-12:39.

48 For example, sweetening the bitter water at Marah (Exodus 15:23-25).

49 "The LORD threw Sisera, all his charioteers, and all his army into a panic before Barak's assault. Sisera left his chariot and fled on foot. Barak pursued the chariots and the army as far as Harosheth of the Nations, and the whole army of Sisera fell by the sword; not a single man was left." (Judges 4:15–16).

50 [The Lord said,] "I will put hostility between you and the woman, and between your offspring and her offspring. He will strike your head, and you will strike his heel." (Genesis 3:15).

51 [The Lord said to Abraham,] "All the nations of the earth will be blessed by your offspring." (Genesis 22:18).

52 [Moses said,] "The LORD your God will raise up for you a prophet like me from among your own brothers. You must listen to him." (Deuteronomy 18:15).

53 [Nathan said to David,] "The LORD declares to you: 'The LORD himself will make a house for you. When your time comes and you rest with your fathers, I will raise up after you your descendant, who will come from your body, and I will establish his kingdom. He is the one who will build a house for my name, and I will establish the throne of his kingdom forever'." (2 Samuel 7:11–13).

reason, Jesus did numerous miracles, a fact that annoyed his enemies because they could not deny them, although they tried desperately to do so.[54] His miracles included controlling the forces of nature, healing diseases, restoring normal function to body parts, casting out demons, feeding the hungry, and raising the dead. These miracles were not part of a social program to aid the poor and oppressed, however, but rather they were done to demonstrate that Jesus was the messenger of the Lord and, in fact, the promised Messiah.[55] Jesus had the ability to heal everyone in Canaan, to make them comfortably wealthy and to drive out the Romans, all by the power of his Word. However, Jesus' mission was to save souls, not to repair the sinful world. While his miracles benefited a relatively small number of people, their real purpose was to show the power of the One who was doing them to many more people both then and now. The following selections show the range of miracles that Jesus did.

Jesus Walking on Water[56]: Walking on water is easy when it is frozen, but totally impossible for a human being when it is in liquid form, as it certainly was on the night that Jesus took a stroll on the Sea of Galilee. What is the physical reason for this? The density (i.e., the weight per volume) of people is nearly the same as that of water. If people try to stand upright in water, most of their bodies will be below the water surface. The weight of the water which they displace must be the same as the weight of their entire bodies. If they are denser than water, they will completely sink. To be able to walk on the surface of the water would require that a person had no weight. Since it is the force of gravity which gives people weight, the law of gravity, as it was applied to Jesus, would have had to be cancelled for his body to enable him to walk on the watery surface. But because the Lord controls the laws of nature and can abrogate any of them at will, this was a simple feat for Jesus and showed his deity. A much greater miracle occurred once he reached the boat: namely, the

---

54 John 9:13-34.

55 "As he was passing by, he saw a man blind from birth. His disciples asked him: 'Rabbi, who sinned, this man or his parents, that he was born blind?' 'Neither this man nor his parents sinned,' Jesus answered. 'This came about so that God's works might be displayed in him.'" (John 9:1-3).

56 "Meanwhile, the boat was already some distance from land, battered by the waves, because the wind was against them. Jesus came toward them walking on the sea very early in the morning. When the disciples saw him walking on the sea, they were terrified." (Matthew 14:24–26).

storm immediately stopped. The winds and waves could do nothing without the command of the Lord, and when Jesus, as the Lord, told them that their services were no longer needed, they shrank away to nothing. Jesus' almighty power meant that what happened to him and those around him was totally under his command. His disciples immediately recognized what had happened and worshipped him as the "Son of God." They could see the evidence and had been around the sea long enough to know what it meant. They had witnessed a miracle of the first order.

Curing Diseases[57]: Curing Peter's mother-in-law of a fever might not seem like much; she might simply have been on the verge of becoming healthy. But Jesus' healing word and touch extended to many more diseases. These included paralysis, bleeding, leprosy, skin diseases, and general maladies.[58] Some might say that he was just a good physician, who could recognize the causes of disease and recommend courses of treatment. Therefore, because his advice caused a much higher percentage of people to recover, he would have been thought to be working miracles. Yet, people are only so gullible. People in the first century knew that it took time for a person to recover from a disease, and Jesus' cures were miraculous also in the sense that they happened instantaneously. In addition, where did an untrained country preacher get the knowledge to diagnose and treat so many people successfully through available natural remedies? If he were divine, of course, he would have had such knowledge, but he would have also had the power to do the miracles, meaning that he could have effected the cures as the Bible reports. If he were not divine, his knowledge would have been limited by his environment, and people would soon have realized he was no more capable than they to perform healing.

Restoring Normal Function to Body Parts[59]: While diseases come and go, fixing non-functional body parts is another matter. The inability to see, hear, speak or walk are not short-term, easily addressed problems. This is particu-

---

57 "Jesus went into Peter's house and saw his mother-in-law lying in bed with a fever. So he touched her hand, and the fever left her." (Matthew 8:14–15).

58 "Jesus continued going around to all the towns and villages, teaching in their synagogues, preaching the good news of the kingdom, and healing every disease and every sickness." (Matthew 9:35).

59 "Jesus replied to them, 'Go and report to John what you hear and see: The blind receive their sight, the lame walk, those with leprosy are cleansed, the deaf hear, the dead are raised, and the poor are told the good news'." (Matthew 11:4–5).

larly true when the handicaps date back to birth or early childhood. People in an area would know who was thus afflicted, so Jesus could not come into town after some front man had arranged for a few people with imaginary diseases to appear on cue to allow Jesus to "cure" them to build his reputation. Restoring a withered hand was not a parlor trick, nor was healing those with speech impediments or the blind. Even if the common people might have been willing to believe anything, the religious leaders certainly were not. They were diligently seeking cases which could be shown to be fraudulent, and they were frustrated that they were limited to using rhetoric because they could not find any hard evidence against Jesus' miracles. In fact, it is Jesus' enemies who are better witnesses than his disciples in this matter. His disciples might have tried to help him look good, but the teachers of the law, the Pharisees, and the Sadducees, would have destroyed his reputation if they could possibly have done so. They failed because Jesus really was performing miracles through the divine power that was part of his being.

Casting Out Demons[60]: One of the strongest objections people have against Jesus' miraculous actions is the numerous accounts of him driving out demons. They will point out that one does not see demon-possession in the world today. If there are any legitimate cases, they are rare. What one does see instead are cases of people with mental diseases which make them behave abnormally according to common standards of judgment. Skeptics argue that it was these that Jesus healed and not people who were possessed by demons.

There are three points to consider here. First, if these people really were only mentally ill and not demon-possessed, then Jesus' curing them was still a significant miraculous feat. Nevertheless, accepting that cases indicated as demon possession were really only mental illness is incompatible with the inerrancy of the Scriptures, which, in general, carefully distinguish between normal illness and demon possession.[61]

Second, cases of demon possession are actually quite rare in the Bible. Outside of the life of Christ and the immediate period of the apostles, it's almost unknown in the Scriptures. Even in the book of Acts, the further one

60 "Also, demons were coming out of many, shouting and saying, 'You are the Son of God!' But he rebuked them and would not allow them to speak, because they knew he was the Christ." (Luke 4:41).

61 "Sickness and Disability," *Lexham Theological Wordbook* (Logos Software online, Faithlife, 2018).

gets from Jesus' ascension, the less common it becomes. It is entirely possible that the Lord may have allowed demons to take possession of people at this moment in history to demonstrate Jesus' power over Satan's angels. Demons cannot do this without God's permission because he is still the ruler of the universe and people are the Lord's special creation, not the devil's possession. While the Lord is always able to keep devils out of people, to demonstrate the horridness of demon-possession to the inhabitants of Canaan at Jesus' time and to show that Jesus had the same power over demons as God the Father himself, he might well have permitted incidents of demon-possession to skyrocket in Jesus' lifetime.

Third, the Bible indicates that sometimes physical illness and other types of suffering and loss were caused by the devil, whom the Lord had allowed to torment the person. Certainly, demon possession can include physical symptoms, so mental or emotional damage could have been the result of demon possession at the time of Christ. This may still happen today. Perhaps, some cases of mental illness are caused by the devil, either directly through demon possession or indirectly by his manipulating "natural causes". Jesus said that a woman was crippled because Satan had tortured her for 18 years.[62] St. Paul wrote that a messenger of Satan afflicted him to keep him humble.[63]

We do not know the extent to which the agents of Satan are allowed to torment the people of the world, but it is clear that in at least some cases the Lord did permit it. Consequently, we know that if Jesus could heal physical illness, then he could also heal mental illness and cure any ills that the demons might have been allowed to inflict. The Bible speaks, and anything beyond that is speculation.

Feeding the Hungry[64]: Several times Jesus found himself in remote areas with hungry people. The Bible lists two instances specifically where 5,000 and where 4,000 men plus women and children were involved. Each time Jesus took a small amount of food and multiplied it so that it fed the whole assembly, with food even being left over. Skeptics sometimes claim that the people really had food with them, and they just needed Jesus to begin the sharing process for them to bring out their own food and pass it around. It would hardly seem necessary that such a popular speaker would have had to

62 Luke 13:10-17.

63 2 Corinthians 12:7.

64 Feeding five thousand (Matthew 14:13-21) / Feeding four thousand (Matthew 15:32-39).

resort to such a crude hoax. For the Creator of Heaven and Earth, adding a few thousand sandwiches to the material complement of the universe would have been child's play. If Jesus was who he claimed that he was—namely God—then who can doubt that he did what he told us he did? If he isn't God, then his whole ministry was a sham.

Raising the Dead[65]: Jesus' raising people from the dead was the most troubling of his miracles to the Jewish religious leaders.[66] Once people had died, their bodies were considered unclean. Anyone who came into contact with, or even into the close proximity to, a dead body would become ceremonially unclean and not be able to participate in the worship life of the nation or even to return to their homes without a week-long cleansing ritual.[67] This fear of being in the presence of a dead body shaped the attitude of the priest and Levite in the parable of the Good Samaritan.[68] That this man Jesus could make the unclean clean merely by removing the source of the uncleanness (i.e., being dead) had deep theological significance. Only God was supposed to be able to do that, and only a priest was able to remove uncleanness through the ritual sanctioned by God. Jesus was creating a new way to become clean before God. The terrible thing from the standpoint of the Aaronic priesthood was that the fears of the religious leaders were justified: Jesus had come to earth to give people a new way to become clean (i.e., justified) before God without their priesthood.

Modern skeptics of Jesus' raising of the dead do not look at these theological issues but at the fact that the processes of physical death cannot be reversed. Once the blood clots and the proteins begin to denature, there is no going back. Therefore, the thinking goes, Jesus could not have raised to life any person who was truly dead. These miracles must have been phony. Yet, if there was anything that the Jews would have wanted to make certain of, it was the death of a person. The issue of uncleanness forced them to be very

---

65 The raising of the son of the widow of Nain (Luke 7:11-17) / The raising of Jairus' daughter (Mark 5:35-43) / The raising of Lazarus (John 11:38-44).

66 John 12:9-11.

67 [The Lord said to Moses,] "The person who touches any human corpse will be unclean for seven days. He is to purify himself with the water on the third day and the seventh day; then he will be clean. But if he does not purify himself on the third and seventh days, he will not be clean. Anyone who touches a body of a person who has died, and does not purify himself, defiles the tabernacle of the LORD. That person will be cut off from Israel." (Numbers 19:11-13).

68 Luke 10:25-37.

careful. Death was a major inconvenience for the living. As a result, Jesus would not have gone near a dead body if he were not going to raise it, because doing so would put a seven-day crimp into his ministry while he purified himself. He could not go shopping among the funeral processions, hoping to issue the call to life and find a respondent. No, those involved with the people whom Jesus raised to life knew these people were dead,[69] and Jesus knew that they would return to life when he commanded them to do so. Because every particle in the universe only acts at his command, directing the particles in a dead human body to reverse their course and to be prepared to function as part of a living body again was no different to the Lord from directing them to begin the decay mode after death. If one believes in an almighty God, one must accept that he can act as an almighty God, particularly when he states that he did so.

Summary

When a discussion about miracles seems to be going nowhere, we need to go back to the definition of what it means for the Lord to be almighty and the definition of a miracle as the Lord merely doing something in a different way to carry out his will. If people do not accept these definitions, we must discuss with them more the fundamental problems with their set of beliefs.

---

69 "After he [Jesus] came to the house, he let no one enter with him except Peter, John, James, and the child's father and mother. Everyone was crying and mourning for her. But he said, 'Stop crying, because she is not dead but asleep.' They laughed at him, because they knew she was dead. So he took her by the hand and called out, 'Child, get up!' Her spirit returned, and she got up at once. Then he gave orders that she be given something to eat." (Luke 8:51–55).

7

God's Plan of Salvation

In the last three chapters we have considered the God of the Bible from the viewpoint of his eternal majesty and his control of nature. God's power and majesty should make us tremble—they are so much greater than anything we human beings can imagine. Yet, those qualities would mean nothing if God did not direct his attention to us personally. Many teachers down through history have conceived of God as being *transcendent*—far beyond any human experience or contact. To such a God, we humans are no more interesting than ants on a sidewalk are to us human beings. That concept of transcendence lurks beyond much agnostic and even pantheist thinking (see Chapters 2 and 4). But the reality is that God does interact with us. While there is a sense in which God is far above and beyond us, he kneels down to our level and reveals himself to us in his Word. More than that, he comes to us in the person of Christ. It is these actions of God that make apologetics essential to our witness.

The God of the Bible

God reveals himself in the Bible as being "*triune*" or as the holy Trinity. As Jehovah's Witnesses and others like to point out, the words trinity and triune do not occur in the Bible. They were coined by later generations to express the church's consensus of what the Bible teaches about God. But there are many theological terms that don't occur in the Bible. While some are more useful than others, we develop these terms to make it easier to talk about complex truths. We speak of the Trinity or the Triune God so that we don't have to constantly say "the God who is one and three" or "who reveals himself as one God in three persons" or even "the God who is the Father, the Son and the Holy Spirit." We could say it that way, but it would grow tiresome.

The Doctrine of the Trinity is What the Bible teaches.[1] While whole books have been written about the subject (and a detailed treatment is outside the scope of this book), the apologist should have a grasp of the basic scriptural evidence for the Trinity. The Bible demonstrates the reality of the Trinity by balancing two truths: 1) there is one and only one God,[2] and 2) yet, the Bible clearly presents that one God as consisting of three persons.[3] The Athanasian Creed summarized this complex theological reality by saying, "We worship one God in three persons and three persons in one God, without mixing the persons or dividing the divine being."[4,5]

God has one essence or substance. Since God is not part of this universe (see Chapter 1), this is difficult to express clearly, but there is one being that is God. However, there are three persons in that essence/substance/being. Yet, that does not mean that we can split that essence into three parts and say, "This part is the Father" or "This part is the Son." One essence means that all of God is the Father and all of God is the Son. On the other hand, the Father, the Son, and the Holy Spirit are separate persons who cannot be interchanged or confused for one another. We have never met a being like this in the physical world, so we cannot comprehend how such a being can exist and function. Yet, the Bible declares that this is the nature of the Lord, and then it explains why and how each of these persons are important to God's relationship to man.

---

1 In Chapter 10, we consider the modern questioning of whether we can really organize all that God says into a creedal formulation and a Trinitarian formula.

2 See Deuteronomy 6:4 and 1 Corinthians 8:4, as well as the many statements like Isaiah 43:14 and Deuteronomy 32:12 which state there is no other God than the God of the Bible.

3 For example, Matthew 3:16-17, Matthew 28:19, John 15:26 and 2 Corinthians 13:14.

4 *Christian Worship: A Lutheran Hymnal* (Northwestern Publishing House, Milwaukee, 1993), 132. Hymnals tend to simplify the language a little.

5 The *Book of Concord* reads, "We worship one God in trinity and the Trinity in unity, neither confusing the persons nor dividing the substance." *The Book of Concord: the Confessions of the Evangelical Lutheran Church,* Robert Kolb and Timothy J. Wengert, eds. (Fortress Press, Minneapolis, 2000), 24.

The Trinity Enters the Creation. The Bible tells us that God created man after he had created the rest of the universe and its contents. It shows us that from the very beginning man was special to God, and that he created him in the "image of God,"[6] that is, with an understanding of God's eternal will and an ability to keep it. This will equates to God's moral law, which will be discussed in detail shortly. God also gave man at least one special commandment and a promise that punishment would follow if man did not keep this commandment. Of course, man did not keep the commandment, and God's punishment kicked in. Henceforth mankind was subjected to the wrath of the Almighty God.

Yet, rather than simply destroying man and moving on, God promised that he would provide a Savior who would rescue mankind from the punishment it deserved.[7] God's rescue of mankind is called the gospel, and God unfolded his plan for that rescue over a very long period of time. God chose (and even brought into existence) a special people, Israel, to be the instrument that he used to bring that Savior into the world. God controlled all human history so that Jesus would be born in just the right time and place.[8] God established a special relationship with Israel to demonstrate his love and patience and to prepare them to be his messengers to the world. He instituted a set of ceremonial and civic laws to train them, and his moral law to help them realize that they could never please him on their own. They needed him to rescue them.

When the right time had come, God the Father sent God the Son to assume a human nature into his divine nature to become Jesus, the Christ and Savior that mankind desperately needed. This is called the *incarnation*—literally, "the coming into the flesh". The Son of God existed from eternity.[9] As God, he participated in the Creation and in all the rest of God's mighty acts in the Old Testament. But he also entered the womb of the Virgin Mary and assumed a real and complete human nature. At that moment, God gave him a new name: Jesus.[10]

---

6 "So God created man in his own image; he created him in the image of God; he created them male and female." (Genesis 1:27).

7 First given in Genesis 3:15.

8 "When the time came to completion, God sent his Son, born of a woman, born under the law, to redeem those under the law, so that we might receive adoption as sons." (Galatians 4:4-5).

9 John 1:1-4.

10 Matthew 1:20-24.

The Person of Christ. The study of the person of Christ is called *Christology*. The union of the Son of God with a human nature is sometimes called the *personal union*. It is perhaps the most complex theology the Bible reveals, and we don't have the space to study it in detail here. But in order to prepare the apologist to explain what the Bible teaches (especially to those who challenge the idea that the Trinity is a biblical doctrine), there are four ways that we usually demonstrate that the Bible teaches that Jesus is true God. First, the Bible simply calls him God or some equivalent term.[11] Second, the Bible repeatedly ascribes to Jesus qualities or characteristics that only God has, such as being eternal and unchangeable[12] or omniscient.[13] Third, the Bible goes further and repeatedly depicts Jesus doing things that only God can do, like creating the world,[14] sustaining all creation,[15] giving life,[16] and many more (not least of which are his miracles). Finally, the Bible depicts God as jealous—as insistent on the glory that is due to him alone (see Chapter 4).[17] The Bible then commands us to honor Jesus just as we do the Father.[18]

The other side of the coin is Jesus' humanity, which in the modern world is not often questioned (except when skeptics deny that he existed at all), unless we are talking to someone with beliefs similar to those of a Jehovah's Witness. We use three basic arguments to demonstrate that the Bible teaches Jesus is a man. That the Bible calls him a man must be our first argument.[19] Second, we point to passages which clearly state that Jesus had a human body and soul.[20] Finally, we point out that Jesus did all the things a normal human being does: he grew[21], he slept,[22] he ate,[23] he died[24] and more. Yet, in one way he did differ from us: he had no sin (Hebrews 4:15).

---

11 Matthew 1:23; John 20:28-29; John 1:1-2; Colossians 2:9.
12 Hebrews 13:8.
13 John 21:17.
14 John 1:3.
15 Hebrews 1:3.
16 Act 3:15.
17 Isaiah 42:8.
18 John 5:22-23.
19 Such as 1 Timothy 2:5, and also passages like Hebrews 2:14 which state that Jesus shared our humanity and 2:17 which say that he was like us in every way.
20 For example, Luke 24:39 and Matthew 26:38.
21 Luke 2:40.
22 Mark 4:38.
23 Luke 24:41-42.
24 Luke 23:46.

This union means that the person of Christ had all the qualities of God and of man, without mixing them into something new or existing as two separate beings joined together. God could die because Christ was man and Christ died. A man could do miracles because Christ was God and Christ did miracles. Once Jesus died and rose, he ascended into heaven, where he continues to be God and man, united in one person, for all eternity. That means that Jesus is present everywhere, both as God and as man. (That's why he can be present in communion and why millions of Christians can receive his body and blood, but these elements are never exhausted.) Jesus—God and man—hears our prayers and answers them. Jesus—God and man—will return to judge the living and the dead and remake the world.

This union is different from those times in the Old Testament when God assumed a human form to interact with people (see Chapter 4). That was an accommodation to our limited minds and hearts. In Christ, God did something unique and truly overwhelming—the Creator entered the creation, the Maker of the universe made himself part of the universe. Unlike any other religion, Christianity does not teach that we have to reach up to God. He knelt down to us in the person of Jesus. Then he lifts us up to him.

Jesus' Active and Passive Obedience. Why does Christology matter? Finally, only faith in the true Christ will save us, which is why Jesus warned us to be on our guard against false Christs and false prophets.[25] What did we need in a Savior? We needed someone who could fulfill the law in our place (theologians call this his *active obedience*). We needed someone to pay for our sins (theologians call this his *passive obedience*). That someone had to be a real human being, because God's laws apply to us. But that someone had to be able to rescue not just Adam and Eve, not just the people of Israel, but the whole human race—billions of unborn people. How could that happen?

This was the genius of God's plan. St. Paul wrote, "When the time came to completion, God sent his Son, born of a woman, born under the law, to redeem those under the law, so that we might receive adoption as sons."[26] The Savior had to be born of woman—he had to be a real human being. Why? So that he could fulfill the law of God in our place. Thus, the Book of Hebrews says, "Now since the children have flesh and blood in common, Jesus also

---

[25] Matthew 24:11, 25.
[26] Galatians 4:4-5.

shared in these, so that through his death he might destroy the one holding the power of death—that is, the devil—and free those who were held in slavery all their lives by the fear of death."[27] Jesus shared our humanity to free us from death and sin.

In the early church, theologians wrestled with what it meant that Jesus was both God and man. It didn't seem logical to argue that one man could have two full and complete natures, so many different theologians tried to combine the two natures by having Jesus' divine nature replace some aspect of his human nature: his heart, his mind, his reason, and so forth. But God led a man named Gregory of Nanzianzus (AD 329-390) to the insight that ultimately ended all those efforts. He said, "That which was not assumed by Christ was not healed."[28] Jesus had to be all that we are so that he could take our place and free us from sin. Therefore, he was a true, human being, with body and soul, mind, and heart, just as we are.

However, Jesus had to be more than that. Psalm 49 says that the price to redeem someone's life—to keep them from dying—is too costly for any person to pay.[29] The Savior we needed had to be able to cover the actual cost of our sin. He had to do it for the entire world—that's what John 3:16 tells us, "For God loved the world in this way." Only the blood of God's Son could pay that debt. Finally, in a sinful world, only the Son of God could face the devil and be without sin.[30] To accomplish all this, God did a miracle. The Holy Spirit descended on the Virgin Mary and the Son of God entered her womb where she conceived his human nature. God gave us a Savior who is fully human and one who is fully divine so that he could accomplish our salvation.

To spread the news of God's redemption of the world through his Son, Jesus commissioned his followers to tell everyone they encountered about it. He promised that God the Holy Spirit would teach them and sustain them in this world. He promised to create faith and gather the elect into his family, which he calls "*the church*." With his commission and promise, we go forward as messengers and apologists, everywhere teaching and defending his law and his gospel. Let us, therefore, consider attacks on God's plan of

---

[27] Hebrews 2:14-15.

[28] Gregory of Nanzianzus was a monk and a bishop who was a leader at the First Council of Constantinople.

[29] Psalm 49:7-9.

[30] Hebrews 4:15.

salvation and our responses to it, knowing that we must always be careful to properly distinguish between the law and gospel.

Setting the Stage

Martin Luther famously said, "Therefore whoever knows well how to distinguish the Gospel from the Law should give thanks to God and know that he is a real theologian."[31] His point was simple: the message of Scripture comes down to two main teachings: the law and the gospel. Ever since Christ preached both, people have wrestled to reconcile the two, and have, at times, engaged in selective or wholesale misrepresentation of one or the other or both.

Nevertheless, understanding the two doctrines and how they fit together is the key to understanding the Bible. In that sense, the discussion of law and gospel can be framed as a question of *hermeneutics* or as how to properly interpret the Bible. A detailed discussion of that discipline is outside the scope of this book. Still, the key to understanding the message of God's Word is comprehending what the law actually says, what the gospel actually says and how they relate to each other.[32]

Each doctrine is true in its own right. Still, at the same time, each doctrine stands in opposition to the other. Luther said, "These two things are diametrically opposed: that a Christian is righteous and beloved by God, and yet that he is a sinner at the same time. For God cannot deny His own nature."[33] Not surprisingly, most people try to solve the problem of relating the law and the gospel by changing or weakening or outright eliminating one or the other. We cannot accept or even be silent in the face of any of those approaches. Both law and gospel are the inspired and inerrant Word of God. We, as apologists, must be prepared to deal with the way that these two doctrines are twisted and

---

31 Luther's Works, **26**:115.

32 The *Formula of Concord* says, "The distinction between law and gospel is a particularly glorious light. It serves to divide God's Word properly and to explain correctly and make understandable the writings of the holy prophets and apostles. Therefore, we must diligently preserve this distinction, so as not to mix these two teachings together and make the gospel into a law. For this obscures the merit of Christ and robs troubled consciences of the comfort that they otherwise have in the holy gospel when it is preached clearly and purely. With the help of this distinction these consciences can sustain themselves in their greatest spiritual struggles against the terror of the law." Solid Declaration, V:1 (Kolb, Wengert, ibid., 581).

33 Luther's Works, **26**:235.

manipulated in the modern world.

The Reformed[34] theologian W. Robert Godfrey wrote in a popular treatment of the Reformation:

> "Luther said the most important word in medieval theology was the Latin word *ergo* ("therefore"). He said the besetting sin of Latin theology was "therefore"—constantly resting their theology on the conclusions of human reason. He said the real word that should be at the center of our theology is the German word *dennoch* ("nevertheless"). Theology operates not by therefores but by neverthelesses. We as Reformed theologians following that nice, balanced lawyer, John Calvin, may tend to be more sympathetic to therefores. But if we are going to understand Luther, we have to understand his use of the nevertheless to drive home his point."[35]

Godfrey was on to something. The realization that the gospel is not a logical extension of the law was the insight that made Luther the teacher he was. It's not a "new law" like the Roman Catholic Church taught (and still teaches today).[36] The law and the gospel are two equally valid, equally true revelations of God which in a sinful world must stand in contrast to each other. Yet, they meet and are resolved in the cross of Christ.

Unfortunately, the "nevertheless" relationship between the law and the gospel is counterintuitive. Even many Christians struggle to understand it, let alone explain it. If we Christians struggle to distinguish between law and gospel, what can we expect from unbelievers? The apologist almost has to expect that this distinction will be lost on people who attack Christianity. To be fair, there are well-informed unbelievers who do, in fact, know what the Bible teaches concerning this matter. Still, we are far more likely to encounter people who simply do not understand this most basic teaching of Scripture. Our task as apologists is to explain the message to them.

Distinguishing Between the Law and the Gospel

One way to summarize the contrasts between the law and the gospel is to think in terms of five questions: Where is each teaching written? Who does

---

[34] See Chapter 10 for the different meanings of the word "Reformed." Godfrey is a Calvinist.

[35] Robert Godfrey, *Reformation Sketches: Insights into Luther, Calvin, and the Confessions* (P & R Publishing, Phillipsburg, NJ, 2003), 5.

[36] *Catechism of the Catholic Church* (Doubleday, New York, 1995), par. 1965-1974.

what to reach heaven under each teaching? What verdict does each teaching render on us? What does each teaching promise us? How does each teaching motivate us to live a Christian life?

Where is Each Teaching Written? The Bible teaches that every human being is born with at least some knowledge of the law.[37] Sometimes we call this knowledge *natural law*[38] or better, *the natural knowledge of the law.* In addition to this inborn knowledge of the law, God also built a conscience into each individual. What is the difference between the two? The conscience is the ability to compare a person's words and deeds and even thoughts and feelings with a standard of behavior—"*the law*," at least as much as that person knows it. Most people think of the conscience primarily in terms of guilt, but St. Paul wrote in Romans 2:15 that Gentiles' thoughts accuse or even excuse them. When a person is falsely accused of something, they have an in-born desire to be vindicated.

Now unfortunately, because sin has corrupted every human heart (except that of Jesus), God's perfect design is broken at every level. People don't live according to the law, even to the degree they know it. The natural knowledge of the law is not just incomplete; it's positively damaged so that conscience doesn't have a certain standard to compare with. It must be supplemented with the written law that God gave in his Word. The conscience itself functions imperfectly. People can train their conscience to ignore certain kinds of sins or lull it into a false security through rationalizations and justifications. People can be made to feel guilty for things that aren't really their fault. But the point remains: God wrote the law into human hearts. However imperfectly the whole system functions, it is there. To supplement the failures caused by sin, God gave the law a second time in his Word; therefore, it is really written in two places: the human heart and the Bible. Of course, the Bible also makes clear that there is a great difference between having the law and keeping the

---

37 "So, when Gentiles, who do not by nature have the law, do what the law demands, they are a law to themselves even though they do not have the law. They show that the work of the law is written on their hearts. Their consciences confirm this. Their competing thoughts either accuse or even excuse them." (Romans 2:14-15).

38 This can be an unfortunate term, because the same term is also used in philosophy, but it doesn't always mean the same thing. It has also been used in jurisprudence. In recent years, the term has gotten a lot of play among advocates of the political right in the U.S, but again, not really in the same sense that it is being used here.

law.[39] Just because God tells us to do or not do something, doesn't mean we can follow his command, even when we know what it is.

The gospel is totally different. When the jailor at Philippi was pulled back from the brink of suicide, he asked Paul and Silas, "Sirs, what must I do to be saved?"[40] He didn't know! Again and again, St. Paul called the gospel a "mystery"[41]—by which he means something that we could never understand unless God revealed it to us. He said that he proclaimed "God's hidden wisdom" which none of the rulers of this age understood because no eye has seen, no ear has heard, no heart has conceived what God has planned for us. These things must be made known to us through the Holy Spirit.[42]

So, it really shouldn't surprise us that unbelievers don't understand the gospel. God has to reveal it to us. He does that through his Word. Thus, while the law is written both in the Bible and in our hearts, the gospel is written only in the Bible—at least until the Holy Spirit creates faith, at which point he does plant the gospel in our hearts as well. Yet even then, if we don't continue to hear it and strengthen our faith, that faith can die. Those who neglect the means of grace invariably have their understanding of the gospel gradually reduced to rules about being a good person.

---

39 See, for example, Romans 2.

40 Acts 16:30.

41 For examples: "Now to him who is able to strengthen you according to my gospel and the proclamation about Jesus Christ, according to the revelation of the mystery kept silent for long ages but now revealed and made known through the prophetic Scriptures, according to the command of the eternal God to advance the obedience of faith among all the Gentiles—to the only wise God, through Jesus Christ—to him be the glory forever! Amen." (Romans 16:25-27) / "When I came to you, brothers and sisters, announcing the mystery of God to you, I did not come with brilliance of speech or wisdom. I decided to know nothing among you except Jesus Christ and him crucified." (1 Corinthians 2:1-2) / "In him we have redemption through his blood, the forgiveness of our trespasses, according to the riches of his grace that he richly poured out on us with all wisdom and understanding. He made known to us the mystery of his will, according to his good pleasure that he purposed in Christ as a plan for the right time—to bring everything together in Christ, both things in heaven and things on earth in him." (Ephesians 1:7-10) / "You have heard, haven't you, about the administration of God's grace that he gave to me for you? The mystery was made known to me by revelation, as I have briefly written above." (Ephesians 3:2-3).

42 "We do, however, speak a wisdom among the mature, but not a wisdom of this age, or of the rulers of this age, who are coming to nothing. On the contrary, we speak God's hidden wisdom in a mystery, a wisdom God predestined before the ages for our glory. None of the rulers of this age knew this wisdom, because if they had known it, they would not have crucified the Lord of glory. But as it is written, **What no eye has seen, no ear has heard, and no human heart has conceived—God has prepared these things for those who love him.** Now God has revealed these things to us by the Spirit, since the Spirit searches everything, even the depths of God." (1 Corinthians 2:6-10).

Who Does What to Reach Heaven Under Each Teaching? Under the law, every person has to be perfect in his thoughts, desires, words and actions to reach heaven.[43] There are no exceptions. There are no technicalities. There are no other options. God is perfect and he demands perfection. Conversely, the gospel proclaims that God gives us that perfection because Jesus was perfect in our place.[44] Jesus died to pay for our sin.[45] Jesus rose and conquered death.[46] The law commands us to be perfect to get to heaven. The gospel proclaims that Jesus already was perfect, so we go to heaven.

What Verdict Does Each Teaching Render on Us? God uses the image of a courtroom because he is the eternal judge. Under the law, the verdict is simple: guilty.[47] Nothing can hide our sinful words or deeds from God. He even sees our thoughts and feelings and inner desires.[48] The gospel offers a different ruling in God's court: not guilty. Most English Bibles regularly use the words "*justification*" and "*justify*" to make this point. Unfortunately, those words can mislead us. Today, we justify ourselves when we're making excuses for bad behavior or when we're trying to get out of trouble. The Greek that lies behind the words "justify" and "justification" was used in court when

---

[43] "But the law is not based on faith; instead, **the one who does these things will live by them.**" (Galatians 3:12) / "Be perfect, therefore, as your heavenly Father is perfect." (Matthew 5:48) / "For I am the LORD, who brought you up from the land of Egypt to be your God, so you must be holy because I am holy." (Leviticus 11:45) / "For whoever keeps the entire law, and yet stumbles at one point, is guilty of breaking it all." (James 2:10).

[44] "For we do not have a high priest who is unable to sympathize with our weaknesses, but one who has been tempted in every way as we are, yet without sin." (Hebrews 4:15) / "For just as through one man's disobedience the many were made sinners, so also through the one man's obedience the many will be made righteous." (Romans 5:19).

[45] "Love consists in this: not that we loved God, but that he loved us and sent his Son to be the atoning sacrifice for our sins." (1 John 4:10) / "He made the one who did not know sin to be sin for us, so that in him we might become the righteousness of God." (2 Corinthians 5:21).

[46] "But as it is, Christ has been raised from the dead, the firstfruits of those who have fallen asleep. For since death came through a man, the resurrection of the dead also comes through a man. For just as in Adam all die, so also in Christ all will be made alive." (1 Corinthians 15:20-22).

[47] [David wrote,] "God, you know my foolishness, and my guilty acts are not hidden from you." (Psalm 69:5) / [Jesus said,] "When he [the Holy Spirit] comes, he will convict the world about sin, righteousness, and judgment." (John 16:8).

[48] "For the word of God is living and effective and sharper than any double-edged sword, penetrating as far as the separation of soul and spirit, joints and marrow. It is able to judge the thoughts and intentions of the heart." (Hebrews 4:12) / "Everyone who hates his brother or sister is a murderer, and you know that no murderer has eternal life residing in him." (1 John 3:15).

the judge ruled a person not guilty.[49]

What Does Each Teaching Promise Us? God's law condemns every sin and every sinner to death and hell. Already in the Garden of Eden, God announced, "For you are dust, and you will return to dust."[50] Or, as Paul announced, "For the wages of sin is death."[51] Death—in all the ways that the Bible uses that word—is the result of sin.

Most of the time, the basic idea behind death in the Bible is separation. *Physical death* is the separation of the soul from the body.[52] On the other hand, death can also refer to the sinner's separation from God,[53] something Lutheran theologians often call *spiritual death.* At times, the Bible also uses death to refer to hell.[54] In one sense, one might say that this is because existence in hell is so bad that it doesn't seem right to call it "life." But in a greater sense, it's because the essence of hell, the heart of the suffering and sorrow, is to be locked out of God's presence forever.[55] Sometimes we call this *eternal death.*

---

49 "The righteousness of God is through faith in Jesus Christ to all who believe, since there is no distinction. For all have sinned and fall short of the glory of God. They are justified freely by his grace through the redemption that is in Christ Jesus." (Romans 3:22-24) / [Jesus said,] "Anyone who believes in him is not condemned, but anyone who does not believe is already condemned, because he has not believed in the name of the one and only Son of God." (John 3:18) / "That is, in Christ, God was reconciling the world to himself, not counting their trespasses against them, and he has committed the message of reconciliation to us." (2 Corinthians 5:19). / "Who can bring an accusation against God's elect? God is the one who justifies. Who is the one who condemns? Christ Jesus is the one who died, but even more, has been raised; he also is at the right hand of God and intercedes for us." (Romans 8:33-34).

50 Genesis 3:19.

51 Romans 6:23.

52 For example, "And the dust returns to the earth as it once was, and the spirit returns to God who gave it." (Ecclesiastes 12:7).

53 For example, "And you were dead in your trespasses and sins in which you previously lived according to the ways of this world, according to the ruler of the power of the air, the spirit now working in the disobedient. We too all previously lived among them in our fleshly desires, carrying out the inclinations of our flesh and thoughts, and we were by nature children under wrath as the others were also. But God, who is rich in mercy, because of his great love that he had for us, made us alive with Christ even though we were dead in trespasses. You are saved by grace! He also raised us up with him and seated us with him in the heavens in Christ Jesus." (Ephesians 2:1-6).

54 For example, [Jesus said,] "Let anyone who has ears to hear listen to what the Spirit says to the churches. The one who conquers will never be harmed by the second death." (Revelation 2:11).

55 "They will pay the penalty of eternal destruction from the Lord's presence and from his glorious strength on that day when he comes to be glorified by his saints and to be marveled

The gospel promises something completely different—"For the wages of sin is death, but the gift of God is eternal life in Christ Jesus our Lord."[56] Or to go back to the Garden of Eden, even before God pronounced the sentence of death on all mankind, he cursed the devil. In the Bible, most of the time the "curse" has nothing to do with bad language or casting spells. Curse means to condemn someone to hell.[57] When God cursed the devil, he promised a Savior who would crush the devil's head and be struck on the heel by a poisonous snake, that is, the Savior would die.[58] This would bring us back to God. This was the first promise of a new and different result for us.

When Jesus died on the cross, he suffered death in every sense of the word, including hell. That can be seen in his crucifixion. The sun stopped shining. Jesus sometimes called hell "outer darkness"[59]—the place where the light of salvation does not shine. At the height of his suffering, Jesus quoted Psalm 22: "My God, my God, why have you abandoned me?"[60] At that moment Jesus suffered hell itself *in our place.*

That is the resolution of law and gospel. The law condemns us to die and go to hell. The gospel calls us holy and righteous in God's sight and promises us eternal life. How can both things be true? Because Jesus took our place in life and in death. Jesus rose to announce that all our sins are paid for now and forever. The law and the gospel meet at the cross of Christ. This is the thing that most people simply do not understand. This is the key to all apologetic efforts to dealing with questions of how the law and gospel relate.

---

at by all those who have believed, because our testimony among you was believed." (2 Thessalonians 1:9) / [Jesus said,] "Then he will also say to those on the left, 'Depart from me, you who are cursed, into the eternal fire prepared for the devil and his angels!' And they will go away into eternal punishment, but the righteous into eternal life." (Matthew 25:41,46).

56 Romans 6:23.

57 "For all who rely on the works of the law are under a curse, because it is written, **Everyone who does not do everything written in the book of the law is cursed.** Now it is clear that no one is justified before God by the law, because **the righteous will live by faith.** But the law is not based on faith; instead, **the one who does these things will live by them.** Christ redeemed us from the curse of the law by becoming a curse for us, because it is written, **Cursed is everyone who is hung on a tree.**" (Galatians 3:10-13).

58 [The Lord said,] "I will put hostility between you and the woman, and between your offspring and her offspring. He will strike your head, and you will strike his heel." (Genesis 3:15).

59 For example, [Jesus said,] "But the sons of the kingdom will be thrown into the outer darkness where there will be weeping and gnashing of teeth." (Matthew 8:12).

60 Matthew 27:46. Also compare Psalm 22:1.

How Does Each Teaching Motivate Us to Live a Christian Life? The law motivates us to obey out of fear. We don't want to "go to hell." Lutheran theologians speak of the *opinio legis*, which is a Latin term that could perhaps be translated as "a law-oriented outlook." We naturally[61] think that if we do good, God will reward us, and that if we do bad, God will punish us. We naturally think that the best way to ease our conscience is by doing something good to offset the bad things we've done. Fear of being smacked down by God or a desperate need to feel better becomes the driving motivation for living a new life. This, however, is really not a new life at all. It's the old life just dressed up in Christian clothes. Living in such a manner either leads us to despair (when we cannot silence our conscience) or to becoming Pharisees (when we deaden our conscience and convince ourselves that our manmade rules are good enough for God—something that is all too common in the church today).

The gospel motivates us to obey God out of a sense of joy and gratitude for what Jesus has done.[62] More than that, the gospel changes us and drives us to be new and different people.[63] This does not mean that the law has no place in a Christian's new life. The law tells us imperfect believers what really pleases God. As Lutherans, we like to say that it is a guide. This is because the law does not produce a new life; only the gospel can do that.

If a Christian can keep the distinction between law and gospel straight in his or her head, that Christian is a real theologian. He or she will be on the right path to answer the challenges we face on these issues.

---

[61] In theology, "naturally" means something different from what it means in ordinary speech today. When we speak of natural ingredients, we mean things that nature produces (instead of manmade substitutes). When we speak of natural processes, we mean the way the world (nature) works. Natural often carries the implication of the way things are supposed to work. In theology, it's just the opposite. "Naturally" or "our natural man" is the way we were born. It is the way things always work, but only because we live in a sinful world. If we worked the way we are designed to work and the way God intended for his creation to work, we should be sinless, and everything should be perfect. But due to the fall, "by nature" means "in the way we are born and in the way the world is condemned to function until Jesus comes," that is, sin reigns.

[62] "And whatever you do, in word or in deed, do everything in the name of the Lord Jesus, giving thanks to God the Father through him." (Colossians 3:17).

[63] "For the love of Christ compels us, since we have reached this conclusion: If one died for all, then all died. And he died for all so that those who live should no longer live for themselves, but for the one who died for them and was raised." (2 Corinthians 5:14-15).

Two Main Teachings in All of Scripture

As we said earlier, most people solve the problem of relating the law and the gospel by changing, weakening, or outright eliminating one or the other or both. One of the most common ways of doing this is to portray the Old Testament God as a God of wrath and punishment while the New Testament God is portrayed as a God of love and forgiveness. This is often done in a very crude way on TV or in movies. However, it can also be done in a much more refined way. The more refined way is to hold that there is an evolution of religion. The Old Testament law represented a new development in ethical thinking that was very advanced for its time. Yet, it was still very mechanical in nature—we do this and God will do that (i.e., a *quid pro quo*). Even though progress was made over the centuries, threats and rules were still the main focus until Jesus came and introduced a religion of the heart. St. Paul then took the very Jewish thoughts of Jesus and turned them into a whole new religion with a whole new answer to how we deal with God and with our own conscience.

The apologist needs to understand that this position is nonsense in both its crude and refined form. The law is found all through the Bible. St. Paul and Jesus called people to conform their lives to God's Will as it is revealed in the Ten Commandments. Likewise, the gospel is found all through the Bible. We've already seen that in the Garden of Eden, on the day Adam and Eve fell, God promised a Savior, the Seed of the Woman. Throughout the Old Testament, God repeated that promise of a coming Savior, which is the gospel in its purest form. Moreover, God also demonstrated the gospel by repeatedly forgiving his people, both as a nation and as individuals. God showed his power to save by rescuing his people repeatedly. He dealt with their hearts through his constant call to repentance. In fact, God told Isaiah that mechanical offerings did them no good without a religion of the heart.[64]

---

64 "'What are all your sacrifices to me?' asks the LORD. 'I have had enough of burnt offerings and rams and the fat of well-fed cattle; I have no desire for the blood of bulls, lambs, or male goats. When you come to appear before me, who requires this from you—this trampling of my courts? Stop bringing useless offerings. Your incense is detestable to me. New Moons and Sabbaths, and the calling of solemn assemblies—I cannot stand iniquity with a festival. I hate your New Moons and prescribed festivals. They have become a burden to me; I am tired of putting up with them. When you spread out your hands in prayer, I will refuse to look at you; even if you offer countless prayers, I will not listen. Your hands are covered with blood.'" (Isaiah 1:11-15). / [The Lord said,] "Is this the kind of fast I have chosen, only a day for a man to humble himself? Is it only for bowing one's head like a

It is true, however, that God's people developed in their understanding of his plan and his purpose. But it is not true that God's revealed religion "evolved." Evolution means change. God's religion did not change, in the sense that what he wanted from his people or his plan of salvation changed. What did change was the manner in which God taught those truths. Sometimes, we speak of *progressive revelation*: Isaiah (lived around 700 BC) understood more of God's plan than King David did (lived around 1000 BC). King David understood more than Moses did (lived around 1500 BC). Moses understood more than Abraham did (lived around 2100 BC). Yet, none of them had the detail which we believers have today. What's the difference? It is the degree to which the plan of salvation had been written down at the different moments in history when David or Moses or Isaiah or any other Old Testament believer lived. As God gave more and more of his Word to the prophets and then to the apostles, he revealed more and more of his plan. So, the Old Testament believer had a more limited revelation, but he or she still had what God wanted them to know.

Someone might still ask why the tone of the Old Testament is so much harsher than that of the New Testament. While this observation is true, it is often overstated. The Old Testament has many rich expressions of God's love, and it might be useful to point some of them out.[65] Likewise, there are texts in the New Testament which threaten God's wrath.[66] Certainly, the ratio of wrath to mercy is different. There is a reason for that—much of the Old Testament was written to people who had turned away from God and were hardening their hearts. God needed to wake them up so that they would be spared eternal judgment. Conversely, the whole New Testament is directed to the church, which, by definition, is made up of repentant believers. To be sure, many of the epistles take issue with sins and problems in doctrine and practice. However, the assumption is usually made that God is dealing with weak believers, rather than those who have turned away. On those occasions in the New Testament when hardened unbelievers or fallen away Christians appear, the apostles and even Jesus do sound an equally harsh note—because

---

reed and for lying on sackcloth and ashes? Is that what you call a fast, a day acceptable to the LORD?" (Isaiah 58:5).

[65] For example, Psalm 23, Psalm 46, Lamentations 3:22-24 and Ezekiel 33:11. Many more could be added.

[66] For example, Matthew 25:46, Romans 2:1-3 and 2 Thessalonians 1:6. Many more could be added.

sin brings death and hell.[67]

Most critically, the apologist needs to keep in mind that law and gospel fit together at the cross of Christ. The Old Testament was given before Jesus came, so God dealt with his people differently from how he did after Jesus came. Nevertheless, his message is always that sinners deserve hell, but that the Savior rescues us.

Efforts to Weaken or Eliminate the Law

The law-gospel dynamic is the heart of the Christian faith, so it's not surprising that there are many different ways that it comes under attack today. In addition to pitting the law and the gospel against each other, each teaching is denied at times. In our world today, the more common attack seems to be against the law. In some ways, that really shouldn't surprise us. No one likes being told they're sinners or that they deserve to go to hell. No one likes being told they cannot do or think what they want to.

The Effect of Evolution on Guilt. One very effective technique that modern skeptics use against the law proceeds from the assumptions our society makes about evolution. In Chapter 5, we considered the apologetic approach to the teachings of evolution. Here, we want to consider one way that assumptions about evolution affect the worldview that prevails in our society.

The Bible teaches that God is the ruler of the heavens and the earth. Again and again, both the Old and New Testaments record the praise that men and angels, and indeed all creation, render him. The Bible calls on us to praise God.[68] Our praise is not an option. It is what the Creator of the universe deserves and even demands. On Judgment Day, all people who have ever lived will bow before him.[69] The Bible presents that Creator as both the Lawgiver[70] and the Judge of the whole world.[71] That God should and must be obeyed. At the same time, the Bible shows us a God who makes mankind the crown of his creation and the object of his endless love and care. Such a Father deserves

---

67 For example, Matthew 23:13-39, Galatians 5:7-12, 1 Timothy 1:18-20, 2 Timothy 4:14-15 and 2 John 7-11.

68 [A psalmist wrote,] "From the rising of the sun to its setting, let the name of the LORD be praised." (Psalm 113:3).

69 Philippians 2:10-11.

70 See Exodus 20 and Deuteronomy 5.

71 Genesis 18:25.

the obedience of his children. When we human beings fail to honor and obey our Father in heaven, we have sinned. In that sense, all sin really breaks the First Commandment.

But that whole perspective fails if God is not the Creator and mankind is not his special creation. The greatest damage that the theory of evolution does to the church is not undermining the truth that God made the world. It's undermining our responsibility to him.

Hand in hand with that damage goes the fact that evolution undermines our understanding of the nature of sin. According to Genesis 3, Adam and Eve disobeyed God and corrupted his entire creation. Romans 5 makes it clear that the sin of one man brings death on us all, because we inherit Adam's sin and then we sin ourselves. Sin is wrong and it deserves God's condemnation. On the other hand, evolution says something totally different. It says that man was not created to love and serve God. Instead, we evolved from lesser creatures. Part of that evolution is the development of human morality. As primitive man began to organize into families and groups, it was advantageous to have allies and family members one could trust. Society was born from a need to defend ourselves against threats all around us. Little by little, that need developed into a higher social conscience and a sense of right and wrong. Religion of all kinds played a part in this development, but so did philosophy, art, and literature.

Of course, the variations on this theme are endless, and we don't need to consider them here. Conversely, we do need to understand the end result—sin is regarded as a church construct. It was a way for ancient and medieval thinkers to make sense of a world that is full of injustice and misfortune. It was a way of explaining plagues and natural disasters as the wrath of God. It was a useful tool in the development of a higher morality. Nevertheless, it does not actually mean that any person has to answer to a holy God on Judgment Day nor on the day he or she dies.

Most people who follow this line of thinking will view the concept of sin as detrimental to society today. They may be willing to allow that the concept served a purpose in the past (otherwise it would not have evolved or become so deeply rooted in Western culture). Now, however, we need to move past this kind of thinking. We need to allow that many things which the Bible calls sin are valid choices for people to make as we progress to a new and better future. We need to recognize that guilt is an unhealthy emotion. It leads to self-destructive behavior and destroys a person's self-esteem. We need to free people from feeling guilty, not proclaim a law that compounds their guilt.

Of course, if an individual really thinks this way, they are going to be very difficult to deal with. On the other hand, we do have an ace in the hole, namely, their own conscience. As we said earlier, God designed it to compare their lives with the law as they know it. Its power to make a person feel guilty is tremendous, even in consciences that have been conditioned to ignore God's law and reflexively justify all that a person says and does. (If this were not true, the entire therapy industry would collapse.)

Part of using the law is recognizing that God designed guilt, just as he designed physical pain. Physicians tell us that physical pain often serves a purpose. It warns us that we are damaging our bodies so that we pull our hand back from the stove or buy shoes that give us better arch support. Guilt is God's warning system. It tells us that we are breaking his law and endangering our eternal salvation. A solution is needed before the damage is irreversible. Knowing that allows the apologist to focus on the personal guilt of a skeptic so that person realizes they need a solution. The solution, of course, is Jesus.

Denying Original Sin. Even if a person does not have an evolutionary approach to morality, chances are that he or she will have a problem with original sin. By *original sin* we mean that every human being (except Adam and Eve when they were first created and Jesus who was conceived by the Holy Spirit) inherits sinfulness from their parents. Already at the moment of conception, every human being is a sinner. That by itself is difficult to accept, but the corollary is even harder: already at conception, every human being is guilty of sin in God's eyes and, therefore, deserves eternal damnation, which can only be avoided if that person comes to faith in Christ.

The Lutheran Confessions admit: "This inherited sin has caused such a deep, evil corruption of nature that reason does not comprehend it; rather, it must be believed on the basis of the revelation in the Scriptures."[72] In other words, no one would believe in original sin if God didn't teach it in his Word.[73] This is one of those places where every thought has to be taken cap-

---

72 *Smalcald Articles*, Part III, Article 1, Kolb Wengert, ibid., 311.

73 The article continues by offering four passages to demonstrate that original sin is, indeed, the Scriptures' teaching: Psalm 51 (see verse 5), Romans 5 (see especially verse 12), Exodus 33 (specifically verse 20) and Genesis 3 (the fall into sin—the pertinent section being verses 6-24).

tive by the Word of God. This couldn't be truer in our time. The vast majority of Americans believe that people are basically good. If they are evil (like child molesters or racists), then something happened to make them that way. People look at little babies and think how innocent they are, so they take offense at the clear teaching of Scripture.

When discussing this issue, we as apologists need to make sure that we are speaking clearly. Original sin is not an action or a deed that a baby does or even a thought or feeling that a baby has. It is a quality that children inherit from their parents. All physical characteristics are inherited. The color of a baby's eyes, the maximum height they can attain, an innate disposition to music or sports are inherited traits. Sometimes, in a broken world, children inherit bad things. Genetic defects, such as the one that causes sickle cell anemia, are passed from parents to children. Some studies indicate that there may be a genetic factor that makes some people more susceptible to substance abuse. Some people have argued that even personality traits might be inherited. So, it is not outside the realm of reasonability to see sinfulness as an inherited trait.

Actual sin, both in the form of sins of the heart and sins of word and deed, springs from the sin that we inherit. Obviously, God holds us guilty of the sinful things that we do and say. The Bible makes clear that he also convicts us for the sins of our hearts and minds. Still, the difficulty many people have with original sin is that God counts us as guilty already in the womb, before we have done anything good or bad. "That's not fair!" is the gut reaction.

This is a difficult doctrine—and it doesn't hurt to admit that. Even we struggle with it sometimes. But it helps to see that God is not making something up. Our sin is real. In one sense, the heart of sin is selfishness. I put what I want and what makes me feel good ahead of everyone else. Why do I do that? Because I'm sinful. Babies are the most selfish people on earth. When a baby wakes up in the middle of the night, he or she doesn't care that mommy and daddy have to get up in a couple of hours. That child wants to be attended to *now*. Children don't have to be taught to be selfish or to insist on what they want. They have to be taught to share, to respect other people, to speak the truth and to show love. These things show that the contamination that is original sin is real and active in every child's heart.

Sometimes, people answer by quoting a popular saying, "God doesn't create junk!" That's true, as far as it goes. The Bible does not teach that God created Adam and Eve sinful. That Jesus could take on human flesh without being sinful shows that being sinful is not part of the essence of being human. It's something that was done to us by the fall into sin. Jesus came to restore us to the state of holiness with which Adam and Eve were born. When we reach heaven, we will be free from our original sin. Even here, the gospel works in our hearts to gradually restore our holiness. But that original sin is always there pushing back.

Sometimes skeptics will assert a false idea that too many Christians also teach, namely, original sin cannot mean that we are completely sinful (see chapter 10). It means that we are damaged and that it is harder to be good. However, if we work at it, we can achieve a God-pleasing life. There are many variations of this argument both inside and outside the church. Nevertheless, this just is not what God's Word says. St Paul wrote, "For I know that nothing good lives in me, that is, in my flesh."[74] We often call this *total depravity*. There is nothing good in us the way we are born, no matter how innocent a baby looks. God has to do a miracle to reclaim us and plant the new man in us.[75]

Sometimes, this question will veer off into a discussion of baptism. This will probably happen because we bring up baptism as a means of grace for infants. As true as this is, it might not help. From the perspective of the skeptic, it leaves untold billions of babies condemned to hell because their parents don't get them baptized. A truly sharp critic might point to a Lutheran family that loses a baby, perhaps even before it is born, and ask if that child is really condemned to hell. Generally, at this point, we fall back to the (true) position that God does not speak to this situation in his Word and that, therefore, we have to trust his grace. Luther, in dealing with this narrow question, pointed out that Christian parents pray that God would grant their unborn child faith and that we should trust that God answers such a prayer, even if we don't know how he does it.[76] Lutherans often also point out that babies in the womb can hear the gospel proclaimed to their parents and sometimes

---

[74] Romans 7:18a.

[75] Again, the Lutheran Confessions speak clearly on this issue: "On the other hand, we believe, teach, and confess that original sin is not a slight corruption of human nature, but rather a corruption so deep that there is nothing sound or uncorrupted left in the human body or soul, in its internal or external powers." *Formula of Concord*, Epitome, Article I. (Kolb Wengert, p. 488).

[76] "Comfort for Women who Have Had a Miscarriage," Luther's Work **43**:247-8.

assert that the Holy Spirit can work in this way. In truth, this last argument raises more questions than it answers, since babies don't understand words. There is no other situation in which we would argue that preaching the gospel in words that a person cannot understand would give them faith. Moreover, it doesn't answer the horror we and skeptics may feel at the thought of the babies of non-Christians going to hell.

The apologist needs to bring the question back to the reality of sin. It is not unfair for God to condemn sin. Forgiveness is really the unnatural thing. God overrides his justice by punishing his Son in our place. However, those who do not trust in Jesus will not have the benefit.

In the end, we must recognize that this issue is offensive, but it is also a red herring. Most of the time, the real reason to bring it up is to sidetrack the conversation, just as the woman at the well of Sychar brought up theological disputes to get Jesus off track.[77] We cannot ignore this issue, but we need to bring the discussion back to our challenger's own standing before God. Is he or she truly willing to stand before God and say, "I tried to be a good person"? Don't all people have to admit what their own consciences tell them—that they just haven't been good enough?

Disregarding the Law Written in the Bible. Modern American society simply denies a great deal of what God says. The attitude which has emerged regarding homosexuality and gay marriage is instructive. Some people will seriously argue that the Bible doesn't really condemn homosexuality. It condemns abusive homosexual relationships. This kind of argument tends to come either from people with some kind of academic background that makes them believe they have some expertise in what the Bible says or from people who have attended classes or even services in the many churches today that hold to an opinion like this. The answer is very simple: show us where in the Bible God limits his condemnation of homosexuality to abusive relationships. There simply is no context that says this. A quick examination of the key passages will show that God's Word is clear on this issue. Marriage is made for a man and a woman.[78] Sexual relations are confined to two people who are married to each other. Homosexuality is a sin that brings consequences, even

---

77 John 4:20.

78 "This is why a man leaves his father and mother and bonds with his wife, and they become one flesh." (Genesis 2:24).

in this life.[79]

We live in a time when the Word of God is no longer held in high esteem. People inside and outside the visible Christian church are willing to try to change its clear message so that they can feel as they are "on God's side" and in tune with our society at the same time.

Other people have no problem disagreeing with the Bible. Generally speaking, they begin with the idea that there really is no such thing as objective truth, so there really is no such thing as an objective standard of right and wrong. There is only what is right or wrong for each individual. Therefore, anytime the Bible presents something as being morally right or wrong, it's automatically dismissed as the product of a more primitive understanding of religion. The reason, of course, for advancing this kind of argument is that Christians point to God's Word and say that homosexual relations, abortion, no fault divorce, and sex outside of marriage are morally wrong. Yet, people want to do all these things. Since the Bible really does teach all these things are wrong, they need a way to evade this truth.

Attacks like these come in many different forms, but they can be answered relatively easily. The apologist simply asks, "Was kidnapping and enslaving Africans wrong?" "Was the Nazi extermination of the Jews wrong?" Almost no one today will (publicly) argue that those things were justifiable. The apologist can then ask, "What makes those things wrong?" Invariably, the answer will revolve around hurting people. Whatever answer is given, however, almost certainly it will appeal to a higher standard of right and wrong than some subjectively chosen moral code. Some things are objectively right and wrong. God did write the moral law in our hearts. It isn't actually necessary at that moment to then equate those things with what God says about homosexuality or abortion. In fact, if an apologist does that, they could easily find themselves sidetracked by accusations that he or she is equating homosexuality with the Holocaust. That kind of emotional assault will end the discussion. The point is to make it clear that God does give us standards. He records them in his Word. Every human being has violated those standards and deserves God's judgment. Of course, this opens the door to a discussion of Jesus.

---

79 "For this reason God delivered them over to disgraceful passions. Their women exchanged natural sexual relations for unnatural ones. The men in the same way also left natural relations with women and were inflamed in their lust for one another. Men committed shameless acts with men and received in their own persons the appropriate penalty of their error." (Romans 1:26-27).

God says many things that are offensive to modern sensibilities. They were often offensive to the sensibilities of the people God spoke them to originally! We should not hide those things or deny them. On the other hand, we also don't need to make it easy for unbelievers to dismiss our testimony by bringing those things up in our first conversation. The apologist needs to establish the law as a threat to the eternal life of the person with whom he or she is speaking. Only when the Holy Spirit uses the gospel to create faith is a person open to considering the other hard things that God says. It is an act of faith to deny the sensibilities of our culture and subscribe to God's view of right and wrong.[80] We cannot win arguments on these points. We need to turn the conversation to Jesus and use the law the way God intended it to be used.

Denying Hell and Judgment. Of course, unbelievers have other strategies for evading the law and its consequences. A common way to deny the law today is by denying hell or any kind of divine punishment in the life to come. If people can convince themselves that God does not judge our actions and there will be no consequences, all that Christ came to do is lost. Sometimes, this can be part of a general denial of an afterlife. While that is becoming more and more common, the overwhelming majority of people in the United States (and indeed throughout the world) do believe in some kind of afterlife. It's prominent in many modern movies and works of fiction—even the Harry Potter books had a major subtheme about death leading to just another plane of existence.

One could argue that a belief in life after death is built into the natural knowledge of the law, so it's not surprising that most people believe in some kind of afterlife. But such a belief does not mean they have a Christian understanding of the afterlife. Indeed, huge numbers of people today who believe that death leads to a new plane of existence do not believe in the resurrection of the body. They do not believe in a final judgment at which Christ will raise the dead and purify this world. They do not believe in heaven.[81] Instead, they believe in a gathering of all loved ones, or an opportunity to spend eternity doing the things a person most liked to do. Even in Christian churches, one sometimes hears someone say, "Dad has got his first bucket of bass and now

---

80 "We demolish arguments and every proud thing that is raised up against the knowledge of God, and we take every thought captive to obey Christ." (2 Corinthians 10:4b-5).

81 Strictly speaking, heaven is the intermediate state. It's where we go after we die until Jesus returns.

he's starting his next one!"

When many of these key elements are missing from people's understanding, the Bible's concept of hell is bound to be denied or twisted. Nevertheless, some people who don't believe in a specifically Christian afterlife, do fear what's coming. "The Great Unknown" is terrifying to them, in part, because they do have a conscience and because it does tell them that God is going to collect what is due. But at the same time, their knowledge of what the Bible says about hell and judgment is going to be limited and inaccurate in most cases. The apologist needs to choose carefully what ideas to engage. It is not necessary to debate every aspect of hell to make the point that God's judgment is real and terrible, and we need Jesus to rescue us.

Another form of denying judgment is simply to say that God would never do that. If there is a Judgment Day, God is going to just take everyone to heaven. Naturally, there are many varieties of this view. One of the more thoughtful ideas is that it doesn't seem fair for God to condemn someone to eternal punishment for sins that only lasted for a brief time in this life. The person who advocates this kind of argument will often ridicule a God who judges as vengeful and even evil. This kind of argument can sometimes be mitigated by pointing out that momentary actions often have consequences far beyond what seems fair. If a young man or woman steps out in front of a bus, they may spend the next fifty years dealing with crippling injuries. Likewise, criminal courts regularly sentence offenders to sentences far longer than the time it took to commit a crime. Unfortunately, if a person insists that eternity is different, we Christians don't always have an answer that will satisfy a skeptic. All sin is an offense against the eternal God and merits eternal punishment. Whether an individual accepts this or not does not affect its validity.

Many people move very easily from this point to the idea that people are basically good. (Although nearly everyone is willing to modify this statement if they are asked about child molesters or Adolf Hitler.) Most people who are willing to admit that some people are so bad they deserve to go to hell want to limit that number to a very small group of really bad people. This is because they want to believe that they themselves are basically good people. Their sins are more "mistakes" than outright rebellion against God. Gently but firmly, the apologist has to make it clear that God does not limit his law in that way. Fortunately, the law also is part of God's Word, so it has the power of the Holy Spirit built into it. This is why unbelievers are so desperate to deny it. It is our trump card as we continue to testify to what God says.

Misusing Old Testament Regulations. Some people adopt another approach to attacking the Bible's record of God's law: they cite Old Testament dietary laws and purity laws and ask if we accept them. They point to laws that forbade weaving different kinds of cloth together or to growing different crops in the same garden.[82] Sometimes they point to severe punishments God commanded for far more serious offenses and imply (or say) that God also commanded the same punishments for these lesser offenses. Their real goal is to accuse us of trying to bind modern society to Old Testament law. To some degree, that false accusation lurks behind the media's fascination with the term "fundamentalist,"[83] which is never a compliment in modern discourse.

The apologist needs to emphasize that God gives different kinds of laws, just as civil authorities do. Some laws apply only in certain situations. Commercial health codes are enforced in restaurants and hotels, but not in private homes. Other laws are general or even universal in scope. Murder is wrong, even when there are mitigating circumstances. Sometimes, one kind of law overrides another. Soldiers can shoot enemy soldiers in battle but not in other situations. God's law works in much the same way. Not every law God gave applies to every situation. God gave many commands in the Bible that were very specific and applied only to the situation at hand (e.g., when God told Moses ten times to inflict plagues on Egypt). Other laws had a more general application.

Lutherans often divide biblical law into three general types: *civil law*, which dealt with how Israel was supposed to run its country; *ceremonial law* which dealt with Old Testament worship; and *moral law*, which deals with what is right and wrong. The civil law dealt with inheritance and taking care of the poor. It dealt with contracts and marriage and the relationships between

---

[82] [The Lord said,] "You are to keep my statutes. Do not crossbreed two different kinds of your livestock, sow your fields with two kinds of seed, or put on a garment made of two kinds of material." (Leviticus 19:19).

[83] Fundamentalism has a complicated history. Originally, the word was used for people who agreed with *The Fundamentals*, a series of articles written between 1910 to 1915 to defend traditional Christian teaching, as Darwinism and historical critical approaches to Scripture made their way into American seminaries (See chapter 10). By the last decades of the twentieth century, the term came to be applied to any religious group of any faith that took its writings literally, such as fundamentalist Islam. Tying that term to Christian fundamentalism allows the media to create an impression of uneducated, unthinking fanatics who might be dangerous.

people. It assumed either a monarchy or a tribal society governed by elders and family heads. The ceremonial law dealt with purity issues and sacrifices and the priesthood. It told how to dress and what to eat and not eat and what kinds of false religious practices to avoid. The Old Testament civil and ceremonial laws often had some moral law principal behind them, but these laws were specific applications of those principals to an ancient people who were in a covenant relationship with God while they waited for Christ to come. New Testament Christians are not bound to these regulations.[84] The apologist must make that point clear to those who distort the Old Testament record of God's law.

Moral laws state God's standard of right and wrong so that we humans can measure our actions against this standard. They also announce what constitutes God's punishment for sin. Moral law applies to all people everywhere, which is why it is so common in the New Testament. The apologist needs to make the case that moral law continues to apply to us today.

The Command to Exterminate the Canaanites. Skeptics like to zero in on one specific set of commands that God gave. They use these commands to question God's authority to define what is right and wrong. When Israel conquered the Promised Land, God commanded his people to exterminate the nations that were there.[85] Many people today are troubled by this. Many people today see this as the natural result of fundamentalism, and they use this command to equate with Islamic fundamentalist terrorism all those who believe that the Bible is the inspired Word of God. They maintain that activities like the Crusades and the persecution of Jews in the Middle Ages are exam-

---

84 "Therefore, don't let anyone judge you in regard to food and drink or in the matter of a festival or a new moon or a Sabbath day. These are a shadow of what was to come; the substance is Christ." (Colossians 2:16-17).

85 [Moses said,] "When the LORD your God brings you into the land you are entering to possess, and he drives out many nations before you—the Hethites, Girgashites, Amorites, Canaanites, Perizzites, Hivites and Jebusites, seven nations more numerous and powerful than you—and when the LORD your God delivers them over to you and you defeat them, you must completely destroy them. Make no treaty with them and show them no mercy. You must not intermarry with them, and you must not give your daughters to their sons or take their daughters for your sons, because they will turn your sons away from me to worship other gods. Then the LORD's anger will burn against you, and he will swiftly destroy you. Instead, this is what you are to do to them: tear down their altars, smash their sacred pillars, cut down their Asherah poles, and burn their carved images. For you are a holy people belonging to the LORD your God. The LORD your God has chosen you to be his own possession out of all the peoples on the face of the earth." (Deuteronomy 7:1-6).

ples of Christians engaging in similar undertakings.

The apologist needs to emphasize that God never commanded the New Testament church to spread the gospel by force. He did not make the extermination of unbelievers part of the moral law, nor does the Bible record even one example of a Christian using violence of any kind to advance the church's mission. Those Christians who have undertaken evangelism by conquest were not fulfilling the Great Commission.

Further, the destruction of the Canaanite peoples was part of God's judgment on them for their unbelief and their religious practices.[86] God simply will not tolerate idolatry. [87] Nor does he have any tolerance for sinful acts committed in his Name. He does not permit us to sit in judgment over his judgments, a truth that is difficult for an unbeliever to accept, but ultimately one with which every Christian must come to terms. At the same time, God intended Israel to serve as the medium for sending Jesus into this world. The idolatry of the Canaanites presented a serious spiritual risk for the people of God—as he himself pointed out.[88] The coming of the Savior of the world was God's overriding concern, so ultimately this command had a loving goal, even while it maintained the strictness of God's justice.

In the end, defending God's law can lead to anger and condemnation from unbelievers. That doesn't mean we shouldn't try. As apologists, we point out what God has said. We try to help people understand it. We use the law above all else to lead people to Jesus who rescues us from all that our sin deserves. Certainly, some people will harden their hearts against that message. They may attack us to justify their own sins and their own rejection of the natural law which God has written in their hearts. They may call us homophobes and all manner of other insulting things. They may persecute us in this life. The

---

[86] [The Lord said to Abram,] "In the fourth generation they will return here, for the iniquity of the Amorites has not yet reached its full measure." (Genesis 15:16) / [The Lord said,] "You are to keep all my statutes and all my ordinances, and do them, so that the land where I am bringing you to live will not vomit you out. You must not follow the statutes of the nations I am driving out before you, for they did all these things, and I abhorred them. And I promised you: You will inherit their land, since I will give it to you to possess, a land flowing with milk and honey. I am the LORD your God who set you apart from the peoples." (Leviticus 20:22-24).

[87] Lyle Lange, *One God – Two Covenants* (Northwestern Publishing House, Milwaukee, 2010), 69-74.

[88] [Moses said,] "You must destroy all the peoples the LORD your God is delivering over to you and not look on them with pity. Do not worship their gods, for that will be a snare to you." (Deuteronomy 7:16).

apologist has to remember that all power is in God's Word. Our job is not to win arguments or even to win converts. It's to testify to the truth. When we are condemned, we remember what Jesus said: "Blessed are you when people hate you, when they exclude you, insult you, and slander your name as evil because of the Son of Man. Rejoice in that day and leap for joy. Take note—your reward is great in heaven, for this is the way their ancestors used to treat the prophets.... Woe to you when all people speak well of you, for this is the way their ancestors used to treat the false prophets."[89]

Attempts to Weaken or Eliminate the Gospel

The most natural response to the gospel is to simply disbelieve it. Since the gospel is not written in our hearts, our old man has a tremendous advantage. It requires a miracle of grace to make a believer and God's continuous supernatural intervention to keep our faith alive. As a result, until God brings the gospel to bear on an individual sinner, the devil's job is easy. Unfortunately, the devil is not content to sit back and keep the followers he has. He actively works to push the gospel back. One of his most effective strategies for attacking the gospel is to attack the law because the gospel means nothing if we aren't sinners. We don't need to be rescued if we aren't on the way to hell. Therefore, every attack on the law is, in fact, an attack on the gospel.

Nevertheless, the devil and the unbelieving world also level a series of attacks against the gospel itself. Perhaps the most common way to attack the gospel is simply to convert it into a new law. This is the approach of the Roman Catholic Church, and it can be seen in many Arminian churches today. "What would Jesus do?" becomes the axis that a Christian's faith revolves around. Jesus is portrayed as an example of a truly good person. True Christians follow his example. Obviously, Jesus is an example for us. Yet, this is only because he kept the law perfectly in our place so that we can be counted as righteous before God. The Christian life is a very important issue, and when we Christians don't live good lives, we make our job as apologists harder. Nevertheless, we must be aware that there is a fine line between living our faith and turning Jesus into a new law giver.

Another common attack on the gospel is to say it doesn't make sense. How can one man's death pay for the whole world? Why does Jesus' death erase

---

89 Luke 6:22-23,26.

our sins? Sometimes, people will even go so far as to ask what kind of a savage God would require payment in blood for the sins of the world. The apologist needs to have a good understanding of the gospel to answer those questions.

Jesus as a Force for Change. Another set of related challenges center on what some people call *atonement theory. Atonement* usually refers to Jesus' payment for our sins. Atonement theory is the effort by theologians to explain how Jesus' death wins us eternal life. Many different explanations have been offered. [90] A full explanation of these theories goes beyond the scope of this book. Nevertheless, there is an apologetics application when people attempt to explain Jesus' death.

Perhaps the most common challenge to Jesus' death is related to the least biblical of the atonement theories. It is sometimes called the *moral influence theory.* In essence, this theory holds that Jesus died to show us what real love is like and in the process, become a catalyst for societal change. Accordingly, Jesus becomes a martyr to the cause of making society more just and loving. Even in its most popularized form, this attack on the gospel involves two key ideas. First, Jesus' death does not accomplish any *satisfaction* in a technical sense. It provides no payment for sin. In general, the moral influence theory of atonement rejects the idea that God would demand a payment or that Jesus could possibly make one. Skeptics may ridicule the whole idea. In what area of life do we allow one person to pay for another person's crimes? We simply cannot imagine a judge knowingly and intentionally executing one person for another person's crime and calling that justice.

The other idea that is almost always present in this approach is the idea of *free will.* Lutheran theologians often avoid this term, preferring instead to

---

90 Some of the more common ones (in an oversimplified form) are the ransom theory (Jesus paid the devil to free us from hell), *Christus Victor* (Latin for "Christ the victor"—Jesus won the battle against the forces of evil and freed us), the Satisfaction Theory (Jesus paid God as our sacrifice), the Penal Substitution Theory (Jesus took our place in God's courtroom and suffered our legal punishment—this is the biblical concept at its fullest), the Governmental Theory (Jesus did not pay our exact penalty, but he suffered to show God's displeasure over our sin; the payment does free us, but only because the church becomes a hiding place for us sinners from God's wrath), the Scapegoat Theory (a modern theory which focuses on the Old Testament scapegoat in Leviticus 16; in essence, this theory holds that Jesus is killed by a crowd that believes him guilty, but he is proven innocent, so the crowd is guilty). Some of these theories reflect biblical truth and biblical ways of talking about Jesus' death. He did defeat sin, death and the devil. He did pay a ransom. But most are too narrowly focused to give a complete treatment of Jesus' work.

speak of "freedom of choice." Whichever term we use, we Lutherans mean that God allows us to make decisions for our lives here on this earth. He doesn't predestine us to be farmers or doctors or even pastors. God allows his children to decide among the options he presents, even as he guides and directs our lives (a paradox, to be sure). Still, most people mean something else by free will. They mean that we can choose to be good and, in the process, earn eternal life. Maybe we cannot earn it all, but we can at least contribute to some degree. This concept is false, however, because we can contribute nothing. St. Paul wrote, "For I know that *nothing good* lives in me, that is, in my flesh."[91] This approach appeals to our natural man because it allows us to be good.

The apologist should be prepared to encounter some version of the moral influence theory. It is simply the easiest way for an unbeliever to think about Jesus without having to deny his existence or "take on" Christians. He or she can feel like they are reasonable and respectful of Christian faith. Nevertheless, the moral influence theory once again changes Jesus from a Savior into an example. The apologist must focus on personal responsibility for sin so that the person we are talking to sees the need for a personal Savior. When the skeptic is pulled up short by their own sense of responsibility before God, the Holy Spirit will work through the good news of Jesus' payment for our sins and removal of our guilt.

The key teaching that answers the moral influence theory is the Bible's teaching on atonement. Jesus took our place in God's punishment. We sometimes call this *forensic righteousness.* The term has nothing to do with a medical examiner. "Forensic" refers to a courtroom. In God's courtroom, every one of us would be guilty. He has all the evidence. He has video of our entire lives with a voice-over playing all our sinful thoughts and feelings. We cannot escape the verdict of guilty. We cannot escape the death and hell that must follow. At this critical instant, Jesus—whom the Bible sometimes calls our Advocate,[92] our Lawyer—steps into our place and takes the punishment we deserve.

This is the point of all the biblical language that speaks of sacrifices. In the Old Testament, God demanded sin offerings and guilt offerings to atone or to pay for the sins of the people. The New Testament makes clear that those

---

91 Romans 7:18.
92 1 John 2:1.

bloody sacrifices were teaching tools.[93] God wants people to understand that there is a price that has to be paid for sin. Jesus paid it with his death on the cross. For the apologist, understanding the relationship between Old Testament sacrifice and Christ's payment is one way of illustrating that God does, in truth, teach the need for atonement.

Attacks on the Ministry of Christ. Attacks on Jesus' ministry can take numerous different forms. One kind is to engage in critical discussions of what the text really should have been. Scholars dissect the gospel accounts, argue about where this or that expression might have come from, and then eliminate those things they believe are wrong or inventions. They subsequently try to present what Jesus really might have said, or more common today, what the original tradition might have been, without really considering whether any of it actually happened. To counter this, the apologist must insist on dealing with the text as it is. If a person doesn't want to believe it, that can be granted, so long as they will allow us to keep talking about it. No one believes the gospel until the Holy Spirit works faith in their heart.

Another attack on Jesus' ministry is to portray him or his apostles as being hopelessly male chauvinistic, or as viewing the world through a limited, first century Jewish viewpoint. It follows, then, that Jesus made mistakes and held superstitious beliefs that were common to the people of his day. Again, the important thing for us is to focus on what Jesus said and did, not on their preconceived notions of his work. When Jesus speaks for himself, most of these attacks will fail.

A further problem arises because Jesus preached a great deal of law during his ministry. He drove the moneychangers out of the temple with a whip. He called Peter "Satan." He condemned the Pharisees again and again. Even beloved parts of the gospels, such as the Beatitudes, are really law. People who don't understand the gospel will point to those things and argue that Jesus really taught us a way to live. He wasn't interested in doctrine. In fact, they will argue, Jesus didn't have much respect for church leaders. He was a radical who attacked them and subverted their authority. They want to turn him into someone who basically denied God's Word, because, they argue, "Jesus accepted everyone." Consequently, we dare not condemn homosexuality or adultery or other obvious sins, because Jesus didn't.

---

93 See Hebrews 9 and 10.

But is this picture of Jesus' ministry true? Of course not. What is true is that Jesus accepts everyone who repents. He did associate with tax collectors and prostitutes who were penitent. In his day, people who thought they were more righteous than these "sinners" looked down on him for that. Yet, Jesus did not excuse their sin. The most complete interaction with this kind of person which the gospels record is the account of Zacchaeus.[94] In that account, Jesus took the initiative. He spoke to Zacchaeus and invited himself to Zacchaeus' home, and in the process caused a lot of muttering. However, only after Zacchaeus repented did Jesus say, "Today salvation has come to this house, because he too is a son of Abraham. For the Son of Man has come to seek and to save the lost."[95] Why was Zacchaeus lost? Because of sin. How did Jesus reclaim him? Through repentance and faith. The reason Jesus did not accept the religious leaders of his day was not because they were "the Establishment" and that he was some kind of radical revolutionary. They did not think they were sinners; therefore, they were unwilling to repent.

In John 12, Jesus said, "As for me, if I am lifted up from the earth I will draw all people to myself." John continues, "He said this *to indicate what kind of death he was about to die.*"[96] Being "lifted up" meant his crucifixion. He did not come to create social change or to subvert the institutionalized church. He came to lay down his life to win the world. While it is true that Jesus accepts everyone, he does that on the basis of their justification. They believe and they are counted as righteous in God's sight. That's a far cry from simply accepting everyone, no matter how they choose to live their lives. Again, the point must be made; Jesus preached a great deal of law—because the new life still has to conform to God's standards of right and wrong.[97]

The Challenge of Universalism. A more direct assault on the gospel is found in universalism. In essence, this philosophy says that all roads lead to God. The Christian conception of God is therefore just a human way of thinking about God who is far beyond our understanding. The Hindu gods, the Muslim god, the spirits, and animistic gods of tribes out in the jungle have just as valid a relationship with God as Christians do. Therefore, people don't really need the gospel. They need the relationship with God that works for them. In the

---

[94] Luke 19:1-10.
[95] Luke 19:9-10.
[96] John 12:32 and 33.
[97] Romans 3:21-26.

United States this has led to the phenomenon of "spiritual but not religious." This is the fastest growing self-designation of religious orientation in America today. It makes God totally subjective. He's whatever the individual wants him to be.

The apologist needs to stake the claim for the exclusivity of Christianity. God simply does not allow the Humanistic point of view. Again and again, God says, "I alone am God and there is no other."[98] We did not invent the claim that the Triune God is the one true God. That's God's own claim. Christianity must not back away from that claim. As apologists, we need to assert it within the context of Christ as the true Savior. Jesus said, "No one comes to the Father except through me."[99] The only answer to this kind of unbelief is to lead people to the Father through the Son.

A different type of attack which is sometimes brought against the gospel is that it undercuts the Christian life. If religion doesn't make demands and if the church just forgives and lets people off, they are encouraging sinful behavior. This is not a new attack. It was used already in Luther's lifetime. Nor did it start then either. Paul said in Romans, "And why not say, just as some people slanderously claim we say, 'Let us do what is evil so that good may come'? Their condemnation is deserved!"[100] From the very beginning of the New Testament church's outreach to the world, people have used this attack.

Moreover, those who raise this argument do have a point. That is what makes this such a powerful attack. Sinners *do* often use forgiveness like a get-out-of-jail-free card. They do often use it as a license to sin and to not think about how serious sin really is. This kind of misuse of the gospel is frequent among lapsed Christians, and some unbelievers pick up on it as a line of argument against the gospel message. But St. Paul already dismissed that as blasphemy. When we confront those attacks, we need to make the point that true Christianity encourages a real Christian life. The gospel works not just to

---

98 For example, [Moses said,] "You were shown these things so that you would know that the LORD is God; there is no other besides him.... Today, recognize and keep in mind that the LORD is God in heaven above and on earth below; there is no other." (Deuteronomy 4:35, 39) / "I am the LORD, and there is no other; there is no God but me. I will strengthen you, though you do not know me, so that all may know from the rising of the sun to its setting that there is no one but me. I am the LORD, and there is no other. I form light and create darkness, I make success and create disaster; I am the LORD, who does all these things." (Isaiah 45:5-7) / [Peter wrote,] "There is salvation in no one else, for there is no other name under heaven given to people by which we must be saved." (Acts 4:12).

99 John 14:6.

100 Romans 3:8.

change behavior, but to change hearts. While some people twist it into something else, that doesn't mean the message itself is invalid. As always, the best way to demonstrate this is to get back to why we need Jesus, and then let the Holy Spirit do his work.

Summary

God reveals himself as more than just the Creator of the universe who is high above us and distant from life as we know it. He reveals himself as the God who loves us and saves—the Holy Trinity: the Father, Son, and Holy Spirit. To rescue us, the Second Person of the Trinity took on flesh and lived and died and rose again.

The law and the gospel are the two chief teachings of Scripture. The only way to understand what God says is by understanding what each of these teachings means and how they come together at the cross of Christ. Because that's true, we face attacks on three lines: the denial of the law, the denial of the gospel or an attack on how they fit together. The apologist needs to understand what God teaches about these things and be prepared to lead the skeptic to Christ.

8

Challenges from Archaeology and Historical Research

Christianity takes place in history. Events are dated throughout the Bible. Historical figures are referenced. Events take place in real geographical locations and reflect real cultural settings. The study of those times and societies inevitably impacts our understanding of those events and the context in which they took place.

This approach is different from many religions (like Shinto, Hinduism, various tribal and animistic religions) that set their great events in a mythical or legendary past. There is no real effort to reconstruct that time period. Conversely, there are other religions (like Islam and Buddhism) that claim specific historical figures as their founders and which engage in historical examination of those founders and of the events those religions emphasize. Christianity is deeply focused on its historical claims. They are an essential part of the message of the gospel, and that has led to extensive examination and debate about the historical background of Christianity.

Christians should welcome these examinations. Yet as apologists, we must be aware that those disciplines which study the past are a double-edged sword. At times, they provide useful insights that help us understand the Bible's account. However, today no academic discipline is dominated by Christians. In both history and archaeology, there are many scholars who are overtly hostile to Christianity and who consistently interpret the evidence that has come down to us in a way that seems calculated to attack the historic basis of Christianity. Certainly, since these are academic fields, there is a process to challenge misleading information. Yet, because the media often reports the attacks and fails to report the corrections, many people absorb these arguments in an uncritical way. The apologist must be prepared to deal with this situation.

History

In its simplest form, history is the study of the past. Sadly, almost no academic discipline adheres to the simplest definition. In fact, there is quite a philosophical debate about "what is history?" Thankfully, we can forego that discussion here. However, that doesn't mean we can just use the simple definition. History is practiced today with great rigor and is subject to the same kinds of academic challenge processes that exist in the sciences. That is sometimes called "academic history." Yet, most historians don't consider themselves to be scientists in the way that archaeologists do. If anything, they consider themselves to be social scientists.

History is actually one of the oldest disciplines of study. It was practiced in ancient times. Yet, ancient historians like Herodotus or Josephus were not doing research to learn what had happened in the past or why. They were primarily writers who chose history as their topic because it was interesting to many people. The best ancient historians did do research. In fact, we know of a number of them who traveled to different places, interviewed people and read all that was available on specific topics. Herodotus, for example, is often viewed as one of the first writers to attempt a critical history; he gives more than one version of an event and then identifies the one he thinks is correct and why. This was the seed of academic history. In the end, however, most ancient historians were like the majority of history writers whose books we find in modern bookstores. Most of them are not historians by training. They're journalists or writers. Their purpose is to entertain. That's not a bad thing. There are certainly far worse things a person could read or do for entertainment than read history. Yet, it does affect what a person writes and why. Jodi Magness, an archaeologist, summarized the difference between history and archaeology:

> "History is the study of the past based on information provided by written documents. In other words, although both archaeologists and historians study the past, they use different methods or sources to obtain their information. Archaeol-

ogists learn about the past through the study of the material remains left behind by humans, whereas historians study written records (texts). These sources of information often provide different (although not necessarily mutually exclusive or conflicting) pictures of the past."[1]

Historians often use an interdisciplinary approach to reach conclusions—that is, they often use the conclusions of other disciplines, such as archaeology, anthropology, or even chemistry or astronomy. For example, in 2018, the *Journal of Archaeological Science* reported on the chemical analysis of beer cups in the Khani Masi excavation in northern Iraq.[2] Historians working with ancient Mesopotamian texts have found clear references to beer (even pictorial representations of people drinking beer), but the archaeological evidence for beer up to this point has been quite rare. Archaeologists conducted complex chemical analyses of various types of ceramic vessels and identified evidence that they had held beer. This shed light both on the usage of certain kinds of ceramic vessels and on some of the cultural implications. Thus, history established a well-accepted fact based on textual evidence but used archaeological and chemical evidence to support and elaborate that knowledge.

Yet, as the example also shows, historians' primary resources are records—texts—that can be analyzed. So they put great emphasis on *primary sources*—records that come directly from what they're studying. A primary source might be the annals that many kings had recorded on a day-to-day basis, or an ancient law code, or records of sales and transactions or a description of an event in a letter. The closer the writer was in time to an event, the more weight historians give his or her account. Eyewitness testimony is of greater value than second-hand testimony which is of greater value than rumors or general reports that were floating around.

Nevertheless, a historian's work is more than just finding ancient texts. Those texts have to be evaluated, so historians conduct a critical analysis of any text they use. They ask questions such as: when and where was this document produced? By whom? What was its source? What was its original form?

---

1 Jodi Magness, *The Archaeology of Qumran and the Dead Sea Scrolls* (Wm. B. Eerdmans Publishing Company, Grand Rapids, 2002) 4-5.

2 E Perruchini, C Glatz, MM Hald, J Casana, JL Toney, "Revealing invisible brews: a new approach to the chemical identification of ancient beer," *Journal of Archaeological Science* (online, June 27, 2018).

How credible is the author? They often compare contradictory sources to try to find hints of bias or error. They have principles for determining reliability and for examining eyewitness evidence. Perhaps the most important criterion they use is sometimes expressed with the Latin expression *Cui bono?*—"for whose benefit?" Whom does the text make look good and whom does it make look bad? Who would have sponsored the production and the hand-copying of such a text?

What does all that mean for the apologist? We are dealing with ancient history. Jesus, the apostles and all the Old Testament prophets and kings lived in a world that no longer exists. The British novelist L.P. Hartley once said, "The past is a foreign country; they do things differently there."[3] Historians try to understand that past and translate it for the present. But the farther into antiquity one goes, the fewer the sources there are to work with, due to decay caused both by natural processes and ongoing human intervention. For instance, in 2010, the city archive of Cologne, Germany, collapsed due to nearby subway construction. Millions of pages of original sources were damaged and some were lost forever. That same year in Augsburg, Germany, an infestation of bread beetles was discovered to be consuming their archive. These archives held records that were centuries closer to us than anything from the biblical world.[4]

What is left of ancient Roman and Greek writings are often only mere fragments. There are many works that we know existed, but we don't have a page remaining to read. There are many works that are quoted or summarized for us in other works or translated (in whole or in part and immediately the question arises as to how well) but the original is gone. Roman tax records for Bethlehem simply don't exist. Whatever archive contained Pontius Pilate's death sentence for Jesus has disappeared long ago. When studying the world of the Old Testament, the situation is far worse. Israel has been a battlefield among competing cultures and superpowers for millennia. All that makes historical study much harder to do.

There is a certain accidental quality to what has survived from the past. This necessitates another layer of analysis and another set of questions which are very important for an apologist. What does the absence of records or evi-

---

3 LP Hartley, *The Go-Between* (Hamish Hamilton Limited, London, 1953).

4 B. Ann Tlusty, *Augsburg During the Reformation Era: An Anthology of Sources* (Hackett Publishing Company, Indianapolis, 2012).

dence really mean? One of the richest fields for modern New Testament research consists of Egyptian papyri.[5] The largest group of these fragments comes from a rubbish heap in Oxyrhynchus, where there are thousands of papyri fragments from many different kinds of ancient documents. The reason they were preserved is the climate. The Egyptian desert is hot and dry, so it prevented decay. It would be easy to conclude that Egypt had more records than other places in the Roman Empire. Yet, that would be an illogical conclusion. What information has been lost from the record in Egypt and in other parts of the Roman Empire? It is difficult to know. What records of the twenty-first century church will exist 500 years from now? What conclusions will future historians draw from them? It's easy to see how fragmentary evidence can lead to false conclusions.

Those who study the history which the Bible records do extensively use the sources that exist. This leads to the most contentious issue when it comes to history: what is the role of the Bible as a historical record? Christians rightly see the Bible as *the* historical record. We hold that it is inerrant even when it speaks of history and geography. Skeptics disagree. At best, they consider the Bible to be one source among many. There certainly are historians who use the biblical account in a respectful way. Nevertheless, because they don't approach it with the presuppositions of faith, they do not—indeed, they cannot—regard it as the final say on anything. Even when it is the only source for a given event, they will subject it to the kinds of analysis that they would apply to any other historical document. They will then construct a hypothesis about what really happened. When colleagues evaluate that hypothesis, they will attack or defend it based on the accepted principles of their discipline, not on whether God's Word takes their every thought captive.[6]

A final comment is perhaps in order about the difference between academic history and church history. Many academic historians (even those whose subject is church history) will sniff at "denominational histories". They tend to view the writers of those works as less interested in history than in glorifying a tradition or a denomination. Certainly, they have a point. It's far too common and too easy for histories of denominations and even histories of the Christian church to become uncritical justifications, or worse, glorifications

---

[5] Papyri are documents written on papyrus, which can be thought of as an early form of paper. Among the thousands of papyrus documents found so far in Egypt, as of 2018, 139 were copies of some portion of the New Testament.

[6] 2 Corinthians 10:5.

of the people in the institution. Still, there is also a great difference between academic history and legitimate church history as a discipline. Church history is really historical theology. It is the attempt to trace the finger of God as he fulfills his promises across the centuries. Because we live in this sinful world, the identification will always be halting and tentative. We will always have questions as to why the God of grace allows disasters to strike his people. We will want to use the tools of academic history when appropriate, to see sin and grace as clearly as possible. But the apologist needs to know the difference between the two when answering the challenges raised by history.

Archaeology

For a Christian, perhaps no area of scholarship is more subject to expectation, debate and even disappointment than archaeology. It stands to reason that if Moses and Solomon and Jesus lived, we should find evidence in the archaeological record. To Christians, this seems like it should be an opportunity to prove what God's Word says is true. But sadly, for a number of different reasons, it doesn't often work out that way. Some of those reasons have to do with what is left in the ground for us to find. Some have to do with what archaeology is and is not, and how it works. In this section, we want to give a thumbnail sketch of what archaeology is and how it helps but also hinders the Christian's work of apologetics. Later in the chapter, we will briefly mention some of the more famous case studies in archaeology and history. The reader should be aware that whole books have been written about everything which we will mention here. Our main purpose is to give some guidance as to how to use and how not to use archaeology in our task of defending the faith.

In Chapter 1, three broad types of science were discussed. Hard sciences, like physics and chemistry, are disciplines where the scientist can isolate and/or control the variables and conduct experiments. Soft sciences, which include fields like sociology and many fields related to medicine and biology, are disciplines in which experiments can be conducted, but the scientist cannot control all the variables, so some level of statistical probability is necessary to relate results to meaningful conclusions. Observational sciences are those disciplines like astronomy or geology where the primary source of information is the study of phenomena that the scientist happens to encounter. The encounters are usually the result of deliberate planning and exploration, and some limited experimentation may be possible. But for the most part, the scientist turns his telescope to the heavens or digs into the earth and finds what he or she finds. The data is recorded and analyzed and compared to other known data, and models are constructed to explain what has been observed. Archaeology is an observational science.

The word *archaeology* comes from a Greek expression that means "the study of ancient things". As a science, it's the discovery and study of the material remains of past cultures. It focuses primarily on physical objects often called *artifacts.* Because many artifacts have writing on them, (such as the Dead Sea Scrolls or ancient inscriptions on statues or the notes jotted on ostraca—see below) there is an obvious crossover to history. The term archaeology usually refers to a method of studying the remains of ancient cultures, but it can also be used to refer to the data and interpretations that come from that method.[7]

Archaeology is extremely limited by what can be found. Archaeologists often cite "the two percent rule": they excavate two percent of the area of two percent of the known sites and find two percent of what was once there.[8] From that fragmentary evidence, conclusions have to be drawn. Why is the evidence so fragmentary? The most obvious reason is the passage of time. Erosion, decomposition, new generations of people living in the same place (and in the process changing the environment) all destroy some of what was once there. The further into the past we look, the greater the destruction. Certain kinds of artifacts are simply very hard to preserve. For example, textiles rot or are eaten by insects. Clay pots break. Dyes made from plant or animal products bleach out in sunlight.

Another reason why so much is lost to us is that ancient peoples almost never left valuable things lying around for future generations to discover. If it was still valuable, people took it with them if they could. There are exceptions, such as coin hoards that were buried for safekeeping but never recovered. Sometimes things were buried when a building burned or was abandoned suddenly, like the artifacts from Pompeii, which were buried by a volcanic eruption or like those found in cities that were attacked and destroyed. Perhaps the most famous kind of exception consists of burial treasures, such

---

[7] John Brug, *Digging for Insights: Using Archaeology to Study the Bible* (Northwestern Publishing House, Milwaukee, 2016), 7-8.

[8] Brug, ibid., 9.

as those found in King Tut's tomb. However, intact burial hoards are the exception, rather than the rule. Almost all known burial sites were plundered thousands of years ago. To date, no burial site has been found in Israel that contains a hoard of treasure.

Even with all that being said, there is still presumably a rich trove of archaeological material to be discovered in Israel and throughout the Mediterranean world. In cities like Rome and Jerusalem, every time a new foundation is dug, the possibility exists that the workers will discover something apparently ancient and work will have to stop while an archaeological assessment is performed. If the discovery is significant, it could lead to an extensive excavation. There is no evidence that this process of accidental discovery is going to stop in the foreseeable future.

Even in known and famous sites, such as Pompeii, the modern archaeological community is determined *not* to excavate the entire site. They want to leave discoveries for the future, because they believe that future archaeologists will be working with better tools and techniques and with a fuller understanding of the past. That means that they may well see something very different in a site and a set of artifacts from archaeologists do today.

There are other, less idealistic reasons that sites go unexcavated. Archaeology is expensive and time-consuming. Unless some wealthy person or some funding organization sponsors a dig, hopefully for several years, a site won't be excavated. Some sites, like the Temple Mount in Jerusalem have a political or cultural importance that makes excavation impossible. Sometimes, war or social upheaval makes it difficult to conduct a scientific excavation and survey.

When a dig is undertaken, what do archaeologists find? Rarely do they find the kind of rich and valuable pieces that Indiana Jones movies lead people to think are found. In Israel, the most common thing they find is pottery shards—broken fragments of pottery. Pottery was the packaging of the ancient world. Just as our landfills are filled with plastic wrap and cardboard boxes, ancient sites are filled with broken pottery. Some shards were used as notepads (sticky notes wouldn't be invented for thousands of years). These are called *ostraca* (singular *ostracon*), and they are especially valuable. But many other kinds of things are also found—often broken or fragmentary, often everyday things. Still, these artifacts tell us a great deal about the site, such as what it was used for and when it was in use.

Dating of finds is an incredibly important and technical question. In Israel, many sites were used over hundreds or even thousands of years. When artifacts are found, archaeologists engage in a great deal of analysis to try to date when the items got there. Sometimes, the dating can be fairly exact. Sometimes, archaeologists will say something like, "Sometime in the eighth or ninth century," which may seem to us a little like saying, "Sometime between the American Revolution and World War II." Yet, when one is dealing with thousands of years of history, sometimes that's as close as it is possible to get.

There still remains the critical question of what an artifact means. Someone once said, "What archaeology yields is not facts, but artifacts—which then have to be interpreted."[9] Much of that interpretation depends on when and how the artifacts are found. Archaeologists talk about seeing an artifact *in situ* (Latin for "in its place"). Modern archaeology is a slow, painstaking process of carefully locating, uncovering, and documenting artifacts as they are found. When a dig is finished, a final report is supposed to be issued that details everything that was found, and under what circumstances *in situ.* Sometimes, it can take years for that final report to be released. Since only the people who actually worked on the dig can be eyewitnesses to the discovery of any artifact, the final report is what all subsequent scientists must use to evaluate the setting of an artifact. Of course, the artifact itself can still be studied. Yet, relating it to what was around it is the key to a complete analysis of what it does or doesn't tell us about the people who once possessed it.[10]

Modern archaeology encounters a difficult problem exactly at this point: there are many artifacts in museums and collections all over the world—and on the antiquities market—that cannot be studied *in situ* and that will never have a final report published. Archaeologists call the chain of possession of an artifact its *provenance.* Careful documentation of the provenance of an

---

9 Michael Wise, Martin Abegg, Jr. and Edward Cook, *The Dead Sea Scrolls: A New Translation* (HarperCollins, New York, 1996).

10 Some people like to point out that the inability of other scientists to exactly duplicate the discovery process means there is no way to prevent investigator bias from influencing what appears in the report of the dig. Archaeologists try to control for this by the documentation of the finding process, which includes visual representations (either photos or drawings) of artifacts as they were found, the soil as it appeared, and even diagrams with three dimensional spatial references that cover each *locus* or specific location/feature within a dig site. Yet, it is still true that archaeology is finally a process of controlled destruction of a site. Once excavated, it can never be re-excavated. This is particularly a problem with sites excavated when archaeology was much more of an Indiana Jones style treasure hunt than the careful scientific discipline it is today.

artifact from its original discovery to its current ownership and resting place is extremely important for analyzing what it means.

There are at least two challenges to examining the provenance of an artifact. First, a huge number of artifacts in museums and collections all over the world were excavated before archaeology had developed into a science. It used to be much more like a treasure hunt sponsored by wealthy Europeans and Americans who wanted the best and most impressive pieces for their museums or private collections. This approach led to very limited documentation of excavations and to the destruction or discarding of artifacts which at the time didn't seem to be valuable, but which today would be considered extremely important for doing a proper analysis. It also often left sites contaminated and confused, so that modern archaeologists who return to them have difficulty determining how the original excavations changed them.

A second problem is the difficulty in policing the modern antiquities market. As is often the case, the laws and treaties that govern what is legal to sell can be manipulated by unscrupulous and profit-oriented marketers. Poor people living on top of ancient sites might care a great deal more about how much money they can get for an artifact than about preserving the knowledge that would come from a careful examination of an undisturbed site. This has sometimes led to fakes and to false provenances. Sometimes, a real artifact has a fictionalized provenance to protect its illegal origin. Sometimes, clever people pass off fake artifacts as genuine. Even very knowledgeable people are taken in, at times, by these deceptions.

Further, what scientists are interested in today is different from it was when Howard Carter opened King Tut's tomb in 1922. At that time, history, archaeology and anthropology were very focused on the study of "great men," i.e., kings, nobles, military and political leaders. Today, there is much greater interest in the lives of ordinary people in all these disciplines. This contributes to a shift in the focus of what archaeologists want to study.

In recent decades, archaeology has begun to confront a set of moral and cultural concerns that didn't trouble early treasure hunters. The descendants of ancient peoples have begun to challenge the right of modern scientists to disturb the graves of their ancestors. Hand in hand with this has come a push to return artifacts to the nations from which they came. This has proven to be a thorny issue for artifacts that have belonged to museums in the West for generations. It has also affected almost all new efforts to excavate ancient sites. In Israel, any artifact that comes from any excavation done after 1978 is automatically the property of the state of Israel.

A final word of caution is in order. Archaeological digs are going on all the time. Reports are being tabulated and written. There is such a lag time between each step that anything written or published about an issue in archaeology can be obsolete by the time it appears in print.

The Purpose of History in the Bible

It is very common to read of a Jewish tradition of writing history that begins with Moses and extends through Josephus and into the modern world. That observation can lend itself to a misunderstanding of the many historical writings in the Bible, especially in the Old Testament. None of them was written as a purely historical document. None was written to satisfy academic curiosity about how the world as we know it came to be. It that sense, the authors were not writing history the way that many authors do today.

What were they doing? They were writing under the inspiration of the Holy Spirit to give us a record of man's sin and God's grace. In the book of Deuteronomy, Moses retells the history of his people from the time they left Mt. Sinai until they were camped in the Plains of Moab about to enter the Promised Land. Now, everyone over forty years old had lived through those years in the desert (even if they were children then). But Moses retold the story to make a point about God's grace and forgiveness in the face of their rebellion. In truth, all the historical accounts in the Bible are selective retellings of some of the things that happened to some of the people of God so that the whole world could see the grace of God who sent Jesus to save us. Because God was so selective about what he recorded—indeed because he omitted so much detail that was obvious to ancient readers—historical research and archaeology can be very useful tools in expanding our understanding of specific biblical issues and incidents.

However, history and archaeology can be seriously misused. The most basic problem that they can pose is giving the impression that we cannot understand the Bible without them. Someone who knows almost nothing about the ancient world can still understand the basic truth of God's grace and man's sin. That shines through clearly even if specific actions by ancient prophets and kings seem to be totally nonsensical due to the reader's not having the cultural knowledge to understand why they did the things they did. Any use of history or archaeology that would call this basic message into question should be treated with extreme skepticism. The basic information that an artifact or an ancient text communicates may be real, but we must not allow an interpretation to lead us away from the clear words of the Scriptures.

There is a related and very common issue that is especially true with archaeology but can also apply to historical research: the research is often used to attempt to prove someone's pet theory or belief. Likewise, it is often misused to disprove something that a specific person doesn't like. Even if the theory being supported is true or the idea being attacked is false, if the archaeological or historical evidence does not really demonstrate what the writer or researcher wants it to, that person is misusing that evidence. This is an example of the fallacy of confirmation bias.

In the modern world, academic history and archaeology have been used to challenge a great deal of what the Bible says. Time and space don't allow us to go through all the different challenges to the historical accuracy of the Bible's accounts. We can perhaps divide them into three broad categories. One group is events that are denied because they are miracles (see Chapter 6). We need to make a distinction here between something someone might say in an argument with us as we share the gospel with them and what a serious historian would put into print. The skeptic who is arguing might blatantly deny miracles as pure nonsense injected into the Bible. That would be rare for a serious historian or archaeologist to do. More likely, they would argue that the worldview of the biblical authors included a belief that God or the gods directly involved themselves in human affairs, sometimes even causing things to happen that are scientifically impossible. Our worldview no longer allows for such beliefs. Of course, they have denied the miracles when they say these things. They point to secular sources that record the same event (such as the destruction of Sennacherib's army in 2 Kings 19) and deny that there was a true miracle. They may also point out that some miracles in the Bible are not recorded anywhere else, such as Nebuchadnezzar's madness in Daniel 4.

A second group involves issues of dating or of geographical or genealogical information. Dates or events or people don't seem to match what has come down to us through non-biblical documents. Examples of this would include challenging the statement that Darius the son of Ahasuerus was ruling in

Daniel 9.[11] (Cyrus would have been ruling the Persian Empire and no "Darius the Mede" is known to us from history.) Another example is the statement that Belshazzar was Nebuchadnezzar's son in Daniel 5. (He was really his grandson.)[12]

The third group consists of words and actions of historical figures that are recorded only in the Bible. This includes such things as proclamations made by heathen kings that recognize the true God and interactions with (even marriages to) Old and New Testament figures. Historians doubt or deny these kinds of events. Why? Sometimes they rely on an *argument from silence* which in classical logic is a fallacy and, therefore, proves nothing. In the humanities, the situation is a little more complicated. An author's silence on a topic can be significant, if it would be reasonable to expect him to comment on it. But that doesn't mean it didn't happen. Absence of evidence is not evidence of absence.

Some skeptics may express the belief that what is recorded is simply too fantastic to have really happened. At times, they seem to consistently assume that other sources are more accurate than the Bible. Sometimes they fail to take into account the insights that careful study of the biblical accounts in their original languages provides (for instance, in Daniel 5, "father" and "son" are probably being used in the wider sense of an ancestor and descendant, which Aramaic permits, but which is less common in modern English).

In this regard, history shows its relationship to other social sciences, especially anthropology, which is more concerned with what the worldviews of a society or group of people tell us about them, than about whether these worldviews are true. As believers, we trust in the Word of God even when we cannot demonstrate that every claim it makes is true. As apologists, we need to ask the skeptic to articulate why these things cannot be true. We dealt with objections to miracles in Chapter 6. Objections to the historicity of the Bible can be answered at least in part by pointing out the antiquity of the Bible's own account. That is, the writers of the biblical text were much closer to the

---

11 "In the first year of Darius, the son of Ahasuerus, a Mede by birth, who was made king over the Chaldean kingdom." (Daniel 9:1).

12 "King Belshazzar held a great feast for a thousand of his nobles and drank wine in their presence. Under the influence of the wine, Belshazzar gave orders to bring in the gold and silver vessels that his predecessor Nebuchadnezzar had taken from the temple in Jerusalem, so that the king and his nobles, wives, and concubines could drink from them." (Daniel 5:1-2).

events than we are. In many cases, their testimony is the closest surviving record of an event. To simply dismiss the biblical account in favor of non-biblical sources because they are non-biblical is not in keeping with principles of academic history. The apologist should also always remember that the historical accounts in the Bible have a clear purpose and that determines what they record and what they don't. Again, recognizing the purpose of an account is part of modern historical research, and we shouldn't be afraid to use that principle. In many cases, the issues skeptics raise have reasonable explanations, and the more we study God's Word, the more prepared we will be to answer those objections.

Now, this does not mean that we can always answer every objection raised by historical or archaeological research. Sometimes, we don't know enough about the ancient world to give a definitive answer to every objection. For example, a very knowledgeable critic might know that up to this point, the archaeological evidence that the conquest of the land of Canaan occurred in the way the Bible describes it is mixed at best. That does not mean that archaeology disproves the biblical account. But it does present issues (and interpretations of issues) that are difficult to explain, given our current level of knowledge. For the believer's personal faith, it is important to remember that faith is being certain of things we do not see.[13] So we read the Bible with the presupposition that God is speaking the truth.

From an apologetic perspective, we should be firm enough in our faith to admit when we don't have answers. But we also need to be sure that we know the difference between data and interpretations, as well as the difference between evidence that presents difficulties and evidence that positively disproves something. This is where God's gift of logic comes in, and we should understand how logic works and demand that critics be rigorous and honest in evaluating the evidence they present. Just as it is wrong to force evidence to demonstrate what God's Word says, it's also wrong to force it to deny God's Word. Artifacts always have to be interpreted. Historical sources must be subjected to rigorous analysis. Underlying biases, agendas and assumptions cannot be allowed to make legitimate difficulties into clear proof that God's Word is false.

---

13 Hebrews 11:1

Is There Such a Thing as Biblical Archaeology?

Biblical archaeology is actually an ancient undertaking. The Empress Helena (who died AD 330), the mother of Constantine, traveled to the holy land from AD 326 to 328 to search for relics and to identify famous biblical sites. In the early years of the discipline, many archaeologists working in Israel assumed that they were uncovering artifacts that related to the biblical narrative.

Today the situation is far more complex. Many Christian seminaries and colleges continue to sponsor archaeological digs. They obviously hope to find evidence that they can legitimately tie back to the biblical narrative. Many other people, however, are not working with that expectation. In fact, most archaeologists today regard the Scriptures as a heavily theologized interpretation of reality rather than as a reliable guide to persons who really lived or to events that really happened. Some of them still consider that they contain at least a vague outline of Old Testament history, or they consider them to be one source of information among many—a source that must be carefully analyzed to determine how useful or truthful it is. On the other hand, many disregard most of what the Bible says.

In 2015, the Biblical Archaeological Society posted an interview between the society's founder Hershel Shanks and Duke University archaeologists Eric and Carol Meyers. They observed that when the society's periodical *Biblical Archaeological Review* was begun in 1975, the field was dominated by men and women who thought of themselves as *biblical* archaeologists (even though many of them did not believe in inspiration). Since then, a shift has taken place with many archaeologists today arguing that there is no such thing as "biblical archaeology." Rather there is "Syro-Palestinian archaeology". The reason for this is a perceived misuse of the Bible and of the archaeological evidence. In the view of people who hold this position, it is a mistake to read the Bible, pick a spot based on a narrative, dig and then claim, "See! We found what the Bible was talking about!" Shanks and the Meyers' observed that the pendulum seems to have swung back a little bit. But even they clearly thought there was merit to the concern.[14] The debate goes on. In 1998, the American Schools of Oriental Research changed the name of their periodical from *Biblical Archaeologist* (a title it had used since 1938) to *Near East-*

14 Hershel Shanks, "Biblical Archaeology: Whither and Whence," *Biblical Archaeology Review 41:2* (online, March/April, 2005).

ern Archaeology at least in part to separate itself from association with the view that the Bible is authoritative or inspired.[15]

Today, the archaeological community views much of the Bible with skepticism. King Solomon is generally regarded as a myth. The existence of King David is difficult to deny, since the term "house of David" has been found on a ninth century stele at Tel Dan. But so far, archaeology has not produced direct evidence of King Solomon's existence.[16] In 2010, Eilat Mazar excavated a wall that she dated to the tenth century BC and argued "We don't have many kings during the tenth century that could have built such a structure, basically just David and Solomon."[17] But other scholars immediately challenged that identification. The debate has not been resolved.

A further issue which is part of this question is the problem of identifying a biblical site. Archaeologists don't dig up signs that say, "Welcome to Ai, population 2387." Many Christians assume that we can simply read the Bible, and it will tell us where a city was. This, however, is rarely the case. When a site is excavated, there can be an intense debate about whether it is an Israelite or a Canaanite site. Does the presence or absence of things like pig bones answer that question for us? If the site was inhabited for a long time, were all the layers Israelite or not? There is often a very long chain of arguments from the artifact to the conclusion. Those scholars who want to move away from "biblical archaeology" often have real concerns about forcing evidence into a theological perspective. We apologists would be wise to be very careful that we understand the argumentation before we use specific sites to "prove" the biblical narrative.

---

15 Shanks, ibid.

16 A stele (also spelled stela) is an upright stone or column, usually with a commemorative inscription or a carved picture. The Tel Dan stele was erected in Galilee near the Golan Heights by an Aramean (Syrian) king, probably Hazael, to commemorate a victory over Israel and Judah in battle. Its fragments were discovered in 1993 and 1994. This stele has been called "the first historical evidence of King David." It recounts the victory of the Arameans over two enemies, "the king of the house of David" and "the king of Israel." It does not mention King David specifically (since he would have been dead for almost 200 years when it was engraved). It is also broken with pieces missing. But it is part of a growing body of archaeological evidence that challenges the notion that David, at least, was legendary.

17 Mati Milstein, "King Solomon's Wall Found—Proof of Bible Tale?", *National Geographic News* (online, February 27, 2010).

The Role of the Media

A Lutheran young man found himself in a situation where he was interacting on a daily basis with unbelievers. As time went on, he witnessed to his faith more and more. Some of the people he dealt with regularly began to engage with him and even debate with him, in much the way the authors of this book envision our members talking to people who don't believe and who want to argue against the gospel. One day, one of these friends walked up to the Lutheran with a big smile on his face and a news article in his hand. He said, "See! They found Jesus' coffin!" He was smiling because he was a Muslim, and he thought he had proof that the central claim of Christianity has to be false. The news article in his hand dealt with an *ossuary*—a box used to collect and store bones. This particular ossuary has caused an enormous amount of ink to be spilled, and we will consider it in a little more detail later in this chapter when we look at a few famous archaeological case studies. But our interest here is how the media uses archaeology and how unprofitable their use is, both for people who want to defend God's Word and even for those who want to attack it.

The news business in the modern world is a time-sensitive occupation. When a disaster strikes or something dramatic happens, journalists have a very limited amount of time to collect and verify information, compose an article or broadcast and put it online, on the air or in print. This was a problem in the 1950s and 60s when the main reason to race something into print was the danger of being "scooped" by another news organization. Today, the problem is magnified many times over by the "on-demand" nature of our society. Content has to be available instantaneously. There simply isn't time for careful research. Given some examples of what is said about archaeology and the Bible in the media, apparently, there often isn't even time to digest and understand the information that is available.

The media is a for-profit industry. The money comes in through advertising. The number of papers sold, the number of people who watch or listen, or the number of "hits" on a website determine how much businesses are willing to pay to advertise on a specific platform. The end result is that quite often headlines are misleading. They are designed to draw readers/viewers in. Sometimes, reporters feel a certain pressure to make their product engaging or salacious or controversial because those things tend to get more "hits." The situation is made even more complicated by the current trend of people to cherry-pick their news feeds so that they never encounter a perspective that disagrees with their own.

Yet, even when journalists are doing their best to give a clear and accurate explanation of what an archaeological discovery is and what it means, they have one more problem that really applies to almost everything in apologetics: the difficulty of summation. News articles need to be short and to the point. Complex information needs to be simplified. But whenever something is simplified, details must be omitted—sometimes very important details. When that happens, the people reading or listening to the abridged account will be tempted to supply information that they think was left out so as to make the material feel complete or so that it makes sense in their minds (see memory formation in Chapter 9). Sometimes, what they assume is just plain false. The ability to summarize without creating false impressions is a real art. The person who can do it well is a master communicator. Sadly, we live in a world full of average communicators.

A classic example of these difficulties coming together was the reporting that took place on 9/11. Those who were watching the news will remember the attempts by reporters all day long to get a handle on how many casualties the attacks on the World Trade Center had generated. As the day went on, numbers like 10,000 and even 20,000 were mentioned. Of course, the truth is that just under 3,000 people died that day. Where did the media get their numbers? Various people were making their best guess as the day went on. The news was coming so fast and furiously that there was very little time or ability to check the numbers or to consult with people who might have said those numbers were high. People wanted a number immediately, so the media reported the numbers they had. Moreover, they did something that the media often does. They generally said, "The total number of casualties could be as high as 20,000." Did they say that there were 20,000 casualties? No, in actual fact they didn't. They said that there could be that many. Still, is that what most people heard? Or did they lock on to the number 20,000 and accept it for days until a new and better estimate was released?

When it comes to archaeology, the media will often do something similar. "Scientists may have found Jesus' coffin!" Does that say they did? Technically, no. But does it leave the impression that they did? Will people walk around saying, "They found Jesus' coffin!"? Almost certainly.

Like most disciplines, archaeology has breakthrough moments that change our understanding of the past. The media loves "breaking news" so reporting such a discovery is not surprising. Yet, when it comes to biblical archaeology, any claim that something new and revolutionary has been discovered should be viewed with caution. It is possible—the Dead Sea Scrolls were certainly a revolutionary discovery. Still, most archaeological discoveries that the media reports as "breaking news" were actually known about by archaeologists for many years before the media "discovered" them. Careful reading and cross checking will usually reveal when this is the case.

Because there are so many nominal Christians in the United States and because Christianity has had such an enormous impact on our culture, stories that seem to shake the foundations of the faith, or even that seem to provide confirmation of our faith, will attract media attention. That isn't going to change in the near future. However, when it comes to archaeology—or any other complex issue in apologetics—the news media cannot be our first source. Not only do reporters not have any more training in scientific disciplines than the average person does, they have a vested interest in putting together a piece that will get attention. Fortunately, in the modern age, quite often more serious and detailed discussions of the issues raised by reporters trying breathlessly to beat each other to the punch are available. We need to take the time to research them.

Testimonies and Travails of History and Archaeology

There are certainly times when archaeology and history can be used profitably by students of the Bible. The New Testament was written almost 2,000 years ago. The last book of the Old Testament was written 2,400 years ago. The gap between our culture and the cultures to which the Bible originally spoke is enormous. There have been many instances of historical texts and archaeology illuminating the past. Ancient records can give us information that the Bible omits. For example, King Ahab gets major treatment in 1 Kings 16 to 22, while his father Omri gets only eight verses (16:21-28). Yet Assyrian records and the Mesha inscription[18] in Jordan show us that Omri was a dynam-

[18] The Mesha Stele, also known as the Moabite Stone, is a black, basalt monument with an inscription by King Mesha of Moab (erected around 850 BC). It was discovered in Dhiban (biblical Dibon), Jordan in 1868. It was damaged and reconstructed. It is currently at the Louvre in Paris.

ic and powerful ruler, while his son Ahab is hardly mentioned. The archaeological excavations of Omri's palaces at Tirzah, Samaria and Jezreel give further evidence of the wealth and power of his reign.[19] Jesus' parables often reference farming techniques. Biblical accounts frequently picture people undertaking everyday activities in work and trade and even relaxation. Archaeology can often give us a better idea of how these activities were actually carried out by excavating ordinary Israelite homes, finding their tools and even studying their graves. Historical texts can sometimes give us additional details on how the ancients lived. These sources tell us things that were obvious to the ancient reader but which are harder for us to see.

In the sections that follow, we will look at several case studies of historical research or archaeological finds and discuss their import to the apologist. We won't come close to hitting every controversy. We certainly won't give anything like a catalogue of archaeological discoveries in Bible lands. Rather, our goal is to give the reader a sense of how this work is done and what the apologist can and cannot say about these cases. We hope the reader will then be able to apply a similar approach to investigating historical and archaeological challenges to the Bible's message—and even a similar skepticism to historical or archaeological claims that seem to be too good to be true.

The Dating of Jesus' Birth

One of the most common examples of secular history challenging the testimony of the Bible deals with the date of Jesus' birth. Most scholars consider this to be an open and shut case of the Bible contradicting itself and history as a whole. There are many different presentations of it. For our purposes, we will examine the discussion by historian Adrian Goldsworthy in Appendix II of his book *Augustus: First Emperor of Rome.*[20] There are several reasons for using this particular discussion. Goldsworthy is an eminent historian in his field who has written widely on Roman history and has specifically covered Jewish history within the Roman Empire. His book is recent and is also written in a popular style. In his discussion, Goldsworthy is trying to be fair and balanced. He does not have an ax to grind, and he often uses the gospels and St. Paul's writings as valid historical documents. Still, at the same time,

---

[19] Bryant G. Wood, "Omri King of Israel," *Bible and Spade* (Winter, 1998).

[20] Adrian Goldsworthy, *Augustus: First Emperor of Rome* (Yale University Press, New Haven, 2014), 487-492.

his treatment of the question is fairly typical. He also subjects the gospels to the kind of analysis that most secular historians believe is necessary to be intellectually honest.

Goldsworthy begins by stating, "The date and circumstances of the birth of Jesus of Nazareth rely entirely on the Gospel accounts. It is not mentioned by any other sources until much later, and those accounts were certainly influenced by—and probably wholly dependent on—the Gospels." He notes that this is different from the crucifixion which is mentioned in other early sources. Moreover, he also points out that this is fairly common. Even Julius Caesar's date of birth is uncertain. There are stories about Augustus' birth, but they too were recorded much later.

Goldsworthy dates Matthew, Mark, and Luke (and maybe John) to the end of the first century. He explicitly states that they are theological writings, not histories, so he's not surprised by their lack of detail. However, he notes, "Matthew 2:1 firmly dates the Nativity to the reign of Herod the Great. Luke 1:5 specifically dates the birth of John the Baptist to Herod's lifetime, and by implication dates the birth of Jesus to that same period."[21] Since Herod died in 4 BC,[22] Goldsworthy suggests somewhere from 7 to 4 BC as the year. He states that this would allow for Jesus' crucifixion to take place during Pilate's prefecture, which was from AD 26-36.

Yet, he continues, "Luke 2:1-2 poses a problem." This is the reference to the empire wide census that took place while Publius Sulplicius Quirinius was governor of Syria.[23] He goes on, "No other source mentions a single decree imposing a census and levy throughout the provinces. This does not mean that we can say with absolute certainty that Augustus never issued such a decree, but it does mean that we should be cautious about accepting this purely on one piece of evidence." He goes on to excuse Luke from any obligation to be

---

21 "After Jesus was born in Bethlehem of Judea in the days of King Herod, wise men from the east arrived in Jerusalem." (Matthew 2:1) / "In the days of King Herod of Judea, there was a priest of Abijah's division named Zechariah. His wife was from the daughters of Aaron, and her name was Elizabeth." (Luke 1:5).

22 There is a general consensus among scholars that Herod died in 4 BC, and Goldsworthy does not even discuss any other possibility. For the purposes of this review, the authors accept this consensus. It should be noted, however, that some scholars have contested that date. For an example, see Andrew E. Steinmann, "When Did Herod the Great Reign?" *Novum Testamentum*, **51**:1-29 (2009).

23 "In those days a decree went out from Caesar Augustus that the whole empire should be registered. This first registration took place while Quirinius was governing Syria." (Luke 2:1-2).

technically correct in describing the government tax practices of the Roman Empire "given how few people today really understand all aspects of the taxation system in their own countries." He allows that under Augustus the tax system was "tidied up" and most, perhaps all, provinces had to conduct a census at some point, for the first time in their history. Still, he goes on to charge Luke with confusion about Quirinius.

This is the key point for historians who challenge Luke's account: Quirinius was the legate of Syria. He *did* conduct a census of Judaea, but not until *AD* 6 when Archelaus (Herod the Great's son) was deposed and the Romans changed Judaea from a client state to a province, being placed under the control of a proconsul (later Pontius Pilate) who reported to the legate. In 6 *BC* Quirinius' predecessor, Publius Quinctilius Varus, took over as legate of Syria. He held that office through the death of Herod the Great in 4 BC. Varus replaced a man who had been in office since 9 BC, so there was very little room for Quirinius to hold the office during the reign of Herod the Great.

The AD 6 census caused outbreaks of resistance in Judea. Goldsworthy believes that Luke, writing seventy or more years later, was confused by the cultural memory of the outrage over Quirinius' census, so he attached his name to an event that must have happened ten or twelve years earlier, conducted by Herod the Great. Goldsworthy goes on to allow that Quirinius could have held the office of legate very briefly around 6 BC when Jesus was born, and we just don't have a record of it. He seems to have been serving "in the wider area" but there is no record of an involvement in the census.

This is very instructive for us as apologists. Goldsworthy is trying to be fair, and he is careful not to rule out the possibility that Luke's reporting is accurate. He even allows for further confusion caused by the fact that although Herod styled himself as a king, he was viewed by the Jews as a stooge of the Roman government and maybe Luke and other Jews figured that any census Herod would have conducted would have to have come from Rome originally. But in the end, Goldsworthy treats the gospel account the way that historians treat virtually all documents that come down to us from ancient times. He does not dismiss it outright. On the other hand, he does not regard it as infallibly accurate either. He tries to come up with an explanation that would preserve as much of the ancient account as possible, but that leaves the modern historian as the arbiter of what is possibly true.

From an apologetics perspective, the answer here is to admit what Goldsworthy also admits several times. The records simply are too incomplete to definitively say what did or didn't happen. No one can demonstrate that a census of the Roman Empire did not take place sometime in the last couple years of Herod the Great's rule. Luke and Matthew are ancient documents—even if one accepts Goldsworthy's dating them to last quarter of the first century (which is a little late). They are the closest documents to the event which relate the circumstances of Jesus' birth. They agree that Jesus was born during the reign of Herod the Great (which Goldsworthy does not contest). The apologist must insist that those who want to demonstrate that Luke is wrong actually do so.

The Dead Sea Scrolls

Almost everyone agrees that the most important biblical archaeological find of the twentieth century was the Dead Sea Scrolls. The scrolls were found in eleven caves west of the Dead Sea, near the Wadi Qumran.[24] Sometime between about 134 BC and 100 BC, a Jewish settlement was established at Qumran. Scholars have been debating the exact nature of that community for nearly 70 years. It existed until the Romans destroyed it in AD 68, as part of the First Jewish War (which also led to the destruction of Jerusalem two years later). Qumran lies south of Jericho. Several ancient sources report that scrolls were discovered in jars near Jericho. Origen (AD 185-254), a Christian Bible scholar who lived in Israel, reported that he used such a scroll in compiling the *Hexapla.*[25] The church historian Eusebius (AD 260-340) notes (in reference to Origen's *Hexapla*) that Greek and Hebrew manuscripts had been found in a jar near Jericho during the reign of the Roman Emperor Caracalla (AD 211-217). Somewhere around the year 800, a Nestorian patriarch[26] named Timotheus I reported that Arab hunters had found a rock chamber with many Hebrew books inside about ten years before he wrote.

---

24 A wadi is a riverbed that is dry part of the year.

25 This was a six-column comparison of different Greek and Hebrew manuscripts of the entire Old Testament. Origen reported that he used a manuscript found in a jar near Jericho for one of the Greek versions of the book of Psalms.

26 The Nestorians were followers of Nestorius (died sometime after AD 451). They followed a false understanding of Christology, or how Jesus is God and man. A patriarch is a high-ranking bishop.

But no further discoveries are known until late 1946 or early 1947. A Bedouin shepherd was throwing rocks into an opening in the cliffs at Wadi Qumran when he heard something shatter. Eventually he and some friends climbed up and entered the cave where they found ten jars, about two feet high. One contained three scrolls. Later, four more scrolls were removed from the cave.

The scrolls were taken to an antiquities dealer in March of 1947, known as Kando—short for Kahlil Iskandar Shahin. He was a Syrian Orthodox Christian, and the Bedouins thought that the scrolls might be written in Syriac.[27] He arranged for the Syrian Orthodox Metropolitan (or presiding bishop of the city) Athanasius Yeshua Samuel to buy four of the scrolls for 24 pounds (about $100 at that time).[28] The metropolitan showed them to a professor named Eleazar Sukenik from Hebrew University in Jerusalem. Sukenik made a secret trip to Bethlehem on November 29, 1947, the very day that the United Nations passed the resolution to create the state of Israel, to visit Kando. He purchased the other three scrolls. In April 1948, he announced the discovery to the world. In his old age, he recounted how the reporters had to dodge artillery shells coming to his press conference, but in the end, the importance of the discovery excited scholars and lay people all over the world.

Between 1947 and 1956, eleven total caves were discovered which contained manuscripts. (More than thirty others contained pottery and other signs of habitation.) There were also ruins of a Roman era settlement, including a cemetery. Since then, in spite of many attempts using sophisticated technologies, no more caves have been found with manuscripts in them.[29]

Scholars believe that the original repository at Qumran may have contained one thousand different works. At least 870 separate scrolls have been identified. The original seven scrolls were more or less intact. Their content could be read fairly easily, as could a few other more or less intact scrolls. But the vast majority of what was discovered in these eleven caves were fragments of manuscripts—sometimes tiny fragments. They had to be pieced together like a jigsaw puzzle. In cave No. 4 alone, 15,000 fragments were discovered.

They were written by hand, some in flowing beautiful script, some in an almost illegible cursive. Most of the scrolls were in Hebrew, but about one in

---

27 Syriac is a dialect of Aramaic.

28 Mar Athanasius sold his four scrolls in 1955 for $250,000. They were then donated to the State of Israel.

29 James C. VanderKam, *The Dead Sea Scrolls Today* (Wm. B. Eerdmans Publishing Company, Grand Rapids, 1994), 1-18.

five were in Aramaic. A handful were in Greek. There were two different kinds of texts: copies of books of the Bible (every book except for Esther has at least fragments present) and nonbiblical (but still religious) writings. Some of the nonbiblical works include previously known Jewish works.[30] Some were unknown before the Qumran discoveries. The copies of the Scriptures are a thousand years older than any previously known copy of the Old Testament. Today, they are available in translation and in their original languages.[31]

What value do the Dead Sea Scrolls have for the apologist? That is a complicated question. Many scholars today focus on the identity of the Qumran sect and what their teachings tell us about the rise of the New Testament church.[32] Some scholars have argued that Jesus or John the Baptist were present at Qumran or that they are referenced in the sectarian writings[33] found among the scrolls. Very few scholars today would agree with those assertions (although the media and some websites do sometimes repeat those out-of-date theories). Still, some scholars have noted that ways of speaking about religious topics and some practices of the Qumran group echo New Testament statements and concerns. It is probably best to see these parallels as representing the religious ferment that possessed Jewish society immediately before and after the time of Christ. Parallel ways of speaking don't necessarily mean similar teaching. Many Baptists and Evangelicals think that Lutherans are "just like the Catholics" because some of our vocabulary and practices are similar. The authors of this book strongly disagree. God used the men he raised up in a specific time and place, and he inspired his Word to be written in the vocabulary and terms they had mastered.

---

30 Although in some cases, these are the only known *Hebrew* or *Aramaic* versions of these Jewish writings.

31 Wise, ibid., 1-12.

32 The leading hypothesis is that the Qumran community was one variation of a group known as the Essenes. This sect is not mentioned in the New Testament, but several ancient writers (Josephus, Pliny, and Philo) do mention them. Part of the difficulty in the scholarly endeavor is comparing what those three authors say with what is written in the documents recovered at Qumran. There is not perfect alignment, and scholars still debate what that means. The archaeological evidence recovered at the settlement and in some of the caves adds further layers of debate, especially since no final report of the excavations there (done in the 1950s!) has ever been published.

33 The nonbiblical writings among the scrolls have been classified in several different ways. Most scholars agree that there are some writings which seem to be unique to the group that gathered at Qumran. These are often called "sectarian writings" in literature about the Dead Sea Scrolls.

A great deal of literature has been written on what the Dead Sea Scrolls reveal about the development of the Old Testament canon. Prior to the discovery of the Dead Sea Scrolls, the oldest known copies of the Old Testament were from about one thousand years *after* the time of Christ. The oldest complete manuscript of the Old Testament is known as the Leningrad Codex. It has been dated to AD 1009. There are several other related partial manuscripts, but none is more than a hundred and fifty years older than the Leningrad Codex. These manuscripts have formed the basis for Old Testament texts for centuries. Together, they are called the Masoretic Text (named for the Masoretes, the scholars who copied them from older manuscripts which no longer exist).

Theories about the evolution of the Old Testament text abounded for years and it was not uncommon for skeptics to question whether Jesus really had the same Old Testament that we do today. The Dead Sea Scrolls changed all that. It is now very difficult to argue that the Masoretic Text is dramatically different from what was available at the time of Christ. In fact, from an apologetic point of view, we can show that 1,000 years of hand copying did, in fact, preserve the text of the Old Testament—no small point.

However, there are two significant issues about the text that the Scrolls raise. Not surprisingly, hand copying a book of the Bible can lead to copy errors. One issue is that there are literally thousands of differences between the readings of one or more of the scrolls/fragments and the Masoretic Text. These differences are called *variants* (see Chapter 3). But the vast majority of them can be explained as copy errors. So, the Dead Sea Scrolls form one part of the evidence used to determine what the original reading was.

The second issue is related but is more complicated. There are times when the Dead Sea Scrolls preserve a significantly different reading from the Masoretic Text. Sometimes, this reading coincides with one or another of the other ancient witnesses we have.[34] Some scholars argue that the Dead Sea Scrolls are evidence that at least these books did not exist in their final form (the form

---

[34] These ancient witnesses consist of the various Greek translations of the Old Testament (the most famous being the Septuagint), the Samaritan Pentateuch (a revision of the five books of the Moses made for the Samaritans who emerged after the Assyrians conquered the northern kingdom of Israel – See 2 Kings 17:24-41 for a possible hint at the origins of both the Samaritans and the Samaritan Pentateuch), and the *targums* (Aramaic language translations and commentaries made during or after the exile for Jewish people whose knowledge of Hebrew was weak).

we know today) until centuries after the original authors wrote them or that different textual “traditions” existed among the Jewish people, which all had more or less equal weight. They speak of different versions of books being in circulation or being developed.

However, does the evidence really support such a broad conclusion? Certainly, the Dead Sea Scrolls are evidence that varying forms of the text of specific biblical books did exist among the Jews near the end of the Old Testament period. Yet, not every book of the Old Testament has an alternate form at Qumran. What we cannot tell from the collection there is how wide the circulation for these alternate forms was. Did other Jewish communities recognize these alternate forms? Did they consider them to be equally authoritative? We simply do not have the evidence to say. Where did the alternate forms come from? To use them to construct a whole theory about the evolution of the Old Testament text seems to be pushing well past what the evidence actually shows. We should not pretend that this evidence does not exist or overstate our theological position. Still, we absolutely can insist that theories built on this evidence acknowledge what is evidence and what is conjecture.

To be clear, the authors of this book consider the Scriptures to be the inspired, inerrant Word of God, and we trust that God has preserved them for us accurately. Then again, that does not mean we can answer every question about the original text which discoveries like the Dead Sea Scrolls raise. We must remember that God is hidden in this sinful world and that he does not always give us all the information we might need to give a definitive answer to these questions. The overwhelming majority of the text of the Bible is not in doubt. In the end, none of the differences changes a single scriptural teaching—always a very significant point for the apologist to make. In spite of millennia of hand copying, the message of the Bible is clear.

A final concern for the apologist is what the variety of works at Qumran indicates about the Jewish concept of a theological *canon* or an authoritative set of books, given by God, which we use to measure and rule all religious thinking and teaching. Practically speaking, “the canon” means that we can identify a specific set of writings as the inspired Word of God—these 66 books (or 39 in the Old Testament) and no others. “Canon denotes a closed list," Eugene Ulrich wrote.[35,36]

The Dead Sea Scrolls contain a number of books that today are called apocrypha (those that are in the Catholic Bible but not in Protestant Bibles) and pseudepigrapha (books rejected by the mainstream of Jewish and Christian thought). In some cases, the only known Hebrew versions of these books come from Qumran. Some of the pseudepigrapha found there were unknown before their discovery at Qumran. Did the Qumran sect view these writings as Scripture? Perhaps. However, it is difficult to make a final determination because no one has found a list of which books these people considered to be divinely inspired.[37]

The Qumran Sect preserved quite a large number of religious writings, not all of which are in complete agreement with each other. They seem to show us a group that was extreme in their views of sacrificial purity and perhaps monastic in practice. Yet, does the fact that they kept multiple copies of religious writings which are not part of the Bible mean that they considered those books to be on an equal level with the books of the Scriptures? The evidence is not clear. There are multiple copies of several sectarian works which clearly were influential in expressing their theological positions. They probably were viewed as authoritative. But an archaeologist excavating a Lutheran seminary a thousand years from now would probably find multiple copies of catechisms, hymnals and theological textbooks. That would not mean that the

---

[35] Eugene Ulrich, *The Dead Sea Scrolls and the Origins of the Bible* (Wm. B. Eerdmans Publishing Company, Grand Rapids, 1999), 57.

[36] There is an enormous body of literature on what the concept of a canon means and how early the concept entered into the thinking of the church. (The term is not used in this sense until the 4th century AD.) Most scholars admit that the Jewish people had a concept that certain books were given by God and were authoritative. The debate involves the making of lists: which books to include and which books to exclude and when and to what degree did all the Jewish sects agree with those identifications.

[37] Even if one allows that the collection contains works that this group considered to be equal to the Scriptures, it should be noted that the discoveries at Qumran represent the perspective of one Jewish group. They never actually engage in a discussion of the relative importance of the different works found there, so scholars are left to draw conclusions from other kinds of evidence. One of the most important criteria would seem to be the question of which books the Qumran community wrote commentaries about. The answer: biblical books, books that today are in the Old Testament. VanderKam lists "continuous commentaries" (verse by verse, running commentaries) on Isaiah (six different ones!), various psalms, Hosea, Micah, Zephaniah, Nahum, and Habakkuk (pp.44-45). He also notes "thematic commentaries" which "assemble a number of biblical passages that pertain to a single or a few themes". The passages listed, overwhelmingly, are from books that are clearly part of the Old Testament (pp. 51-54).

students or faculty viewed these documents as being equal to the Bible, even if they viewed them as having a certain level of authority.

Even if it could be demonstrated that this particular sect held other books to be as authoritative as the Scriptures, would that mean that the Jewish people had no fixed concept of a canon? Would that mean that all Jewish people followed the Qumran beliefs about a canon? It simply would not. The Qumran sect died out.[38] That may be because their unique views were no more meritorious in their day than the Jehovah's Witness perspective is today, so even if it could be demonstrated that they held this or that position, what difference would it make?

Jericho

Another case study that illustrates the value of archaeology for the apologist—and also contains a warning—is that of Jericho. Jericho is regarded as one of the oldest more or less continually inhabited sites in the world. Like many Middle Eastern sites, today it consists of a *tel*—a mound of earth that has multiple layers of inhabited city beneath. Generally, earlier layers are lower, later layers are higher. Recent excavations have shown that the walls of the city fell down in the 1400's BC. This is significant because it squares with the biblical account (the walls fell, they weren't knocked down by siege engines) and the biblical date. (Many scholars today deny that the Exodus took place this early. They put it at 1200 BC. The most influential earlier excavation of the site, in the 1950s, concluded that Jericho was uninhabited at the time the Bible says Joshua conquered it.) The excavation also showed that the site was not plundered or subject to a siege. (There were multiple containers of food still resting in their jars.) It furthered showed that the site was burned, all of which agrees with the account in Joshua 6.

The evidence, however, does not specifically link the fall to Joshua. While some scholars are ready to accept this as confirmation of the biblical account, others point out that it could be the result of an earthquake or perhaps the city was abandoned for another reason and the walls just fell down on their own. (The site gives evidence of being abandoned for at least a couple of hundred

[38] Most scholars consider modern Judaism to be descended specifically from the Pharisees. Other schools of thought that existed at the time of Christ and that can be traced in the archaeological and historical record simply did not survive the destruction of Jerusalem and the diaspora—the scattering of the Jewish people.

years, again as the Bible records—see Joshua 6:26 and 1 Kings 16:34.[39]) Even those who want to see the evidence as corroborating Joshua's account have to admit it doesn't prove that it happened that way.[40] However, many scholars have pointed to the conclusions of the 1950's dig (which are still widely accepted) as demonstrating an error in the biblical chronology. Nevertheless, even professional archaeologists are not in agreement on the chronology and there is substantial evidence to allow for the biblical account. While we cannot *prove* from the archaeological evidence that the Joshua account is true, it is not *disproven* by the archaeological evidence either. We, as apologists, need to insist that skeptics make their cases.

There is a New Testament adjunct to the issue. Matthew 20:29-34, Mark 10:46-52 and Luke 18:35-52 all record the healing of a blind man named Bartimaeus. (Luke does not give his name.) Matthew and Mark both state that this happened as Jesus was *leaving* Jericho. But Luke states that it happened as Jesus *approached* Jericho. This has often been used to demonstrate that there is clear contradiction in the Bible. Archaeology indicates that there are actually several tels at the Jericho site. At the time of Christ there was the ancient city that had been inhabited since the time of King Ahab. There was also a Roman city, built at the time of King Herod and used by the Romans to collect tolls. This allows for the possibility that Matthew, Mark and Luke all recorded the same event. Matthew and Mark viewed it from the perspective of one of the cities and Luke from the perspective of the other.

As comforting as this reasoning is, it has to be handled with the greatest of care because it is not a God-given explanation. The Scriptures simply do not resolve this difficulty for us. (And we are foolish if we do not admit that there are passages in the Bible which are difficult for us to reconcile or understand properly.) This is a possible explanation. As such, it *does* allow us to defend the Bible against an accusation that there is a contradiction here. There is at least one possible, understandable explanation for the difference in the way

---

39 "At that time Joshua imposed this curse: The man who undertakes the rebuilding of this city, Jericho, is cursed before the LORD. He will lay its foundation at the cost of his firstborn; he will finish its gates at the cost of his youngest." (Joshua 6:26) / "During his [Ahab's] reign [874/3-853], Hiel the Bethelite built Jericho. At the cost of Abiram his firstborn, he laid its foundation, and at the cost of Segub his youngest, he finished its gates, according to the word of the LORD he had spoken through Joshua son of Nun." (1 Kings 16:34).

40 Bryant G. Wood, "Did the Israelites Conquer Jericho? A New Look at the Archaeological Evidence", *Biblical Archaeology Review*, **XVI**:2:44-58 (March/April, 1990).

the event is recorded. There could be additional explanations. Who knows? But there is at least one, so the charge of a contradiction fails.

The Isaiah Bulla

In 2018, Professor Eilat Mazar of Hebrew University of Jerusalem announced the discovery of a *bulla*—the impression made from a seal—that *might* have belonged to the prophet Isaiah. A bulla was made by pressing a seal into clay. Bullae served a number of different purposes, such as serving as signatures on documents or as receipts for payment. This particular bulla was found *in situ* in debris dated from the seventh or eighth century BC. (Isaiah lived at the end of the eighth century.) About ten feet away, another bulla was found that clearly did belong to King Hezekiah, who often had dealings with Isaiah. The site appears to have been the royal bakery for the palace. Yet, there is a question about the Isaiah bulla—it's broken. It's only about half an inch wide. It clearly has the name "Isaiah" written in Hebrew characters and the beginning of another word which may be "the prophet." On the other hand, it might simply be a name, "Navi." There is no way to know for sure, since the rest of the seal is gone.[41]

What does this bulla evidence prove? Nothing. That is unfortunate because it would be the only archaeological discovery to date with Isaiah's name on it. We Christians would love to be able to point to physical evidence of a relationship between King Hezekiah and the prophet Isaiah, as we see it depicted in 2 Kings, 2 Chronicles and the book of Isaiah. Unfortunately, all we have is something that might reflect that relationship. There's nothing wrong with holding the *opinion* that this is Isaiah's bulla and that he shopped at the royal bakery, just as King Hezekiah did. Yet, this evidence doesn't prove that. At most it gives some pause to people who want to question whether there really was an historic Isaiah at all.

The James Ossuary

An ossuary is a box that is filled with bones. During the last half of the century before Christ and for most of the first century AD, it was customary for Jewish families to lay their dead out in a tomb (usually a burial cave) and

---

41 Megan Sauter, "Isaiah's Signature Uncovered in Jerusalem," *Bible History Daily* (online, February 22, 2018).

then to return when the flesh had decayed and to gather the bones into a box called an ossuary (from the Latin word for "bone"). Sometimes, but not always, the name of the deceased would be inscribed on the ossuary.

In 2002, the periodical *Biblical Archaeology Review* announced the finding of an ossuary with an Aramaic inscription that read "James the son of Joseph the brother of Jesus." People immediately connected this inscription with James, the brother of Jesus, who wrote the epistle of James and who was a leader in the Jerusalem congregation after Pentecost.[42] If this inscription is authentic and if it really is talking about the James of the New Testament, this would be the oldest known reference to Jesus outside the Bible. The box itself is about twenty inches long, and the inscription is just twenty letters in Aramaic. Everyone acknowledges that the ossuary comes from the first century. The controversy involves the inscription. Some experts in ancient handwriting have held that it is genuine. Others have argued that it appears to have been added much later. The case was made much more dubious because the ossuary did not come from an approved dig, so its provenance is unknown. When the original announcement was made, the owner remained anonymous. Later, it came out that it belonged to Oded Golan, a private collector with one of the most extensive collections of privately-owned artifacts in Israel.

In March of 2003, the Israeli Antiquities Authority (IAA) appointed a committee of 14 scholars to evaluate the authenticity of the inscription. That same month, Israeli police searched Oded's home. Eventually, the IAA ruled that the inscription was a fake—but the scholarly community is still divided on that ruling. Golan was charged with forgery for this and several other pieces he had sold. The trial lasted five years, but in 2012, he and his co-defendants were found not guilty of all charges relating to forgery. (They were convicted of some minor offenses.) To this day, the archaeological community is divided on the authenticity of the inscription.

Even if it is authentic, however, what would it prove? "Jesus" was actually a very common name at the time of Christ, as were "Joseph" and "James." Even if the inscription is eventually proven to be genuine, there is no way to

---

[42] "But I didn't see any of the other apostles except James, the Lord's brother." (Galatians 1:19) / "When James, Cephas, and John—those recognized as pillars—acknowledged the grace that had been given to me, they gave the right hand of fellowship to me and Barnabas, agreeing that we should go to the Gentiles and they to the circumcised." (Galatians 2:9).

know if it refers to Jesus' family or to some other family that lived in Jerusalem during the first century.[43, 44, 45]

The Lost Tomb of Jesus

There have been arguments about the correct location of Jesus' tomb for a long time, although there is significant archaeological evidence supporting the location at the Church of the Holy Sepulchre.[46] But in 2007, a new controversy was generated by James Cameron, the director of the movie *Titanic*, and Simcha Jacobovici, a documentary producer. The two of them made a documentary called *The Lost Tomb of Jesus*. In it, they pointed to a tomb that was discovered in 1980 in Talpiot, a part of Jerusalem. Ten ossuaries were found in this tomb. One has since been lost. Cameron and Jacobovici claimed that this tomb was the family tomb of Jesus and that the ossuaries had his name, the name of Mary Magdalene (whom they claimed was Jesus' wife) and other members of the family. They claimed that the James ossuary discussed above originally came from this tomb. Obviously, if there is a box with Jesus' bones in it, he did not rise. If Mary Magdalene was his wife and they were buried in Jerusalem together with other family members, the entire New Testament is a fraud.

The archaeological community swiftly and completely rejected all these claims. They pointed out that the tomb was nothing new. It had been discovered and analyzed almost 30 years before Cameron made his sensational claims. None of what Cameron claimed held water archaeologically or historically—to say nothing of theologically. Still, the media circus they generated has a certain amount of staying power. Their "documentary" was originally produced and aired on the Discovery Channel. Although it has been debunked on programs like *Nightline,* it's the kind of sensational thing that people will tend to remember and bring up, without actually knowing how ridiculous it was, as evidenced by the Lutheran whose friend brought him a news article about this ossuary and announced that Jesus' coffin had been found. It is, therefore, useful for an apologist to be aware of this situation and others like

43 "Is the 'Brother of Jesus' Inscription on the James Ossuary a Forgery?", *Bible History Daily* (online, August 31, 2015).

44 Brug, ibid., 18,129-132.

45 Mark Rose, "Ossuary Tales," *Archaeology,* **56**:1 (online, January/February, 2003).

46 Brug, ibid., 82-83.

it (the *Da Vinci Code*, for example), so that he or she can derail these arguments when they are brought up.

The Shroud of Turin

One of the most debated artifacts known today is the Shroud of Turin. The shroud is a piece of cloth. It is 14 ½ feet long and 3 ½ feet wide. It is made of flax in a herringbone twill pattern. There are two images on the Shroud—the front and the back of a naked man with his hands folded in front of his groin. The heads of the images are near each other in the middle. The feet are at opposite ends. The man has a beard and mustache and shoulder length hair, parted in the middle. He would have been almost six feet tall and is muscular in appearance. The Shroud is actually light brown in color, but many people have seen a negative image of it. The image of the man is much easier to see in the negative. The Shroud has some reddish stains that some people believe are blood. It also has some holes where it was singed in a fire. The Shroud is kept at the Cathedral of St. John the Baptist in Turin, Italy, which was built specifically to house it. It has resided in Turin since 1578, hence the name.[47]

Many people believe that the Shroud of Turin is Jesus' burial cloth. They often argue that the image was made when Jesus rose from the dead, presumably by a great flash of light or other divine power. However, what is the evidence regarding this cloth?

First, it should be noted that the Bible does not mention any image like this. Nor does the Bible describe Jesus' resurrection. It describes the empty tomb and his appearances after rising. We have no account of his actual rising, and there is no mention of an intense flash of light. When St. Paul lists all the proofs of Jesus' resurrection in his sermons and epistles, never once does he mention the Shroud. Matthew, Mark and Luke all mention a piece of clean, white linen (Greek: *sindon*) in which Jesus' body was wrapped.[48] Their descriptions could mean a piece of cloth like the Shroud. John is more

---

[47] The official website of the Shroud of Turin. Photos of the Shroud can be examined there.

[48] "So Joseph took the body, wrapped it in clean, fine linen, and placed it in his new tomb, which he had cut into the rock. He left after rolling a great stone against the entrance of the tomb." (Matthew 27:59-60) / "After he bought some linen cloth, Joseph took him down and wrapped him in the linen. Then he laid him in a tomb cut out of the rock and rolled a stone against the entrance to the tomb." (Mark 15:46) / "He [Joseph of Arimathea] approached Pilate and asked for Jesus's body. Taking it down, he wrapped it in fine linen and placed it in a tomb cut into the rock, where no one had ever been placed." (Luke 23:52-53).

problematic. He speaks of "linen cloths."[49] The Greek word he uses (*othoniois*) is plural and implies pieces or strips of cloths. He also mentions a single cloth or "wrapping" (Greek: *soudarion*) that had been placed around Jesus' head.[50]

How do these biblical accounts fit together? Our information on first century Jewish burial customs is limited. The practice of using ossuaries described above means that we don't often find a body still wearing its shroud. In 2000, however, such a body was found in the Old City of Jerusalem, dating from the time of Christ. The weave of the shroud was much simpler than the Shroud of Turin, and some have argued that it more accurately represents what would have been used.[51] Still, it does appear that shrouds were used and that the "the linen cloth" mentioned by Matthew, Mark and Luke could be conceived of as a shroud.[52] The strips of cloth that John mentions must have been wrapped around Jesus' body underneath that linen cloth.

Historically speaking, the first definite mention of the Shroud of Turin comes from 1390.[53] That reference, a letter from Pierre d'Arcis, the bishop of Lirey, France (where the Shroud was at that time) to Pope Clement VII[54] actually calls it a forgery and says that the artist had confessed. That is significant, since a genuine relic, like Jesus' burial shroud, would have instantly become the object of pilgrimages which would have enhanced the bishop's see and dramatically increased his revenue. It's hard to see what he would have gained from denying the authenticity of Jesus' real burial shroud.

Radiocarbon testing was done on a fragment of the Shroud in 1988 by three separate laboratories. The tests yielded dates ranging from AD 1260-1390.[55]

---

49 "They took Jesus's body and wrapped it in linen cloths with the fragrant spices, according to the burial custom of the Jews." (John 19:40) / "Stooping down, he saw the linen cloths lying there, but he did not go in. Then, following him, Simon Peter also came. He entered the tomb and saw the linen cloths lying there." (John 20:5-6).

50 "The wrapping that had been on his head was not lying with the linen cloths but was folded up in a separate place by itself." (John 20:7).

51 Bethany Bell, "Jesus Era Burial Shroud Found," *BBC News* (online, December 16, 2009).

52 We are not aware of any translation using the word "shroud" for this cloth, but that isn't compelling evidence one way or the other.

53 There are some earlier references that are disputed, the earliest being from 1349.

54 It should be noted that Clement was the pope at Avignon during the Great Schism, when there were two popes in opposition to each other.

55 PE *Damon et al.*, "Radiocarbon Dating of the Shroud of Turin," *Nature*, **337**:611-615 (1989).

Nevertheless, those tests have been disputed.[56] To date, many different kinds of scientific tests have been undertaken. Most give dates that correspond to the Middle Ages. Some have given much earlier dates. The most recent tests were done by two Italian forensic scientists in 2018. They concluded the Shroud was a fake.[57] All the tests have naturally been challenged by people who disagree with the conclusions that they indicate.

There are a number of different references from the early Middle Ages to burial cloths bearing the image of Christ (especially his face). They clearly were not all the same cloth, so they cannot all be genuine. As is the case with Roman Catholic relics generally, there was a great desire to have physical links to Christ. Just as clearly, there were people either innocently or deliberately passing off fakes as genuine articles, many of which are still held as relics in Roman Catholic churches today.

The burden of proof lies with those who claim that the Shroud is real. There are good reasons to doubt its genuineness: it's unknown before the fourteenth century; the first clear reference calls it a fake; it appears at a time when many supposed relics of Christ were being manufactured and used for financial gain; and the Bible never points to it as a proof of Jesus' resurrection.

Even the Roman Catholic Church has never officially accepted nor repudiated the Shroud. Some popes have spoken highly of it, but the Shroud's official website leaves the question open. Christians need to be careful here. It would seem to be a wonderful blessing to have an artifact from Jesus' actual burial—especially one that seems to have been miraculously formed when he rose. Yet, God doesn't typically give us things like that. Our faith is based on his Word. Even if the Shroud is genuine, the testing and the evidence are equivocal at best and in many cases negative. That it would make it an extraordinarily weak argument for the truth of the Scriptures, and a weak argument is usually worse than no argument at all. For the apologist, there is almost no value in entering the debate on either side. If someone wants to attack it, we don't have to weaken our own credibility by defending it. If someone wants to insist on it, we don't have to antagonize them or be tarred with their weak defense.

---

56 Raymond N. Rogers, "Studies on the Radiocarbon Sample from the Shroud of Turin," *Thermochemica Acta*, **425**:189-194 (2005).

57 Matteo Borrini and Luigi Garlaschelli, "A BPA Approach to the Shroud of Turin," *Journal of Forensic Sciences*, (July 10, 2018).

Noah's Ark

Perhaps no account in the Bible has generated more efforts to find artifacts than the story of Noah in Genesis 5-9. Attention has focused especially on Mt. Ararat on the eastern border of Turkey. Genesis 8:4 states, "The ark came to rest in the seventh month, on the seventeenth day of the month, on the mountains of Ararat." Since at least the eleventh or twelfth centuries, Christians have believed that this was a reference to Mt. Ararat, and legends have proliferated that the remnants of the ark are there. Mt. Ararat's higher peak is over 16,800 feet in elevation and is the highest peak in Turkey. The lower peak is still almost 12,800 feet above sea level. Either height would make sense in the account of the ark floating on the waters of the flood while they receded and coming to rest on a mountain.

Scholars have pointed out, however, that this is a little too simple. First of all, the Hebrew doesn't actually say that the ark came to rest on Mt. Ararat. It speaks of "the mountains" in the plural. This is a typical Hebrew way of referring to a mountain range. The Hebrew name does seem to be related to the Assyrian name Urartu, which is a mountain range in Turkey and Armenia. Yet, it is not very specific. Given the enormous amount of time that has passed, there is no guarantee that the name referred to the same geographic location at the time that Moses wrote Genesis as it did at the time of the Assyrian Empire. (It's not hard to demonstrate that place names sometimes shift in terms of what they refer to, especially over long periods of history and when the names cross linguistic and cultural lines.)

Nevertheless, numerous expeditions have tried to find the ark on Mt. Ararat, fueled by a local legend that the remains are located there. The Byzantine Emperor Heraclius (died AD 641) is said to have made a trip in search of it. As early as 1722, Augustin Calmet wrote in his Bible dictionary, "It is affirmed, but without proof, that there are still remains of Noah's ark on the top of this mountain; but M. de Tournefort,[58] who visited this spot, has assured us there was nothing like it; that the top of mount Ararat is inaccessible, both by reason of its great height, and of the snow which perpetually covers it."[59] Moreover, in modern times, the unstable politics of the region made it impossible for Christians to undertake a serious research expedition until the nine-

---

[58] Joseph Pitton de Tournefort was a French botanist (1656-1708).

[59] Augustin Calmet, *"Ararat," Calmet's Dictionary of the Holy Bible: With the Biblical Fragments, Vol.1, Charles Taylor, tr. (Holdsworth and Ball, London, 2011), 178-179.*

teenth century. A number were attempted. The Cold War put an end to that in the twentieth century (Mt. Ararat is very close to the Russian border with Turkey.) Former astronaut James Irwin led two expeditions in the 1980s without finding anything.

There is a long list of people who have claimed to have seen evidence of the ark on Mt. Ararat (not always at the same location). An Armenian named Georgie Hagopian claimed to have visited the ark twice around 1908-10 (or perhaps earlier). A U.S. Army sergeant stationed in Hamadan, Iran, claimed to have camped above it in 1943. He stated that he could look down into it, but he didn't approach it. In 1955 a French explorer claimed to have found a five-foot wooden beam on Mt. Ararat well above the tree line. Carbon 14 dating reportedly produced conflicting results and his guide later claimed he brought the beam with him. In 1968, a man who claimed to be a Smithsonian volunteer also claimed to have seen pictures and crates of artifacts from the ark collected by a 1968 National Geographic expedition. In both 1977 and 1993, television specials claimed that the ark had been found. Yet, testable evidence was not produced.

All these claims have been dismissed as hoaxes by some, but fervent believers continue to point to them as evidence of the truth of God's Word. It is difficult to take archaeological claims seriously when they cannot be verified. Without doubt, finding real remains of Noah's ark would be one of the greatest archaeological finds in all of history. We Christians would feel a certain sense of vindication. Nevertheless, if that were to happen, it does not mean that the scholarly community would then take the biblical account seriously. Even were the evidence compelling, we would still base our faith on what God says, while we rejoiced at his working to champion his truth. However, to date, nothing conclusive or convincing has been produced.[60]

The story of Noah isn't the only account that has led to almost quixotic quests for physical remains of the past. Because so much time and effort has been devoted to them and so many unsubstantiated claims have been brought forth about them, such quests have become reminiscent of ghost hunters and all their wild claims. Another example would be the Ark of the Covenant. The last historical reference to the ark in the Bible is in 2 Chronicles 35:3 in connection with the reform undertaken by King Josiah (reigned 641/40-609 BC)

---

60 Brug, ibid., 134-137.

and the celebration of the Passover.[61] The Bible does not tell us what became of it, and many people have speculated about it. Again, it would be a wonderful treasure to find. But to date, we can say nothing about it.

What does this sampling of archaeological finds, claims and frauds teach us as apologists? When the findings of archaeologists (or even historians for that matter) appear to contradict the Bible (which does happen), logically, you can draw one of five conclusions:

1) *The Bible was wrong.* This is often the conclusion of scholars, media figures and even the man in the street. Obviously, it's not an option for us. Faith is being certain of what is not seen. We accept what God says.
2) *The Bible was not wrong, but our interpretation of it was.* We understood the biblical text as claiming something that, in fact, it does not. There are lots of reasons why this might be the case. That it is possibly true should encourage us to use archaeological and historical claims as an opportunity to go back to the Word and study carefully what God does and does not say. The Holy Spirit sometimes uses the opposition of sinful human beings to help us reach a clearer understanding of his Word.
3) *The archaeologists' data is not wrong but their interpretation of it is.* They draw conclusions from the data that it does not support. This goes back to the difference between facts and artifacts. Still, we must be very careful with this, since both history and archaeology are serious, rigorous disciplines that require in-depth study to understand and to evaluate. We cannot blindly allow "experts" to undermine our faith, but we do want to be sure that our examination of their claims is credible and defensible.

---

61 "He [Josiah] said to the Levites who taught all Israel the holy things of the LORD, 'Put the holy ark in the temple built by Solomon son of David king of Israel. Since you do not have to carry it on your shoulders, now serve the LORD your God and his people Israel.'" (2 Chronicles 35:3). This verse raises a number of difficult questions, but it does demonstrate the ark was still in Jerusalem at the end of the seventh century BC. Jeremiah makes a reference to the ark in 3:16 ("When you multiply and increase in the land, in those days—this is the LORD's declaration—no one will say again, 'The ark of the LORD's covenant.' It will never come to mind, and no one will remember or miss it. Another one will not be made.") Yet, he doesn't actually say whether the ark was in Jerusalem when he wrote or what condition it was in.

4) *The archaeologists' data is bad.* What they found was not what they thought they had found (hoaxes, false provenances, etc.). This is difficult for us to evaluate. It usually takes time for things like this to come out. Nevertheless, it does happen. Being aware of some instances of such mistakes should give pause to anyone making sweeping claims that conveniently support their position.
5) *With our present state of knowledge, we cannot reconcile what archaeology says with what the Bible says.* This one presents our greatest challenge. As a result, the apologist must remember the two percent rule and the accidental nature of nearly all historical and archaeological evidence. God is in his Heaven, and he does whatever he pleases. Sometimes, he allows sinful people to wallow in their delusions. Sometimes, he allows challenges to our faith to come in order to teach us to cling to him no matter what. Our faith is not based on archaeology or historical research. It's based on the Word of God.

Summary

Philosophers today often talk about "truth claims." Christianity makes many truth claims. As we discussed in the first chapter, it is only possible to establish truth in comparison with a standard. Facts, artifacts, arguments and proofs are all used in one way or another to attach a truth claim to a standard, or an implied standard. Archaeology, like science in general, has a limited, but important role to play in helping to verify our truth claims. Nevertheless, as in other areas of science, it is a complex topic that requires a certain level of professional expertise to use it properly. The rest of us are left to do the best we can to evaluate those experts and their work. None of those experts is without bias—and that bias can complicate the analysis of the evidence. This is true even when the bias is in favor of the truth claims of the Scriptures. We need to be willing to do hard and honest work to evaluate the claims we hear in the media. We need to recognize that many people will parrot or even misquote what they hear someone else say in order to argue for their own point. We need to be very careful about how we use historical research and archaeology.

History rarely generates the same kind of media excitement that archaeology does. Still, it also presents challenges to the truth claims of the Bible. The biggest single challenge in historical studies comes from submitting the Bible to the critical analysis of scholars, as if it were any other document. To be fair, academic history is not theology. To say that the Bible is God's special revelation to mankind, and as such it is infallibly true, is to make a theological statement, not a scientific or historical one. Some scholars in the fields of history or archaeology hold this view of the Bible, but most do not. In any case, history and archaeology as academic disciplines are not based on an assumption that the Scriptures are true, and it would be unrealistic to expect the findings of scholars in these fields to reflect that assumption. Our job is to understand the conclusions these academics make and to study carefully so that we can deal with these challenges and then return to the main goal of apologetics: witnessing to Christ.

So, where does that leave us when it comes to apologetics? There is no replacement for independent study. The vast majority of what people say about archaeology or history and the Bible is going to come from media accounts which are fragmentary and sensationalized. A little online research will often clear the way to permit an evaluation of what is really going on.

We must be careful. When it comes to biblical archaeology, if something sounds too good to be true, it probably is. We need to view breathless reports that claim to have proved the Bible's account with a healthy dose of skepticism. If they do indeed confirm what God's Word says, it will come out over time. Still, we live in a world in which God is hidden. That means that he doesn't always give us proof when we would like it. He often allows misinformation to be circulated by his foes. That will change only on Judgment Day. For now, we live by faith and not by sight.[62]

While we dare not rest our faith on archaeology or historical research, we can use it to help us understand the times and the cultures in which Jesus and the prophets and the apostles were living. This can only enrich our study of the Scriptures. We can rejoice when we encounter solid archaeological and historical evidence for people and events in the Bible. Yet, it is finally the Holy Spirit working through the gospel that creates and sustains faith. Archaeology and history, like all apologetic endeavors, is about clearing the way for the gospel. Therefore, we are back to doing serious research again when tough subjects arise.

---

[62] 2 Corinthians 5:7.

9

Challenges from Cognitive Psychology

The Lord said to Jeremiah, "The heart is more deceitful than anything else, and incurable—who can understand it? I, the LORD, examine the mind, I test the heart to give to each according to his way, according to what his actions deserve."[1] The Bible uses several words to describe man's process of thinking, reasoning, feeling, and believing, namely, "heart," "soul," "spirit" and "mind." Scientists add another, "brain," and then subdivide the brain into numerous components with different functions. Historical theological issues and modern psychological research both play a part in what the apologist faces when trying to address obstacles that block people's path to faith.

In this chapter we will deal with the mental and psychological issues that are important as we present and defend the teachings of the Scriptures. Due to the extensive research in cognitive psychology in recent decades, the educational, advertising and political establishments have learned how to manipulate our minds more than most people realize. Such manipulation by Secular Humanists[2] is poisoning our efforts to spread the gospel and is a major reason that fewer young people are interested in religion than in the past. This

---

1 Jeremiah 17:9–10.

2 The lowercase word "humanism" means being concerned about things of humanity. Classical Humanism, which arose at the time of the Renaissance, is an intellectual movement that emphasized the works of man, particularly literature, art, history, and the thought of Greek and Roman culture. Secular Humanism, also called Radical Humanism, is a movement which is attempting to hasten man's evolution into a being that can create and sustain a utopian society for the benefit of all mankind. Unless otherwise indicated, Humanism will be used in this book in the latter sense when written as uppercase.

is quite intentional. The destruction of Christianity is not just collateral damage in Humanism's effort to build an earthly utopia; for many of its adherents, it is a major objective of that effort. There is no way that we can consider all the issues that the apologist will face, so we will concentrate primarily on understanding why people think as they do[3] and how to deal with the psychological efforts to lead people away from Christ.

Setting the stage

As apologists, we must consider how people arrive at the intellectual state at which we encounter them. Educational psychologists tell us there is no such thing as a *tabula rasa*, i.e., a blank slate.[4] At birth, children already have programmed into them certain tendencies that will come into play when exposed to appropriate stimuli. As Christians, we cannot disagree with this because we believe that we are all born with original sin,[5] which leads us to commit actual sin.[6] As a consequence, in addition to having the tendency to nurse when placed at their mothers' breasts, infants also have the tendency to view the world only in terms of their own needs.

Children also have the inherent ability to place things into categories (e.g., things that are edible).[7] This ability is essential to survival, and it improves with practice. In fact, it becomes almost automatic as the mind attempts both to group things as similar for identification but also to subcategorize them for ease of retrieval. Whenever a person encounters new information, the mind attempts to flesh out its knowledge of the new discovery by relating it to a category and ascribing the attributes of that category to it. Some of this assignment is rule-based while other assignments are done through guessing. These approaches do not always work correctly, which is one reason why

---

[3] Most of the material in this chapter reflects the "dual process model" of thinking. The authors used it because it is well-supported by experimental evidence over diverse areas of study and generally accepted by relevant scientists.

[4] Monisha Pasupathi, *How We Learn* (The Great Courses, The Teaching Company, Chantilly, VA, 2012).

[5] "When the LORD smelled the pleasing aroma, he said to himself, 'I will never again curse the ground because of human beings, even though the inclination of the human heart is evil from youth onward.'" (Genesis 8:21).

[6] "Now the works of the flesh are obvious: sexual immorality, moral impurity, promiscuity, idolatry, sorcery, hatreds, strife, jealousy, outbursts of anger, selfish ambitions, dissensions, factions, envy, drunkenness, carousing, and anything similar." (Galatians 5:19-21a).

[7] Pasupathi, ibid., Lect. 5.

people sometimes misunderstand information. These mistakes can cause problems for the apologist because mis-categorization of information can create obstacles to a person's understanding the reasoning of the apologist. With practice, both rule-based and guess-based assignments improve, but they are never perfect, and past mistakes may also persist in the memory, as will be discussed in the following section.

As they grow older, children also learn *behavioral scripts*[8] by the same two mechanisms mentioned above. Through reward, punishment and observation a person develops a pattern of behavior which we call a *culture*.[9] That culture embraces many things, including attitudes toward religion. These personal behavioral scripts are activated by specific *triggers*[10] and are important to the brain's ability to address issues without excessive thought. Such scripts can greatly affect how a person will react to statements by an apologist. For example, the word "church" (see Chapter 10) will trigger a series of images and feelings. Because people's triggers are attached to scripts that have been developed by each individual and are specific to them, the same argument advanced by an apologist may generate dramatically different results in two apparently similar people based on their past experiences. Scripts will sometimes pour preformed arguments into a person's mind to handle a specific situation, and this can catch an apologist off guard.

Each person whom an apologist meets will already have an established mental matrix of information in the form of categories and scripts guiding his or her beliefs and actions. To present an appropriate and effective defense of biblical truths, the apologist must probe not only the person's beliefs but also the underpinnings of those beliefs, being cautious so as not to trigger defensive reactions. In effect, the apologist will need to act as a psychologist.

---

8 A *behavioral script* is a stored set of expectations and actions which a person will use to guide their visualizations and responses when faced with the situation for which the script was developed. For example, when a parent sees a child falling off a bicycle, the script tells the parent that the child will react in predictable ways (e.g., cry, be dazed, shrug it off). It tells the parent how to treat the child (e.g., comfort, bandage, discipline) and the bicycle (e.g., check for damage, straighten handlebars, readjust seat). Scripts are refined after they are invoked by a learning-through-experience process.

9 *Culture* is a difficult word to define, and its meaning depends on both the field of study and the specific context. It is used here to speak of a great deal of subconscious, assimilated material, including attitudes, opinions and experiences.

10 A *trigger* is a word, phrase or situation which causes subconscious fears, hopes and/or scripts to be brought into a person's consciousness and to assume a dominant role in the person's thoughts and actions.

People develop beliefs, scripts and *mindsets*[11] in an effort to deal with a world which is too complex to understand.[12] To accomplish such development, they need anchor points[13] and screening mechanisms[14] to reduce the number of inputs they receive to a volume which they can mentally process and emotionally handle. In the next several sections we will look at the underlying factors which contribute to the behaviors we observe and at how we must deal with them. We will start with the memory, the place where information and scripts are stored.

Memory

The memory is the mechanism by which the brain holds information for evaluation and manipulation and for subsequent storage of it. It is generally thought to be composed of three parts.[15] The *long-term memory* stores processed information and scripts indefinitely and is located in the *cortex* region of the brain. It has an intricate retrieval system which allows the information and scripts to be brought into the subconscious or conscious mind for processing. *Short-term memory* is the repository for information newly arrived through the senses and is located primarily in the *hippocampus* in the *medial temporal lobe*s. Its capacity is very low, being able to hold about 7 pieces (chunks) of information for up to 30 seconds. The information is then discarded or is transferred, after appropriate processing in which sleep plays an important role, into long-term memory. To a limited extent, suitable exercises can improve the capacity of short-term memory. The *working memory* is also of short duration and is used for learning, reasoning and comprehension. For example, working memory allows us to add 23 and 14 "in our head," without assistance of paper or calculator. It is located in the *prefrontal cortex* and is regarded as part of consciousness.

---

[11] A *mindset* is a set of filters or algorithms which affect how information enters the thinking process. A mindset causes information to be screened for acceptance and modified for usage before the conscious mind begins processing it analytically.

[12] Ryan Hamilton, *How You Decide: The Science of Human Decision Making* (The Great Courses, The Teaching Company, Chantilly, VA, 2016).

[13] An *anchor point*, which will be discussed in detail later, gives us a place from which to measure so that we can make judgments.

[14] *Screening mechanisms* are just specialized scripts used to try to eliminate irrelevant background information.

[15] Thad A. Polk, *The Aging Brain* (The Great Courses, The Teaching Company, Chantilly, VA, 2016), Lect. 1.

It is helpful for the apologist to understand how memories are formed and the limitation of memory recall.[16] The memory system is not a photographic array, that is, it does not record events as they happen. This is true both due to the physical limitations of the memory and, more importantly, because the mind at all levels is operating based on scripts, as described above. If this were not true, every sensory input would be an unrecognized signal that would have to be evaluated individually for potential action. It would be similar to being thrown into an entirely new environment every second and having to attempt to make sense of it. Scripts give the brain the ability to put sensory input into a useable context.

In attempting to use its current script to interpret the sensory inputs, the brain often finds that there is a mismatch between what the senses report and what the script claims should happen. For example, we might be driving down a familiar street following the script for that street when suddenly a ball comes bouncing onto the roadway. If we fail to notice the ball, we will continue using the current script and perhaps run over the child who follows the ball into the street. If we do notice the ball, then we must switch to a new script that deals with objects entering the street. Because the ball has no place in the initial script, we genuinely might not see it at the conscious level, as was shown by the invisible gorilla experiment in Chapter 2. It is important to realize that we cannot remember and therefore cannot act upon something that gets screened out because it does not fit into our current script. Good driving requires a driver's full attention and the development of a *metascript* which watches for deviations from the current script and quickly switches to the appropriate alternate script.

In daily life, our brain is continually comparing our current scripts with our sensory inputs. If everything fits together, the sensory input is allowed to slide out of short-term memory and be forgotten. This is the reason that we quickly forget everything that happened on a routine drive which had no notable incidents. When a notable incident does occur, the brain transfers information about the event from short-term to long-term memory. The memory image of the event, however, is not necessarily a truthful representation of the event that occurred, but rather a blended representation of our sensory inputs with the details of our current script. If some details found in the script are missing from the sensory input, place-holding details from our

---

16 Novella, ibid., Lect. 1-6.

current script may be substituted for them. Because not everyone's place-holders for a specific type of script are the same, eyewitnesses of a particular event often give significantly different accounts to the police because their minds blended things differently.

The poor blending of script and sensory input has produced many tragic consequences. Police have shot unarmed suspects because their scripts were inadequate to correctly interpret their sensory inputs. People have been convicted of crimes that they did not commit due to inaccurate eyewitness testimony caused by the incorrect blending of data. People have spent years feuding over an unimportant incident because they misread what was really happening based upon the different scripts they were using to interpret it. All parties involved genuinely remember the events differently and may even accuse each other of intentional misrepresentation, (i.e., lying). Unfortunately, bad blending of scripts and sensory information is not the only problem leading to incorrect memories.

Once an image of an incident is inserted into our long-term memory, our subconscious mind continues to refine the image to bring it into line with our idealized view of ourselves. If we acted in an inappropriate manner, our brain will automatically diminish the significance of or remove the inappropriate actions. It may add positive information that didn't happen but that we would like to have happened under the circumstances. We tend to see ourselves as more heroic or as more helpless, depending on what makes us feel better about our actions. Our brains may even replace actors in an incident with others it feels are more appropriate to the incident. If someone asks us a question about an event for which there is no information in our memory image of it, we may feel compelled to give an answer consistent with what we do know, and that answer then becomes part of our image of the event. In other words, leading questions can permanently alter our memory. All this is done subconsciously, so that our conscious mind really believes the refined story is an accurate account of the incident. This phenomenon lets people pass lie detector tests and sound completely credible about inaccurate information because they really believe it is true.

The unreliableness of the memory poses a major challenge for us as apologists.[17] We might present the correct reasoning to someone troubled by

---

17 Some claim that unreliable memories account for the differences in synoptic portions of the Scriptures, especially the gospels. Indeed, it might appear to the unbeliever that the

a theological issue and that person might show evidence of understanding the argument at the level of working memory. Yet, when we talk to the person some time later, it becomes evident that his or her memory of the argument was distorted both by a processing script when it was stored and by a memory refinement mechanism that tried to reconcile it with some deeply held belief. We are then forced to backtrack to find the deeper problem before we can address the issue as it was originally presented to us. We must recognize that the person we are dealing with is not intentionally lying to us, but rather that we are dealing with a false memory situation that we have to explore.

Each of us can fall victim to these memory issues, because, due to original sin, we are all internally programmed to justify ourselves at the expense of others. Adam and Eve tried to justify themselves by blaming Satan, each other and even God. But, as was shown, this is not only a problem of our conscious minds, but it extends into our subconscious memory processes. This can negatively impact our witness because we cannot be sure that those to whom we have witnessed have the same memory of what was said as we do. Obviously, we cannot document our whole lives using an internet storage cache or even keep a detailed enough written diary of daily events. However, when we discuss a topic with someone with whom we expect to have a continuing dialogue or with whom we will need to follow up to see whether our previous efforts have been correctly internalized, it is useful to write a note to ourselves so that we will remember our impressions at the time of the conversation. Written notes don't change with time as our memories. We might also want to record the points with which we plan to begin the next session and those items that we want to review.

---

gospel writers were operating with different memories based on different scripts and, therefore, that they recorded specific incidents in different ways. If they had been acting as independent agents, this would be a plausible explanation. However, it is not the correct explanation. The Lord's "memory" is perfect because he is omniscient. We know from the biblical teaching of inspiration that he led his writers to include different details of the same incidents for his purposes. Sometimes, it is a challenge to see how they fit together, but God is not subject to the kind of memory script issues we are. The Bible does employ eyewitness testimony to declare that events had really occurred and were not myths because when the Bible was written, that was the best evidence available. Cameras, fingerprinting and DNA testing would not be invented for many centuries.

Personality Types

Anyone who has lived in a family with more than one child realizes that not all children respond in the same manner to similar stimuli. One child will tough something out while another will be emotionally destroyed by the same situation. Dissimilarity is also true in any group of employees. A boss often must use a convoluted set of instructions and incentives to bring everyone aboard for a critical project. People have different personalities, different goals, and different concerns. A large amount of psychological research has gone into group management, and people who arc good at such management are generally recognized in their organizations. While an apologist will usually be dealing with only individuals or small groups, recognizing the dissimilarity of people is still essential to effectiveness.

Dr. Carl Jung developed four criteria that have been responsible for subsequent work for classifying personality types.[18] His first criterion indicated the source and direction of a person's energy expression, either *Extroversion* or *Introversion*. His second criterion considered the method by which someone perceives information, either *Sensing* from the external world or *Intuition* from the internal or imaginative world. His third criterion noted how a person processes information, either *Thinking* (logically) or *Feeling* (emotionally). His last criterion reflected how a person implemented the processed information, either *Judging* through organizing all life events or *Perceiving* through improvising and exploring alternative options. When these criteria are combined, they yield 16 personality types.

For practical purposes, Jung's types are often combined into four personality styles, which exist to a greater or lesser extent in all of us, although not everyone agrees on the exact combinations. None of us are purely of one style, although a few people may be very close to such purity. Most people, however, are closer to one such character style than the rest. How an apologist deals with different people will depend on their blend of personality types that make up these styles. One style is that of decision-maker. A *decision-maker* wants the key information summarized so that a decision can be made, a plan put into place and an action accomplished. When dealing with such a personality, the apologist will not get a long hearing, so it is important to have one or two major points ready to be presented in a forceful fashion. Christi-

[18] Carl Jung, *Psychologische Typen* (Rascher Verlag, Zurich, 1921).

anity to this type of person is a group of clearly stated doctrines which have implications for personal behavior. The characteristics of this style tend to dominate in business leaders and military officers.

A second personality style is that of the analyst. An *analyst* wants all the detail and a carefully reasoned presentation. Evidence is important, and its organization is critical. When dealing with an analyst, the apologist must be prepared in depth. Analysts accept nothing without being able to see how each step follows sequentially. It probably will take several sessions to make a complete case, particularly on a complex issue. Christianity to this type of person is a set of interconnected doctrines, each related to the overall theme, which needs to be understood to be applied in the Christian's life. The characteristics of this style tend to dominate in engineers and accountants.

Thirdly, there is the personality style of a communicator. A *communicator* wants everyone to feel good about what is happening and needs to understand the people involved. These people are social and need to build a relationship with the apologist to accept Christian concepts from him or her. When dealing with a communicator, the apologist must be willing to spend time talking about peripheral issues. The reasons for the issue being addressed must be highlighted and the inability to resolve the issue by compromise must be explained. The communicator will want to feel good about the position of the apologist and know how he or she can talk about it to and with others. Christianity to this type of person is a community in which correct doctrines are part of the bond between people. The characteristics of this style tend to dominate in clergymen and social workers.

The last personality style is that of the visionary. A *visionary* sees the world differently from the obvious way it appears to others or even to their own senses. These people are like Leonardo da Vinci, who envisioned numerous devices that did not exist and sometimes did not become practical for centuries. They visualize how things might be organized or done differently and sometimes seem completely detached from reality. People in whom the characteristics of this style are strong will pose the greatest challenge to the apologist because they do not like to be bound by what has come before, such as doctrines written in a book. When dealing with such creative people, the apologist will want to seek common ground by discussing God's creativity in the use of miracles to solve problems. The Lord is a master artist, painting in many colors and designs on his canvas of plants and animals. Christianity to this type of person involves interacting with a dynamic God who is continually renewing his people and his creation. This personality style tends to be dominant in artists, performers, and inventors.

To be successful, apologists must remember that they are not trying to convince themselves about the truths of God. They must shape their arguments to the nature of the person with whom they are dealing. Because few people are of one pure personality style, the apologist will have to probe to find which underlying personality type of the person is most easily reachable and which is dominating his or her view of the gospel. If the person is approached from a different perspective, the ability to get a profitable hearing will be greatly diminished. Personality styles are a gift of God, but they can also be obstacles that must be overcome so that each individual can hear the message of the Scriptures clearly. The apologist cannot ignore this because Satan and his human agents are working hard to exploit personality styles for the purpose of making Christianity unappealing.

How We Make Decisions

The authors of this volume do not advocate decision theology, but it is important for us to understand that how people make decisions will affect how we conduct apologetics. Why, for example, do people decide to reject the Bible without knowing its contents? Because decision-making is such a critical topic for advertisers and politicians, it has been the object of considerable research. This research has confirmed what seems fairly obvious, namely, that there is both a conscious and a subconscious component to people's thinking, i.e., their decision-making process. This research does give us a more systematic understanding of the thinking process, and this understanding can be used by the apologist to recognize obstacles which may be confronting him or her.

Psychologists have come to understand the conscious and subconscious components of thinking as two decision-making processes, which have come to be called by the unimaginative names of System 1 and System 2.[19,20] System 1 simultaneously processes many inputs in a parallel manner and tries to synthesize the best solution based on the inputs and its accumulated biases that exist in the relevant script. It is automatic and often works below the level

---

[19] Daniel Kahneman, *Thinking, Fast and Slow* (Farrar, Straus and Giroux, New York, 2011).
[20] Hamilton, ibid., Lect. 2.

of our conscious awareness. This system is what allows us to walk, ride a bicycle and drive a car, all of which require multiple actions to remain in control. When we first tried each of these, we did not do well because System 1 (also called the "automatic brain") had not been trained on the proper responses to make each of these processes work properly. When we have no System 1 process available to address an issue, we must rely on System 2 to handle it. System 2 uses serial processing to analyze the inputs that it receives, which means it must consider the merits of each input, one after the other, relative to the previous inputs and make decisions accordingly. It may even have to backtrack to previous decisions based on the new information. This makes System 2 much slower than System 1 as it sorts out these stimuli and responds to them. Consequently, System 2 may miss critical details because they arrive too quickly to be processed. Yet, it is through System 2 that we learn and do our deeper thinking and analysis.

The important point for the apologist is that System 2 is continually training System 1 to handle as many tasks as possible. For a person to live his or her daily life efficiently, this is critical. On the negative side, some of the inherent shortcuts that System 2 teaches System 1 prejudice the decisions that System 1 makes. For example, if a person has several bad experiences with people in group A, System 2 may train System 1 with the concept (i.e., write it into its script) that avoiding people of group A is a good idea. System 1 will then react in future situations based on this programming. Certainly, System 2 is the master and can override System 1, but such overriding requires a positive action on the part of System 2. Since System 1 is faster than System 2, System 2 is in the position of having to change a decision that System 1 has already sketched out for the person, if such a change is necessary or desirable. If System 2 is distracted or unwilling to countermand that decision, the System 1 decision will prevail. System 2 has only a limited amount of intellectual energy to expend on its activities, which include consciously perceiving the events occurring in its environment, making decisions, switching between tasks and overriding the decisions of System 1. It must periodically rest to regenerate itself. The more intensely that System 2 is forced to work, the less reserve it has to override System 1 decisions. We know that when we are tired, we are prone to allow things to slip by to which we would raise objections if we were well-rested. As Vince Lombardi once said, "Fatigue makes cowards of us all." Many bad habits are the result of improperly programming System

1 and then not exerting the intellectual energy to retrain it.

But how does this functioning of the brain impact our practice of apologetics? Both temptations from the devil and conversion by the Holy Spirit work with System 2. Because of this, apologists must fashion their arguments for consideration by System 2. But System 2 is not the whole person. A large amount of a person's behavior is preprogrammed into System 1. Even if a person accepts an apologist's argument as reasonable and even if the Holy Spirit converts a person to faith, the System 1 programming does not automatically change. When a person becomes a Christian, for example, he or she will still have a large number of pre-Christian attitudes and scripts that System 1 will use to make decisions for him or her. System 2 must in the short-term override these unchristian behaviors and must in the long-term reprogram System 1 to behave differently. However, this takes a good deal of conscious effort by System 2, which will be faced with a war of attrition against continuing improper suggestions from System 1 and temptations by the devil not to work so hard at performing this retraining. This is in addition to the Old Adam who will also discourage the reform of System 1. Failure to give a new Christian adequate spiritual and emotional support can often lead to the new Christian's System 2 becoming weary and giving up, leading to a loss of faith. In the same way, even when a person accepts an apologist's argument, a period of helping that person adjust his or her decision-making processes to the new frame of reference with new anchor points is often critical. (Anchor points will be discussed further in the next section.) The apologist must remember that System 2 nodding in agreement is not the same as System 1 being permanently reprogrammed. The huge backdoor losses of new converts are often a direct result of failing to help these converts reprogram their System 1 scripts.

The Bible makes two statements that emphasize the importance of training what is called System 1 in the current psychological decision-making model. The first involves the training of our children so they will continue to faithfully follow the Lord.[21] Clearly, we want them not only to learn their catechism and memory work lessons well enough to meet their teacher's expectations, which can happen by placing this knowledge in an extended version of short-term memory under the guidance of System 2, but also to

---

[21] "Fathers, don't stir up anger in your children, but bring them up in the training and instruction of the Lord." (Ephesians 6:4).

place this information in long-term memory linked with processes in System 1. It needs to become an integral part of their lives. Secondly, Jesus said that at the final judgment his followers will be unaware that they had served him in many ways through their actions.[22] Perhaps, this will be true to some extent because they have developed such a bias in favor of responding automatically to the situations of life in a God-pleasing way that they did not require conscious effort to take such actions. Their System 1s had been properly programmed for Christian living. The conscious System 2 did not have to agonize over each set of alternatives, but it could accept the decisions of the automatic brain. Under these circumstances, the *new man* is alive and well within us. Naturally, to achieve this requires constant study of God's Word so that Satan will not successfully tempt System 2 to reconsider and to override the good habits of System 1 (e.g., weekly church attendance) and eventually to reprogram it to laxer standards.[23]

Anchor (Reference) Points and Deception

An old adage, attributed to St. Ambrose, goes, "When in Rome, do as the Romans do." It was intended to give people a reference point for establishing their own behavior. A *reference point* gives us a place from which to measure so that we can make judgments about such things as price, value, position or size. In psychology it is also frequently called an *anchor point*, because it restricts us to the vicinity of a value on a scale like an anchor restricts a boat's position. Appropriately setting scriptural anchor points and uprooting secular anchor points is an important task of an apologist.

For example, suppose that sales are a little slow, and a merchant decides to try to improve business. He therefore advertises a sale of "1/3 Off the Manufacturers' Suggested Retail Prices on Specially Tagged Items". He had previously been selling product X at $100, but for the sale he tags the item at 1/3 off of $150, the price the manufacturer had arbitrarily set. People who had not paid much attention to the product before now see it as a good deal. The merchant has changed people's anchor point for the value of product X and increased sales. In the same way, if a merchant charges 5% more for credit card transactions, she will have a lot of unhappy customers, but if she gives a

22 Matthew 25:37-40.

23 "Be sober-minded, be alert. Your adversary the devil is prowling around like a roaring lion, looking for anyone he can devour." (1 Peter 5:8).

5% discount to those who pay cash, she will have a lot of happy customers. Buying decisions and general happiness will be influenced by the setting of anchor points.[24]

Anchor point manipulation is important in marketing, but it is also used by Secular Humanists to attack Christianity. For example, God's law says that "You should treat others as you yourself want to be treated," i.e., the *Golden Rule*.[25] This has long been considered by many as the anchor point for interpersonal relationships. The gospel encourages us to "go the extra mile,"[26] particularly when dealing with fellow Christians,[27] and to "treat others as they want to be treated." This has been called the *Platinum Rule* and is a higher standard because it forces us to think about the real needs of the people with whom we deal. It is, therefore, a different anchor point. Humanists through the Civil/Human Rights Movement have tried to change this standard of behavior to be "You shall treat others as they have a right to be treated". This, however, is a variable anchor point because people can always insist that they have rights that we are not respecting and move the position of the anchor point. It is reminiscent of the phony laws of the Pharisees[28] and of the papacy which were used to emotionally control people. Political correctness is just the "tradition of the elders" in another guise. The purpose of this "Rights Rule" is to leverage guilt to gain advantage. Here, the apologist must point out the difference between taking offense and giving offense, which was discussed in Chapter 1. As Christians, we should never intentionally mistreat people, always taking into consideration human weaknesses as articulated in the Golden and Platinum Rules.[29] If we fail to do this, it is our sin. On the other hand, we cannot prevent people from wanting to feel victimized or offended and looking for someone to blame for their own shortcomings. We must reject the attempt to use guilt to manipulate us so that we do not become

---

[24] Hamilton, ibid., Lect. 19.

[25] [Jesus said,] "Therefore, whatever you want others to do for you, do also the same for them, for this is the Law and the Prophets." (Matthew 7:12).

[26] Matthew 5:39-42.

[27] "Therefore, as we have opportunity, let us work for the good of all, especially for those who belong to the household of faith." (Galatians 6:10).

[28] "For the Pharisees and all the Jews do not eat unless they give their hands a ceremonial washing, keeping the tradition of the elders. When they come from the marketplace, they do not eat unless they have washed. And there are many other customs they have received and keep, like the washing of cups, pitchers, kettles, and dining couches." (Mark 7:3–4).

[29] [Jesus said,] "Blessed are the merciful, for they will be shown mercy." (Matthew 5:7).

enslaved by human standards and no longer have our Christian freedom (see Chapter 10).[30]

A second anchor point manipulation by Humanism is its effort to change our sense of the nature of God. This issue was broached in Chapter 4, but the way the manipulation occurs is of relevance here. The question is often posed as, "How can you believe in a God who does X or lets Y happen?" The goal is to cause us to change our anchor points to exclude X and Y from what we would consider a God capable of doing. Sometimes this attack is stated as "I refuse to believe in a God who does X or lets Y happen!" Despite the emotion often associated with this question or statement, it is the previously discussed logical fallacy of wishful thinking. Whether we believe in a particular god or whether we believe that God has a particular attribute does not change whether God exists or whether he actually has the attribute mentioned. Sadly, through progressively limiting suggestions by Humanists about God's nature (i.e., by their moving the anchor point of divine acceptability), most people have come to believe that for a being to be a God it must have much more humanistic characteristics than the Bible ascribes to the Lord.

When dealing with issues where Humanism has been successful in resetting the anchor points of expected behavior or characteristics regarding a matter, the apologist must attack the legitimacy of these new anchor points. He or she must show that Humanists have been trying to mess with our minds. One of the common phrases they use in their effort to adjust our anchor points is "Certainly, we can agree that…." This phrase is an example of the fallacy of false compromise and is used to prevent looking at the messy details that will call into question the ideas that Humanists are pushing, as they hope to get people to use their System 2 process to train System 1 to automatically reject anything that doesn't fit what they are trying to cover with their "agreement". The phrase should be a signal that someone is trying to bamboozle us. Faced with this, the apologist always needs to pursue the subject down one level and often two to see whether what is being advocated includes buried attacks upon biblical teachings.

For example, someone might say, "Certainly, we can agree that everyone has a right to be treated with human dignity!" But what is human dignity? If it means that no one should be starved or tortured or held without trial, we

30 "Why do you submit to regulations: 'Don't handle, don't taste, don't touch'?" (Colossians 2:20-21).

might readily agree. If it means, however, that no matter how antisocial people act, they must be given total freedom and all the comforts of life, then the apologist must point out that the Bible calls on the magistrates to administer justice and curb evil.[31] We cannot agree that people who act against society should be shielded from punishment for their deeds, such as confinement, reduction to poverty or even execution. This is the first level down, but there is a second level that needs to be reached. The apologist must press onward to the issue of whether people are to be afforded dignity based on some intrinsic property of being human or because people are a special creation of God for whom Jesus died. When we allow our anchor points to be manipulated, we can be backed into the trap of having to reject that which we had previously agreed was the appropriate behavior or course of action or to reject some doctrine of the Scriptures that conflicts with it. In either case, we become hypocrites. This is the reason that it is so critical to detect and attack efforts to change our anchor points.

Birds of a Feather

In old western movies, the critical scene was the one in which the hero walked into the street to face the bad guy coming to meet him one-on-one. The preceding story, the background music and the camera angles were all tuned to create a feeling of intense anxiety in the pits of the stomachs of the viewers. Yet, it is precisely this type of situation that most people try desperately to avoid. We do not want to be forced into a life-or-death scenario where we face some villain alone. We want allies, and we want to place the feeling into our opponent's mind that it is better to yield and do it our way without a struggle or at least be willing to bargain for a mutually acceptable compromise. Naturally, the bigger the coalition that we can build, the better our chances to avoid the "gunfight" that we fear. In this regard, theological issues are no different from any other issues.

Certainly, those who wish to develop a temporal paradise want harmony among all religious groups to gain this purpose. Atheists, agnostics and many people for whom religion has only a social and/or cultural meaning think that it is important to downplay critical doctrines for the common human good.

[31] "For it is God's servant [i.e., civil government] for your good. But if you do wrong, be afraid, because it does not carry the sword for no reason. For it is God's servant, an avenger that brings wrath on the one who does wrong." (Romans 13:4).

But there is a much larger issue behind the scenes gnawing at many people who have some consciousness of religion, particularly as they grow older. They fear the scenario of arriving at Judgment Day and discovering that they have bet on the wrong religious horse or that their deeds are much worse in God's sight than they had imagined. They need to believe in a plan that deals with this worst-case scenario. They realize that no one is going to "beat God to the draw," so they are moved to adopt a strategy sometimes used in those old westerns, namely, "He can't shoot all of us." They tell themselves that surely there must be some truth in all religions, although some might say only in all Christian denominations. Therefore, they reason, if we all agree to recognize each other as fellow children of God, or as fellow Christians, then we can all stand together and present a united front before God when the moment of judgment occurs. While they might seldom express it this overtly, they comfort themselves by the thought that God wouldn't dare damn everyone. The apologist must sense this and respond, "Yes, he would!" In the Old Testament, the Lord spared only eight at the time of the flood.[32] He chose only the relatively few children of Israel as his people. He sentenced all but two out of more than 600,000 fighting men to die in the wilderness.[33] Jesus himself said that few would be saved.[34] In blunt words, it is the Lord's plan of salvation or eternity in hell. No mass of humans is big enough to force the immutable Lord to change his mind.[35]

Even many who accept the previous paragraph in principle are prone to believe that if we could assemble a larger group of the faithful, even if they have some diversity in beliefs, we could accomplish a great deal of good. This belief is held by some at the level of all Christians, by some at the level of all Protestants, by some at the level of all Evangelicals and by some at the level of all Lutherans. This is the principle that if you are the enemy of my enemy, then you are my friend. It was the approach of various Reformed leaders after the Reformation who wanted to form military or religious alliances with Luther and his followers. Luther vigorously opposed all such efforts because he knew that such close cooperation in some matters would quickly lead to

---

32 1 Peter 3:20.

33 Numbers 14:30; Exodus 38:26.

34 [Jesus said,] "How narrow is the gate and difficult the road that leads to life, and few find it." (Matthew 7:14).

35 [The Lord said,] "From today on I am he alone, and none can rescue from my power. I act, and who can reverse it?" (Isaiah 43:13).

erosion of doctrinal positions. The Lutheran apologist must point out that it is the Holy Scriptures that draw the line between what we can and cannot accept. No matter how good the deal for forming a common front with others, we cannot "go down to Egypt," as Isaiah said,[36] or we will all be lost.[37] Accepting the apologetic "help" of other Christian bodies by forming a common front on some doctrine is asking for trouble. Things become even worse when the burden of the battle is shifted to us, even though they also benefit. It's the old "let's you and him fight" because he is our common enemy. The Lutheran apologist must not be suckered into such battles.

While we all believe that we are strong enough not to fall into the trap of making common cause with false teachers, we are in reality no stronger than Peter who denied the Lord when the circumstances appeared compelling.[38] A favorite tactic of people, regardless of their beliefs, is to put social pressure on the Christian to join in some activity with them. It can involve merely wasting time, immoral or criminal behavior, doctrinal compromise or showing a *false flag*.[39] The apologist must be ready to answer the question, "What's wrong with a little X?" If there is anything wrong with any amount of X, then we must resist going along with X even if it costs us friends, harmony within the family, opportunities for promotion or our standing as rational people in the community. When faced with the opportunity to flock together with other birds, we must be certain that in the matter at hand, they really have the same type of feathers.

Faith and the Goals Hierarchy

The Lord, the God of the Bible, makes it abundantly clear that he expects the first place in our lives. From Mount Sinai he said to the Israelites, "Do not have other gods besides me."[40] Moses wrote, "Fear the LORD your God, wor-

---

[36] "Woe to those who go down to Egypt for help and who depend on horses! They trust in the abundance of chariots and in the large number of horsemen. They do not look to the Holy One of Israel and they do not seek the LORD." (Isaiah 31:1).

[37] [Solomon wrote,] "There is a way that seems right to a person, but its end is the way to death." (Proverbs 14:12).

[38] Galatians 2:11–21.

[39] People give a "false flag" when they behave in a way which is different from what they claim to believe. This can place a stumbling block in the path of other Christians. See Galatians 2:11-21. The term comes from the days when pirates flew false flags to deceive other ships into approaching them.

[40] Exodus 20:3.

ship him, and take your oaths in his name. Do not follow other gods, the gods of the peoples around you."[41] Jesus said, "But seek first the kingdom of God and his righteousness, and all these things will be provided for you"[42] and "If anyone comes to me and does not hate his own father and mother, wife and children, brothers and sisters—yes, and even his own life—he cannot be my disciple."[43] These statements show the immense importance that the Lord places on having the top spot in our lives.

There will be, of course, other things that are of importance to people, and how these gain importance has been well studied. Psychological research has shown that both positive and negative incentives are critical to controlling human behavior and establishing goals.[44] People are naturally drawn to things that give them pleasure, and they learn to avoid things that cause them pain. Yet these two motivators cannot always be separated; the pleasure of good grades, for example, requires enduring the pain of studying. People set their goals based on the amount of pleasure they hope to gain for the incurring of a certain amount of pain. The acceptable pain/pleasure ratio will vary by individual. Moreover, both intrinsic motivators (e.g., a sense of accomplishment, a feeling of guilt) and extrinsic motivators (e.g., public acclaim, financial loss) play a role in goal setting, with extrinsic motivators often trumping intrinsic motivators. Goal-confusion for the Christian can occur because the goal-motivators of the Christian faith are intrinsic, while many of the motivators for temporal goals are extrinsic. Jesus declared that those who seek their rewards in the eyes of men will receive such rewards, but they will receive no reward from God the Father.[45]

The lure for the Christian to elevate temporal goals above spiritual goals is ubiquitous. Those selling products, services and ideas are always trying to get their wares high on the list of our goals, preferably on top. For example, an auto dealer might want us to believe that a new car is the critical factor to

---

41 Deuteronomy 6:13-14a.

42 Matthew 6:33.

43 Luke 14:26.

44 Hamilton, ibid., Lect. 8.

45 [Jesus said,] "Be careful not to practice your righteousness in front of others to be seen by them. Otherwise, you have no reward with your Father in heaven. So whenever you give to the poor, don't sound a trumpet before you, as the hypocrites do in the synagogues and on the streets, to be applauded by people. Truly I tell you, they have their reward. But when you give to the poor, don't let your left hand know what your right hand is doing, so that your giving may be in secret. And your Father who sees in secret will reward you." (Matthew 6:1-4).

our happiness. A university administrator may warn us that we cannot make a good salary without a college degree. A coach might stress the importance of our children being involved in the school sports program. A politician may argue that better infrastructure is the key to future prosperity. On a continuing basis, numerous "sellers" are attempting to provide the appropriate motivation to make us feel that there are certain things that we just must do or have.[46] While these tangible or temporal things may have some importance in the short-term, as they come cascading onto our list of goals, they may overwhelm the ability of our System 2s to properly evaluate them in terms of their long-range significance. We become victimized by the "tyranny of the urgent". Moreover, those proposing diversions of our time and resources to their causes are often very good at the psychological manipulation needed to create the illusion of urgency. Christians are then tempted to put their faith on autopilot for "just a little while until this crisis is over." In the process, their goals hierarchy is often permanently reshuffled.

The apologist frequently encounters such a problem with goals hierarchy with someone who is either a professing Christian or a mission prospect when discussing his or her spiritual life. The person may say, "I know that I should be more committed to God, to the church, to reading my Bible, to living a godly life, to …, but …." What follows the "but" is often a clue to how his or her heart has fallen under the psychological manipulation of the things of this world. The apologist must probe the person's thinking with pointed questions about their feelings concerning the Lord: "What do you want out of life?" "What are you afraid of if you don't do X?" "Why do you think God will be satisfied with you if you behave in manner Y?" Such probing is essential to determine what factors people regard as important in establishing their goals hierarchy, so that the law and/or the gospel can be presented effectively.

The Christian's best defense against the temptations of the world is to have a life strategy which begins with the regular study of the Word of God.[47] The second step is to compile a list of the blessings and the challenges which the

---

[46] "For those who live according to the flesh have their minds set on the things of the flesh, but those who live according to the Spirit have their minds set on the things of the Spirit." (Romans 8:5).

[47] [A psalmist wrote,] "How happy is the one who does not walk in the advice of the wicked or stand in the pathway with sinners or sit in the company of mockers! Instead, his delight is in the LORD's instruction, and he meditates on it day and night. He is like a tree planted beside flowing streams that bears its fruit in its season and whose leaf does not wither. Whatever he does prospers." (Psalm 1:1-3).

Lord has provided.[48] The third step is to decide how each of the blessings will be used and how each of the challenges will be addressed. Priorities in terms of how these fit into a life of service to the Lord can then be established. The Lord does not promise us a scripted life that can be planned out until our deaths. He will certainly allow us to experience surprises. Yet, by drafting a plan and by periodically revising it when we are not faced with the need to make immediate decisions, we can consider new opportunities and challenges within a framework that will prevent our making hasty judgments which will have long-term negative consequences to our faith. The devil is always seeking a way to lead the believer into sin and despair.[49]

To help people prevent their spiritual goals from being manipulated by worldly influences, the apologist might consider how to use *thought experiments* as a constructive tool. These experiments have become popular in such diverse fields as philosophy, physics, and diagnostic medicine. For example, suppose a high school lad is considering a particular secular career. He needs to ask himself some questions. "How will I serve the Lord throughout my life if I pursue this career path? Will I be able to attend a college where there is a nearby church of our fellowship? Are jobs in this career located in places where our fellowship has churches? How will this career affect my ability to establish a Christian family and be a good father? Will my education cost me so much money that it will hamper my other goals? Will this career put me into situations where I will find it difficult to maintain Christian ethics?" All these questions and more are important as a thought experiment in Christian service. If the apologist can guide people facing life choices into developing an approach oriented to a life of service to the Lord instead of an effort just to make a living or to muddle through, then the psychological influences of the secular rewards and punishments can be put into perspective and not become overwhelming or force faith-destroying choices to be made. Proactively strengthening people's intrinsic goals of the Christian faith vis-à-vis the extrinsic goals of the secular world will diminish the amount of work that the apologist needs to do later to repair the damage which has been done to people's goals hierarchy by the sellers of things which have no eternal importance.

---

48 [David wrote,] "LORD, you are my portion and my cup of blessing; you hold my future." (Psalm 16:5).

49 "Be sober-minded, be alert. Your adversary the devil is prowling around like a roaring lion, looking for anyone he can devour." (1 Peter 5:8).

Cognitive Lessons about Education

The more we learn about cognitive psychology, the more we realize that someone is always trying to yank our chain. Hidden messages are programed into much of the communication that we get.[50] Displays in stores are organized to encourage the purchase of specific items. News stories are frequently written to elicit emotion as well as to provide information. Advertisements are designed not only to inform about the real advantages of the product but also to make us think that it will also fulfill unrelated desires (e.g., respect, envy, sexy companions). Issues are framed to cause directed, rather than unbiased, decisions. Secular education likewise openly sells the benefit of a multicultural society while delivering the message that those who do not view all lifestyles as equal are obstructionists to reaching a better world and, thus, are to be avoided. Apologists face the daunting task of teaching people to question everything that is presented to them. In the same way that the Bereans checked out in the Scriptures what Paul told them,[51] so apologists must point people to those portions of the Scriptures which are relevant to the messages being delivered to them in this secular age.

The System 2 decision mechanism can only herd so many cats at one time. Moreover, while the brain has a large long-term storage capacity, it is not limitless. The result of these two phenomena is that we can learn only so much and that we can learn only so fast.[52] Each type of informational bin has a functional limit, and when that limit is reached, the materials must be moved to an overflow bin. Organization of the information must be done by System 2, and this becomes more stressful as the amount of information grows. As mentioned above, this wears it down so that it cannot handle other decision-making tasks. The result of overloading System 2 is that new information "goes in one ear and out the other." This is the reason that the mammoth amount of new technology is a threat to the Christian church. The amount of time and effort needed to gain technical knowledge is time and effort which is not available to study God's Word. Young people are particularly enamored with such technology, so it is a real danger to the study that they need in order to grow in their faith. For many people, this technology is becoming their real

---

50 Hamilton, ibid., Lect. 14.
51 Acts 17:11.
52 Pasupathi, ibid., Lect. 3.

god, and the apologist must forcefully point this out. The glow of the smart phone will not replace the oil of faith as the requirement to get into heaven.

"Where did you hear that?" used to be a common question of the doubter before the invention of the internet search engine. Now people can check on the truthfulness of any statement on the omniscient internet. However, simply because someone posted something does not make it true, no matter how many "likes" it has. But even without the internet, much of the information that we hear is of questionable truthfulness. Moreover, the American public is highly gullible.[53] Worse yet, the first thing that we hear about a subject frequently sets the anchor point for judging all subsequent information, giving a "first-heard" bias. The apologist must warn people to avoid this bias by treating all information as being probably wrong until its source has been checked. It is important to collect knowledge *about* the sources of information so that reliability of the information *from* the source can be determined.[54] This is particularly true when someone claims that the Bible says a particular thing. Most people do not know very much about the Bible, so they easily fall for the ruse that "if something seems like it ought to be in the Bible, then it is actually there". Even just looking at one or two verses might not be enough to determine what the Bible is actually saying. The apologist must direct those who are challenged by people making strange claims about the Bible to check with knowledgeable teachers.

The greatest lesson that one can learn from cognitive psychology is that failing to study is the surest way to be deceived.[55] Not everyone is a scholar, yet almost everyone in this world does learn the things they want to learn and that they think will be important to them. Both failure to learn and learning from the wrong sources will place souls at great risk. "Putting in one's hour a week" in a worship service was wholly inadequate for sound faith 150 years ago, and it is no more adequate now. The apologist must be proactive in urging people to read selected materials at their level of comprehension on a continuing basis. It is gluttony to feed the body but not to feed the soul. Therefore, to make his or her work easier in the long term, the apologist must

---

[53] Novella, ibid.

[54] It is important, however, not to disregard the information from a source merely because the source has biased motives for supplying the information. (See the *appeal to motive* fallacy from Appendix I.)

[55] Hamilton, ibid., Lect. 24.

work to cultivate a desire to learn in everyone whom they can influence.[56]

Neural Research

The human brain is the center of the nervous system. It contains many billions of neurons, each connected by synapses to many other neurons.[57] The brain is divided into a number of sections, such as the cerebrum, thalamus, hypothalamus, tectum, tegmentum, cerebellum, pons and medulla. In recent years, an effort has been made by neurologists to map the various regions of the brain to determine what activities performed activate which portions of the brain. Thanks to the development of such procedures as Computed Axial Tomography (CAT), Magnetic Resonance Imaging (MRI), Magnetoencephalography (MEG) and Positron Emission Tomography (PET), this is now a routine type of study. The brain map gives surgeons the ability to determine which areas of the brain to treat when particular symptoms are seen elsewhere in the body, as well as much information about where it is safe to operate if the brain itself is diseased.

It was natural for those studying the brain to want to know what effect emotional stimuli had on it because such knowledge would be useful for anticipating how a person's actions and personality would be altered after surgery in a particular area of the brain. Some researchers also felt that it would be interesting to know what effects performing certain religious practices would have on the brain.[58] Studies started in 1993 on nuns doing centering prayers. Studies continued on people speaking in tongues, different types of religious people in various forms of meditation, and atheists doing some of the same activities as a reference, although these atheists were not a formal control group. Such studies showed consistent patterns for the various types of religious activities, although there was some variation based on the participants' familiarity with the practices. The researchers concluded that religious practices were firmly rooted in brain activity. The patterns differed by the type of activities, but not necessarily by the beliefs of the subjects.

The observations of the neural researchers have both good and bad news for the apologist, and frequently, it is the same news. Religious practices im-

---

56 Pasupathi, ibid., Lect. 24.

57 DP *Pelvig, H Pakkenberg, AK Stark & B Pakkenberg, "Neocortical glial cell numbers in human brains," Neurobiology of Aging,* ***29****:1754–1762 (2008).*

58 Newberg, ibid.

prove mental alertness and health, particularly among the senior population. That is good, but the effects seem independent of the belief system. Therefore, one cannot claim these findings are a result of worshiping the Lord. Secondly, the research indicated that religious activity activated those parts of the brain that increased contentment and a sense of well-being. Once again, however, these changes were independent of the religion of the participants. In short, there is a benefit to religion in general, so the need for god should not go away soon from the standpoint of brain health. On the other hand, similar effects can be gained by other disciplined practices. This should convince the apologist not to sell Christianity as a way toward the earthly benefit of better mental health. While some Christian practices might be good for both the physical and mental health of the church members, it is the eternal salvation that Christ promises, not some temporal blessing, that people should seek from their spiritual life.

Perhaps the most alarming result of neural research is that our brain changes our concept of god.[59] The various parts of the brain want (i.e., chemically find favorable) a god with which they can relate. The interrelationships of the parts of the brain and the degree to which they respond to various stimuli related to religious practices seem to cause people to assign specific attributes to their image of god. For example, some processes in the brain cry out for an authoritative god, while others might seek a god who can be accessed, such as a friend with whom to talk. The relative strength of these processes will drive the brain to seek one or the other type of god. Some brain patterns are more consistent with desiring an angry god that punishes its enemies, while other patterns correlate to seeking a god that is benevolent. The apologist must talk with people to try to sense how they are being pushed by their brains to seek certain characteristics within a god and then talk about how the Lord acts in that manner. This does not mean that the people should be allowed to redesign the Lord, but rather that they should be taught that he can relate to them in the way that they need to establish a relationship with him within the framework of his law and gospel. Some will need to see his anger at sin, some will need to see his authority over the affairs of men and others will need to know they have a friend in Jesus. If we recall the personality styles that we discussed earlier in this chapter, we will see a relation-

[59] "American Piety in the 21st Century," Baylor Institute for Studies of Religion, 2006 (online).

ship.[60] We need to start where people are so the Holy Spirit can bring them to where they need to be.

The Lord did not create humans to die, but since the fall, death is inevitable. Therefore, it is thought that many human minds have developed a script to deal with dying, just as they have developed scripts to deal with other scenarios from slipping on the ice to witnessing a bank robbery.[61] Certainly, the script for dying will be incomplete because no one has a lot of experience with dying. It will also be colored by the person's culture and by what he or she has previously heard about dying. Some, but not all, people who enter the near-death state will have their minds at some lower level implement such a script and begin feeding the conscious mind the information from the "dying" script. Things in the script will seem real because the normal sensory inputs will have been shut down in anticipation of dying and because the brain is being "doped" by lack of blood circulation. People often have a sensation of becoming detached from their bodies, seeing bright lights, meeting people they know or being met by a supernatural being. While what happens in the dying script may seem very real to the person involved, the person is not really dead because the brain is still functioning at some level. Neurons are still firing and messages are still being passed.[62] If the person is revived from the near-death state, the items supplied by the script seem as they have just been observed by the senses. The person, therefore, believes that they really happened and transfers the images to long-term memory. If the person is not revived, we cannot know how the dying script plays out. Because the details of what happens are uncertain and because the phenomenon continues to be a focus of scientific research, the apologist should not interpret any figures or events in these near-death experiences as being real, but should rather assure the person that at the time of death their soul will be brought before God for judgment.[63] The apologist need not challenge experiences which people believe that they have had, but they certainly should not use claims of people's going to Heaven and returning to support our faith.

---

[60] 1 Corinthians 9:19-22.

[61] Newberg, ibid., Lect. 15.

[62] Due to the difficulty of studying the brain of a person in this state, this explanation might be subject to later refinement.

[63] "Just as it is appointed for people to die once—and after this, judgment." (Hebrews 9:27).

Analytic Paralysis

We will end by considering two difficult psychological hurdles that an apologist will sometimes face. As we discussed previously, our long-term memories are not reliable. Rather than recording what actually happened, they record a blended account of our scripts and our sensory inputs. They become further corrupted because our sinful nature wants to make us look the best in our memories, even if that means altering what we observed. These mechanisms also try to protect what we remember to be true from alteration by new evidence which we do not like. We all have a tendency to be closed minded, refusing to honestly consider new things if our memory has been refined to the point of believing that we know the real truth about a subject. Healthy skepticism about new information is warranted to prevent being gullible and being blown to and fro by every wind of change.[64] However, the unwillingness to consider or discuss an issue can be a sign of a deeper psychological problem. As apologists, we cannot address such deeper problems, but we can do two things that will help us in our witnessing. First, we can explore whether there really is a deeper problem or whether we are just facing an issue on which there is a major misunderstanding that can be approached from a different angle. Second, we can look at our own approaches to be certain that we have not so biased ourselves that we have abandoned our standard of truth, namely the Scriptures, and have made our own ideas and feelings the source of our beliefs.

We introduced the topic of denialism in Chapter 5 in our discussion of those who deny certain aspects of science. Denialism[65] is rooted in the fallacy called the *appeal to absurdity*. Something is claimed to be absurd; therefore, it cannot be true. Certainly, some things are absurd. For example, if someone claimed to have thrown a baseball over the Atlantic Ocean, we might reject this out of hand as being impossible. However, denialism goes further because it refuses to accept evidence. For example, reformers in southern Germany and Switzerland in the sixteenth century denied that the body and blood of Christ were substantially present in the Lord's Supper because it was "absurd" that a human body could be present in many places at the same time. This mindset prevented them from even considering scriptural evidence that was opposed to their position. They denied there could be such evidence. In effect,

---

64 Ephesians 4:14.

65 Novella, ibid., Lect. 20.

such people have created a script that filters out anything that does not support their position.

Denialists often resort to another logical fallacy called *moving the goalposts*. In an effort to appear willing to discuss an issue rationally, they sometimes are willing to agree to consider evidence that could prove them wrong if it is produced. In effect, they claim to be willing to engage in a falsification challenge. However, when such evidence is presented, they "move the goal posts" by demanding further evidence. By repeating this strategy, they can continue to declare that they have never been disproved by evidence. For example, when machine intelligence (artificial intelligence) was being developed in the 1960s, some people claimed that computers could never have "real intelligence," that is, intelligence like only humans could possess.[66] They claimed that computers would never be able to read handwriting or understand spoken human speech. When computers began to do these things, the definition of "real intelligence" was changed to mean being able to play complex games such as chess. When the chess-playing computer Deep Blue beat the reigning world champion under tournament conditions in 1997, once again the goalpost of "real intelligence" had to be moved so that computers could not have it.

The apologist may need to probe the apparent denialist's position from several directions to see whether it really is denialist or whether it is merely excessive caution. If a position is truly denialist, then the apologist is not going to make any progress reasoning with the person because his or her heart will not accept scriptural arguments, just as the Calvinists didn't. The apologist must rather try to contain the damage that the denialist does to others by teaching other Christians the appropriate way to address the issue under discussion.

Another form of thinking impairment is to believe in a grand conspiracy theory.[67] With this impairment, people so strongly believe they are right about some matter that the only explanation which they can accept for why other people do not think the same way is that they have been duped by a broad-based conspiracy which is suppressing the evidence that supports their position. For example, the reason that conspiracy theorists cannot produce defini-

---

66 Hubert L Dreyfus, "Alchemy and Artificial Intelligence" (RAND Corporation, Santa Monica, CA, 1965).

67 Novella, ibid., Lect. 19.

tive evidence that aliens are visiting Earth in flying saucers is that the American government and other world governments are engaged in a conspiracy to confiscate and hide all such evidence. Those who try to raise objections to this line of reasoning are accused of being part of the conspiracy. The claim that there is a wide conspiracy among scientists to suppress evidence supporting creationism is an example of such a grand conspiratorial theory.

Certainly, there is conspiracy and collusion in this sinful world. For example, sometimes competitors will agree to divide up construction jobs by assigning some to each company and then adjusting their bids so the appropriate company is the low bidder, albeit at a higher bid than would have been made in a competitive situation. Fraternity brothers might use an "old-boys' network" to steer jobs and contracts to members of that fraternity without giving others an opportunity to compete for them. Police officers, neighbors or family members might agree to hide evidence of a crime to shield a prominent person. Some of these conspiracies, such as engaging in insider stock trading, are actively investigated by government agencies. However, these are small-scale operations with a very limited number of players. To be correct, grand conspiracies would require so many players that it would be impossible to maintain the secrecy imperative for a conspiracy to be successful.

In addressing the issues of grand conspiracies, the apologist must be realistic about the nature of a world where the demons are continually trying to cause havoc. People will conspire and act dishonestly for their own advantage and to promote causes which are harmful to the faith of Christians. On the other hand, the Lord will not let the devil so organize the world against the beliefs of his elect so as to destroy them, but he will cause the hellish hosts to frequently fall all over themselves in their opposition to the divine will.[68] We should remind people never to blame malevolence for what can be explained by mere incompetence or ignorance or to assert that people's natural hostility to the gospel must imply that they are part of a conspiracy. When facing those who are obsessed with the idea that scientists or government agents are working in a concerted fashion to destroy our faith, the apologist must point out that the Lord is in control and is more powerful than any set of conspirators. Instead, the apologist must direct people to the teachings of the Scrip-

---

[68] "No temptation has come upon you except what is common to humanity. But God is faithful; he will not allow you to be tempted beyond what you are able, but with the temptation he will also provide a way out so that you may be able to bear it." (1 Corinthians 10:13).

tures, which are the firm foundation against which even the gates of hell cannot prevail.

Summary

Like the discoveries in any science, those of cognitive psychology can be used for good or evil. The apologist should be very concerned by how easy it is to manipulate human thinking by altering its reference points and by changing the environment in which people make their decisions and formulate their opinions. We are all gullible by nature, and it is even worse in matters concerning our souls, because Satan and his hosts are working to deceive us.[69] As a result, people must be urged to study the Word of God diligently, and the apologist must study even more so as to be able to point out particular dangers. While the Holy Spirit can overcome any obstacle, it is sinful to tempt him.[70] We must use System 2 reasoning with wisdom and must train System 1 to detect and flag efforts to manipulate our faith by psychological means. "Jesus told them, 'Watch out that no one deceives you.'"[71]

---

[69] "Let no one deceive you with empty arguments, for God's wrath is coming on the disobedient because of these things." (Ephesians 5:6).

[70] "Do not test the LORD your God as you tested him at Massah." (Deuteronomy 6:16).

[71] Mark 13:5.

10

The Christian Church

It might surprise some people to have a chapter on the Christian church in a book about apologetics. Yet the church is what people see. By God's design, the Holy Christian Church is his chosen instrument to spread the gospel until Christ returns. It's the only way that the elect will hear the message that will bring them to faith. Yet, until Jesus comes back, the church exists in this world "warts and all." Because it is made up of sinners, the skeptics and opponents of the gospel find a lot to criticize about God's chosen instrument. For many people, the church and the people who belong to it are the best arguments to not accept the good news about Jesus. In this chapter, we are going to review what the church is and how it works. We will remind ourselves of the mission God gave us and the means he appointed for us to use. We will also look at some of the attacks that skeptics bring against the church to discredit the gospel.

Setting the Stage

The word "church" can mean many different things. If someone says, "What a beautiful church!", we all know they're talking about a building. But if a congregation's building burns down, does that church cease to exist? Obviously not, because the people that belong to that congregation are the church. So we often use the word "church" to refer to a specific congregation, as when we say, "My church is facing a tough time right now, but we're going to rebuild." We can use the word for a larger group (a "church body") like a

Lutheran synod or the United Methodist Church or the Roman Catholic Church. We can also use it for closely related traditions that may encompass more than one denomination. For us, the most obvious example is the "Evangelical Lutheran Church," but we also might speak of the Baptist Church, the Episcopal Church etc. We sometimes speak of "houses of worship," but when we unpack that expression, we usually say, "churches, mosques or synagogues." We reserve the word "church" to refer exclusively to Christians.

For Lutherans, the *Holy Christian Church* is a technical term that means all true believers in Jesus Christ of every time and place. We often shorten that expression to just the *church* and mean all believers. The Holy Christian Church includes Old and New Testament believers, those in heaven and those still on this earth, those who live in Wisconsin or Michigan or China or South America. If you have faith in Jesus, you belong to the church, no matter what church body you belong to here.

We use a variety of terms to refer to gatherings of believers here on this earth: congregations, church bodies, denominations, synods, conferences, and many more. Strictly speaking, all those groups are "church" only because there are members of the Holy Christian Church (i.e., believers) there. Also strictly speaking, those groups only function as "church" when they do the work Christ has commanded his church to do. The gathering transcends any sort of social club or political movement or effort to remake our society.

The Invisible Church

In the Apostles' Creed, we confess, "I believe in the Holy Christian Church, the communion of saints." These words already raise the very point that makes apologetics both challenging and necessary concerning the issue of the Christian church: it is an article of faith. We believe in the Holy Christian Church because God says it exists. We believe that even when the evidence we can see with our own eyes or can gather through the media or can deduce from history makes the church look anything but holy or Christian. Here again, the words of Hebrews 11:1 apply: "Now faith is the reality of what is hoped for, the proof of what is not seen."

Lutheran theologians like to speak of the visible church and the invisible church. The *visible church* is every congregation and church body we can see. The *invisible church* is everyone who shares faith in Christ. Because only God can look into the heart and see faith, only God knows for sure who is in the invisible (true) church.[1]

So how do *we* know who is included? We can draw a relative conclusion based on two objective indicators. One indicator is the presence of the gospel in Word and sacrament, which Lutherans call the *marks of the church*. Marks can be important. One might think of animals with patterns on their coats, such as zebras or cheetahs. Scientists who study them in the field learn the pattern that is unique to each animal, and they can identify individuals by their markings. It is the same with religious organizations. The gospel makes the church present because God's power always accomplishes his purpose.[2] Therefore, wherever you find the gospel (even if it is somewhat adulterated by false teaching), you can assume there are believers present.[3] But still you cannot tell *for certain* which member is a true believer and which is a hypocrite masquerading as a believer. That's true even for leaders in the church.[4]

This brings us to the second indicator: a person's confession of faith. This lets us make a provisional identification of who is and who isn't a member of the invisible church. An individual's confession really consists of three parts. The first and most obvious part is what they say, for example, "I believe in Jesus Christ, true God ...." An equally important part of their confession is what they actually do. A person, for example, who continues in unrepentant sin but claims to be a faithful church member is lying and should be excommunicated, which is to say, recognized as an unbeliever.

---

1 "Nevertheless, God's solid foundation stands firm, bearing this inscription: **The Lord knows those who are his,** and let everyone who calls on the name of the Lord turn away from wickedness." (2 Timothy 2:19) / "One believes with the heart, resulting in righteousness, and one confesses with the mouth, resulting in salvation." (Romans 10:10).

2 [The Lord said,] "For just as rain and snow fall from heaven and do not return there without saturating the earth and making it germinate and sprout, and providing seed to sow and food to eat, so my word that comes from my mouth will not return to me empty, but it will accomplish what I please and will prosper in what I send it to do." (Isaiah 55:10-11).

3 We must be careful here to distinguish between the outward form of the gospel and the inner content of the gospel. Any religious group that uses the Bible in its teaching and preaching has the outward form of the gospel when clear statements about Jesus' work are read from the Scriptures. Some groups, however, deny the content or the actual meaning of those gospel words. Antitrinitarian groups, such as Latter Day Saints or Jehovah's Witnesses, fall into this category. Likewise, modern Judaism has rejected Christ, even though prophecies of his coming are read regularly in their synagogues. [St. Paul wrote,] "Yet still today, whenever Moses is read, a veil lies over their hearts, but whenever a person turns to the Lord, the veil is removed." (2 Corinthians 3:15-16).

4 [Jesus said,] "Be on your guard against false prophets who come to you in sheep's clothing but inwardly are ravaging wolves." (Matthew 7:15).

Most people are willing to grant these first two indicators. It is the last one which is more difficult, but which absolutely must be considered a part of an individual's confession: what church and/or other religious organizations they claim membership in. This last part may require some explanation. In the past, most people would have accepted the proposition that belonging to an organization meant that you agree with all that it stands for. Today, many people will say that it is generally accepted that someone might not agree with everything that a church or an organization says or does, but he or she can still be a part of it, because they agree with the important things. They might compare it to membership in a political party, in which someone might vote a straight ticket, but still might disagree with some aspects of the party's platform. In the church, this is complicated by the tendency of some church organizations to specifically reject any confessional (i.e., doctrinal) identity.

Membership without complete commitment to a church's teachings creates a dilemma. How does the world at large know which things a specific member agrees with and which ones he or she disagrees with? It is still true that if someone is a member of a church or a lodge or a society of any sort, they are saying to the world, "I approve of what this group stands for." They might claim all kinds of reservations privately, but that does not change the impression they give to all who know of their membership and participation. In fact, if their church does something offensive, people might blame them because they belong to it. They might even resign their membership in protest. What does that say, except that they don't want to be tarred with the public confession of that church?

A person's confession is not a perfect indicator of faith. Sometimes, believers (especially new believers) hide their faith, as Joseph of Arimathea did.[5] Sometimes, people join a visible church and echo its confession without actually believing it. A young man might be about to marry a young Christian woman who might desperately want him to join her church, so he does, just to please her. Similarly, a young person might participate in the confirmation ceremony at the end of eighth grade to avoid a fight with his or her parents. Despite these kinds of issues, one's confession is a functional indicator of who is a believer, and so God tells us to use it.[6]

---

[5] John 19:38.

[6] Matthew 7:15-20.

The invisible church is really a grouping of people. The Bible uses different images to talk about that grouping: "the body of Christ,"[7] "the house/household of God,"[8] "the new (or heavenly or spiritual) Jerusalem,"[9] "the people of God"[10] and many more. On the one hand, it is made up of individuals who personally trust in the life, death, and resurrection of Christ to give them eternal life. On the other hand, it is a community, a people, a body. Its members are interconnected in their faith. Both of these two truths are part of what it means to be the church.

The Holy Christian Church is holy not in the sense that we Christians stop sinning. It is holy in the sense that God declares us to be holy on the basis of the life, death and resurrection of Christ. Now, this does lead to a new and holy life here on this earth.[11] Still, on this side of heaven, the new and holy life is never complete. The church is Christian in the simple sense that it hopes in—and only in—Christ (see Chapter 7). The modern emphasis on religious diversity and coexistence simply is not part of the Christian faith. Nevertheless, the Holy Christian Church transcends denominations. Just as it is possible for hypocrites to pretend to be believers and so have membership in a visible church, all those who truly trust in Jesus are part of his church no matter what the sign in front of their building calls them. There will be Catholics and Methodists and Baptists in heaven along with Lutherans.

If this is true, why can't everyone worship together? In heaven we will. We will enjoy perfect fellowship with all members of the Holy Christian Church. On earth, however, our church membership is still a part of our confession of faith. When people join a Baptist church, they are confessing that they approve of Baptist teachings, which includes a denial of the Real Presence of Jesus' body and blood in the sacraments and an affirmation that we must make a decision for Christ to be a true believer. Those errors will not always destroy faith (although they very well could). Moreover, God tells us to watch out for those who teach things that are contrary to what we have learned and to avoid them.[12] This does not mean that we must refuse all con-

---

7 See, for example, Ephesians 1:22-23, 4:12,16 and Romans 12:4-5.

8 See, for example, 1 Peter 2:5, 4:17 and 1 Timothy 3:15.

9 See, for example, Galatians 4:25-26, Hebrews 12:22, Revelation 3:12 and Revelation 21:2,10.

10 1 Peter 2:10.

11 "What should we say then? Should we continue in sin so that grace may multiply? Absolutely not! How can we who died to sin still live in it?" (Romans 6:1-2).

12 Romans 16:17-18.

tact with Christians who disagree with us, but it does mean that we must not join with them in supporting common ministries or in proclaiming the gospel. Nevertheless, we look forward to the day when we will enjoy perfect fellowship with those believers in heaven.

Because we cannot tell who truly has faith, we cannot separate the invisible church from the visible church. But God does know the difference. It is the believers within visible churches that make those bodies "church". This means that Jesus' command to proclaim the gospel is really directed at those of us who actually trust in him. It is possible—even probable—that some members and even some ministers have proclaimed the gospel without believing it.[13] Are those ministrations valid? Yes. Paul wrote, "For I am not ashamed of the gospel, because it is the power of God for salvation to everyone who believes, first to the Jew, and also to the Greek."[14] The power is in the gospel, not in the preacher. As Paul noted in Philippians, as long as Christ is preached, the Holy Spirit works. That comforts us when we act as apologists. The gospel is God's power. It will accomplish his purpose.

The Mission of the Church

Everything that is made by someone else has a purpose. It might be to dig ditches (e.g., a shovel or an industrial piece of machinery). It might be to enlighten or educate (e.g., a book or a magazine). It might be simply to entertain (e.g., a movie) or to bring pleasure through beauty (e.g., a painting). God made the church. It has a purpose. For the church to thrive on this earth, it needs to function according to its God-given purpose. Jesus pictures the church's function in terms of giving light and being salt.[15] The church exists to enlighten the hearts and minds of those who are inside of it and those who are not. The church exists to prick consciences in this world, like salt, by proclaiming the law and the gospel. If the church ceases in these functions or replaces them with something that seems to be more "in tune" with our age, then it loses its function. Jesus said, "it is no longer good for anything". In the paragraphs that follow, we will identify the purpose God gave the church and address various ways that the modern world attacks that mission or tries to distract it by focusing on peripheral questions.

---

13 See, for example, Philippians 1:12-18.

14 Romans 1:16.

15 Matthew 5:13-16.

God gave the Christian church a mission here on this earth: to proclaim the gospel. This command assumes some nonverbal communication. Jesus told us, "Let your light shine before others, so that they may see your good works and give glory to your Father in heaven."[16] It has been said, "A Christian's life is the only sermon some people will ever hear."[17] Yet, living a Christian life is not enough. We need to tell what Jesus has done. When Jesus gave the Great Commission,[18] he told us to make disciples of all nations. Making disciples is more than just sharing the gospel. It's leading Christians to follow their Lord for as long as he gives them life here.

Making Disciples. Jesus specifically told his followers to make disciples *of all nations.* This means that mission work—sharing the gospel with those who don't believe—is an essential part of our task. The church engages in outreach in different ways. Individual Christians simply talk about their faith.[19] Congregations organize efforts to reach out into their own communities, and they support efforts to send missionaries to places they cannot reach personally.[20] While unbelievers often have a negative reaction to people knocking on their doors and inviting them to church, we do not have to defend our efforts to reach out. Christ commanded us to, and any fair-minded person would have to acknowledge that if we believe that Jesus is our Lord, we need to do the work he sent us out to do.

Sometimes, a side question comes up about "sheep stealing," which is a term that is sometimes used for bringing people who are already Christians into our own churches. Traditionally, Lutherans have avoided this practice, because all true believers will go to heaven, regardless of what church they belong to. However, we have never hidden our defense of the truth. Sometimes, people in other churches hear the truth from Lutheran pastors or members, and they desire the clarity with which God has blessed our church body. It is not sin to give his clear Word to them or to receive them into mem-

---

16 Matthew 5:16.

17 "But even if you should suffer for righteousness, you are blessed. **Do not fear what they fear or be intimidated,** but in your hearts regard Christ the Lord as holy, ready at any time to give a defense to anyone who asks you for a reason for the hope that is in you. Yet do this with gentleness and respect, keeping a clear conscience, so that when you are accused, those who disparage your good conduct in Christ will be put to shame." (1 Peter 3:14-16).

18 Matthew 28:18-20.

19 See, for example, Acts 8:1-4.

20 This is what the church in Antioch did when it sent out Paul and Barnabas (Acts 13:1-3).

bership. Today, with so many Christian churches abandoning the Scriptures wholesale, it should not surprise us when faithful Christians flee to a church that stands on God's Word. Conversely, it is not our job to pry those people out of their churches. Outreach efforts should primarily target those who do not know their Savior.

Jesus contrasts baptism with teaching to underline the need to bring people to faith and then to disciple them for as long as they live here. In practical terms, we make disciples on numerous levels. Not only do we baptize our children, but we also teach them to know their Savior. We often hear it said that parents should let their children make up their own minds about religion when they're older. This sounds very open-minded. But in reality, it reinforces the sinful nature that lives in the hearts of our children. [21] God commands parents to raise their children in the faith.[22]

Another key component to making disciples is discipline. Jesus himself lays out the basic format for church discipline in Matthew 18:15-20. The purpose is love. It's easy to portray church discipline as unloving and hypocritical, especially when it reaches the point of excommunication. The apologetic task is to unmask this posturing and explain that love demands discipline. When Jesus was confronted by a self-righteous man, the evangelist Mark wrote, "Looking at him, Jesus loved him and said to him …"[23] He went on to proclaim the law. Love demands that we risk wrath and hurt feelings by confronting issues of sin before a lack of repentance destroys faith and robs that person of eternal life. Of course, in our society, people who don't accept the Bible's teachings on morality will never accept the necessity of disciplining unrepented sin. We should not allow ourselves to be sidetracked on this point. It should be enough to find an issue that both parties agree is an evil and ask whether the church can allow its members to continue in that evil. From there, we can work backward to the point that God calls us to discipline other things, too, even things that the person we're talking to does not recognize as sin.

Another part of making disciples is the church's ongoing need to provide comfort for the troubled and the afflicted. But we need to be careful here. The

---

21 [David wrote,] "Indeed, I was guilty when I was born; I was sinful when my mother conceived me." (Psalm 51:5).

22 "Fathers, don't stir up anger in your children, but bring them up in the training and instruction of the Lord." (Ephesians 6:4).

23 Mark 10:17-21.

comfort of the gospel is different from the comfort that comes from therapy. The true comfort of the gospel is that our sins are forgiven and that we will live with Jesus. In addition, he then promises to hear our prayers and make all our sufferings work for our good. Many medical professionals point to studies that show that religious people often respond to treatment better than non-religious people and that pastoral care in the hospital can help with the healing process. However reliable these studies may be (see Chapter 9), the real work of a pastor in such situations is to point the sick and troubled to the Lord who loved them so much that he sent Jesus to save them. Then God demonstrated his power over all that hurts us by raising him from the dead. That is the one who promises to hear our prayers.

The Holy Ministry. Jesus himself established the blueprint of the work of the New Testament church when he called the twelve disciples and designated them as "apostles" so that they could learn from him and then go out and preach the gospel.[24] St. Paul made clear that the public ministry is God's will when he wrote that Jesus himself gave some to be apostles, prophets, evangelists and pastors and teachers.[25] He also asked how anyone can preach unless they are sent.[26] The church in this world will always have ministers who represent Christ to his people and who represent Christ and the church to the world. God never defined what exactly goes into any public ministerial office, beyond being a servant of the Word. The Lutheran church has traditionally focused most of its attention on the offices of pastors and teachers. In Lutheran thinking, the administration of the sacraments, under ordinary circumstances, is a pastoral function.

Ministers are one of the most visible parts of the church's operation, so it's not surprising that the ministry has often been a lightning rod for controversy and attacks. Some of those attacks derive from the very concept of the ministry itself. The next section will briefly touch on the development of bishops into a full-blown episcopate in the Roman Catholic and Eastern Orthodox communions. These offices are conceived of as having enormous power and authority. On the opposite end of the scale, some churches from the Evangelical or Pentecostal schools of thought effectively have lay preachers who simply follow "an inner call" to preach.

---

24 Mark 3:13-19.

25 Ephesians 4:11.

26 "And how can they preach unless they are sent?" (Romans 10:15).

The Bible does not specify educational requirements for ministers or how we should organize our churches' ministries. If an episcopal system functions best, we are free to employ it. Conversely, the Bible does invest authority in the ministry.[27] It is a very specialized authority, the authority of the law and the gospel. Ministers speak as Christ's representatives and point exclusively to him. Jesus was emphatic in teaching that ministers (and all other leaders in the church) are called to show the exact same kind of humility and self-sacrifice that Jesus himself did.[28] He never hesitated to proclaim hard truths to people who didn't want to hear them (once he even used a whip![29]). Despite this, he still came as one who served and who gave his life as a ransom for many. An attitude of humble self-sacrifice that is always courageous to speak the truth is the model for the church's ministry, whatever offices we institute.

A common way to attack the church today is to attack *organized religion* (sometimes called *institutionalized religion*). This attack generally assumes dishonesty on the part of Christians, but it especially attacks leaders in the church. Some people assert that the church has changed from a movement that challenged entrenched and corrupt religious leadership into an organization that is all about power. They usually go on to argue that the church has become an instrument to help elites stay in power—whether political elites in society or elites within the church. The church is an instrument to subjugate people, especially women and minorities.[30]

Is it true that over time, the "institutional church" became obsessed with power? In some cases, yes, and this is not just a Roman Catholic problem. But Jesus instituted the ministry to serve the spiritual needs of his people and to proclaim the gospel. He warned those who lead that they were to be servants, not masters, just as he came to serve.[31] The testimony of Christian people who

---

27 "Remember your leaders who have spoken God's word to you. As you carefully observe the outcome of their lives, imitate their faith. ... Obey your leaders and submit to them, since they keep watch over your souls as those who will give an account, so that they can do this with joy and not with grief, for that would be unprofitable for you." (Hebrews 13:7,17).

28 See, for example, Mark 9:33-37 and Luke 22:24-30.

29 John 2:13-22.

30 Of course, this was the position of people like Karl Marx, but today one does not need to go that far left to find it. This kind of thinking pervades university classes and even much writing and thinking in liberal churches.

31 "Jesus called them over and said, 'You know that the rulers of the Gentiles lord it over them, and those in high positions act as tyrants over them. It must not be like that among you. On the contrary, whoever wants to become great among you must be your servant,

have benefited from the gospel ministry might be the strongest antidote to these oft repeated attacks.

The Roles of Women in the Church. When people portray the church as an institution that is all about power, they usually claim that the early church had both male and female ministers but that once the pursuit of power took over, women were sidelined. They often further assert that the early leaders were lower class, uneducated people who were revolutionary in their outlook. They then maintain that once the church became institutionalized, freedom gave way to hierarchy and power structures. Priests and bishops became authority figures. Wealth and status became more important than people.

To answer this attack, the apologist should begin with the true purpose of the church: to rescue all people, male and female, slaves and free, of all races, from the power of sin. St. Paul wrote, "There is neither Jew nor Gentile, neither slave nor free, nor is there male and female, for you are all one in Christ Jesus."[32] This *Big Lie*[33] about Christianity has to be opposed by the true purpose God gave the church.

After this, the subordinate arguments need to be countered with the Word of God. The holy ministry was established by Christ. A careful reading of the gospels tells us that some women supported Jesus' ministry. Matthew, Mark and Luke all state that women "followed" Jesus from Galilee to Jerusalem.[34] Luke also tells us once that they were "with" Jesus during his ministry.[35] What

---

and whoever wants to be first among you must be your slave; just as the Son of Man did not come to be served, but to serve, and to give his life as a ransom for many.'" (Matthew 20:25–28).

32 Galatians 3:28. See also Colossians 3:11.

33 A "Big Lie" is a blatantly false statement that is repeated frequently and emphatically so that it appears to gain an air of truth from its constant repetition.

34 "Many women who had followed Jesus from Galilee and looked after him were there, watching from a distance. Among them were Mary Magdalene, Mary the mother of James and Joseph, and the mother of Zebedee's sons." (Matthew 27:55-56) / "There were also women watching from a distance. Among them were Mary Magdalene, Mary the mother of James the younger and of Joses, and Salome. In Galilee these women followed him and took care of him. Many other women had come up with him to Jerusalem." (Mark 15:40-41). / "The women who had come with him from Galilee followed along and observed the tomb and how his body was placed. Then they returned and prepared spices and perfumes. And they rested on the Sabbath according to the commandment." (Luke 23:55-56).

35 "Afterward he was traveling from one town and village to another, preaching and telling the good news of the kingdom of God. The Twelve were with him, and also some women who had been healed of evil spirits and sicknesses: Mary, called Magdalene (seven demons had come out of her); Joanna the wife of Chuza, Herod's steward; Susanna; and many others who were supporting them from their possessions." (Luke 8:1-3).

exactly that looked like is difficult to say because the gospels don't say any more than that. It is clear that at least some of these women were well off, but how regularly did they really travel with the disciples and Jesus? We just don't know. What is clear is that these women are never mentioned in the gospels as taking part in Jesus' ministry. Every reference that is used to support the idea of women preaching in the early church is questionable at best. There simply is no clear statement or example that this was the case.

Of course, the underlying agenda for this argument is to promote "equality" in the church. The assumption is made that woman are treated badly in the church. They are only allowed to do the most menial functions. It is pure male chauvinism to deny women any office that is open to a man. If one examines that line of thought carefully, he or she will discover a completely unbiblical set of assumptions: being a follower is less important and less beneficial to the church than being a leader, "humble" service is really demeaning, and a person should have the right to pursue any service that they have the natural gifts to pursue. Yet, doesn't that fly in the face of Jesus' words about coming to serve? God calls pastors to serve and sacrifice. God sees leadership—in the home, in the church and even in the state—as service, as hard work that is done for the benefit of others. To make the assumption that denying women the opportunity to be pastors or bishops or church councilmen is demeaning is to misunderstand the relationship of the mutual interdependence that God has created.

Should women be allowed to preach? God himself denies women any role in the church where they teach or exercise authority over men.[36] It is difficult to see many real-world situations in which women could preach publicly or function as pastors with those restrictions. Faith accepts God's words and plan; it does not distort them. God never says that a woman would be a poor preacher or that women are less intelligent (and so worse writers, worse at biblical languages, or worse teachers) than men. God simply assigns them a different role.

---

36 "As in all the churches of the saints, the women should be silent in the churches, for they are not permitted to speak, but are to submit themselves, as the law also says. If they want to learn something, let them ask their own husbands at home, since it is disgraceful for a woman to speak in the church." (1 Corinthians 14:33b-35) / "A woman is to learn quietly with full submission. I do not allow a woman to teach or to have authority over a man; instead, she is to remain quiet. For Adam was formed first, then Eve. And Adam was not deceived, but the woman was deceived and transgressed." (1 Timothy 2:11-14). Concerning the general principal of male headship, see 1 Corinthians 11:3,8-9.

In the twenty-first century, this is a difficult issue to defend. The apologist would do well to distinguish between *role* and *value.* A person's value is what they are worth. Every human being is worth the blood of the Son of God to the Father. Conversely, not every human, not even every man, is called to be a pastor. Not every man who wants to serve in that way gets the opportunity to do so. The secular world regularly operates with this distinction. When a young man or woman joins the military or gets a new job, they usually start at the bottom. Does that mean that their supervisor is smarter or more gifted than they are? Does it mean that their supervisor contributes more to society and so is worth more than that young person is? Does it mean that God loves that supervisor more than that young person? No. It merely means that God has assigned them different roles in life.

When the leadership role is done in the manner God describes it (this is true even in government—study Solomon's many instructions about justice and wisdom for governing officials in the book of Proverbs), it is a function that requires the greatest humility and self-sacrifice. Of course, we should not pass by without making mention of the sin of male chauvinism. Women are created by God and gifted, just as men are. If upholding the biblical roles of men and women becomes a useful tool to implement a chauvinistic attitude, such an action is not God-pleasing. The apologist should not try to justify the many demeaning statements and actions in the history of the church on earth. Rather, we recognize that it is difficult for sinners to implement the will of God in an imperfect world. We want to commit ourselves to giving women the full scope of opportunities to service that God allows in his Word.

The Priesthood of All Believers. Proclaiming the gospel is not just the job of pastors and teachers. Luther had two key insights that are essential for the work of the church. One is sometimes called the *priesthood of all believers*. Priests in the Old Testament were the only ones who could approach God. They served as mediators for the people. (The Catholic Church incorporated that approach into its practices and teachings.) The New Testament, however, teaches that all believers have access to God. All believers can ask for forgiveness and approach him directly. Moreover, the gospel—the primary tool of all church work—is not restricted to a priestly caste. All believers can share it and apply it.

Luther's other key insight about the church was the doctrine of vocation. Vocation comes from a Latin word that means "to call," and we rightly say that our pastors and teachers are called by God to serve the Church. Luther also saw vocation as applying to secular jobs and even to different roles in life. Being a doctor or a farmer or a truck driver, as well as being a husband and father, or a wife and mother, is a gift of God. Christian people serve the Lord when they fulfill those roles.

How do pastors and members relate to each other in God's plan for the church? God calls ministers to proclaim the good news in order to equip the saints (believers) for a life of serving God and to build up the church in faith, which is the only route to unity.[37] God's people then know the truth, and they can defend their faith both from false teaching and from the attacks of the devil. Pastors and members work together and support each other as they make their way to heaven.[38] Ministers serve as Christ's representatives to the church and as the church's representatives to the world. As such, they provide leadership in the visible church. Yet, the message belongs to the whole church. In many situations, members will be on the front lines, defending the faith.

Public Sin in the Church. Jesus warned us that we would face opposition and persecution until he came back. Sometimes, we say that the church on earth is the church militant—the church at war. In one sense, God doesn't call us to defend ourselves, except by the testimony of our lives. St. Peter wrote, "Conduct yourselves honorably among the Gentiles, so that when they slander you as evildoers, they will observe your good works and will glorify God on the day he visits" (1 Peter 2:12). Notice that the vindication truly comes only when Jesus returns. Before that day, we may experience lies like those Jesus himself experienced when he rose from the dead. The enemies of the gospel know their claims aren't true, but they make them anyway.[39]

---

37 "And he himself gave some to be apostles, some prophets, some evangelists, some pastors and teachers, equipping the saints for the work of ministry, to build up the body of Christ, until we all reach unity in the faith and in the knowledge of God's Son, growing into maturity with a stature measured by Christ's fullness." (Ephesians 4:11-13).

38 "Then we will no longer be little children, tossed by the waves and blown around by every wind of teaching, by human cunning with cleverness in the techniques of deceit. But speaking the truth in love, let us grow in every way into him who is the head—Christ. From him the whole body, fitted and knit together by every supporting ligament, promotes the growth of the body for building up itself in love by the proper working of each individual part." (Ephesians 4:14-16).

39 "As they were on their way, some of the guards came into the city and reported to the chief priests everything that had happened. After the priests had assembled with the elders and agreed on a plan, they gave the soldiers a large sum of money and told them, 'Say this, "His

This doesn't mean, however, that we should never engage people when they attack the church. We need to present a defense because the attacks on the church have a purpose, namely, to discredit our message by discrediting the messenger. Therefore, it is necessary to correct lies and misrepresentations. This is especially true when people use their lies to avoid thinking about the message of the gospel.

Because the church on earth is made up of sinners, sometimes members (and even church leaders) fall into public sin. While the Bible does point out how important it is that unbelievers see our testimony confirmed in our lives, we cannot allow the public sins of Christians to be used to deny the truth of the gospel. It isn't even necessarily a question of actually seeing the sins of Christians. Many people simply assume that all Christians are hypocrites. This assumption is reinforced in the media. When conservative, Bible-believing Christians are depicted in the media, almost always they are judgmental, uneducated, and generally unattractive people. The apologist needs to point out that Christians do not claim to be without sin. As a bumper sticker once read, "Christians aren't perfect, just forgiven." The apologist needs to be prepared to acknowledge sinful failings on the part of believers in every generation and then to point out that is why we trust in Christ, not in ourselves.

Another attempt to discredit the church is to claim widespread corruption. "The church is all about money" is a frequent statement. A related attack is to paint church leaders as hypocrites who engage in illicit sex or financial shenanigans, who make under-the-table deals with politicians or who kowtow to wealthy members. Of course, the spectacle of televangelists' empires falling due to sexual or financial scandals only reinforces that perspective. Even though the most famous cases are decades old, they are still brought up as evidence of the corruption of the church. The pervasive nature of the sex abuse problem that has come to light in the Roman Catholic Church is sometimes used to paint all churches with the same brush.

It is undeniable that instances of immoral behavior happen, and they are always tragic. We never want to defend sexual abuse by clergy or any type of sinful behavior that makes the news and discredits our testimony. Jesus

---

disciples came during the night and stole him while we were sleeping." If this reaches the governor's ears, we will deal with him and keep you out of trouble.' They took the money and did as they were instructed, and this story has been spread among Jewish people to this day." (Matthew 28:11-15).

certainly warned us about wolves in sheep's clothing.[40] It is worthwhile, however, to make the point that the vast majority of pastors and teachers ministering in Christian churches in America serve congregations where fewer than one hundred people gather for Sunday worship. These servants of the Word drive old cars and live on much less money than most people with their level of education do. They do it out of love for the Lord and his people.

The apologist should point out that the same type of corruption happens in all areas of life. Politicians get caught in compromising situations, and they suffer the consequences of their behavior. Still, does such deviant behavior mean that democracy is a bad idea? Teachers sometimes go to jail for their misbehavior with their students and rightfully so. Despite this fact, would anyone argue that we should get rid of schools because all teachers are hypocrites? In the same way, some trusted Christian leaders have been guilty of sinful behavior. Yet, these tragic cases do not change the truth of our testimony. Thankfully, God in his grace has filled the gospel with his power. That power does not depend on the one who uses it. Consequently, the gospel proclaimed by a pastor who turns out to be a child molester was still the gospel. It worked when believers heard it because the Holy Spirit was working. It strengthened faith and comforted the hurting, which makes the sin of the preacher all the more tragic and disturbing.

The Visible Church—A Broken Church?

Even the most casual observer can see that the church today doesn't look much like the church of the first century. There were no denominations in Jesus' day. There were no creeds, at least not in the sense that we think of them today. The worship life of the church, the organization of the church, the forms of ministry the church used then might all seem very exotic to Christians in the twenty-first century. A skeptic might ask a number of loaded questions about the path the church on earth has traveled over the last twenty centuries.

They might then move on to an equally obvious reality; the Christian church today is deeply divided. The modern church has two great branches, the Eastern (or Orthodox) and Western branches. While the Eastern church

---

[40] [Jesus said,] "Be on your guard against false prophets who come to you in sheep's clothing but inwardly are ravaging wolves." (Matthew 7:15).

has fewer doctrinal divisions, it is hardly one monolithic whole.[41] Conversely, the Western church is fragmented into many different pieces. One can draw a line of demarcation between Roman Catholicism and all other Western churches (sometimes called Protestant churches), but that doesn't come close to summarizing the reality that exists.

The Early Church. The ancient church may not have had denominations in the modern sense, but it was far from united. The apostles themselves make numerous references to false teachers working in their name and dividing the church.[42] The New Testament speaks of a number of issues that are sometimes called *Judaizing* and deal with the question of what the Old Testament law means for the New Testament believer. Galatians 2-3 and Acts 15 give us a glimpse of the efforts undertaken already during the times of the apostles to preserve unity and at the same time to identify and to separate the church from false teachings.

The New Testament may also have begun[43] to address doctrinal concerns that came to be called *Gnosticism,* which became a major issue in the second century and divided the church.[44] Gnosticism was a religious movement that probably began outside the Christian church. It absorbed elements from many different religions and in turn burrowed into Christianity, introducing false teachings which then multiplied and mutated into various forms. The early church fathers (men like Irenaeus, AD 140-202) were at pains to differentiate their teaching from the things that various gnostic preachers taught.

The first great series of internal controversies to break up the unity of the visible church is sometimes called the Trinitarian Controversies, which began sometime around the beginning of the second century and lasted until the end

---

41 Eastern Orthodoxy has had its share of controversies over the centuries, but its divisions today are more organizational. The Eastern Orthodox communion is led by the Ecumenical Patriarch of Constantinople (modern Istanbul), but he has nothing like the authority of the Roman Catholic pope. He is "first among equals" of the *autocephalous* or independent Eastern Orthodox churches. Generally speaking, these churches are organized by nationality (Greek Orthodox, Russian Orthodox, etc.).

42 See, for example, Acts 20:29-31, Philippians 1:15-18 and 1 John 2:18-19.

43 Many scholars feel that 1 John, Colossians and the pastoral epistles (1 and 2 Timothy and Titus) address issues that represent incipient Gnosticism, but that movement became full blown only after the New Testament was written.

44 Justo L. Gonzalez, *A History of Christian Thought, Vol 1: From the Beginnings to the Council of Chalcedon* (Abingdon Press, Nashville, 1971), 126-141.

of the fourth century.[45] These controversies dealt with what it means that we worship the Father, Son and Holy Spirit. They have a complicated and extensive history, which we will not deal with here. The Nicene Creed, which was promulgated in two forms first in AD 325 and then later in AD 381, represents the summary of the church's answer to this controversy. The Christological Controversies grew out of the Trinitarian Controversies.[46] They became the center of attention as the Trinitarian Controversies died out.[47] They lasted until the fifth century. These controversies dealt with what it means that Jesus is both God and man. The church's answer to the Christological Controversies is summarized in a creed called the Definition of Chalcedon, which was promulgated in AD 451. All these controversies resulted in divisions in the church.

The Great Schism As these controversies diminished, the church did not enter into an era of peace and tranquility. It remained the church militant, but it faced many different challenges. It also remained a gathering of people who were conditioned by their cultures and the times and places in which they lived, so the visible church evolved. It developed practices and structures and liturgies. Its members wrote works of theology and devotion, which affected the generations which followed. Unfortunately, because it was the church on earth and filled with sinners who are by nature weak and easily led astray, it did not always follow the Bible carefully or teach its doctrines clearly.

The early centuries of the church's existence produced two great streams of theology and tradition, an Eastern and a Western stream. The Eastern stream was dominated by Greek-speaking theologians. Its main centers were Antioch in Syria and Alexandria in Egypt. The Western stream was dominated by Latin speakers centered in northern Africa and Rome.

The efforts to differentiate between true and false teachers naturally led to a discussion of what constituted the true church. In the East, the early church leader Ignatius (c.35-c.107) emphasized the importance of the office of the bishop as the rallying point of the church against false doctrine. He argued that by God's design, each congregation is united under one head, the bishop.

---

45 Dating the beginning and ending of these controversies is difficult, and it depends on which movements and teachers one includes. Gonzalez gives a general overview in the course of several chapters, starting about page 126.

46 Gonzalez, ibid., 335-6.

47 Some scholars would consider Arianism to be the beginning of the movement from the Trinitarian to the Christological controversies. This movement is named after Arius (AD 260-336).

He urged the faithful to close ranks around their bishops because the bishops were the successors to the apostles, and therefore, they were the guarantors of true doctrine. He also linked the sacraments to the bishops. The bishops therefore embodied the unity of the church.[48]

The central issue that dominated Western thinking about the church revolved around the doctrine of penance. Tertullian (c.160-c.225) laid the foundation for Roman Catholic thinking about penance. Rather than seeing it as something that involves the heart (that is, the law striking a sinner with guilt and fear but the gospel assuring that sinner of forgiveness and giving peace to the conscience) Tertullian conceived of penance as a way to get back into God's good graces. In his view, when we sin, we fall under God's wrath, so we must "do" penance to be set free. He did conceive of this as meritorious on the sinner's part. He articulated the classic Roman Catholic view of penance as consisting of contrition (feeling sorry for sins), confession (to a priest) and satisfaction (a work undertaken to remove the penalty of sin).[49]

The key issue in Western thinking dealt with those Christians who had committed a mortal sin after their baptisms. Could they do penance and be received back into the church? Tertullian and his followers argued that only God could forgive sins, so the church could not receive them back. Other Western theologians argued that the bishops could forgive those sins, thus laying the groundwork that would develop into the Roman Catholic *penitential system*.[50]

Over the succeeding centuries, these ideas in the East and West continued to grow and develop. In both parts of the church, the episcopal structure took hold and became entrenched. The emphasis on the bishops as guarantors of doctrine, as the transmitters of the sacraments and as judges of repentance gradually led to a very hierarchical structure in both the East and the West. Almost inevitably, this led to conflict over authority in the church. When Constantine made Christianity the favored religion of the empire starting in AD 313, the conflict intensified. In the West, the bishop of Rome, already known as the pope, claimed authority over the entire church. The bishops in the East saw several key bishoprics as being equal to the bishop of Rome,

---

[48] Brent Hagglund, *History of Theology*, Gene J. Lund, tr. (Concordia Publishing House, St. Louis, 1968), 107-8.

[49] Hagglund, ibid., 108.

[50] Hagglund, ibid., 108-9.

although they often accorded the pope special honor. Eventually, the patriarch of Constantinople assumed leadership of the Eastern cause.

In AD 1054, after centuries of doctrinal and practical disputes, the two churches separated in what history has come to call the *Great Schism*. They had much in common: the primacy of bishops, a sacramental system that included seven sacraments (in place of the two that the Scriptures describe), a reverence for monasticism (although the East tended to embrace hermit-based monasticism, while the West tended to embrace monasticism organized into monasteries), and a very liturgical structure (although the liturgical traditions developed separately, even embracing a different church year). In both branches of Christianity, the emphasis on human works in the sacramental system obscured the gospel. In the West, bishops were often secular rulers as well as church leaders, and the pope claimed authority over all rulers, secular or religious. Many theologians in the West were advancing the idea that the pope spoke with God's own authority and, as a result, was practically infallible, although this doctrine was not officially proclaimed until 1870.

The Reformation. Without ever meaning to do it, a monk in the German city of Wittenberg set off the Lutheran Reformation and changed the world. All he wanted to do (at first anyway) was to debate a practice that he thought was obscuring the gospel. When he was done, the Western church was irreparably torn apart and a whole host of new perspectives on theology had entered the church. Martin Luther often stated his willingness to back down from his teaching if he could be persuaded from Holy Scripture. To put it in modern terms, Luther was offering a falsification challenge—so long as his opponents used the same standard of truth he did, the Word of God.

Sometimes, we summarize Lutheran teaching with the three *solas,* by which we mean three Latin expressions Luther used to summarize his approach to theology.[51] *Sola gratia* means "by grace alone." God's grace is the

---

[51] Luther himself never put these three solas together as a programmatic slogan for the Reformation, although all three were used at various times by him and most other Protestant Reformers. Using them as a summary of Luther's work and thought seems to date from a 1916 essay published to commemorate the 400th anniversary of the Reformation [see Theodore Engelder, "The Three Principles of the Reformation: *Sola Scriptura, Sola Gratia, Sola Fides"* in *Four Hundred Years: Commemorative Essays on the Reformation of Dr. Martin Lutheran and its Blessed Results* (Concordia publishing House, St. Louis, 1916), 97-109]. Since that time, some people have added two other related ideas, *solus Christus* "Christ alone" and *soli Deo gloria* "to God alone be the glory" – both very Lutheran thoughts and concerns.

heart of all theology. The way that a church defines "grace" reveals a great deal about what it teaches. For example, the Roman Catholic Catechism defines grace as "the *free and undeserved help* that God gives us to respond to his call to become children of God [emphasis in the original]."[52] "Help" is a deliberately chosen word, because it implies some ability on our part to "respond to his call".

The Lutheran church, on the other hand, understands grace as God's work and his alone. Any teaching that in any way makes human beings responsible for the things that God does runs contrary to all Lutheran and biblical theology. The Lutheran church derives its definition for grace from the way the Bible itself presents God's grace. On one level, the Greek word (*charis*) literally means a gift. Therefore, grace is not something that people earn; it's something that God gives them just because he loves them. The Bible uses that Greek word for various gifts God gives (such as Paul's ministry[53] or the generosity to help others[54]) and even for gifts that people give each other.[55] Of course, the greatest example of grace is God sending his Son to live and die and rise again in the place of every sinner. The forgiveness of sins won through Christ and the eternal life that follows are further examples of God's grace. But there is a deeper truth here, reflected in passages like John 1:14 which describes Jesus as being "full of grace and truth" or the many times St. Paul and other New Testament writers speak of God's grace as a quality that lives in him[56] or as something in God that moves him to love and save mankind.[57] Grace refers to God's favor, his internal disposition to love sinful humans. Again, this love is not based on any merit or worthiness within any individual. God loves those who are simply unlovable. The Lutheran shorthand definition of grace then is "God's undeserved love".

Sola fide means "by faith alone". The point here is to remove any hint of merit on the part of fallen mankind. God saves the elect by faith. God calls them righteous by faith. Our Lutheran forefathers liked to call faith "the hand

---

52 *Catholic Catechism*, Para. 1996.

53 See, for example, Romans 5:15-16 and 1 Corinthians 3:10.

54 See, for example, 2 Corinthians 8:1.

55 Modern translations don't always use the word "grace" where the Greek word *charis* occurs, making this somewhat harder to see, but examples would include Acts 24:27, 1 Corinthians 1:16 and 2 Corinthians 1:15.

56 See, for example, Ephesians 1:6-14 and 2 Thessalonians 1:12.

57 See, for example, 2 Thessalonians 2:16, 2 Timothy 1:9, Romans 5:15 and 2 Corinthians 8:9.

that grasps God's grace". Faith is simply trust. God makes promises, and those who are saved cling to them because he gives the promises. Lutherans prefer to speak of faith in terms of "trust" rather than "belief" because "believing" can seem to be an action of our will or a choice we make (so it has been used in decision theology, see below). Trust, on the other hand, is a response that the love of God calls forth from us. It is something that God works in us. Faith *alone* emphasizes the fact that we are not saved by "faith and" something else, e.g., faith and our decision, faith and works of love, or any-thing else.

God gives us faith. But that does not mean that God believes for us. The Christian trusts in what God has done in Christ. God then views that Christian as holy. St. Paul wrote, "The righteousness of God is through faith in Jesus Christ to all who believe, since there is no distinction."[58] After pointing out that all have sinned and deserve to go to hell, but are justified freely by God's grace, and then pointing again to Christ's sacrifice, he disallows any thought of boasting on our part. Why? He explains, "For we conclude that a person is justified by faith apart from the works of the law."[59] So there can be no "faith and...". There is nothing we can point to that we did that justifies us. When God gives us faith, he covers us with Jesus. St. Paul pictures it like putting on a garment.[60] Christ's righteousness covers and hides our sin. In other words, God calls us righteous just as Jesus was. Hence, the horror that Lutherans feel at any expression that adds any human work to faith or that reduces faith from a gift God gives to a decision we make or an act of will or any other human undertaking.

Sola scriptura means "through Scripture alone". The Scripture is inspired by God. He gave every word of the Bible (in its original languages) to the men who wrote it; therefore, it is the only source and standard for doctrine and a Christian life. It is the standard to which all our claims of truth must be compared, as discussed in Chapter 3. This position assumes that God has built his power into the Word. Luther understood with a rare degree of clarity how that power works in both the law and the gospel (see Chapter 7).

---

58 Romans 3:22.

59 Romans 3:28.

60 "But since that faith has come, we are no longer under a guardian, for through faith you are all sons of God in Christ Jesus. For those of you who were baptized into Christ have been clothed with Christ." (Galatians 3:25-27).

Because God speaks through the Word, Lutherans believe that it is possible to clearly state what the Bible's teachings are. Luther himself began the process of writing confessions for this purpose. Since his time, the Lutheran Church has adopted a set of writings called the Lutheran Confessions[61] to summarize its teachings. Lutheran pastors and teachers take an oath to conform all their teaching and preaching to the Lutheran Confessions, because we do see them as authoritative. Nevertheless, we are always careful to distinguish between them and the Bible. The Bible is the source of all doctrine. The Confessions are true and authoritative because they give clear testimony to what the Bible really teaches. In other words, they establish doctrinal truth by holding propositions up to the standard, the Bible. Because they do this so well, they become a kind of interim standard gauging the truth or falsehood of individual writing and teaching. Holding to the Confessions is called *subscribing* to them.[62]

Luther died in 1546. The next hundred years were an era of challenge and consolidation for the Lutheran Church. Early seventeenth century Lutheranism was dominated by a movement known today as Lutheran Orthodoxy. The men who led this movement tried hard to secure the teachings of the Lutheran

---

61 The Lutheran Confessions consist of the Apostles Creed, the Nicene Creed, the Athanasian Creed, the Unaltered Augsburg Confession, the Apology [Defense] of the Augsburg Confession, Luther's Small Catechism, Luther's Large Catechism, the Smalcald Articles, the Tractate on the Power and Primacy of the Pope (usually appended to the Smalcald Articles) and the Formula of Concord. The official collection of the Lutheran Confessions is called the Book of Concord. It was assembled in 1580.

62 Lutherans are very careful to state that we subscribe to the doctrinal content of the confessions. There are statements in the confessions of a historic and even of a scientific nature that are clearly in error. Likewise, one can occasionally find a Scripture reference that is incorrect. Modern students of Scripture may even disagree with the way a passage is used to support a specific doctrinal point. But in the end, we subscribe to the truth the Confessions teach (the doctrinal content). Historically, there has been a debate among Lutherans about whether we subscribe to the Confessions *because* they agree with the Scriptures (expressed with the Latin word *quia* which means "because") or only *in so far as* they agree with the Scriptures (expressed with the Latin word *quatenus* "in so far as"). At first glance, "in so far as" might seem to be the right answer because it allows for human error and limitations. However, hidden behind that assertion is a doubt about whether it is possible for humans to clearly and definitively articulate the truth that God's Word teaches. We will further discuss that later in this chapter, but confessional Lutherans maintain that a *quatenus* (in so far as) subscription means nothing because it doesn't tell which things in the confession a person thinks are biblical. The whole point of writing confessions is to state clearly what God has taught us, so confessional Lutherans insist on a *quia* subscription. We subscribe to the Lutheran Confessions because they are a clear and correct exposition of the Word of God.

Confessions and pass them down to the next generation. The era was a time of controversy between Lutherans, Catholics, and a wide variety of emerging theological movements. Late in the 17th century, *Pietism* arose in the Lutheran Church. At its best, this was a movement to restore piety to the practice of Lutheran churches and people. There was some need for this, because the Thirty Years War (1618-1648) had devastated Germany and because some theologians of the era did have a tendency to neglect the care of souls which Luther himself had taken very seriously. The situation was made worse as a result of all Lutheran churches being departments of their territorial governments. Political leadership did not always serve the gospel well. Pietism began with a legitimate concern for Christians living their faith, but it deteriorated into an indifference to doctrine, especially the doctrine of justification. The subjective nature of this movement left the Lutheran Church less prepared to deal with the rising crisis of Rationalism (see below).

Protestant Christianity. The churches that emerged from the Roman Catholic Church at the time of the Reformation are generally called Protestant. They can be divided into three groups: Lutherans, Calvinists and Arminians. Lutherans tend to call both of the other groups *Reformed*, but outside the Lutheran world the label Reformed is usually reserved for Calvinists.

All three groups have seen further divisions. The Arminian churches have produced the widest variety of different subgroups, each with its own theology and approach. Examples include Anabaptism, Methodism, Holiness bodies, Pentacostalism, Adventism and Restorationism. A survey of all this bewildering complexity is beyond our purpose. Still it exists, and it serves as fodder for skeptics in their attacks against the Christian Church.

In the sixteenth century, Lutheranism claimed most of northern Germany and spread into Scandinavia. In Switzerland, the reform movement had come under the leadership of John Calvin (1509-1564). He would give his name to a very different approach to theology from the one Luther embraced. Calvinism is characterized by a rigorous intellectual approach to matters of faith. It has been summarized with the Five Points of Calvinism, often taught with the acronym *TULIP*. TULIP stands for *total depravity* (the teaching that all people are thoroughly sinful), *unconditional election* (God does not choose people for salvation based on their merits—unfortunately, most Calvinists go farther and make this, in effect, universal election, that is, that God chose some to be saved and others to be damned), *limited atonement* (Jesus died only for the elect, that is, for believers), *irresistible grace* (when God calls someone to faith, they cannot resist), and *perseverance of the saints* (a true believer cannot fall away—often expressed as "once saved, always saved"). The first point does correctly express the Bible's teachings,[63] the second one starts out in the right place, but goes too far,[64] and the other three do not agree with what the Bible teaches.[65] [66] [67]

The Lutheran critique of Calvinism boils down to the role of human reason. Whether he intended to do so or not, Calvin made human reason the judge of theology. (Lutherans call this the magisterial use of reason—see chapter 1). For the same reason, Calvin argued that the "real presence" of Jesus' body and blood in communion had to be a spiritual presence, not a bodily or a substantial one, since Jesus' body is in heaven and no human body can be everywhere at once, nor can any human body possibly supply communion for the millions of Christians who have lived since the time of Christ. Calvin reasoned that if God elected some people to heaven before the world began, he must have elected the rest for hell. Lutherans have always acknowledged that Calvin's views are very logical, but they are simply not in accord with what the Bible says.

Today, Calvinism is relatively rare. Nevertheless, the apologist should be aware of it because the elevation of reason, which is the heart of Calvinism, pervades our world today. The modern reliance on science and observation to determine the origin of the universe is an example. Most Americans operate as if all that God says in his Word only applies if it makes sense to the reader.

---

63 See Romans 3:9-20,23 and Romans 7:14-25, especially verse 18 which explicitly states, "Nothing good lives in me."

64 See Ephesians 1:3-14 and Romans 8:29,30. Of particular interest is 2 Thessalonians 2:13-14, which teaches that we are elected to faith "through sanctification by the Spirit." Romans 8:33, 9:14-16 and 11:5-6, as well as 1 Corinthians 1:27-28, all teach that election is not based on our merit, but on God's grace and choosing. For scriptural testimony against the idea that God elects anyone to damnation, see 1 Timothy 2:4.

65 Jesus died for all: John 3:16; Romans 3:23-24; 5:15-19.

66 Believers can fall away: 1 Timothy 1:19; 3:6-7; 6:9-10; Hebrews 6:4.

67 Irresistible grace is a little more difficult. The Calvinist position is that God offers the message of salvation to all people, but this is only an "external call" that can be resisted. But to the elect, God offers an "internal call" that cannot be resisted. There is a sense in which we might say this—the Holy Spirit takes a thoroughly corrupt heart that resists God with all its might and then God makes that person a believer in spite of their resistance (see 1 Corinthians 12:3, Ephesians 2:8-9). Still, the way it is expressed must be disputed. God's grace is truly resisted even by those who eventually come to faith (see, for example, Matthew 23:37 and Acts 7:51). God holds unbelievers accountable for their resistance.

While we might criticize this as woefully subjective and completely biased (the opposite of rational), most people believe that they are eminently reasonable and rational people, so they demand that God's Word make sense *to them*. This attitude infects the vast majority of visible Christian churches.

In reality, the majority position of conservative Protestant churches today resulted from a direct reaction against Calvin's thinking, without abandoning the way he placed reason as the judge of Scripture. However, this position also exalts the role of feelings, which is why emotionalism is so prevalent in the church today. This branch of Christianity is often called *Arminianism*, after Jacob Arminius (1560-1609), a Dutch theologian. The history of Arminian thought is wide-ranging and bewildering. John Wesley (1703-1791), the founder of Methodism, is one of his most important successors. The whole Evangelical movement is Arminian in outlook. Pentecostal/Charismatic groups and Holiness bodies are subdivisions. Baptists in all their rich variety of theological outlooks also claim this heritage. This strain of thought is the majority view of conservative, non-Catholic Christianity in America today.

Arminius' theological heirs have challenged every one of the Five Points of Calvinism. Instead of total depravity (the Calvinists' most scriptural point), most Arminians believe that sin damages us (more or less severely) and leaves us in need of God's grace. Nevertheless, we still have some good left in us, or we could not respond to God's call. Their teaching on election is confusing. They correctly reject the idea that God predestined some people to go to hell, but they cannot escape seeing some kind of merit or choosing on our part. Often, this becomes some version of God calling those that he saw would respond.[68]

Since the last three points of the TULIP acronym are not scriptural, it would appear that the Arminians must be right about those. The actual theological situation is more complicated than that. Limited atonement creates an enormous doubt in the mind of the believer: did Jesus die for me? How can I know? Arminians correctly argue that Jesus died for all people, even for those who never come to faith. They also generally acknowledge that it is possible for believers to fall away. On the other hand, they replace irresistible grace by

---

[68] When some Lutherans adopted a version of this position, they expressed it with the Latin phrase *intuitu fide* or "in view of faith." In the United States, there was a major controversy among confessional Lutherans over this teaching at the end of the nineteenth century (the "Election Controversy"), although it's questionable whether the seventeenth century originators of the Latin expression meant it in the sense that Arminians do.

some form of participation or agreement or acceptance on the part of the individual Christian. In the twentieth century, this became the conversion experience and "making a decision for Christ," which is still a staple of Arminian churches' outreach efforts. In their pastoral care, they often point to their members' conversion experience as proof that they are saved, rather than simply pointing to Christ. Arminians have an imperfect understanding of the relationship between the law and the gospel. Lutherans preach the law in order to be able to proclaim the gospel. Evangelicals tend to be more concerned about improving people morally.

There is a great deal more to all the different varieties of Arminian churches and the mind-boggling diversity of teachings to which different groups have held in this branch of Christianity. Perhaps we can summarize it by saying these Christians see the necessity to make the teachings of Scripture reasonable *to the individual Christian.* Sadly, we live in an age in which the logical content of an argument is no longer sufficient to convince most people of its merits. Today, the emotional impact of an argument is every bit as important as its logical consistency and rigorous conformity to a standard of truth. People often speak of "knowing something in their hearts", and they express opinions in terms of what they feel to be true. Additionally, the postmodern climate of the twenty-first century has made truth relative and subjective. "It's true" has been replaced by "It works for me" in our culture. Arminian theology is very much a blend of reason, emotion, and subjectivity.

In this respect, Arminian thought is more in line with twenty-first century American thought than is confessional Lutheranism. Confessional Lutherans point to what God says. If all his points line up into a logical system, that is wonderful. Yet, there are times when what God says doesn't satisfy our limited human reason. A Lutheran simply says, "Thus says the Lord" and accepts all that God says, whether he or she can understand it or not. In truth, this is the approach that led the early church to correctly teach the doctrines of the Trinity and the Person of Christ. To say that God is three and God is one does not make logical sense. Likewise, it does not make logical sense to say that Jesus was wholly and completely human, like us in every way, and that he was wholly and completely God, without mixing the two natures into some other form, but still recognizing him as only one person. Nevertheless, this is what the Bible teaches.

When it comes to apologetics, we must beware of the Arminian-friendly world we live in. Christian bookstores are flooded with apologetic books. Cyberspace has countless apologetic websites. There are at least three major "museums of the Bible" in existence as of the writing of this book. Some—maybe even much—of what exists in these sources has some value. Still, we find again and again that the Arminian blend of reason and feeling into a subjectively satisfying argument produces something that will only be satisfying to someone who already holds to all those Arminian positions. If our goal is to clear a way for the gospel, we must approach these questions in a manner that addresses the doubts of unbelievers and that gives answers that will withstand scrutiny and attack.

The Ecumenical Movement and Modern Liberalism in the Church. The Enlightenment, an intellectual movement that swept Europe in the late seventeenth and early eighteenth centuries, gave birth to a new series of challenges to the Christian church. It entered the German university system in the form of Rationalism, which sought to subject Christianity's truth claims to standards of human reason and knowledge. Rationalism developed theories about the composition of the Bible that assumed an evolution of the text, and it doubted or denied the authorship that many biblical books claim for themselves. It accepted Darwin's theory of evolution and, in time, it embraced the scientific arguments for the extreme age of the earth. It questioned miracles or sought rational explanations. Rationalism crossed the Atlantic in the nineteenth century, and by the 1920s, outside of the South, it was triumphant in almost all Protestant churches.

In the twentieth century, American churches went through a series of theological controversies, schisms, and mergers. The key issue in many of these battles was the inspiration and authority of the Bible. Conservative churches embraced the traditional teaching of *plenary* or full inspiration of the Bible. Liberal churches denied that teaching and advanced other models for what the Bible means, what it represents, and how carefully it needs to be followed.

Lutherans experienced the same battles. However, Lutheranism in America was helped by a phenomenon that took place in Germany. In the early nineteenth century, the Confessional Awakening caused many Lutherans in Germany to recall the historic roots of the Lutheran Church. This Awakening was carried to the United States by German immigrants, and confessional Lutheran churches took root in the United States. They were well established by the time rationalism overwhelmed the American universities, which were originally founded to prepare pastors.

The divisions in the Lutheran world today derive directly from this debate. Liberal Lutheranism, like liberal Christianity in general, does not see the Bible as the inspired and inerrant Word of God. Nor does it see the Confessions as witnesses to timeless truth. Rather, they see the Confessions as the witness to the struggle and insights of the times that produced them—useful, to be sure, but not authoritative. Conversely, the Lutheran Confessions proved a powerful weapon for conservative Lutherans, since they were already an exercise in subjecting doctrinal truth to the standard of God's Word. By the end of the twentieth century, conservative Lutherans preferred to call themselves "confessional Lutherans" because the term "conservative" seemed to run the risk of identifying with a political party or program, instead of focusing on God's Word.

As the twentieth century moved on, the ground shifted under all visible churches in the United States and in much of the world. Internal theological arguments within the conservative and liberal branches of the church began to seem less important than the divide between liberals and conservatives. At the same time, more and more people began to think that what united Christians was much more important than what divided them. Little by little, this led to *ecumenism* or the ecumenical movement. The ecumenical movement was originally an idealistic vision of uniting the Christian church on earth into one organization. It was driven by the belief that fighting over doctrine gave a bad witness to the world and was a waste of resources. For a while, it was a burning issue in the visible church. Today it is more of an assumption that lies in the background. Most Christians today—even those who do not take strong doctrinal stands and who do not really accept the Bible as the Word of God—speak of the importance of the different traditions of the various churches. They speak of respecting the differences that exist among Christians without trying to change anyone. In many ways, their way of speaking is parallel to the kind of political conversation that is often labeled as "political correctness."

The ecumenical movement downplayed doctrine. Liberal theology came to dominate the so-called "mainline churches" in America. Its effects can be seen in the way that even ancient, fundamental teachings like the Trinity and the Person of Christ are handled in these churches today. Many people argue (as Jehovah's Witnesses and other non-trinitarian groups do) that the Bible does not actually teach these doctrines, rather that they were developed by the early church. Liberal theologians take a more nuanced approach. Rather than denying outright that the Bible teaches the Trinity and the Person of Christ in the sense of the ancient creeds, they argue that what the ancient church taught is one valid way of organizing all that the Scriptures say about God and Christ. But they would also argue that there are other equally valid ways to do that. They claim that one finds different views on the nature of God and on Christology in different books of the Bible. Some of them would point to the political machinations of emperors and bishops throughout the centuries of these controversies and argue that the classic formulations of the Trinity and the Person of Christ were accepted more for political than for spiritual reasons.

In the end, their key issue is simply this: can what the Bible says about God and about Christ be expressed in a set of universally valid propositions, like the Nicene Creed? They answer "no". As Lutheran apologists, we insist that the only possible answer must be "yes". This is the heart of *confessionalism*. Certainly, we would freely grant that the Nicene Creed does not and cannot exhaust these topics. Yet, one key difference between confessional Lutheranism and all modern liberal theology is our insistence that it is possible to put clear, objective statements about God into human language. These statements can be measured against the standard, the Bible, and must, therefore, be considered to be true. These truth claims will then be unchangingly true, even if the ground of the debate may shift and the applications that the church needs to make may differ over time.

Is it accurate that emperors and even ancient theologians and bishops mixed politics and theology? Undeniably. Even some of the men who gave us the most enduring statements about the Trinity and the Person of Christ were not above using the power of the state or even mob violence to accomplish their goals. Still, the apologist does not have to defend the sinful failings of ancient churchmen and politicians. The doctrines of the Trinity and the Person of Christ are derived directly from Scripture (see Chapter 7). The apologist needs to understand the scriptural basis for these teachings and to be able to demonstrate that this is what God's Word teaches. This reality allows us to view the human process that led to the creeds, with all the sinful foibles of man that it exhibits, as a tremendous testimony to the grace of God. He preserved the truth in his church.

As an apologetic issue, ecumenism comes up when skeptics look at the divisions in the Christian church and dismiss them as so much fighting about nothing. They speak of doctrinal disputes as arcane arguments among ministers that no real person would be concerned about. They see those things as sapping the life out of whatever efforts the church might undertake that would be of value. When Christians point to God's Word, critics often dismiss this explanation with a very difficult argument: if the Bible is true, why can't all Christians agree about what it says?

The apologist must understand that divisions in the visible church are inevitable so long as we live in a sinful world. St. Paul told us, "Now I urge you, brothers and sisters, to watch out for those who create divisions and obstacles contrary to the teaching that you learned. Avoid them, because such people do not serve our Lord Christ but their own appetites. They deceive the hearts of the unsuspecting with smooth talk and flattering words."[69] Jesus told us, "Be on your guard against false prophets who come to you in sheep's clothing but inwardly are ravaging wolves."[70] The skeptic may think that the divisions in the church prove that our testimony cannot be trusted. The Bible tells us that in a sinful world, the truth will come under attack, not just by outside enemies, but also by some who are inside the visible church. Jesus told us to be prepared to face them, to separate from false teaching and to continue to do the work he has given us, trusting in the power of the gospel to overcome the best arguments of the church's enemies.

Finally, when it comes to the development of doctrine in the ancient church, at the time of the Reformation, or even today, the apologist needs to understand the difference between the evolution of doctrine (with the implication that the church decides what to believe) and the growth in our understanding of scriptural truth. God's teaching does not change. The apologist should be ready to admit that we human beings do grow in our personal ability to understand what God says. We twenty-first century Christians stand on the shoulders of the theologians of the early church and the Reformation when we study his Word, so we get to the heart of the Trinity, the Person of Christ, and the role of reason faster than they did because we can use what they discovered. All areas of study work this way. We should not allow the skeptic to subject Christianity to a different standard than any other field of study. We

---

69 Romans 16:17-18.
70 Matthew 7:15.

must insist that growing in our understanding of the message is very different from developing a doctrine or choosing what we will believe.

The Church and Society

The visible church does not exist in a world where people have no social connections. In this world there are both formal and informal connections between people. People are related to others through birth and marriage. They have personal friends. They work at jobs, and they belong to clubs of various types. They live in regions ruled by government of their own choosing or imposed on them by the will of others. Because Christians are involved with other organizations as well as the church, the church cannot pretend these organizations do not exist. At some level there will be a relationship[71] between the visible church and the other organizations which are involved in its members' lives. The most important of these other organizations is the government, often formally called the "state".

Distinction between Church and State: The church and the state are both agents of the Lord[72] and assigned different missions by him.[73] The mission of the church was discussed previously. The mission of the state is to maintain the peace and security for those who reside within its dominion in this sin-riddled world. It is to protect the lives, liberties, property and honor of its citizens and to promote their physical and economic wellbeing.[74] In other words, the mission of the state is restricted to the things of the physical universe. It has the authority to use force, including deadly force, to carry out its mission.[75] The nature of the relationship between the church and state must always be the direct result of their specific missions.

---

71 This does not necessarily mean a *formal* relationship, or even any level of cooperation. Finally, even antagonists have a kind of relationship.

72 "Let everyone submit to the governing authorities, since there is no authority except from God, and the authorities that exist are instituted by God." (Romans 13:1).

73 Augsburg Confession, Art. XXVIII in *Concordia:The Lutheran Confessions, 2 ed.* (Concordia Publishing House, St. Louis, 2006).

74 See Daniel Deutschlander, *Civil Government: God's Other Kingdom* (Northwestern Publishing House, Milwaukee, 1998).

75 "For it is God's servant for your good. But if you do wrong, be afraid, because it does not carry the sword for no reason. For it is God's servant, an avenger that brings wrath on the one who does wrong." (Romans 13:4).

From the description of their missions, it should be clear that the church and state are complementary organizations.[76] One works in the spiritual realm and the other in the physical realm. The church should not attempt to force its teachings on any who are not its members, and it should comply with the laws in indifferent matters (see *adiaphora* below) to the greatest extent possible. The state, on the other hand, should not create laws which inhibit the church from carrying out its mission or propagate its own standard of morality (e.g., *political correctness*). In short, teachings of moral personal behavior before God belong to the church,[77] and rules of conduct among people are the domain of the state.[78]

Nation states will sometimes seek the blessing of the church's moral authority to strengthen their hands in certain policy areas by claiming their programs have divine sanction. Churches will sometimes seek the state's support to coerce obedience from their members, fund their projects or leverage their opponents. The apologist should speak against both these practices because they mix the separate authority God has given to the church and state. Invariably, such arrangements divert the church from its mission and drag it into the politics of the state. It can also corrupt the clergy and muzzle its moral witness, as has often happened in state churches.

Moral Suasion: Nevertheless, it seems that there are times when the church should say something. When the state permits, or actually carries out, actions that are sinful in the eyes of God, should the church remain silent? Here the difference between programs and principles is the critical point. The church certainly must proclaim the moral law that forbids its members to engage in sinful actions mandated by the government.[79] It also must remind the government that as God's agent, it does have specific responsibilities that it must carry out. However, it should never endorse any particular program of the government to meet its responsibilities because the supervision of the physical

---

[76] "Then he [Jesus] said to them, 'Give, then, to Caesar the things that are Caesar's, and to God the things that are God's.'" (Matthew 22:21).

[77] [Jesus said,] "Teaching them to observe everything I have commanded you." (Matthew 28:20).

[78] "Submit to every human authority because of the Lord, whether to the emperor as the supreme authority or to governors as those sent out by him to punish those who do what is evil and to praise those who do what is good." (1 Peter 2:13-14).

[79] [The Lord said,] "As for you, son of man, I have made you a watchman for the house of Israel. When you hear a word from my mouth, give them a warning from me." (Ezekiel 33:7).

world is not the church's mission. For example, the church might call upon the government to address the rise of crime in an area, but it must not lobby for specific solutions. To do so will draw the church away from its mission and involve it in politics. Once a church becomes a political combatant, it has established a stumbling block for those of different political beliefs to hearing its saving message.[80]

Religious Politics: In the middle of the twentieth century, liberal mainline Protestant churches became involved in the civil rights and anti-war movements. They argued their theology was useless if it was not applied to critical social issues. They endorsed candidates, mostly Democrats, and used their pulpits to promote civil causes which they favored. Their witness was strengthened because many of their leaders had worked together in the ecumenical movement. Some of the churches argued it was the only way to retain their politically active young people. Eventually, many Protestant worshippers began to have concerns over their leaders making common cause with political radicals and even revolutionaries. Political violence and the moral and political corruption of several American presidents during the era led to a religious backlash, leading to the election of Jimmy Carter as President in 1976.

In subsequent years, the religious right came into its own as a political force. Its roots lie in the alienation of the Evangelical movement from mainstream society during this period and from the isolation of conservative Christians in the South for almost one hundred years after the Civil War. In the 1980s and 1990s, organizations like the Moral Majority, the Christian Coalition and Focus on the Family built on earlier Evangelical networks and entered politics, primarily in the Republican Party. Their main issues were abortion and family values. During the Reagan administration, they believed that their moment had arrived. Yet, for the most part, they were disappointed by the actual policies of the Republicans they helped to elect. By the twenty-first century, the movement found that it had become an object of ridicule in the media. It has been demonized by opponents and demoralized by defeats, such as the Supreme Court's decision allowing gay marriage.

---

80 "Instead decide never to put a stumbling block or pitfall in the way of your brother or sister." (Romans 14:13).

The attempt to make Christian values a political issue opens a line of attack for enemies of the gospel. Even when the political strategy succeeds, Christian-backed candidates win elections as part of a coalition and then have to make tradeoffs. They need to decide which of their values to cling to and which ones to bargain away. Even more troubling for the church, the whole process of trying to advance a Christian agenda through political action undercuts its dependence on the gospel to make disciples and its recognition that Jesus called Christians to walk the hard road of persecution and scorn, just as he did.[81]

There is no reason for a Lutheran apologist to defend the compromises of religiously driven politicians. At the same time, the sanctity of human life, the sanctity of marriage, the sinfulness of sex outside of marriage (of both the heterosexual and the homosexual variety) and the sinfulness of homosexual behavior are issues to which God's Word speaks. When we need to debate these matters, we should remain calm and give the opponents of the gospel no reason to dismiss our testimony because of our angry words.

Yet, as apologists, we must realize that debating homosexuality or gay marriage or abortion will not bring anyone into the kingdom of Heaven. We should not be surprised that unbelievers have suppressed the natural law that God wrote in their hearts on these issues. All these issues grow out of selfishness and a refusal to let God tell us what is right and wrong. It takes growth in faith to accept everything that God says. We will have more success focusing on things that the other person knows are wrong and feels guilty about. We can bring the gospel to bear on these questions. We don't have to settle every question in one conversation. Patience and love combined with consistent Christian witness will give the Holy Spirit the opportunity to work.

The Christian and the State: The church is composed of numerous individual Christians. While the visible church's relations with the state must be restricted based on their differing missions, the church's members are integral parts of the state as well as the church and need to behave as good citizens of the state. This means that Christians must obey the laws of the state because each Christian serves the Lord by doing so. Still the question arises, are there

---

81 [Jesus said,] "You are blessed when they insult you and persecute you and falsely say every kind of evil against you because of me. Be glad and rejoice, because your reward is great in heaven. For that is how they persecuted the prophets who were before you." (Matthew 5:11-12).

times when a Christian may or must disobey the laws of the state? Here the words *may* and *must* have very different meanings. A Christian must disobey the laws when the laws require the Christian to blaspheme the Lord or disobey his clearly stated will.[82] For example, if told to worship an idol, the Christian must refuse and take the punishment. However, a Christian may not disobey the law simply because he or she does not like it or because the law is "stupid". As a result, a Christian cannot engage in civil disobedience by replacing the demands of the laws with his or her own sense of justice.[83] For example, hosting an underage drinking party is a sin even if one thinks the 21-year-old drinking age is an insult to Germans and Poles.

In the same way, Christians cannot refuse to pay taxes because some of the money is used for purposes they find immoral or reprehensible.[84] If that were acceptable Christian conduct, the ability to collect taxes would become impossible as everyone's consciences became hypersensitive to any possible questionable act of the government. It would undermine the government and create anarchy. Just because the state permits immoral behavior, however, does not mean that a Christian may engage in it. An action being legal does not override it being immoral. The apologist needs good familiarity with the moral law and its implications to correctly handle these issues which can be very troubling to people.

Christian Liberty versus Civil Liberties: The nature of Christian freedom impacts almost all that we do and say as Christians. Unfortunately, this freedom is not well understood in the modern world, even in large parts of the Christian Church. It is not political freedom as it is understood in American discourse today. It is not the right to do whatever we want, so long as we don't hurt anyone. It is not the concept that was encoded into the Declaration of Independence, "We hold these truths to be self-evident, that all men are created equal, that they are endowed by their Creator with certain unalienable Rights, that among these are Life, Liberty and the pursuit of Happiness."[85] The Bible never speaks of freedom or liberty as a right. God did not give it to us so that we can pursue happiness in this life. Christian freedom or liberty is,

---

82 "Peter and the apostles replied, 'We must obey God rather than people.'" (Acts 5:29).

83 "So then, the one who resists the authority is opposing God's command, and those who oppose it will bring judgment on themselves." (Romans 13:2).

84 "Pay your obligations to everyone: taxes to those you owe taxes, tolls to those you owe tolls, respect to those you owe respect, and honor to those you owe honor." (Romans 13:7).

85 Introduction, *Declaration of Independence* (Philadelphia, 1776).

rather, a spiritual state in which the Christian is liberated from the slavery that sin has inflicted on us all. (For a more complete treatment, see Appendix III.) One way that Christian liberty manifests itself is in the freedom to choose how to behave in those matters which are neither commanded nor forbidden by God.[86] Such matters are called *adiaphora*. The Bible, for example, does not tell us what to eat for breakfast, what type of car to drive or whom to marry. However, it does tell us that we should not judge others when they use their Christian liberty, even if we do not agree with their choices.[87] Yet, the choices a Christian makes should not be self-centered, but rather should reflect a heart changed by the gospel so as to glorify God and to serve our fellowmen.[88] In the words of Luther, "A Christian is a perfectly free lord of all, subject to none. A Christian is a perfectly dutiful servant of all, subject to all."[89] Christian liberty, therefore, is not about either civil liberties or even political freedom.

Civil liberties indeed are quite a different matter. In angry confrontations, people can often be heard to say, "I have a right to…" or "my civil rights are being violated." In a nation created by a revolt that was justified by a document declaring that people are "endowed…with certain unalienable rights…," we could hardly expect otherwise. Although some people might prefer the word "freedoms" to "rights" when discussing what they feel their society owes them, everyone does expect some level of respect for their personal prerogatives by the nation in which they reside. Indeed, every culture and every society develop a frame of reference, that is, a set of anchor points (see Chapter 9), by which its members gauge how well they are being treated by those in authority. As a result, civil rights and their relationship to authority are legitimate subjects of debate in the political forum.

The church's concern over civil rights is solely in regard to issues that affect its ability to carry out its mission and to the individual Christians' ability to practice their religion. The apologist must, therefore, not confuse Christian liberty with civil liberties and be drawn into political causes related to

---

86 "For freedom, Christ set us free. Stand firm then and don't submit again to a yoke of slavery." (Galatians 5:1).

87 "Therefore, don't let anyone judge you in regard to food and drink or in the matter of a festival or a new moon or a Sabbath day." (Colossians 2:16).

88 "For you were called to be free, brothers and sisters; only don't use this freedom as an opportunity for the flesh, but serve one another through love." (Galatians 5:13).

89 *Luther's Works* **31**:344.

them. The church has no specific program concerning how secular societies should operate, and individual Christians can have different opinions. St Paul discussed freedom[90] and authority[91] in this context.

Religious Persecution: There is a long history of unbelieving rulers using the power of the state to suppress the Christian Church and to attempt to silence its witness. At times, even governments that have claimed to be Christian have attempted to silence the testimony of those who pointed out the ways they did not follow the Scripture. Physical brutality is still part of Satan's arsenal, but during the last two centuries he has added the use of well-developed psychological warfare methodology to undermine the faith of Christians.

Efforts to use psychological manipulation of popular opinion[92] concerning authority and freedom date back to the French Revolution.[93] Soon such tactics were being used to change the public perception of the proper role of the Christian church in society as well. It was, however, after Karl Marx called religion the "the opium of the people"[94] that real efforts to root out biblical Christianity began in the developed world. Ever since that time, Radical Humanists and Fascists have worked to undermine and destroy the Christian church. Marx's writings called for the shifting of the meaning of the words "authority" and "freedom" as a way of liberating the masses from a reliance on a divine being and replacing it with a reliance on those who had been enlightened by Marxist thought.[95] Vladimir Lenin and Leon Trotsky were determined to remove religious influence from the Russian Empire by using mind-bending propaganda to accompany their widespread use of murder and

---

90 "'Everything is permissible,' but not everything is beneficial. 'Everything is permissible,' but not everything builds up. No one is to seek his own good, but the good of the other person." (1 Corinthians 10:23–24).

91 "Rulers are not a terror to good conduct, but to bad. Do you want to be unafraid of the authority? Do what is good, and you will have its approval. For it is God's servant for your good. But if you do wrong, be afraid, because it does not carry the sword for no reason. For it is God's servant, an avenger that brings wrath on the one who does wrong. Therefore, you must submit, not only because of wrath but also because of your conscience." (Romans 13:3–5).

92 See Chapter 9.

93 Linda S. Frey, Marsha L. Frey, *The French Revolution* (Greenwood Publishing Group, Westport, CT, 2004).

94 Karl Marx, "Zur Kritik der Hegelschen Rechtsphilosophie," *Deutsch-Französiche Jahrbücher*, 1843.

95 Marx and Engels, ibid.

torture of Christian leaders.[96] Their goal was to deify the Communist Party in the minds of the people and to dethrone God. Adolph Hitler and other Fascists used these same methods in the name of glorifying the state and eliminating Christian teachings.[97] Those who successfully resisted the psychological onslaught of the government's propaganda often fell victim to its sword.

In recent history, violent methods have not been used against Christian churches in North America. Nevertheless, the second half of the twentieth century has seen a major shift in the outlook of American society toward religious institutions. Radical Humanists hid behind legitimate political issues and used them to direct resentment against the Christian church as a pervasive bulwark of entrenched obstructionism. The entertainment media has represented traditional Christians as bigots, and the news media has dwelt on the misbehavior of a small number of religious leaders. The apologist must realize that these ill social winds will not dissipate on their own, but they could blow up a storm that will lead to active persecution of the church in the future. Guarantees written in constitutions mean nothing if the public attitude changes to such an extent that everyone looks the other way when churches are restricted in their mission and their teachings. Amazingly, the constitution of the Soviet Union guaranteed religious freedom, but the Soviet government totally ignored that guarantee.

Dealing with Malicious Attacks: Efforts to destroy the church by physical or psychological means generally arise from strongmen, who desire to crush any organization that might serve as a nucleus of resistance against them, or from militant utopians, who view the church's promise of an eternal paradise as a threat to their efforts to build an earthly paradise. The apologist needs to carefully untangle the knotty political and religious issues that may be involved in these scenarios. The structure of a government and the nature of the civil liberties it grants are legitimate political issues, with no direct bearing on the church. A religious issue arises, however, when proponents of any political position attempt to impose their own sense of morality upon Christians or use psychological manipulation in an attempt to gain their objectives. The apologist must be concerned because these efforts often try to influence Christian consciences and to impose legal restrictions on the teachings of the

---

[96] Vejas Liulevicius, *Utopia and Terror in the twentieth century* (The Great Courses, The Teaching Company, Chantilly, VA, 2003), Lect. 7-10.

[97] Liulevicius, ibid., Lect. 11-16.

church. Common psychological tactics include ascribing corporate guilt to the church, assigning guilt through association, feigning offense as a method of leveraging a situation, telling a "Big Lie" and/or using *ad hominem* argumentation. While all these tactics are unscriptural or based on logical fallacies, those dreaming of utopia or personal glory are seldom interested in truth or fair play. They have a religious zeal for their goal, even if they are atheists, and they have deluded themselves into believing that attaining the goal justifies the means employed to get it.

While apologists must avoid taking sides on political issues to prevent becoming a party to the dispute and, thereby, losing their moral authority, they must point out the fallacies in the arguments to the extent that they affect Christian consciences. First, corporate guilt involves blaming church members as a whole for the sinful actions of a few or for historical events in which current members had no involvement. This is done to leverage the practices of the church or to undermine its legitimacy. The Lord condemns such wholesale efforts to tar the innocent who are following correct doctrine and practice.[98] Apologists must emphatically reject such efforts to "guilt" the church. Everyone will be held accountable for his or her own sins, not the sins of others.[99] Second, merely because the church shares some of the same goals or opinions with some other person or some other group does not mean that it is of one mind with them in all matters. This is the fallacy of the undistributed middle, which was discussed in Chapter 1. Third, if, as Christians, we are proclaiming God's truth in love,[100] then we are not accountable before God if others take offense at what is being said. Fourth, we must answer a Big Lie with the Big Truth, namely, that Jesus died for the sins of everyone. If people have sinned, they need to repent, but if they are the victims of the lies of others, the Lord will judge the liars. Apologists should challenge every accusation by demanding to see the evidence. Finally, apologists must address *ad hominem* arguments by shaming the opponents for having such a weak case that they have to resort to such tactics. As Christians, we must be willing to be the objects of harassment and dishonesty and to have the enemies of the

---

98 [The Lord said,] "In those days, it will never again be said, 'The fathers have eaten sour grapes, and the children's teeth are set on edge.' Rather, each will die for his own iniquity. Anyone who eats sour grapes—his own teeth will be set on edge." (Jeremiah 31:29-30).

99 Ezekiel 18.

100 "But speaking the truth in love, let us grow in every way into him who is the head—Christ." (Ephesians 4:15).

church attempt to manipulate public opinion against us. If they persecuted Jesus, they will also persecute us.[101]

Faced with utopian dreams wrapped around a godless morality, the apologist needs to remember the church's early history. Paul realized that he could avoid being persecuted if he adjusted his message to match it to what the Jewish and/or the Roman authorities desired, but that was not his commission from the Lord.[102] True Christians will always be in conflict with those who want to build their own paradise because they do not want to hear that it can never happen. A comfortable Christianity is not Christianity at all. Belonging to a church and attending regularly does nothing to gain favor before God even if it helps us to appear to be respectable before men. God's Word requires that we label sin for what it is, no matter what the current social environment may be. The Lord said that whatever is not hot or cold he would spit out of his mouth.[103] The world may market to the middle, but the Lord looks for commitment in the extreme.[104]

Summary

The Holy Christian Church is a spiritual reality. In its truest form, it is something only God can see. We accept its existence and the mission God gave it by faith. Because the Church is still in this world, at war with sin and death and the devil, and because it is made up of sinners, it's easy for critics and skeptics to find issues to use to attack the work and existence of the church. Still, we are the people of God. We have the gospel in Word and sacrament and Christ's promise that the Holy Spirit is working when we proclaim that Word. Our job is to deal with objections honestly and thoughtfully and to return the conversation to Jesus, who won forgiveness for us depraved sinners in the Church and for those to whom we are witnesses.

---

[101] [Jesus said,] "If they called the head of the house 'Beelzebul,' how much more the members of his household!" (Matthew 10:25).

[102] "Now brothers and sisters, if I still preach circumcision, why am I still persecuted? In that case the offense of the cross has been abolished." (Galatians 5:11).

[103] [Jesus said,] "Because you are lukewarm, and neither hot nor cold, I am going to vomit you out of my mouth." (Revelation 3:16).

[104] Matthew 10:37-39.

Afterward

Where do we go from here?

Throughout this book, the authors have tried to present a great deal of information about many different topics. It may have seemed like too much, too fast. We apologize if that was the case. Unfortunately, one needs to start somewhere, and our purpose was to help you, the reader, get or strengthen your bearings, biblically, theologically, and also logically. We hope that you have a better idea of what apologetics is and isn't and that you are more prepared to engage in it yourself.

This, however, isn't and cannot be the last word on the subject. Until Jesus comes back, the topic of apologetics will be in constant flux as the devil and his hosts regroup and find new ways to attack the gospel message. His purpose is to keep people out of heaven. Since the only way anyone gets to heaven is through the gospel, his goal is to discredit and silence our message. That should tell us something important about all our efforts at apologetics, namely, they must always lead back to the only real weapon we have, the gospel. St. Paul said, "For I am not ashamed of the gospel, because it is the power of God for salvation to everyone who believes, first to the Jew, and also to the Greek."[1] God builds his power into our witness about Jesus. Finally, it is the only thing that will change hearts. It is the only thing that will transform an unbeliever into a believer. It is the only argument we have that can win. Again, St. Paul said,

> "For although we live in the flesh, we do not wage war according to the flesh, since the weapons of our warfare are not of the flesh, but are powerful through God for the demoli-

[1] Romans 1:16.

> tion of strongholds. We demolish arguments and every proud thing that is raised up against the knowledge of God, and we take every thought captive to obey Christ."[2]

The gospel demolishes arguments. The gospel takes every thought captive to Christ. We began this book by saying that apologetics is about clearing the field for the gospel. That is also where we want to end it. We have no purpose when we engage in apologetics, other than to give a clear testimony about Jesus Christ, the Savior of the world.

The Importance of Personal Growth

One of the subtle realities of being a believer in an unbelieving world is that our faith never reaches a point of equilibrium. We never grow to the point where we can say that we have mastered the faith. All we need to do is read the historical portions of the Bible to see that reality. Again and again, we see great "heroes of faith" confessing the Lord in one verse and falling into sin or tripping over their own weakness in the next. Lutherans use a Latin expression to summarize this reality: *simul justus et peccator* (literally "at the same time a saint and a sinner"). Practically speaking, there is a war going on in our hearts between our sinful nature and our new man, the believer that God put inside us. The war will end only with our dying or Jesus' return. Then the sinner within us will die. Until that day comes, that *old man* lives inside us and fights against all that God is doing.

The old man makes apologetics hard. He overthinks everything and demands logical or scientific or historical facts that God simply doesn't give us. He raises doubts in our own minds—and let's be honest, part of apologetics is dealing with our own weakness and doubt. It is clearing the field so we ourselves hear the gospel and so the Holy Spirit strengthens our faith.

Practically speaking, that means that if someone wants to be a skilled apologist, that person needs to be in the Word. He or she needs to personally read it regularly.[3] He or she needs to hear God's Word in the worship service regularly and to go to their pastor's Sunday morning Bible class regularly. If there are Bible studies during the week, these should be considered as well. Nothing

---

[2] 2 Corinthians 10:3-5.

[3] [A psalmist wrote,] "How happy is the one who does not walk in the advice of the wicked or stand in the pathway with sinners or sit in the company of mockers! Instead, his delight is in the LORD's instruction, and he meditates on it day and night." (Ps 1:1-2).

prepares us to engage in effective biblical apologetics like studying the Bible.[4] That is true first of all because the means of grace, that is, the gospel in Word and sacrament, are the only way that God gives us to grow in our faith. A knowledgeable faith is the most important thing we need to present and defend the gospel's teaching.

Apologetics can be challenging. Success rarely comes from one conversation. In fact, we may find that God puts people into our lives that we will spend years talking with. They will repeatedly challenge what we say, but still they will leave the door open. They are like the Roman governor Felix,[5] who kept calling Paul in to talk for a variety of reasons, none of which were particularly sanctified. Yet, because he did, he kept hearing the message. It probably seemed to Paul at times as he was beating his head against a wall. It might feel that way for us, too, sometimes. What will keep us going? Refresh-ing our faith with the gospel. That's where God's power is—the power to re-new our strength and enthusiasm for the work and the power to convince the people whom God places in our lives.

There is another important reason to constantly study God's Word, and we have already mentioned it: we need to know what the Bible actually says so that we don't let skeptics set the terms of the debate. The truth is that most skeptics don't know the Word very well. They have been *told* that the Bible is full of contradictions and impossible stories, such as that a whale swallowed Jonah, most of which, at best, are combinations of truth and falsehood. We need to be able to say, "That's not what the Bible says. And if you don't believe me, I can show you." Apologetics is never about what detractors say the Bible says. It's always about what God really says in the Bible. If we are going to engage in this kind of work, it is impossible to know the Bible too well.

Knowing the Times We Live In

We also need to know our audience. We live in the last days, but that's been true for two thousand years. We need to be current on what is and isn't happening in our culture. Satan shifts the grounds of his attacks from time to

---

4 [Moses said,] "These words that I am giving you today are to be in your heart. Repeat them to your children. Talk about them when you sit in your house and when you walk along the road, when you lie down and when you get up. Bind them as a sign on your hand and let them be a symbol on your forehead. Write them on the doorposts of your house and on your city gates." (Deut 6:6–9).

5 Acts 24.

time. In the lifetime of the authors of this book, we've seen "the Christian Right" rise and fall as a political force. That rise and the fall shifted the ground of debate about God's Word. Hollywood, political leaders, musicians and many other people serve as opinion makers. They speak and other people accept their thoughts as authoritative. We Christians need to have some clue about what is going on so that we can give answers that address the real questions people are asking and the real arguments they are making.

Beyond that, it helps to have an inquiring mind. We said earlier that it would take considerable effort and education to stay abreast of all the developments in the natural sciences. We also noted that archaeology changes so fast that books are out of date by the time they're published. So, no one can realistically expect to become an expert in all these fields. This is the reason that we've been making the point that we don't have to be experts if we understand what God really says and the assumptions that underlie science and history. It is worthwhile to do a little reading or take a course in areas of science and history from time to time, just to understand the context in which people are speaking. Unless we are speaking with experts, the people with whom we engage don't have the time to keep up on all these things either. Therefore, we do not have to cede the ground to them. On the other hand, we also cannot—repeat cannot—found our arguments on the shifting sand of human wisdom. We cannot depend on science or archaeology to prove what God has said. We dare not use outdated and falsified assumptions, theories and arguments to sustain God's Word. That will only undercut that which we want to uphold.

Naturally, Christians who read this book will want to learn more about apologetics itself. This is just an introduction, and there is so much more that could be said about so many topics. Students of apologetics speak of different approaches and schools of thought. They list names and works and again, it becomes a field of study all its own. While a reader may have some interest in it and enjoy reading about it, most Christians probably don't have time to master this wealth of material.

A great deal of it isn't worth mastering. The authors of this book are absolutely convinced that much of Christian apologetics, as it currently exists in print, is counter-productive. When we wrote this book, we submitted every chapter, every idea to extensive review. A statement in the introduction was challenged, even by some Lutheran pastors, namely, the analogy of the poisoned well. We were referring to Reformed efforts at apologetics. Some people thought this was an area where being Reformed doesn't really make that much difference. They urged us to tone it down a bit.

The reader will notice that we didn't. Why not? Because we are convinced that the Reformed approach is not scriptural. It does not mesh with a Lutheran approach to God's Word. In the end, it can do more harm than good. The basic question is the role of reason. By reason, we mean the role of human thought and observation and deduction. God gave us the gift of reason. This paragraph would make no sense if we couldn't express ourselves logically and if the human mind couldn't rationally process what we wrote. Nevertheless, human reason needs to be used the way God intended it to be used. There's an old joke about a man who bought a chainsaw. The salesman assured him that it was the top-of-the line model. He could easily cut four cords of wood a day with it. The man worked all week with it and then brought it back to the store. He told the salesman that he never got more than a quarter of a cord a day out of that machine. The salesman was puzzled and looked the chainsaw over carefully. He engaged the choke and opened the throttle. When he grabbed the handle and pulled the cord, the chainsaw roared to life. "What's that sound?" asked the startled man who had bought the chainsaw. The point is, he didn't use the tool the way it was intended to be used.

Human reason is a gift of God. Properly used, it has saved the lives of millions of children through vaccinations and prenatal care. It has enabled students of the Bible to probe the original languages and explore the meaning of the text of God's Word. It enables pastors to comfort people when they are afraid and call sinners to repentance. Yet, when it comes to eternal life, God gave us human reason so that we can understand and apply his Word. Not so that we can decide what parts of it make sense and what parts don't. Not so that we can reframe science in a desperate effort to sustain a human proposition, namely, that all true science has to agree with what the Bible says. Not so that we can argue people to the point of accepting Christ.

Not all Reformed authors make all those errors, but their assumptions tend to drive people in those directions. As a result, we must be careful about what we read and how we craft our arguments. Just because someone is a Christian and will be with us in heaven, doesn't mean they have given us good apologetic arguments.

The same caution must be made about creation science. Websites like *Answers in Genesis* abound. The Creation Museum in Boone County, Kentucky has become a popular site for Christians to visit. Yet the arguments of creation science are implausible to real scientists, even to ones who believe the Genesis account. In the end, the creation science movement tries to uphold faith with human arguments in an arena where even good arguments can fail.[6] What happens when those human arguments supporting faith do fail? There is much anecdotal evidence, particularly on college campuses, of Christians who defended the Bible with what they thought was good science, only to have their faith shaken or destroyed when their arguments were shown to be false.

Apologetics always needs more study. The authors of this book don't really consider themselves to be experts. We will spend the rest of our time on this earth growing in our ability to present the truth and to counter the attacks of Satan. Yet, our refuge is the armor of God.[7] Our final word to you, the reader, is this: Put on that armor! Trust in the Holy Spirit! Engage the skeptic! The Lord will be with you.

---

[6] Dan Hooper, *What Einstein Got Wrong* (The Great Courses, The Teaching Company, Chantilly, VA, 2017).

[7] Ephesians 6:10-20.

Appendix I

Logical Fallacies

The following logical fallacies commonly occur in both formal and informal argumentation on topics which an apologist is likely to encounter. The list is not complete, but it is given to help the apologist avoid such fallacies in his or her own arguments and to detect them in the arguments of others. The names of some of the fallacies are historical and sometimes a bit strange. An effort has been made to group the fallacies by type and to give examples where the description might not be clear.

General Fallacies: These fallacies include many different types.

***A priori* assertion:** An advocate asserts that because something must be true, opposing arguments are necessarily false and need only to be demonstrated as such by any means the audience will accept. [Example: "The sun must orbit the Earth like the moon does, because anyone can see that when there is a new moon, the sun and moon cross the sky together."]

Association fallacy: An advocate asserts that because two things share or can be implied to share some property, they should be treated in the same manner. (Also called **guilt by association**.) [Example: "People who like sauerkraut are like the Nazis because the Nazis liked sauerkraut."]

Attacking a strawman: An advocate attacks a caricature of an opponent's argument rather than the argument itself. [Example: "If enacted, the real effect of my opponent's proposal would be to starve the poor. No honest person could support such a proposal."]

Begging the question: An advocate includes the conclusion of an argument as a premise. [Example: "We should all eat healthy food because it is good for our health."]

Causal oversimplification: An advocate asserts there is only one cause of an outcome when in reality there are numerous contributing causes. [Example: "Students go to Duke because it has a good basketball team."]

Cherry picking: An advocate selects only those individual cases or that data which seem to confirm a particular position, while ignoring the bulk of the related cases or data that contradict that position. [Example: "Our team has a bad field goal kicker because he missed three field goals in the last game."]

Chronological snobbery: An advocate asserts that the thinking, art, or science of an earlier time is inherently inferior (or better) to that of the present, simply by virtue of its temporal priority. [Example: "The Egyptians used hieroglyphic writing because they just hadn't thought of alphabetic script yet."]

Circular reasoning: An advocate asserts a conclusion which is based on a premise that requires the conclusion to be true. [Example: "We believe in God because the Bible says he exists, and the Bible was given to us by God."] See chapter 3 for the correct statement of this.

Complex question fallacy: An advocate frames a complex issue of multiple components in such a way that only a single answer is allowed. This answer, however, cannot address all the component issues. [Example: "Unless we redistribute all the wealth in America, our poor people will never have a chance to share in America's prosperity."]

Continuum fallacy: An advocate asserts that if doing something is possible, then doing a minute amount more of the something will also be possible. [Example: If it is possible for a person to lift X pounds of sand, then it is possible for him to lift X pounds plus one grain of sand. This process can be continued until it would be claimed that he could lift a ton of sand.]

Confusing cause & effect: An advocate asserts that the consequence of a phenomenon is its root cause. [Example: The faster that windmills are observed to rotate, the stronger the wind is observed to be. Therefore, the wind is caused by the rotation of windmills.]

Conspiracy theory: An advocate claims that any refutation of his or her argument is further proof that it is not getting a fair hearing. [Example: "The 9/11 attacks were planned by the Bush administration, which anyone would clearly see if they were not part of the conspiracy."]

Correlation vs. causation: An advocate asserts that because there is a correlation between two variables, one must be the cause of the other. [Example: Cars are hard to start when people wear fur coats. Therefore, people wearing fur coats make it hard for cars to start. In reality, cold weather causes both phenomena.]

Ecological fallacy: An advocate draws inferences about the nature of specific items based solely upon aggregate statistics collected for a group to which those items belong. [Example: Mr. Sancelli must be a rancher because he comes from rural Montana where ranching is the main business.]

Equivocation: An advocate uses a term with multiple meanings without clarifying which meaning is intended at any particular time. [Example: The word "church."]

Etymological fallacy: An advocate asserts that the original or a historical meaning of a word or phrase is necessarily the same as its current usage. [Example: The word "cleave."]

False analogy: An advocate uses an analogy that bears only a weak similarity to the case of interest. [Example: Party balloons are full of helium. Hot air balloons are somewhat like party balloons. Therefore, hot air balloons are full of helium.]

False compromise: An advocate offers a supposed compromise that, in reality, forces his or her opponents to abandon one of their premises, undercutting the validity of their whole position. [Example: "If you'll concede that Jonah was a myth, I'll concede that David and Solomon really were kings of Israel."]

False dichotomy: An advocate asserts falsely that there are only two choices, either A or B, so that rejecting A is selecting B. [Example: "If you don't fly between Minneapolis and Chicago, you'll have to take a mule cart."]

Gambler's fallacy: An advocate asserts that separate, independent events can affect the likelihood of the next random event. [Example: A coin has come up heads 10 times in row; therefore, it is more likely to come up tails on the next toss.]

Hasty generalization: An advocate quickly draws a broad conclusion without examining all the relevant information. (Also called the **inductive fallacy**.) [Example: "No one in my geometry class speaks French, so people must not speak French anymore."]

Historian's fallacy: An advocate asserts that decision-makers of the past viewed events from the same perspective as currently in vogue and as having the same information as those later analyzing the decision. [Example: "Certainly, the Germans must have known early on in the war that the British had broken the Enigma code."]

Judgmental language: An advocate uses insulting or pejorative language to influence the audience's judgment. [Example: "We all know there is no scientific evidence for the existence of God, so the whole idea of God is utterly simple-minded."]

Kettle logic: An advocate defends a point using multiple arguments that are inconsistent with and/or do not support each other but are merely intended to befuddle the discussion. [Example: "There are 101 reasons why all lawyers are crooked."]

Moving the goalposts: An advocate dismisses all evidence presented in response to a specific claim and demands some other (often greater) evidence. [Example: "Your claim that Fred is a bad baseball player because he has a low batting average and makes a lot of errors doesn't really address the issue of his contributions to the team. More evidence is needed."]

Nirvana fallacy: An advocate rejects a solution to a problem solely because it is not perfect. [Example: "This plan only reduces the unemployment rate to 4%. Anything greater than 0% is unacceptable."]

No true Scotsman: An advocate makes a generalization true by changing the statement of the generalization to exclude a specific counter-example. [Example: "No real Wisconsin resident would root for the Bears, so Larry must have psychological issues".]

***Onus probandi*:** An advocate tries to shift the burden of proof from his or her own shoulders to those who reject his or her assertion. ["If it wasn't true, you would be able to prove it isn't true."]

Out-of-context: An advocate selects words out of their context in a document in a way that distorts the passage's original meaning.

***Post hoc ergo propter hoc*:** An advocate asserts that because something happened first, it must be the cause of a subsequent event. [Example: The rooster crowed and then the sun rose. Therefore, the rooster's crowing caused the sun to rise.]

Psychogenetic Fallacy: An advocate asserts that if an idea arose from a biased mind, then the idea itself must also be faulty. [Example: Compact cars are bad because Hitler started the use of them by promoting the Volkswagen.]

Red herring: An advocate introduces an argument not relevant to the topic of the discussion to lead the opponents into pointless counter-arguments concerning irrelevant material and thereby derailing their case. [Example: "We really can't address the healthcare crisis until we have resolved the issue of illegal immigration." (Illegal immigration is a red herring.)]

***Reductio ad absurdum*:** An advocate asserts that for something to be false (or true) would lead to a ridiculous conclusion; therefore, it must be true (or false). [Example: "If vegetables were really a necessary part of a good diet, we would see carnivores dropping dead all the time."]

Slippery slope: An advocate asserts that a relatively small first step inevitably leads to a chain of related events culminating in some significantly undesirable impact and thus the first step should not be allowed to happen. (Also called the **camel's nose**) [This is not a fallacy if the step actually changes the underlying system, thereby causing it to be more susceptible to further change.]

Special pleadings: An advocate asserts there is something special about a particular case so that it cannot be evaluated in the usual way. [Example: "You cannot see the dragon that lives in my basement because he is invisible, and he does not leave footprints because he floats."]

Vacuous Truth: An advocate asserts something that is technically true but meaningless because nothing is affected. [Example: If there were unicorns in nature, they would all have single horns on their foreheads. True, by definition, but meaningless because there are no unicorns in nature.]

Wishful Thinking: An advocate asserts that something must be true based on it being pleasing to imagine or desirable rather than based on evidence or reason. (Also called the **mind projection fallacy**). [Example: "My pit bull would never bite anyone, because he is so good with me."]

Reasoning Fallacies: These fallacies involve errors in the reasoning process.

Affirming a disjunct: An advocate reasons that one clause of a logical disjunction must be false if the other clause is true. [Example: "There is an apple or a banana on the table. I see an apple on the table; therefore, there is no banana on the table. (Without an "either" in the premise, this conclusion is logically false.]

Affirming the consequent: An advocate reasons that the antecedent in an indicative conditional must be true if the consequent is true. [Example: If Kathy is a waitress, she likes bowling. Kathy likes bowling; therefore, she is a waitress. (False reasoning)]

Base rate fallacy: An advocate makes a probability judgment based on conditional probabilities without taking into account the effect of prior probabilities. [Example: Failure to consider the number of false positives in a normal population in estimating the usefulness of a screening test.]

Composition fallacy: An advocate reasons that something which is true of a part must also be true of the whole. [Example: Since auto windshields are made of glass, therefore, the whole auto must be made of glass. (False reasoning)]

Conjunction fallacy: An advocate reasons that an outcome simultaneously satisfying multiple conditions is more probable than an outcome satisfying a single one of them. [Example: Sandy being a bank teller and a feminist is more probable than Sandy being a teller. (False reasoning)]

Denying the antecedent: An advocate reasons the consequent must be false in a conditional statement if the antecedent is false. [Example: If Jim is a farmer, he likes tea. Jim is not a farmer; therefore, Jim does not like tea. (False reasoning)]

Division fallacy: An advocate asserts that something which is true of a whole thing must also be true of all or some of its parts. [Example: Because a team is good, therefore, all the players on the team are good. (False reasoning)]

False equivalence: An advocate asserts that two situations are logically and/or apparently equivalent when they are not. [Example: Because they are both Europeans, Norwegians and Italians are culturally the same.]

False premise fallacy: An advocate asserts one or more premises that are not well-grounded as the basis for his or her argument. [Example: Hot dogs are made of dog meat; therefore, I do not eat them. (False premise)]

Four-term fallacy: An advocate asserts a categorical syllogism that has four terms, i.e., two middle terms that are not identical so there is no connection between the premises. [Example: All trees are made of wood. My company has a phone tree; therefore, my company's phones are made of wood ("Tree" has a different meaning in the two premises.)]

Prosecutor's fallacy: An advocate asserts that a low probability of false matches occurring means that there is no possibility of some false matches being found. [Example: "Because only one in 10,000 people has the blood characteristic X, the suspect must be the person whose blood we found in a New York City apartment." (False reasoning)]

Regression fallacy: An advocate ignores natural fluctuations and ascribes a cause to a set of observations where none exists. [Example: "The stock market must be going up because it has more 'up' days than 'down' days." (False reasoning)]

Undistributed middle: An advocate reasons that if two things are part of the same thing, one is part of the other. [Example: Every cat is a mammal. Every dog is a mammal. Therefore, every cat is a dog. (False reasoning)]

Unrepresentative Sample: An advocate uses a sample in his argument that does not have the same characteristics as the general population it is asserted to represent (see **cherry picking fallacy**.) [Example: A person randomly selects four red apples from a bin of red and yellow apples and then claims that all the apples in the bin are red. (Bad sampling technique)]

***Ad Hominem* Fallacies:** An advocate attacks his or her opponent personally rather than the arguments that the opponent is advancing.

Appeal to Motive: An advocate dismisses an idea based solely on the supposed motive of its proposer rather than on its merit. [Example: "Only someone who had something to hide would advance such an argument."]

Personal Abuse: An advocate verbally abuses his or her opponent rather than refuting that opponent's argument. [Example: "My opponent is a disgusting excuse for a human being."]

Poisoning the well: An advocate presents adverse information about an opponent in the debate with the intention of discrediting everything that that person says. [Example: "My opponent is a notorious liar."]

Tone policing: An advocate tries to discredit an idea by attacking the emotional envelope of the idea rather than the idea itself. [Example:

"My opponent's whole case is based on injecting emotion into the discussion."]

Traitorous critic: An advocate attacks a critic's affiliation with some group or cause as the underlying reason for his or her criticism in an effort to avoid addressing the criticism. [Example: "My opponent belongs to the Weasel Society, which is always trying to undermine the meaning of Jesus' ministry."]

***Tu quoque*:** An advocate asserts that a certain position is faulty and should be disregarded because its proponent has failed to act consistently in accordance with that position. [Example: "My opponent talks about the importance of complete honesty, but his reputation tells a different story."]

Appeals to False Authority: An advocate appeals to an expert of dubious credentials or an irrelevant, unqualified, unidentified, biased, or fabricated source in support of an argument. [Example: Movie stars making claims about breakfast cereals.]

Absurdity: An advocate dismisses a claim as absurd without demonstrating proof for its absurdity. (Also called the **pooh-pooh fallacy**.) [Example: "It is absurd to think the world is round because the people on the other side would have to stand on their heads."]

Accomplishment: An advocate claims an assertion is true based on the past accomplishments of the person who asserted it, even though those accomplishments do not produce relevant expertise for the issue at hand. [Example: Nobel Prize winner Linus Pauling touting mega-doses of Vitamin C to prevent colds even though his expertise was not in this area.]

Common Practice: An advocate asserts the correctness of a practice because it is commonly accepted or used. [Example: "Binge drinking can't be bad for your health because everybody's doing it."]

The Masses: An advocate asserts that a proposition is true or good solely because the majority of the people in some group believe it to be true or good. [Example: "Four out of five left-handed plumbers recommend…."]

Nature: An advocate asserts that something is better or worse based solely on whether that something is "natural" or "unnatural." [Example: "Our automobiles are made of all natural components."]

Novelty: An advocate asserts that something is superior to the current approach solely because it is new or modern. [Example: "Try our new toothpaste with improved cleaning power."]

Probability: An advocate asserts that something should be taken as true because it is probably the case (or might be the case). [Example: "If I don't bring my umbrella, it will rain."]

Tradition: An advocate asserts that something is true solely because it has long been held to be true. [Example: "We all know that if rain starts before seven, it ends before eleven."]

Appeal to emotion: An advocate manipulates emotions rather than arguing the issue at hand.

Fear: An advocate attempts to increase fear of and/or prejudice towards those rejecting the advocate's arguments. [Example: "If this space shield proposal is not adopted, the Martians will be landing any day to take over the Earth."]

Flattery: An advocate flatters the members of the audience to gain their support. [Example: "Smart people like you can see the importance of this proposal."]

Pity: An advocate tries to induce pity to sway the audience or opponents to his or her position. [Example: "Think of all the sick children who will suffer if we don't build this oil pipeline."]

Poverty: An advocate asserts that because his position aids the poor, it is the only correct position. [Example: "This proposal is the only thing that will prevent people in the inner city from starving."]

Ridicule: An advocate misrepresents his or her opponent's argument in a way that makes it appear ridiculous. (See **attacking a strawman**.)

Social Conformity: An advocate asserts that disagreeing with his or her position will lead to social isolation. [Example: "Only those on the lunatic fringe are lining up to oppose my proposal."]

Spite: An advocate attempts to exploit people's bitterness or spite toward an opposing party. [Example: "The only people in favor of this are the hateful members of the Burger Party."]

Faulty Standards: The standard of truth is perverted in these approaches which are generally described as **argument from ….**

…Credulity: An advocate claims something is so unbelievable that it cannot be taken seriously. [Example: "I cannot imagine how something heavier than air can fly; therefore, airplanes must be somehow a deceptive display."] (Also called **appeal to common sense**.)

…Ignorance: An advocate asserts that because an answer is unknown, perhaps even by the experts, therefore, it is unknowable and an alternative explanation must be accepted or regarded as equally valid. (Also called **appeal to ignorance** or **appeal to the god of the gaps**.) [Example: "Scientists cannot tell us how life originated on Earth; therefore, God must have created it."]

…Moderation: An advocate asserts that a compromise between two positions is always correct. [Example: "It is better to build this high-rise building halfway between San Francisco and Oakland, than to argue over which city to locate it in."]

…Repetition: An advocate attempts to gain acceptance of a position through endless discussion of it, regardless of contrary evidence, until the opposition is worn down. (Also called **proof by assertion**.)

…Silence: An advocate asserts something is true based on the lack of written or spoken evidence from authoritative sources to oppose it. [Example: "The Bible does not say that man should fly; therefore, airplanes are unscriptural."]

Appendix II

Isotope Abundance Studies

This appendix explains why scientists believe that the age of the Earth is "billions" and not "thousands" of years old. Although a large amount of evidence from various kinds of measurements exists, it is the evidence in this appendix which has proven unchallengeable in much the same way as the evidence supporting the heliocentric solar system has proven unchallengeable. The detail presented here is extensive so as to show that these types of investigations are both thorough and reproducible.

All observable and detectable terrestrial substances are composed of chemical elements, and chemical elements are composed of atoms. The atoms of each element have the same number of protons (called the atomic number) in their nuclei and act the same in chemical reactions. For example, all oxygen atoms have 8 protons. The number of neutrons in the nuclei of the atoms of a particular element may vary somewhat without affecting the atom's chemical behavior. Oxygen atoms can have 8, 9 or 10 neutrons and still be stable (i.e., not decay into some other isotope) and behave chemically like oxygen. The sum of the number of protons and neutrons in the nucleus of an atom is called its mass number. Each unique arrangement of protons and neutrons is called an isotope. Oxygen has isotopes called oxygen-16, oxygen-17 and oxygen-18.

If an isotope is unstable, such as oxygen-15, and decays into some other isotope, in this case nitrogen-15, it is called a radioactive isotope or a radioisotope. Each radioisotope has a unique half-life, which is the time for half of its atoms (nuclei) to undergo decay. After one half-life, half the atoms remain unchanged; after two half-lives, one-fourth of the atoms remain unchanged; after three half-lives, one-eighth, etc. After 10 half-lives only about 0.1% of the original number of atoms remains. After 20 half-lives only one atom in a million remains, and after 30 half-lives only one atom in a billion remains. For practical purposes, after 15 half-lives an isotope is considered to have effectively decayed to non-detectability. This type of decay pattern is called *exponential decay* (or more formally *first-order kinetics*) and is a well-understood natural phenomenon. Radioactive decay is governed by what is called the *weak nuclear force* and involves a process called *quantum tunneling*. Half-lives are a function of the energy levels of the particles within the nuclei of the various isotopes. These energy levels are quantized and fixed by natural constants.

In the 1950's, the United States government asked the scientists in one of its national laboratories to do studies to find all the isotopes of elements that occur in nature and the relative abundance of each isotope. The scientists collected samples from diverse places, and then they separated the specimens into their elements and purified these elements. They subsequently injected the elements into mass spectrometers which separated the atoms by mass numbers, similar in effect to how a prism separates the various wavelengths of light. After this, the analysts placed the isotopes found by this method into radiation counters and measured their half-lives. They found several hundred stable isotopes of elements with atomic numbers ranging from 1 (hydrogen) to 82 (lead), except for atomic numbers 43 and 61, for which no stable isotopes were found. They identified additional elements up to mass number 92 (uranium), but these elements had no stable isotopes.

The scientists found 30 radioactive isotopes that had half-lives of at least 730 million years. In the ore samples and ground samples continuing uranium, and only in such samples, they also discovered shorter half-life radioisotopes which were the result of the decay of uranium isotopes into lighter elements (see Endnote). These are called "intermediate decay products of long-lived radioisotopes." They exist in nature because of what is called the bathtub effect, which was explained in chapter 5. The final radioisotope of shorter half-life which the analysts found was carbon-14, whose half-life is 5730 years, but which exists in nature because it is replenished by cosmic ray collisions with nitrogen-14, an isotope which makes up almost 4/5 of the atoms in the atmosphere. All these shorter-lived radioisotopes remain in a steady state caused by the rate at which they decay and the rate at which they are replenished. Without such replenishment, they would soon decay away to nonexistence.

The scientists conducting the isotope abundance study also discovered that numerous isotopes of elements did not occur naturally even though isotopes with adjacent mass numbers of those elements did occur naturally. For example, iron isotopes with mass numbers 54, 56, 57 and 58 were found, but mass numbers 55, 59 and 60 were not found. The scientists were able to make all the missing isotopes using nuclear reactors, and they discovered that these missing isotopes were all radioactive. All the stable isotopes which were also produced as byproducts in the reactors already existed in nature. When the scientists tested the radioisotopes which they had produced, they found that these all had half-lives ranging from tiny fractions of a second to 80.8 million years. They discovered no new long-lived radioisotopes (i.e., half-lives more than 100 million years) in addition to those occurring naturally. As discussed earlier, radioactive isotopes decay away to become undetectable after about 15 half-lives have passed. Because the longest-lived radioisotope (plutonium-244) which was not found in nature would become undetectable after 1.2 billion years, the conclusion was drawn that the Earth must be at least 1.2 billion years old. Because the shortest lived (uranium-235) radioisotope which was found in nature would become undetectable after 11 billion years, the conclusion was drawn that the Earth must be no greater than 11 billion years old. This range is sometimes called the "isotopic age of the Earth." If the Earth were only 6000 to 10,000 years old, then an additional 46 radio-isotopes, those whose half-lives are greater than 1000 years but less than 80 million years, would exist on Earth today because they would not have had time to decay away. None of these radioisotopes exists naturally.

It is reasonable to ask how reliable these measurements are. In fact, they are incredibly reliable because of the simplicity and repeatability of what is being done. There are four possible sources of error, namely, incorrect sampling, incomplete separation, inaccurate measurement by mass spectrometry or inaccurate measurement of the isotopic half-lives by radiation counting. In practice, none of these contribute detectable error. 1) The samples can be collected any place the elements exist naturally, provided the collectors document the collection locations so others can use the same sample source to validate the measurements. There are no further requirements. Specimens from various locations give the same results because all isotopes of an element behave the same way chemically, so they are all found wherever the element exists. 2) Separation technology in chemistry has been refined for centuries and has reached an extremely high level of quality. Even if slight impurities were to remain, they would be culled out in the mass spectrometer because they would have different mass numbers than the element of interest. 3) Mass spectrometry is widely used in industry and healthcare because of its precision. It is based on a well-known principle of physics, and the technology was perfected many years ago. 4) Radiation counters likewise are widely used and extremely reliable. Specimens are usually run in duplicate or triplicate, and when the radiation is weak, controls are run to correct for spurious counts generated by cosmic rays or electrical noise in the counter. In other words, the technology is extremely good. The study of isotopes and their abundances is an example of what is called hard science, that is, science in which the substance of interest can be completely isolated from possible interferences and in which experiments can be exactly reproduced by other investigators using similar equipment. The data is so highly respected that it appears in a table more than 80 pages long in the *Handbook of Chemistry and Physics*, the master reference book of these major fields.

Isotope abundance studies have nothing to do with the efforts to date rocks by geologists. These geological studies have led to an estimated age of the Earth of 4.6 billion years, the so-called "geological age of the Earth." Geologists use more complex sampling techniques and rely on the ratios of the isotopes in the rocks being analyzed. While the physics and the chemical measurement technology behind these analyses are also extremely reliable, creation science advocates have argued that the rock samples have been somehow altered by natural processes, and thus the results do not truly indicate the age of these specimens, even though this argument is very poorly supported by evidence. In any event, no such argument can be given against isotope abundance studies because the only natural process that can be involved is radioactive decay. Anyone who doubts the isotope abundance study results can easily get access to the necessary equipment to repeat the testing for themselves.

In summary, the results of isotope abundance studies show that **all** stable isotopes (250 of them) that can be produced synthetically already exist in nature. In addition, **all** 30 radioisotopes that would exist if the Earth were at least one billion years old do exist, but **none** of the 46 additional radioactive isotopes which would have to exist for the Earth to be only 6000 to 10,000 years old do exist. This evidence is overwhelming, and the experiments have been repeated many times. Every isotope consistent with the Earth being old exists, and every isotope necessary to exist for the Earth to be young does not exist. The results of these studies are widely available, including in the *Handbook of Chemistry and Physics*, as well as in Wikipedia entries for the various elements and from the US Department of Energy (They are summarized in Table 1). The apparent age of the Earth is now, just as it was 6000 years ago, more than a billion years old. How the Earth gained this apparent age is a question that can be given different answers by people making different assumptions about the Earth's origin, but that it is the apparent age of the Earth is certain. The conclusion is as certain as that of the solar system being heliocentric and the Earth being a spheroid.

Endnote: Heavier radioisotopes, such as those of uranium, decay by emitting alpha particles, which reduce their atomic masses by 4 and atomic number by 2, or by emitting beta particles, which increase their atomic number by 1. [An alpha particle has two protons and two neutrons and is the equivalent of a helium-4 nucleus, while a beta particle is an electron.] The path of such radioisotope decays leading to lower-mass stable isotopes is called a "decay chain." Some radioisotopes can decay by either alpha or beta decay, causing the decay chains to branch. To account for all possible radioisotopes, there would need to be four decay chains, one running through each of the uranium isotopes, namely, uranium-235, uranium-236, uranium-237 and uranium-238, because there is no path for these radioisotopes to decay into each other. The four decay chains, which are shown in Figure 1, were named by scientists for ease of reference. The uranium decay series (headed by uranium-238) and the actinium decay series (headed by uranium-235) exist in nature, as does the thorium decay series. The latter series should be headed by uranium-236, but because the half-life of that element is only 23.4 million years, it would have all decayed into Thorium-232, which has a half-life of 14.1 billion years and therefore still exists. The radioisotopes of the neptunium decay series are not found in nature, except for Bismuth-209, because none of the heavier radioisotopes have a half-life of more than 2.1 million years. Radioisotopes of elements of higher atomic number than uranium, numerous of which have been produced artificially, do decay into the members of these four decay chains, but because none of them has a sufficiently long half-life, they do not exist in nature. The longest half-life of this group of artificially-produced radioisotopes belongs to plutonium-244, whose half-life is 80.8 million years. ***Of course, if the fundamental assumption of science is false, then all these measurements are meaningless.***

Table 1 - Table of Radioisotopes of Half-life greater than 1000 years

At. No.	Name	At. Mass	Half Life (in years)	Present
67	Holmium	166m	1.2×10^3	No
97	Berkelium	247	1.38×10^3	No
88	Radium	226	1.6×10^3	*
42	Molybdenum	93	4.0×10^3	No
67	Holmium	163	4.57×10^3	No
96	Curium	246	4.73×10^3	No
6	Carbon	14	5.73×10^3	#
94	Plutonium	240	6.56×10^3	No
90	Thorium	229	7.34×10^3	No
95	Americium	243	7.37×10^3	No
96	Curium	245	8.5×10^3	No
96	Curium	250	9.0×10^3	No
41	Niobium	94	2.03×10^4	No
94	Plutonium	239	2.41×10^4	No
91	Protactinium	231	3.28×10^4	*
82	Lead	202	5.25×10^4	No
57	Lanthanum	137	6.0×10^4	No
90	Thorium	230	7.54×10^4	*
28	Nickel	59	7.6×10^4	No
20	Calcium	41	1.03×10^5	No
93	Neptunium	236	1.54×10^5	No
92	Uranium	233	1.59×10^5	No
43	Technetium	99	2.11×10^5	No
36	Krypton	81	2.29×10^5	No
50	Tin	126	2.3×10^5	No
92	Uranium	234	2.46×10^5	*
17	Chlorine	36	3.01×10^5	No
34	Selenium	79	3.27×10^5	No
96	Curium	248	3.4×10^5	No
83	Bismuth	208	3.68×10^5	No
94	Plutonium	242	3.73×10^5	No
13	Aluminum	26	7.17×10^5	No

At. No.	Name	At. Mass	Half Life (in years)	Present
4	Beryllium	10	1.39×10^6	No
40	Zirconium	93	1.53×10^6	No
64	Gadolinium	150	1.79×10^6	No
93	Neptunium	237	2.14×10^6	No
55	Cesium	135	2.3×10^6	No
43	Technetium	97	2.6×10^6	No
26	Iron	60	2.6×10^6	No
66	Dysprosium	154	3.0×10^6	No
83	Bismuth	210m	3.04×10^6	*
25	Manganese	53	3.74×10^6	No
43	Technetium	98	4.2×10^6	No
46	Palladium	107	6.5×10^6	No
72	Hafnium	182	8.9×10^6	No
82	Lead	205	1.53×10^7	No
96	Curium	247	1.56×10^7	No
53	Iodine	129	1.57×10^7	No
92	Uranium	236	2.34×10^7	No
41	Niobium	92	3.47×10^7	No
62	Samarium	146	6.8×10^7	No
94	Plutonium	244	8.08×10^7	No

Beginning of radioisotopes found in nature

92	Uranium	235	7.04×10^8	Yes
19	Potassium	40	1.25×10^9	Yes
92	Uranium	238	4.47×10^9	Yes
90	Thorium	232	1.41×10^{10}	Yes
71	Lutetium	176	3.78×10^{10}	Yes
75	Rhenium	187	4.12×10^{10}	Yes
37	Rubidium	87	4.9×10^{10}	Yes
57	Lanthanum	138	1.05×10^{11}	Yes
62	Samarium	147	1.06×10^{11}	Yes
78	Platinum	190	6.5×10^{11}	Yes
64	Gadolinium	152	1.08×10^{14}	Yes
49	Indium	115	4.41×10^{14}	Yes

At. No.	Name	At. Mass	Half Life (in years)	Present
76	Osmium	186	2.0×10^{15}	Yes
72	Hafnium	174	2.0×10^{15}	Yes
60	Neodymium	144	2.29×10^{15}	Yes
62	Samarium	148	7.0×10^{15}	Yes
48	Cadmium	113	7.7×10^{15}	Yes
23	Vanadium	50	1.57×10^{17}	Yes
74	Tungsten	180	1.8×10^{18}	Yes
60	Neodymium	150	6.7×10^{18}	Yes
42	Molybdenum	100	8.5×10^{18}	Yes
83	Bismuth	209	1.9×10^{19}	Yes
40	Zirconium	96	2.0×10^{19}	Yes
48	Cadmium	116	3.1×10^{19}	Yes
20	Calcium	48	6.4×10^{19}	Yes
34	Selenium	82	1.08×10^{20}	Yes
52	Tellurium	130	8.2×10^{20}	Yes
54	Xenon	136	2.16×10^{21}	Yes
36	Krypton	78	9.2×10^{21}	Yes
52	Tellurium	128	2.2×10^{24}	Yes

* Isotope is a product (daughter isotope) of radioactive decay of another isotope (parent) with an extremely long half-life. It is not found independently in nature but only in uranium ores which also contain its long half-life parent.

[#] Product of cosmic ray interactions with nitrogen-14.

Figure 1

The Decay Chains of Heavy Elements

Thorium Decay Series

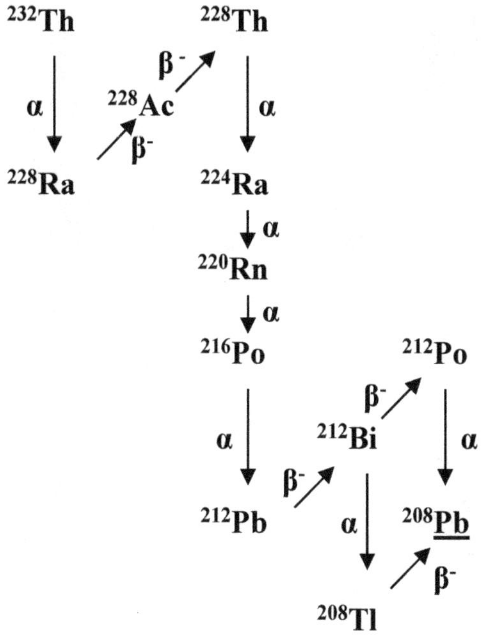

Note the final daughter isotope in the decay chain is underlined.

Actinium Decay Series

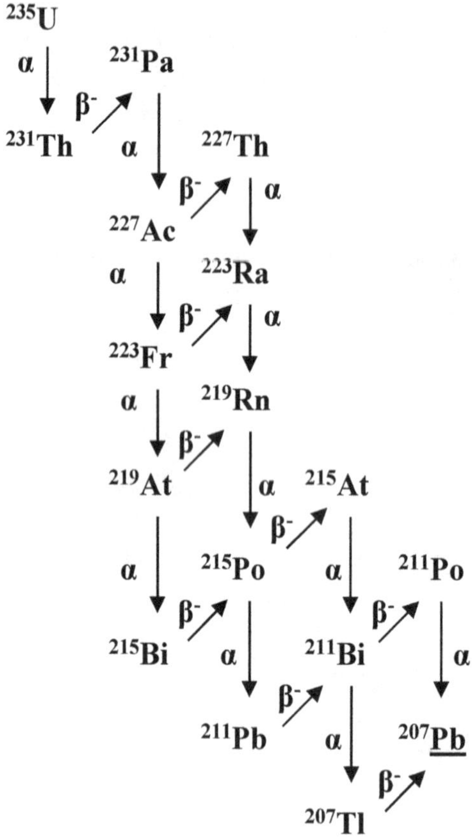

Note the final daughter isotope in the decay chain is underlined.

Uranium Decay Series

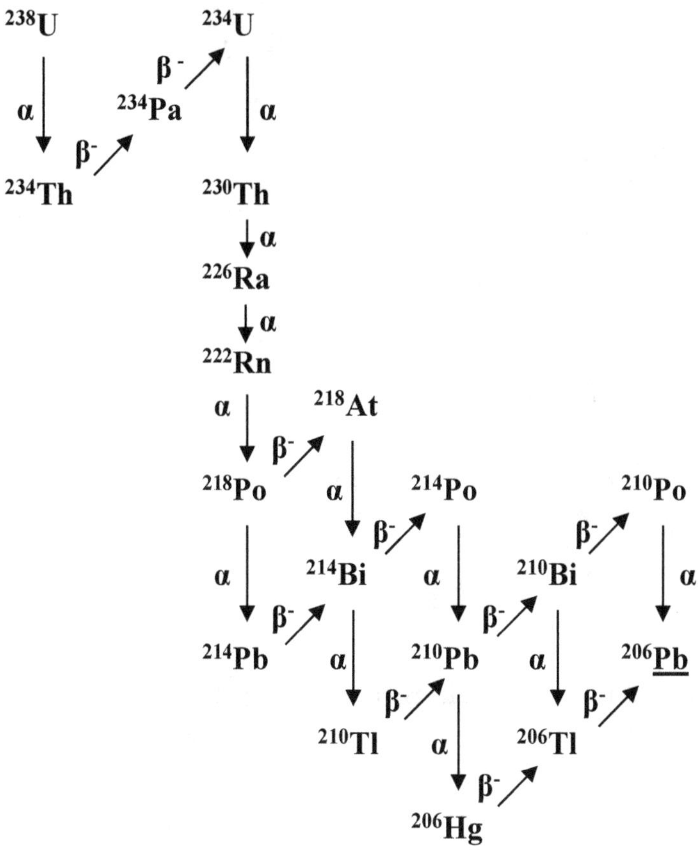

Note the final daughter isotope in the decay chain is underlined.

Neptunium Decay Series

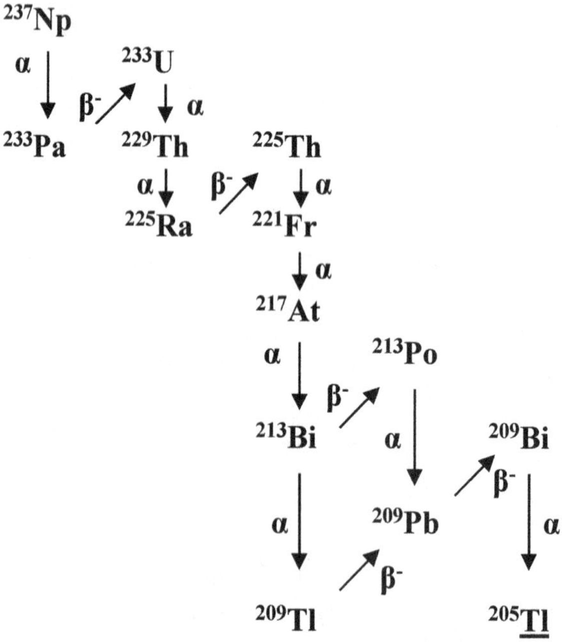

Note the final daughter isotope in the decay chain is underlined.

Appendix III

Christian Freedom and the Bound Will[1]

Christian freedom (also called Christian liberty) is a gift of God in Christ. A central teaching of the New Testament is that God has set us free through the work of Jesus. To understand this freedom, one must understand the nature of human servitude. Luther debated this point in his famous exchange with the Dutch humanist Desiderius Erasmus in 1525. Erasmus argued that people have a free will. Luther countered that people have no free will in spiritual matters. Luther insisted that mankind has a *bound will* or, in other words, is subject to the *bondage of the will.*

The bondage of the will is a spiritual reality, not a physical one. It is not *determinism,* which means that God would ordain every action that every person ever does. While the Bible does often say that God controls our lives,[2] it also clearly and unequivocally makes us responsible for the choices we make.[3] So the bound will does not remove human responsibility for sin. The bound will does not take away our ability to make choices for our lives, such as which job to take or which person to marry.

The bound will means that sinners have no ability to choose God. The human heart, mind and will are totally corrupted by sin, so it is impossible for a sinner to turn to God or approach God. Thus, in conversion, no human being can cooperate or "make a decision for Christ." No sinner can even resist the

---

[1] This appendix follows the basic outline developed by Siegbert W. Becker in his convention essay entitled "Christian Liberty." It was delivered at the 47th biennial convention of the Wisconsin Evangelical Lutheran Synod in 1983. It is available online in the essay file of Wisconsin Lutheran Seminary.

[2] See, for example, Psalm 139:16 and Proverbs 16:9.

[3] See, for example, Matthew 26:24, Romans 1:32 and Acts 17:31.

gospel less forcefully than someone else or can be more likely to come to faith. The whole being—the heart, mind and will, resists God's call to faith with all its strength. When it comes to how he or she lives, the sinner cannot do anything but sin. Every choice is corrupt. Every desire in the human heart is based on selfishness and lust. Even when a sinner chooses to do things that are outwardly good and decent, those actions spring from hearts that are full of sin, and consequently, they express the evil inside him or her, rather than any good.[4]

So the bound will means that all human beings by nature are slaves: slaves to sin, because sinners can only sin; slaves to the devil, because the devil owns the unbeliever and will drag him or her down to hell; slaves to ego, because what by nature drives all people is service to self, not God; slaves to the sinful world, because sinners care so much about belonging to it and learn all their attitudes from it. The practical result is that people are born slaves to works. The natural knowledge of God says that God exists and that all people must answer to him, and as a result, the bound will insists that all people have to win his favor. All human religions, in the end, are products of this slavery and create some kind of system to earn God's favor and avoid his judgment by human efforts.

Christian freedom or liberty means that God has undone all of that. Lutherans almost always trace the concept to Luther's 1520 tract *On the Freedom of the Christian*.[5] In that work, Luther put forth a paradox:

> A Christian is a perfectly free lord of all, subject to none.
> A Christian is a perfectly dutiful servant of all, subject to all.[6]

Each proposition, taken by itself, would completely misrepresent what God has done. But taken together, they explain what it is to be free in Christ. A Christian is a perfectly free lord because God has declared us to be so. Peter

---

[4] The Formula of Concord states, "Therefore, Scripture denies to the natural human mind, heart, and will every ability, aptitude, capability, and capacity to think anything good or proper in spiritual matters by themselves, or to understand, begin, will, undertake, do, accomplish, or cooperate in them." It then provides the following scripture passages as proof texts: 2 Corinthians 3:5, Romans 3:12, John 8:37, John 1:5 and 1 Corinthians 2:14. It continues, "Much less can the fallen human being believe the gospel truly or say 'yes' to it and regard it as true." It then points to Romans 8:7. SD II, 13-14. (Kolb, Wengert, *The Book of Concord*).

[5] *Luther's Works* **31**:327-378.

[6] Ibid, p 344.

calls us a royal priesthood.[7] That does not mean that we rule this world or that our status is visible in the sinful world. It means that we have been elevated by the gospel.

Christian freedom is finally the gospel. God declares that in Christ all our sins are wiped away and that we are freed from all record of them. As a result, we are free from the need to satisfy God by works. This is the crucial point that is lost in so much of the visible church. God does not give us hoops to jump through. Jesus has fulfilled all God's requirements for us to get into heaven. We are free from the need to "do something" to quiet our conscience or to satisfy the judge or to offset our sins. We are free from all consequences of sin. We will not go to hell. No hardship of this life is punishment from God, not even if it is a direct consequence of our sinful behavior![8] God may use things of this sort to discipline us in this life, but he does so only to teach us to follow him here, not to punish us for what we did. Even death itself is no longer a punishment. For the Christian, death is the gateway to life. Christian freedom means that we can say with St. Paul, "I long to depart and be with Christ."[9] Christian freedom means that we are free from fear.[10]

Christian freedom means that the Christian—and only the Christian—is freed from the dominion of sin. Sin is still a power in our lives, and we have to wrestle with it every day.[11] But the Christian no longer is a slave to sin.[12] When the Holy Spirit worked faith in his or her heart, that Christian became a new creation.[13] God placed a new man, i.e., a new nature, in the heart of that

---

7 1 Peter 2:9.

8 "Therefore, there is now no condemnation for those in Christ Jesus, because the law of the Spirit of life in Christ Jesus has set you free from the law of sin and death." (Romans 8:1-2).

9 Philippians 1:23.

10 "Now since the children have flesh and blood in common, Jesus also shared in these, so that through his death he might destroy the one holding the power of death—that is, the devil—and free those who were held in slavery all their lives by the fear of death" (Hebrews 2:14-15). / "There is no fear in love; instead, perfect love drives out fear, because fear involves punishment. So the one who fears is not complete in love. We love because he first loved us." (1 John 4:18-19).

11 Romans 7:15-25.

12 John 8:34-36.

13 "Therefore, if anyone is in Christ, he is a new creation; the old has passed away, and see, the new has come!" (2 Corinthians 5:17).

Christian. That new man lives for Christ.[14] That new man wages war against sin and the devil every day. That new man is our true self: St. Paul wrote, “Set your minds on things above, not on earthly things. For you died, and your life is hidden with Christ in God. When Christ, who is your life, appears, then you also will appear with him in glory.”[15]

Christian freedom means finally that we are free even from the law. We no longer have to work our way to heaven. Christ has done it all. This life, then, is not about constantly checking off lists and jumping through hoops. St. Paul wrote, “But now we have been released from the law, since we have died to what held us, so that we may serve in the newness of the Spirit and not in the old letter of the law.”[16] The Christian life is not one of servitude but one of free service to God. It is not about lists of rules but about a new spirit that joyfully seeks ways to serve God and our neighbor. It is a paradox, but it is true: we are free to serve.[17]

Being made free from all these things does not mean, however, that we can do anything that we desire. Christians freedom is not a license to sin. Rather, it’s a joyful embracing of God’s will as the highest good and of all that is best for us. Therefore, the Christian does study God’s law because in this life our knowledge of his will is still incomplete. We are still in the process of being renewed. We still have a sinful nature to fight against. Yet, Christian freedom means that we do it joyfully, not under compulsion. Only here do we finally arrive at the practical matter that many Christians want to begin with: we are free to live as we choose, so long as we do not do so with sinful intent. St. Paul has several lengthy explanations of what it means to live in freedom,[18] and he calls us not to be enslaved again to works.[19]

This whole discussion has already hinted at Luther’s second proposition: the Christian is a perfectly dutiful servant of all, subject to all. St. Paul begins Galatians 5 with a ringing call to defend our freedom and winds up the dia-

---

14 “Do not lie to one another, since you have put off the old self with its practices and have put on the new self. You are being renewed in knowledge according to the image of your Creator.” (Colossians 3:9-10).

15 Colossians 3:2-4. See also 1 John 3:1-3.

16 Romans 7:6.

17 “For you were called to be free, brothers and sisters; only don’t use this freedom as an opportunity for the flesh, but serve one another through love.” (Galatians 5:13).

18 1 Corinthians 8, 10:23-33, Galatians 5 and Romans 14:1-15:13.

19 “For freedom, Christ set us free. Stand firm then and don’t submit again to a yoke of slavery.” (Galatians 5:1).

logue with a call to use our freedom to serve one another. He then points to God's command to love one another as the summary of the moral law and includes a warning against biting and devouring each other.[20] The Christian life is freedom, but freedom to serve God with all that we are[21] and freedom to serve each other in love that only God can inspire through the gospel working in our hearts. Christian freedom engages in a constant struggle with sin and constantly asks what truly serves our neighbor. Christian freedom even rejoices in poverty and humility for Christ's sake and knows that all that we face in this life is temporary. It is prepared to sacrifice all that we have here for the life to come, because that is our true life in our true home.

---

20 Galatians 5:1-15.

21 Deuteronomy 6:5 and Matthew 22:37-38.

Further Reading

The Apocrypha (Revised Standard Version), (Thomas Nelson & Sons, New York, 1957).

Analytical Instrumentation Handbook, 2nd ed., GW Ewing, ed. (online).

Artificial Intelligence: A Modern Approach, 3rd ed. (online).

The Babylonian Talmud: A Translation and Commentary, Jacob Neusner, ed. (Hendrickson Publishers, Inc., Peabody MA, 2005).

Karl Barth, *Church Dogmatics, Vol I.* (T & T Clark, London, 1969).

Siegbert Becker, *The Foolishness of God* (Northwestern Publishing House, Milwaukee, 1982).

The Book of Concord: the Confessions of the Evangelical Lutheran Church, Robert Kolb and Timothy J. Wengert, eds. (Fortress Press, Minneapolis, 2000).

The Book of Mormon, Joseph Smith, tr. (The Church of the Latter Day Saints, Salt Lake City UT, 1980).

John Brug, *Digging for Insights: Using Archaeology to Study the Bible* (Northwestern Publishing House, Milwaukee, 2016).

Herbert Butterfield, *The Origins of Modern Science* (Macmillan Free Press, New York, 1957).

Catechism of the Catholic Church (Doubleday, New York, 1995).

Christian Worship: A Lutheran Hymnal (Northwestern Publishing House, Milwaukee, 1993).

Concordia, The Lutheran Confessions, 2nd ed. (Concordia Publishing House, St. Louis, 2006).

Daniel Deutschlander, *Civil Government: God's Other Kingdom* (Northwestern Publishing House, Milwaukee, 1998).

Daniel D. Deutchlander, *The Narrow Lutheran Middle* (Northwestern Publishing House, Milwaukee, 2011).

Hubert L Dreyfus, "Alchemy and Artificial Intelligence" (RAND Corporation, Santa Monica, CA, 1965).

Bart D. Ehrman, *Misquoting Jesus: The Story Behind Who Changed the Bible and Why* (HarperCollins, New York, 2005).

Euclid, *The Elements* (Alexandria, Egypt, 300 BC).

Linda S. Frey, Marsha L. Frey, *The French Revolution* (Greenwood Publishing Group, Westport, CT, 2004).

The Generous Qur'an, Usama K. Dahdok, tr. (Usama Dahdok Publishing, LLC, Venice FL, 2009).

Robert Godfrey, *Reformation Sketches: Insights into Luther, Calvin, and the Confessions* (P & R Publishing, Phillipsburg, NJ, 2003).

Adrian Goldsworthy, *Augustus: First Emperor of Rome* (Yale University Press, New Haven, 2014).

Justo L. Gonzalez, *A History of Christian Thought, Vol 1: From the Beginnings to the Council of Chalcedon* (Abingdon Press, Nashville, 1971).

Brent Hagglund, *History of Theology*, Gene J. Lund, tr. (Concordia Publishing House, St. Louis, 1968).

The Handbook of Chemistry and Physics (CRC Press, Inc., Boca Raton, Florida, updated yearly).

LP Hartley, *The Go-Between* (Hamish Hamilton Limited, London, 1953).

Peter Hylton, *Russell, Idealism, and the Emergence of Analytic Philosophy* (Oxford University Press, Oxford, 1990).

Carl Jung, *Psychologische Typen* (Rascher Verlag, Zurich, 1921).

Charles H. Kahn, *Plato and the Socratic Dialogue: The Philosophical Use of a Literary Form* (Cambridge University Press, Cambridge, 1998).

Daniel Kahneman, *Thinking, Fast and Slow* (Farrar, Straus and Giroux, New York, 2011).

Immanuel Kant, *Die Religion innerhalb der Grenzen der bloßen Vernunft* (Königsberg, 1793).

Brian Keller, *Bible, God's Inspired, Inerrant Word* (Northwestern Publishing House, Milwaukee, 2002).

Kelvin Knight, *Aristotelian Philosophy: Ethics and Politics from Aristotle to MacIntyre* (Polity Press, Cambridge, 2007).

Lyle Lange, *One God – Two Covenants* (Northwestern Publishing House, Milwaukee, 2010).

Michael A. Lockwood, *The Unholy Trinity: Martin Luther against the Idol of Me, Myself, and I* (Concordia Publishing House, St. Louis, 2016).

The Lost Books of the Bible (Bell Publishing Company, New York, 1979).

Jodi Magness, *The Archaeology of Qumran and the Dead Sea Scrolls* (Wm. B. Eerdmans Publishing Company, Grand Rapids, 2002).

Karl Marx and Friedrich Engels, *Manifest der Kommunistischen Partei* (London, 1848).

Timothy *O'Keefe, Epicureanism (University of California Press, Berkeley CA, 2010).*

Mark A. Paustian, *More Prepared to Answer* (Northwestern Publishing House, Milwaukee, 2004).

Mark A. Paustian, *Prepared to Answer* (Northwestern Publishing House, Milwaukee, 2004).

Plato, *The Sophist* (Athens, 360 BC).

Bertrand Russell, *A History of Western Philosophy* (Simon & Schuster, New York, 1945).

John Sanford, *Genetic Entropy & the Mystery of the Genome, 3rd ed.* (FMS Publication, Waterloo, NY, 2008).

John Sellars. *Stoicism* (Routledge, New York, 2006).

Friedrich Schleiermacher, *Gesamtausgabe der Werke Schleiermachers in drei Abteilungen* (Berlin, 1834).

B. Ann Tlusty, *Augsburg During the Reformation Era: An Anthology of Sources* (Hackett Publishing Company, Indianapolis, 2012).

Eugene Ulrich, *The Dead Sea Scolls and the Origens of the Bible* (Wm. B. Eerdmans Publishing Company, Grand Rapids, 1999).

James C. VanderKam, *The Dead Sea Scrolls Today* (Wm. B. Eerdmans Publishing Company, Grand Rapids, 1994).

Michael Wise, Martin Abegg, Jr. and Edward Cook, *The Dead Sea Scrolls: A New Translation* (HarperCollins, New York, 1996).

Further Study

Below are college-level courses, collectively entitled *The Great Courses*, created by The Teaching Company located in Chantilly, Virginia, which give background information for topics covered in this book. The information is current, the lecturers are well recognized in their respective fields, and the courses are available in video format, audio format or by online subscription.

David Brakke, *Gnosticism: From Nag Hammadi to the Gospel of Judas* (2015).

Sean Carroll, *Dark Matter, Dark Energy: The Dark Side of the Universe* (2007).

Sean Carroll, *Mysteries of Modern Physics: Time* (2017).

William Dunham, *Great Thinkers, Great Theorems* (2010).

Alex Filippenko, *Understanding the Universe: An Introduction to Astronomy, 2nd ed.* (2007).

Steven Gimbel, *An Introduction to Formal Logic* (2016).

Steven L. Goldman, *Science Wars: What Scientists Know and How They Know It* (2006).

Patrick Grimm, *The Philosopher's Toolkit: How to Be the Most Rational Person in Any Room* (2013).

Ryan Hamilton, *How You Decide: The Science of Human Decision Making* (2016).

Robert M. Hazen, *Origins of Life* (2005).

Dan Hooper, *What Einstein Got Wrong* (2017).

Don Lincoln, *The Theory of Everything: The Quest to Explain All Reality* (2017).

Vejas Liulevicius, *Utopia and Terror in the 20th Century* (2003).

Charles Mathewes, *The City of God* (2016).

Andrew Newberg, *The Spiritual Brain* (2012).

Steven Novella, *Your Deceptive Mind: A Scientific Guide to Critical Thinking Skills* (2012).
Stephen Nowiscki, *Biology: The Science of Life* (2010).
Monisha Pasupathi, *How We Learn* (2012).
Thad A. Polk, *The Aging Brain* (2016).
John J. Renton, *The Nature of Earth: An Introduction to Geology* (2006).
Tyler Roberts, *Skeptics and Believers: Religious Debate in the Western Intellectual Tradition* (2009).
David Sadava, *Understanding Genetics: DNA, Genes, and Their Real-World Applications* (2008).
Benjamin Schumacher, *Black Holes, Tides, and Curved Spacetime: Understanding Gravity (*2013).
Michael Shermer, *Skepticism 101: How to Think like a Scientist* (2013).
Michael Starbird and Edward B. Burger, *The Joy of Thinking: The Beauty and Power of Classical Mathematical Ideas* (2003).
Indre Viskontas, *Brain Myths Exploded: Lessons from Neuroscience* (2017).
Joshua N. Winn, *The Search for Exoplanets: What Astronomers Know* (2015).
Richard Wolfson, *Einstein's Relativity and the Quantum Revolution* (2000).

INDEX

CPSIA information can be obtained
at www.ICGtesting.com
Printed in the USA
LVHW040905040822
725120LV00001B/8

9 780578 223681